FAITHFUL FEELINGS

T0339248

FAITHFUL FEELINGS

Emotion in the New Testament

MATTHEW ELLIOTT

Inter-Varsity Press
38 De Montfort Street, Leicester LE1 7GP, England
Email: ivp@ivp-editorial.co.uk
Website: www.ivpbooks.com

© Matthew Elliott 2005

Matthew Elliott has asserted his right under the Copyright, Designs and Patents Act, 1988, to
be identified as Author of this work.

All rights reserved. No part of this publication may be reproduced, stored in
a retrieval system, or transmitted, in any form or by any means, electronic,
mechanical, photocopying, recording or otherwise, without the prior
permission of the publisher or the Copyright Licensing Agency.

Unless otherwise stated, Scripture quotations are from the New Revised Standard Version of
the Bible, Anglicized Edition, copyright © 1989, 1995 by the Division of Christian Education
of the National Council of the Churches of Christ in the USA. Used by permission. All
rights reserved.

First published 2005

British Library Cataloguing in Publication Data
A catalogue record for this book is available from the British Library.

ISBN–10: 1–84474–079–X
ISBN–13: 978–1–84474–079–6

Set in Monotype Garamond 11/13pt
Typeset in Great Britain by Servis Filmsetting Ltd, Manchester
Printed in Great Britain by Ashford Colour Press Ltd, Gosport, Hampshire

Inter-Varsity Press is the publishing division of the Universities and Colleges Christian
Fellowship (formerly the Inter-Varsity Fellowship), a student movement linking Christian
Unions in universities and colleges throughout Great Britain, and a member movement of the
International Fellowship of Evangelical Students. For more information about local and
national activities write to UCCF, 38 De Montfort Street, Leicester LE1 7GP, email us
at email@uccf.org.uk, or visit the UCCF website at www.uccf.org.uk.

CONTENTS

ACKNOWLEDGMENTS

I would like to thank those who have played an important role in the writing of this book. To Dr Robert Yarbrough and Dr J. Julius Scott, thank you for planting and watering the seed in my heart. To Professor Marshall, thank you for your kindness at Aberdeen. You and Joyce made us feel that Aberdeen was home as you welcomed us so warmly. I have been so thankful for your help on this project. Your input and advice went a long way in making the work ready for publication. To Dr Robert Roberts, thank you for your careful review of my work on emotion. Your comments and input were invaluable. To Dr Brian Rosner, thank you for your encouragement and sticking with me. As your last remaining student from Aberdeen, may I say how grateful I am for your faithful guidance through this project. Thank you for taking my ideas seriously, coming alongside, and being a friend.

I am also very grateful to those who played a role in reviewing and editing the final manuscript. Thank you for catching my mistakes, strengthening my arguments, and adding wisdom. This would certainly be a less valuable resource without your time and hard work. Special thanks go to Dr Philip Duce at IVP and Dr Bob Carling. Your attention to detail was of great value. To Dr Craig Keener, your insight and comments on my arguments were so helpful and encouraging. Thanks for your valuable time. Finally, to Dr Robert Yarbrough, thanks for your final review of the project. You have stood by me from the start of it all. Your faithfulness has meant a great deal.

To my parents, thanks for loving me and dedicating yourself to supporting my dreams. Whatever life brings, you have always been there to support and encourage.

To Laura, thanks. Your patience, encouragement and dedication to me and this project are the reasons I have had the energy to continue.

Thanks be to God for giving us these wonderfully complex and powerful emotions.

Matthew Elliott

ABBREVIATIONS

2d ed. – second edition

3d ed. – third edition

AB – *The Anchor Bible*

ANLEX – *Analytical Lexicon of the Greek New Testament,* Friberg & Barbara (eds.)

Ant. – Josephus. *Antiquities of the Jews*

ANRW – *Aufstieg und Niedergang der Römischen Welt: Geschichte und Kultur Roms im Spiegel der Neueren Forschung*

APQ – *American Philosophical Quarterly*

BWW – *Bible Works forWindows* (http://www.bibleworks.com)

BCE – before the common era

BDAG – *A Greek-English Lexicon of the New Testament and Other Early Christian Literature,* Bayer *et al.* (eds.)

CE – common era

DJG – *Dictionary of Jesus and the Gospels,* Green, McKnight, and Marshall (eds.)

DLNT – *Dictionary of the Later New Testament and Its Developments,* Martin and Davids (eds.)

DNTB – *Dictionary of New Testament Background,* Evans and Porter (eds.)

DPL – *Dictionary of Paul and His Letters,* Hawthorne and Martin (eds.)

EBC – *The Expositor's Bible Commentary,* Gaebelein (ed.)

EBT – *Encyclopedia of Biblical Theology: The Complete Sacramentum Verbi,* Bauer (ed.)

EQ – *The Evangelical Quarterly*

ed. – edited by, edition

EKK – *Evangelisch-Katholischer Kommentar zum Neuen Testament*

HTK – *Herders Theologischer Kommentar Zum Neuen Testament*

ICC – *The International Critical Commentary*

JBL – *Journal of Biblical Literature*

JME – *Journal of Moral Education*

JP – *The Journal of Philosophy*

JPT – *Journal of Psychology and Theology*

JRE – *The Journal of Religious Ethics*

J.W. – Josephus. *Jewish Wars*

Louw-Nida – *Greek-English Lexicon,* J. P. Louw, and E. A. Nida (ed.)

LXX – The Septuagint

NIBC – *New International Biblical Commentary*

NICNT – *The New International Commentary on the New Testament*

NIDOTTE – *New International Dictionary of Old Testament Theology and Exegesis,* Willem A. VanGemeren (ed.)

NIDNTT – *The New International Dictionary of New Testament Theology,* Colin Brown (ed.)

NIGTC – *New International Greek Testament Commentary*
NIV – *New International Version*
NLT – *New Living Translation*
NovT – *Novum Testamentum*
NRSV – *New Revised Standard Version*
NTD – Das Neue Testament Deutsch
NTS – *New Testament Studies*
Phil. – *Philosophy*
Phil. Rev. – *The Philisophical Review*
PNTC – *Pillar New Testament Commentary*

PPR – *Philosophy and Phenomenological Research*
RNT – *Regensburger Neues Testament*
RSV – *Revised Standard Verison*
TDNT – *Theological Dictionary of the New Testament*, G. Kittel and G. Friedrich (ed.)
TNTC – *Tyndale New Testament Commentaries*
vol. – volume
WBC – *Word Biblical Commentary*

Books of the Bible

Old Testament
Gen. – Genesis
Exod. – Exodus
Lev. – Leviticus
Num. – Numbers
Deut. – Deuteronomy
Josh. – Joshua
Judg. – Judges
1 and 2 Sam. – 1 and 2 Samuel
1 and 2 Kgs – 1 and 2 Kings
1 and 2 Chr. – 1 and 2 Chronicles
Neh. – Nehemiah
Esth. – Esther
Ps. (Pss.) – Psalm (and Psalms)
Prov. – Proverbs
Eccl. – Ecclesiastes
Song – Song of Solomon
Isa. – Isaiah
Jer. – Jeremiah
Lam. – Lamentations
Ezek. – Ezekiel
Dan. – Daniel
Hos. – Hosea
Obad. – Obadiah

Jon. – Jonah
Mic. – Micah
Nah. – Nahum
Hab. – Habakkuk
Zeph. – Zephaniah
Hag. – Haggai
Zech. – Zechariah
Mal. – Malachi

New Testament
Matt. – Matthew
Rom. – Paul's letter to the Romans
1 and 2 Cor. – 1 and 2 Corinthians
Gal. – Galatians
Eph. – Ephesians
Phil. – Philippians
Col. – Colossians
1 and 2 Thess. – 1 and 2 Thessalonians
1 and 2 Tim. – 1 and 2 Timothy
Phlm. – Philemon
Heb. – Hebrews
Jas – James
1 and 2 Pet. – 1 and 2 Peter
Rev. – Revelation

Apocrypha, Old Testament Pseudepigrapha and other non-biblical references

1 and 2 Clem. – 1 and 2 Clement
Eth. Enoch – Ethiopic Apocalypse of
Enoch (1 Enoch)
1, 2, 3 and 4 Macc. – 1, 2, 3 and 4
Maccabees

PssSol – Psalms of Solomon
Sir. – Ecclesiaticus (Sirach)
Wis. – Wisdom of Solomon

INTRODUCTION

Everything we do, say and think is, in some sense, emotional. We enjoy it, we dislike it, or we just don't care. We describe our experiences and ourselves by describing how we feel. Life without emotion would be in black and white.

But what is emotion? Where does it come from? Can emotions be trusted? Preachers and theologians share many of the same ideas about specific emotions. These are often negative. For example, some respected Bible teachers say that *agapē* love is not a feeling. Many theologians, theological dictionaries and New Testament scholars teach this view. Is this true?

In my church bulletin recently there appeared two exhortations:

> Pray that you and other believers will develop Christlike self-control: restraint over your own impulses, emotions and desires.
>
> Pray that you and other believers will develop Christlike joy: deep, inner happiness that is unaffected by circumstances.

Is control of emotions stressed in the New Testament? Are they often seen as strong negative influences that are likely to lead believers into sin? Is joy primarily a deep inner theological knowledge? In the words of popular authors Tada and Estes, 'Emotions are one of the least reliable yet most influential forces in our lives. One day we are hopeful; the next, we hate. Despair at one time; delight, the other.'[1]

The lines between reason and emotion are confused and obscure in many scholars' thinking. Morrissey writes:

> The interdependence of mind and heart forms the basic dynamism in human consciousness. In modernity, however, this vital duality has often been obscured by the infamous dualism between reason and emotion, whereby reason is reduced to an abstract rationalism and emotion is identified with irrational passions – a view that has ancient roots. Given this confused state of affairs, the recovery of an authentic emotional life is not only essential for the preservation of human integrity but also for the possibility of authentic religious knowledge.[2]

Clapper argues that it is essential that we seek to understand the role of emotion in the Christian life:

> The 'emotions' are a crucial part of human existence, some would even say they are the defining aspect of a human life. Because of this, theology – the Church's reflections on God and humanity – must, in every generation, come to grips with affectivity. Theology must understand the causes, the nature, and the importance of felt experience within the religious life.
>
> Is the great range of scriptural language about the 'heart' dispensable ornamentation which only clouds the real message of the Gospel, or does this emotion-language itself convey and constitute, in large measure, the real message?[3]

In my own studies I have not found a single scholarly work about emotion in New Testament studies that starts by asking the question, 'What is an emotion?' Answering this question is the foundation of this book.

First we must decide what emotion is and only then can we begin to understand it in the New Testament. It has long been recognized that too often theology stands alone without attempting to interact with other academic disciplines. This book attempts to apply modern studies dealing with emotion to the New Testament. But it is not primarily about the vocabulary of emotion: anger, love, joy, hope, jealousy, fear and sorrow. Instead, it is about emotion

---

1. Tada and Estes, *When God Weeps*, p. 161.
2. Morrissey, 'Reason and Emotion: Modern and Classical Views', p. 275.
3. Clapper, *John Wesley on Religious Affections*, p. 1.

itself, how it was perceived by the writers of the New Testament, and what role they thought it should play in the life of the believer.

As a result of this study, I hope that we can better understand and appreciate our faith. In the words of Jonathan Edwards, the nature of true religion 'consists in Holy affections'.[4]

---

4. Edwards, *Religious Affections* (Smith, ed.), p. 95. See also Sugden, ed., *Wesley's Standard Sermons*, vol. 1, p. 67.

1. WHAT IS EMOTION?

We too easily jump to the conclusion that any amount of an emotion may be dangerous to health or reason – probably a good deal less useful than a two-headed gorilla. With this fear of emotion as the focus, we usually think of learning how not to be emotional rather than whether or not the emotions are being refined and transformed to mature forms. Perhaps it is time for an educated look at emotional intelligence, emotional literacy, emotional work and emotional process.[1]

Introduction

Koteskey writes, 'Strangely enough, emotion has been outside the mainstream of both psychology and Christianity'. Modern psychologists have often considered emotion 'as disorganized processes which interfere with the orderly behavioural laws they are trying to study'.[2] Campos and Barrett write, 'By 1933, some psychologists were predicting that the term emotion would eventually disappear from psychology . . . a prediction that almost came true in the

1. Haviland-Jones, Gebelt and Stapley, 'The Questions of Development in Emotion', p. 250.
2. Koteskey, 'Toward the Development of a Christian Psychology: Emotion', p. 303.

1970s.'[3] Scholars have gone about the academic discipline of New Testament studies without an informed view of what emotions are and how they operate. Counselling classes are separated from the academic teaching of biblical studies and the theologian rarely explains how emotions fit into a theological framework. Contrary to those who stress that emotion in scripture 'is embarrassingly irrelevant for theology', Clapper concludes that theology must deal credibly with the role of emotion in church doctrine and practice.[4]

What do we mean by the word emotion? Aristotle and Plato used the word *pathos* ('passion') to refer to emotions. Under this category they put such emotions as joy, love and fear. Their category was wider than current definitions of emotion but there is an overarching similarity to what we call emotion. Although psychologists often use the term 'affect' to refer to a broader category, which includes emotions, moods, temperament and feelings, here we will use the term 'emotion' for simple emotions and will avoid the use of the term 'affect'.[5]

The New Testament and emotion

Love, joy, hope, jealousy, anger, fear, hatred and sorrow are important words in the New Testament and much has been written on these words in New Testament theology. Insights from other disciplines can shed light on the New Testament. As we learn about the emotions with the help of psychology, anthropology, neurology and philosophy, we may increase our understanding of the role of emotion in the New Testament.

A major reason for including this Chapter is the extensive influence that a 'non-cognitive' approach to emotion (to be defined below) has had on New Testament studies. (A growing awareness of this has been a major guiding and motivating factor for my work.) I do not mean to assert that holding a non-cognitive view has been a conscious choice of most New Testament scholars, but as a non-cognitive approach to emotion has been a part of most academic thinking in the last century, as such it has naturally

---

3. Campos and Barrett, 'Toward a New Understanding of Emotions and their Development', p. 230.

4. Clapper, *John Wesley on Religious Affections*, pp. 4–5. See also pp. 16–17.

5. Young, 'Feeling and Emotion', p. 750. See also Izard, *Human Emotions*, pp. 64–65. For good comments about the difference between mood and emotion see Roberts, 'Emotions and the Fruit of the Spirit', p. 88; Nussbaum, *Upheavals of Thought*, pp. 133–134.

been accepted by most New Testament scholars. However, as we shall see, many neuroscientists and psychologists have now moved from a non-cognitive to a cognitive approach to emotion and the non-cognitive influence on New Testament studies needs to be reassessed in this light. Moreover, as Lyons writes:

> Psychology and psychiatry inherited the study of emotion from philosophy but by and large philosophical work on emotions is now neglected by these other disciplines . . . a cognitive model is still suspect to the majority who work in these other disciplines because it was and is primarily a philosophical theory or model . . . So my, probably vain, hope is that philosophers and psychologists in particular will work together on the emotions and, I am certain, for the benefit of both.[6]

So that we have a better understanding of emotion and its functions in human thinking and behaviour, the goal of this Chapter is therefore to look critically at the major theories that attempt to explain emotion, and to discover which viewpoint gives the best working model.

Theories of emotion

Theories of emotion can be divided into two major viewpoints: cognitive theory and non-cognitive theory.[7] The origin of the ideas expressed in the words cognitive and non-cognitive are ancient. The words themselves give us modern terminology we can use to frame the debate. As we will see, virtually all the major thinkers in ancient Greek philosophy, plays, and poetry recognized and wrote about emotion from one of these standpoints. From church history, Origen, Augustine, Calvin, Wesley, and most notably Jonathan Edwards and Aquinas present us with ideas that are characteristic of cognitive or non-cognitive theory. We all consider emotion in a particular way, we look at it and evaluate feelings through our beliefs about what it is and how it comes upon us. Modern philosophy and psychology have chosen to look at ideas about the

---

6. Lyons, *Emotion*, p. xi. See also Solomon, 'The Philosophy of Emotion', p. 4.

7. For an excellent summary of the views of major theorists on emotion see Strongman, *The Psychology of Emotion*, pp. 14–55. Strongman gives a good summary of Lyons' writing. From the psychologists' viewpoint, by far the most useful philosophical discussion of emotion has been made by Lyons (1980). Strongman, *The Psychology of Emotion*, p. 116.

nature of emotion by using the terms cognitive and non-cognitive. By understanding the modern debate we can come to understand the major question with which all these great figures of our intellectual history have wrestled. When we understand the differences between the two major ideas, we are able to place most of what people say about emotion in one of the two camps. So the question before us is not so much, 'what is the difference between a cognitive and non-cognitive theory of emotion?' but rather, 'what is the nature of emotion itself?' And specifically for our study, what does the New Testament have to say about what emotion is? Using the terms cognitive and non-cognitive will allow us to understand the arguments of Jonathan Edwards, Plato, Aquinas, the apostle Paul, and Jesus himself in the language of the psychology and philosophy of our own day.

The debate between cognitive and non-cognitive approaches to emotion

The debate over the place of emotion in the human psyche is ancient. Plato contrasted emotion with rational thought. Many intellectuals of our time have done the same. Aristotle, on the other hand, believed the emotions are based on intellectual assessment and beliefs. According to Aristotle, a man does not become angry when he feels anger in his senses; rather anger is felt with an intellectual realization that one has been wronged or slighted. In a cognitive understanding, emotions require standards and judgments.[8]

René Descartes is often credited with postulating the first modern systematic non-cognitive theory of emotion. His view subsequently became the dominant philosophical position. Wayne Proudfoot explains, 'This is a view of an emotion as an impression, a feeling, or a unique sort of internal experience that happens to a person, and that can be named and described'. In Descartes' theory, the emotion is not caused by a cognitive process; it is simply experienced. The person can then name the feeling.[9] The sphere of the emotions is the body (soul to Descartes), and not the mind as in the cognitive view.

The primary question is, 'Was the emotion felt and then interpreted or did the cognitive understanding create the emotion?' To put it in another way, are emotions separate from the intellect or are they inseparably linked to the cognitive process?

---

8. Proudfoot, *Religious Experience*, pp. 344–345. Cognition does not imply conscious thought and reflection; it does imply that it is a function of the mind.

9. Proudfoot, *Religious Experience*, p. 348. Schleiermacher shares this view of emotion. Proudfoot, *Religious Experience*, pp. 349–350.

Non-cognitive theories of emotion

What is an emotion?

Non-cognitive definitions of emotion do not stress belief or judgments. Callahan writes,

> Emotions can be loosely defined as distinctly patterned human experiences that, when consciously felt, produce qualitatively distinct subjective feelings and predispositions: 'I am angry and want to attack'; 'I am afraid and want to flee'.[10]

Koteskey, in his review of emotion for theologians, explains the essential elements without any emphasis on cognition as its cause. He states that most psychologists agree that there are three elements present in emotion. These are:

1. 'Conscious Experience' – emotion can be felt and verbalized;
2. 'Emotional Behaviour' – emotional behaviour is epitomized in actions such as laughing, crying and smiling;
3. 'Physiological Events' – these 'events' are primarily the reactions of the nervous system. We begin to sweat when we are afraid, or our heart beats faster when we are getting close to home after a long absence. These reactions often seem completely out of our control.[11]

Different psychologists have put greater emphasis on one of these three elements or defined emotion exclusively as one of these three elements.

The development of non-cognitive theory

Early theorists. The non-cognitive (Cartesian) theory of emotions had its modern beginning in the philosophy of René Descartes. The emotions, to Descartes, are animal spirits reacting to the encountered situation. Lyons explains, 'Thus fear will be a subjective awareness of our limbs being moved in flight and of, say, a constriction around the heart, or increased pulse rate,

---

10. Callahan, 'The Role of Emotion in Ethical Decisionmaking', p. 10.

11. Koteskey, 'Toward the Development of a Christian Psychology', pp. 304–305. For a similar three-pronged generalization of all theories of emotion see Izard, Kagan and Zajonc, introduction to *Emotions, Cognition and Behavior*, p. 3.

and so on'.[12] The emotion is physiological and the change in the body is named by the mind.[13]

David Hume wrote a similar account.[14] He writes, 'Bodily Pains and pleasures are the source of many passions'.[15] In Descartes and Hume we see the tendency of non-cognitive theories to emphasize the primitive or 'animal' like nature of emotions.

Charles Darwin is seen by many as pioneering the modern scientific approach to emotion. His evolutionary model still provides a foundation for many theorists. Young writes, 'Darwin's first principle, which he called serviceable associated habits, states that adaptive behaviour, at first performed voluntarily, became habitual and the habit'.[16] Emotions grew out of the most basic impulse to survive. For example, the physical display of baring our teeth in anger is a reaction learned when our distant ancestors bit in acts of aggression or defence. Although our species no longer uses its teeth as a primary weapon, the reaction remains as a method of communicating the emotion to others.[17]

Facial expressions, according to Darwin, are a universal innate emotional response. Furthermore, these expressions are reflex reactions to stimuli just like a sneeze. Darwin wrote: 'Our third principle is the direct action of the excited nervous system on the body, independently of the will.'[18] In the evolutionary

---

12. Lyons, *Emotion*, pp. 2–5. See Descartes, 'The Passions of the Soul', Art. p. 36.

13. Arnold, *Emotion and Personality*, pp. 95–99. See this section for a good explanation and critique of Descartes and his view on emotion. See also Descartes, 'The Passions of the Soul', Art. p. 51, pp. 378–379; Kenny, *Action, Emotion, and Will*, pp. 7–8.

14. Unfortunately for this perspective, man is both the most intellectually and emotionally advanced animal. Lazarus, Averill and Opton, 'Towards a Cognitive Theory of Emotion', p. 213. For a good summary of Kant and some of the other non-cognitive philosophers see Solomon, 'The Philosophy of Emotion'.

15. Hume, *A Treatise of Human Nature*, Book 2, Part 3, Section 9, p. 438.

16. Young, 'Feeling and Emotion', p. 751. See Darwin, *The Expression of the Emotions*, pp. 27–29, 48, 351. For an effective refutation of this principle see Arnold, *Emotion and Personality*, pp. 100–105. For a prominent advocate of a modern evolutionary model of emotion see the writings of Plutchik, 'The Emotions, Facts, Theories, and a New Model', and see Pomeroy, 'Emotions: A General Psychoevolutionary Theory'.

17. Atkinson and others, *Introduction to Psychology*, p. 429.

18. Darwin, *The Expression of the Emotions*, p. 348.

view, emotion is most often seen to precede cognition. In evolutionary development, it is sometimes argued that emotions developed more quickly than reason. This hypothesis supports the conclusion that emotion is a lower function than cognition.[19]

Descartes and Darwin laid the foundations of the non-cognitive approach. The major principles they laid down remain the guiding principles of non-cognitive theorists. If the idea that there is a fundamental separation of emotion from cognition and that emotion is based on physiology (as opposed to cognition) are proven false, modern non-cognitive theories have also been disproved.

James–Lange. William James took the philosophical framework proposed by Descartes and modified it for psychology. This was the birth of modern psychological theories about emotion. While Descartes emphasized feeling in the soul, James believed that emotion was physiological. He writes, '*the bodily changes follow directly the* PERCEPTION *of the exciting fact, and that our feeling of the same changes as they occur* IS *the emotion . . .* we feel sorry because we cry, angry because we strike, afraid because we tremble.'[20] He rightly points to the separation of cognition and emotion that is implied in this theory: 'Emotion and cognition seem then parted even in this last retreat; and cerebral processes are almost feelingless.'[21]

To James the task of the psychologist was to find the differences in bodily sensation in the different emotions. Emotion without physical arousal or change is impossible. Therefore, emotion is this change. In theory, this allows emotion to be studied, quantified and differentiated by recording the observable changes in physiology.[22] Koteskey writes:'According to James, we feel sorry because we sense that we are crying.'[23] Thus, early clinical study of emotion often tried to equate individual's 'introspective reports of feeling' with changes in physiology. Introspection was seen as the key to studying emotion. However, these studies have been disappointing in their inability

---

19.   Izard, *Patterns of Emotion*, pp. 68–69.

20.   James, 'What is an Emotion?', p. 13. See also James, 'What is an Emotion?', p. 18; James, 'The Emotions', p. 100; Lange, 'The Emotions: A Psychophysiological Study', pp. 62, 80. Lange developed a similar theory independently of James.

21.   James, 'The Emotions', pp. 122–123.

22.   James, 'What is an Emotion?', p. 17; Lange, 'The Emotions: A Psychophysiological Study', p. 68; Lyons, *Emotion*, pp. 14–15.

23.   Koteskey, 'Toward the Development of a Christian Psychology', p. 305. See also James, 'What is an Emotion?', pp. 19, 23–24.

to correlate the same emotion with a particular bodily change in different individuals.[24]

The James–Lange theory dominated psychology in the first part of the 20th century. However, the James–Lange theory was difficult to prove in experimental studies. Animals with major parts of their nervous system missing still reacted emotionally. In other words, even when their senses were unable to send signals to their mind, they still reacted emotionally. Whereas the James–Lange theory implied that each emotion must have a unique physical manifestation, experimental evidence points to the fact that there are identical physical responses for different emotions. W. B. Cannon proposed that the external experience arouses the thalamus in the brain and this in turn sends information to both the body, causing physical emotional reactions, and to elsewhere in the brain, where the emotion is named and interpreted. It is important to understand that this is still a non-cognitive approach. The bodily changes are not a result of the cognitive process but rather are simultaneous with it. This innate and largely generic physical arousal prepares the body for action in different situations.[25] Cannon's work proved many of the details of the James–Lange theory false and his arguments paved the way for non-cognitive theories that give greater stress to cognition.

Schachter and Singer. Stanley Schachter and Jerome E. Singer conducted the most influential experiments on emotion. Their work represents a significant shift toward a cognitive theory. Following Cannon, they observed that different emotions seem to share the same physical phenomenon. How are emotions to be differentiated? Based on extensive clinical research, Schachter and Singer

---

24. Young, 'Feeling and Emotion', p. 751. See also Strongman, *The Psychology of Emotion*, p. 15. For a philosophical argument for the impossibility of this introspective method and its link to Descartes' theory see Kenny, *Action, Emotion, and Will*, pp. 29–31. As a result of James' ideas we often observe a reliance on drugs to cure depression rather than changing the thinking of the patient. Tomkins advocates drug therapy for depression specifically because it controls 'neural firing' which causes the emotion. He writes, 'A warm bath is similarly disinhibiting, and hydrotherapy has been used to successfully control acute anxiety through essentially similar mechanisms.' Tomkins, 'Affect Theory', p. 172.

25. Koteskey, 'Toward the Development of a Christian Psychology', pp. 305–306. See also Cannon, 'The James-Lange Theory of Emotion'. For a good summary of the scientific problems Cannon found with James see Young, 'Feeling and Emotion', p. 759. See Cannon, 'The James-Lange Theory of Emotion'.

proposed that the mind names the physiological reaction to a situation by interpreting the situation.

This has been mislabelled by some as a cognitive theory when it is, in fact, another reworking of the non-cognitive approach. Cognition does not produce the emotion. Rather, it names the physiological changes in the body a particular emotion. This theory takes a step towards the cognitive position by postulating that the physiological change *alone* is not the emotion. Emotion requires interpretation of the event.[26] Carlson writes, 'Thus, to Schachter, emotion is cognition plus perception of physiological arousal. Both are necessary.'[27]

Current non-cognitive theory

Although there has been a move towards a cognitive approach to emotion in recent psychological writing, the James–Lange theory is by no means dead. Non-cognitive theory has gone through changes and revisions, but emotions are still seen by many psychologists as being independent of cognition. Robert B. Zajonc has been an ardent modern advocate of the claim that emotion is possible without cognition. For example, he argues that we can become angry before we have time to think about it.[28]

Similarly, if emotion is cognitive, Carroll Izard wonders how an infant can have emotion before cognitive development.[29] Zajonc points out that the fact

---

26. Koteskey, 'Toward the Development of a Christian Psychology', p. 306. For a good discussion of the work of Schachter and Singer including the problems with their experiment see Atkinson and others, *Introduction to Psychology*, p. 425, and Izard, *Human Emotions*, pp. 32–33.

27. Carlson, *Psychology: The Science of Behavior*, p. 416. According to Lazarus, Schachter and Singer failed to show that what activated the emotion was a physical stimulus and not a cognition. Lazarus, 'Constructs of the Mind', p. 9. We should also note that the major schools of both Behaviorist and Psychoanalytic theory have held to a non-cognitive approach.

28. Atkinson, *Introduction to Psychology*, p. 429. I find Atkinson's examples inadequate as they are reflex reactions that cognitive theorists would not classify as 'emotion'. See also Zajonc, 'Evidence for Nonconscious Emotions'; Zajonc, 'The Interaction of Affect and Cognition'. Against Zajonc's view, recent studies have shown that cognition is actually faster than emotional reactions. These studies indicate that emotion is much more complex than a simple reflex (Mandler, 'A Constructivist Theory of Emotion', pp. 34–38). See this article for a refutation of Zajonc's major experimental evidence.

29. Izard, *Patterns of Emotion*, p. 68.

that cognition may precede emotion does not prove that it is needed for emotion. Emotion is the major element in social interaction and occurs spontaneously and immediately as we interact with others. Therefore, he argues, emotion requires little or no evaluation. Other arguments for a non-cognitive approach include the observation that emotions do not require mental effort, cannot be avoided, and cannot be changed as they happen.

Paul Ekman and Carroll Izard have re-emphasized the role of physical reactions in emotion. Following Darwin's ideas, they rely largely on the input of the face.[30] The expression of a smile may produce greater happiness in the one smiling. The movement of the face plays a major role in determining the emotion. Izard writes, 'The pattern of facial activity or the image of the corresponding pattern of proprioception is a chief determinant of the specific quality of felt emotion.'[31]

Ekman, in recent studies, has shown that the manipulation of the face into emotional expressions may produce other bodily changes which mimic basic emotions. These facial manipulations may also change the actual feelings of the individual. The question that is posed by these studies is whether the facial changes generate emotion or just the physiology of emotion. A physically conditioned, learned or innate bodily change may occur without emotion. This question remains unanswered.[32]

Silvan Tomkins' ideas, in his bold approach to a modern Jamesian theory, provide a good example of the details of a modern non-cognitive theory. He believes that the primary emotions are responses to facial muscles' reaction to a stimulus. The differences in the rate of 'neural firing' differentiate the emotions. A decrease results in joy or a smile while an increase may result in anger or fear depending on the extent of the increase. Tomkins writes, 'Thus, a slap on the face is likely to arouse anger because of the very high density of

30. Carlson, *Psychology: The Science of Behavior*, p. 415. Izard, *Patterns of Emotion*, pp. 2–3. For a summary of Ekman and Izard where Izard is said to be the most influential modern writer on emotion see Strongman, *The Psychology of Emotion*, pp. 50–53.

31. Izard, *Patterns of Emotion*, p. 56.

32. Keltner and Ekman, 'Facial Expressions of Emotion', pp. 367–369. Ekman freely admits that we are a long way from being able to differentiate each emotion by means of physiological reactions (Ekman, 'All Emotions Are Basic', p. 18). See also Atkinson and others, *Introduction to Psychology*, pp. 423–424. Damasio has shown that the brain waves produced by Ekman's experiments differ from the brain waves of normal emotion, thus discrediting Ekman's results. Damasio, *Descartes' Error*, pp. 148–149.

receptors on the surface of the face.' If anger is the result of an increase in neural firing then this slap directly elicits anger.[33] Tomkins writes:

> Affects are sets of muscles, vascular, and glandular responses located in the face and also widely distributed through the body, which generate sensory feedback which is inherently 'acceptable' or 'unacceptable'. These organized responses are triggered at subcortiacal centers where specific 'programs' for each distinct affect are stored . . .
>
> If we are happy when we smile and sad when we cry, why are we reluctant to agree that smiling or crying is primarily what it means to be happy or sad?[34]

Agreeing with Tomkins, Izard insists that each emotion has a unique 'neuro-chemical process'. Evidence for this is given by differing facial expressions for the basic emotions as well as their 'unique motoric and mental representations'.[35]

If emotions are physiologically based they are necessarily a part of a differ-ent system than cognition. A major tenet of non-cognitive theories continues to be the separation of the systems for emotion and cognition. Izard writes, 'the systems have separate functions, and they can and do, under certain con-ditions, operate independently'.[36] However, even though they are separate systems, it is argued that as the individual develops, the emotions form asso-ciations with memories, images and actions that become part of a complicated network linking cognition and emotion. They exert a stronger influence on one another as the network grows.[37]

Although we have seen that many elements of James' theory are still endorsed by many psychologists, in more recent studies there is no longer any

---

33. Tomkins, 'Affect Theory', p. 176.
34. Tomkins, 'Affect as the Primary Motivational System', pp. 105–106; see also p. 110.
35. Izard, 'Emotive–Cognitive Relationships', p. 25.
36. Izard, 'Emotive–Cognitive Relationships', p. 17. See also Izard, *Patterns of Emotion*, pp. 53, 70. For a good criticism of Zajonc's arguments where it is explained how many non-cognitive theorists misunderstand the cognitive approach, see Lazarus, 'Relations Between Emotions and Cognition', pp. 250–253. Lazarus writes, to see them as different systems, 'tests the logical limits of what we might mean about cause and effect' (Lazarus, 'Constructs of the Mind', p. 13). For Zajonc's criticism of Lazarus see Zajonc, 'On Primacy of Affect'. Zajonc, Murphy and McIntosh, 'Brain Temperature and Subjective Emotional Experience', p. 218.
37. Izard, 'Emotive–Cognitive Relationships', p. 33. See also Izard, *Human Emotions*, p. 63, where Izard insists that they are separate systems but writes, 'cognition interacts with the emotion process almost continually'.

question as to whether cognition can be a cause of emotion. Even Izard and Zajonc, probably the most respected modern advocates of a non-cognitive approach, write, 'There is no argument as to whether cognition is a sufficient cause of emotion; the question is whether it is a necessary cause.'[38]

It is clear that the cognitive element in emotion can no longer be ignored. As we have seen, the non-cognitive view has been continually revised in light of new evidence. In order to explain emotion, non-cognitive theorists have gradually had to come closer to a cognitive explanation, often having to revert to cognitive explanations in defining specific emotions. There is no alternative if their definitions are to make sense. These observations make us wonder if it is time to conclude that non-cognitive theory has failed. Do we need to find a theory that does a better job of explaining the operation of emotion?

The case against non-cognitive theory

Beyond the internal failings in non-cognitive theory, there are a number of basic criticisms that can be levelled against it. These include arguments from philosophy and the study of physiology. Simply put, emotion requires cognition. Magda Arnold writes: 'All James–Lange type theories have the same problem. To say that some situations arouse hereditary patterns is no solution. Fear or anger may arouse fight or attack, but they still depend on a realization that something is threatening or annoying, which is an appraisal, however rudimentary.'[39]

There are four basic philosophical arguments that show the inadequacy of all non-cognitive theories of emotion:

1. The problem of naming the specific emotion in non-cognitive theory. Early non-cognitive theorists relied on a person's introspection to associate a certain physical sensation with a certain emotion to identify it. However, people could not necessarily accurately name the emotion that they were feeling.[40] Furthermore, if an emotion is fully internal (a personal naming of a physiological change) to the one feeling the emotion, the content of this emotion becomes impossible to

---

38. Izard, Kagan and Zajonc, introduction to *Emotions*, p. 5. For a good summary of Izard's theoretical framework see Izard, 'Cognition is One of Four Types of Emotion-Activating Systems'.

39. M. B. Arnold, 'Cognitive Theories of Emotion', p. 259.

40. Proudfoot, *Religious Experience*, pp. 352–353. See also Kenny, *Action, Emotion, and Will*, p. 13.

communicate to others. The emotion word is rendered meaningless. In the non-cognitive approach emotion may become only a feeling of bodily change that has nothing to do with the context in which it occurs.[41]

2. In non-cognitive theory emotions can no longer be seen as motives for behaviour. It does not make sense to say 'I ran away from the bear because my heart began to beat faster and I began to sweat.' It does make sense to say, 'I ran away from the bear because I was afraid'. Emotion as a motive only makes sense if it contains an element of evaluation.[42] Non-cognitive theorists (Izard, Tomkins and others) argue that emotions, not physical feelings, are the major motivation for human behaviour. Yet, they hypothesize no good way to differentiate emotion from bodily sensation, thereby creating a circular argument. Emotions cannot be the primary motivation for our actions, as opposed to bodily feelings, if emotions are themselves primarily physical reflex reactions to stimuli.

3. The means by which an emotion can be differentiated from what the body feels; they cannot be said to be physiologically different if the same physical sensations can be interpreted as different emotions in different circumstances. In short, physical sensations are not in themselves emotions.[43] If emotions are only physiological changes, many different phenomena may qualify. For example, a stomach ache or an increase in heart rate caused by drugs both fit this definition of emotion. Cognition is the factor that differentiates an emotion from feeling.

4. In a non-cognitive approach, emotion cannot be evaluated; one emotion cannot be said to be more appropriate than another. If emotion is a sensation in the body (nervous system), no emotion can be, according to Lyons, 'unreasonable, unjustified or inappropriate'.[44] Pain or bodily feelings are morally neutral and cannot be classified as justifiable or unjustifiable. Yet, we are able to make judgments about emotions. We often relate emotion to a cognitive cause. We may say, 'I am angry *because* she did not keep her promise'. It does not make sense to say, 'I am angry because I feel hot and my heart rate has increased'. The link between cognitive function and feeling is broken without proper interpretation of

---

41. Lyons, *Emotion*, pp. 4–7. See also Peters, 'The Education of the Emotions', p. 189 and Lazarus, 'Constructs of the Mind', p. 15.

42. Lyons, *Emotion*, pp. 4–7.

43. Proudfoot, *Religious Experience*, pp. 352–353.

44. Lyons, *Emotion*, p. 8. See also Kenny, *Action, Emotion, and Will*, pp. 47–49.

the cause of the emotion.[45] In summary, emotions are not names of feelings, but rather the results of the interpretations of objects and situations.

There are also a number of powerful physiological arguments against the non-cognitive theory. There has been no definitive success in differentiating the emotions on the basis of differences in physiology.[46] Even if each emotion were linked to different physical reactions it would not prove that the non-cognitive approach was correct. This would only show that different cognitions have different physiological reactions. If it is proven that different emotions have identical physiological expressions, it all but disproves the non-cognitive theory.

As we have seen, non-cognitive theory holds that emotions belong to a different system of the body than cognition. It has been a long-held contention of many non-cognitive theorists that cognition and emotion are primarily dealt with in different parts of the brain. However, from our knowledge of neuroscience, the brain structures used for emotion and cognition cannot be easily separated. Likewise, non-cognitive theorists have often argued that emotions reside in the autonomic nervous system as almost a reflex reaction. Recent scientific evidence has not confirmed this. Modern neurological research points to emotion being largely dependent on the function of the somatic nervous system.[47]

Perhaps the definitive physiological evidence against non-cognitive theory is presented by Antonio Damasio.[48] After extensive study of patients with brain damage that affected their emotions, he found the following:

1. Even when logical facilities are completely intact (as measured in numerous tests) an unfeeling person is unable to function normally or make good practical decisions. People who function as almost a logical

---

45. Proudfoot, *Religious Experience*, pp. 354–355.

46. Lyons, *Emotion*, p. 46. Izard admits this fact (Izard, *Human Emotions*, p. 84).

47. Lyons, *Emotion*, p. 68. See also Strongman, *The Psychology of Emotion*, p. 77. Atkinson, *Introduction to Psychology*, p. 429, and Davidson, 'Affect, Cognition, and Hemispheric Specialization'. The cognitive theory of emotion may also be supported by the development of emotion with the development of the brain. As the infant grows to an adult, emotions change because the cognitive function develops. Kagan, 'The Idea of Emotion in Human Development', pp. 38–72.

48. Damasio, *Descartes' Error: Emotion Reason and the Human Brain*. See also the work of neurologist Richard Cytowic, including his book, *The Man Who Tasted Shapes*.

computer, having a pronounced lack of emotion in normally emotional circumstances, are unable to function rationally;

2. It is beyond doubt that many different parts of the brain, both higher and lower brain sections, play an indispensable role in emotion;

3. It is probable, based on empirical evidence, that specific emotional responses are learned and not innate.[49]

Damasio summarizes:

> Reduction in emotion may constitute an equally important source of irrational behavior . . .
>
> The powers of reason and experience of emotion decline together, and their impairment stands out in a neuropsychological profile within which basic attention, memory, intelligence, and language appear so intact that they could never be invoked to explain the patients' failures in judgment.[50]

In light of Damasio's research it seems impossible to hold that emotion is a lower evolutionary function, that logical, emotionless decision making is possible, or that emotion and reason are two separate systems operating independently. Finally, if emotion is cognitive it does not mean that it would be without fire and passion as some non-cognitive theorists insist. Richard S. Lazarus writes, 'To emphasize cognitive activity in the generation of an emotion is not to equate emotion with cold cognition.'[51] Proudfoot concludes, 'all theories of emotion that assume that the words we possess for describing emotions are terms that refer to discrete impressions, different shades of internal feeling, or traits that dispose one to act in particular ways, are to be rejected'.[52]

In light of the philosophical and physiological arguments against a non-cognitive approach, we can conclude that it has failed in its explanation of

---

49. Damasio, *Descartes' Error*, pp. xii, xiii, 41, 43, 51, 61, 136, 159, 184, 209. See also Ben-Ze'ev, *The Subtlety of Emotions*, pp. 170.

50. Damasio, *Descartes' Error*, pp. 53–54.

51. Lazarus, 'Constructs of the Mind', pp. 6–7. Nussbaum argues strongly that in fact the opposite is true – if emotion were non-cognitive it would have no fire or passion. 'How simple life would be, if grief were only a pain in the leg, or jealousy but a very bad backache. Jealousy and grief torment us mentally; it is the thoughts we have about objects that are the source of agony.' Nussbaum, *Upheavals of Thought*, p. 16.

52. Proudfoot, *Religious Experience*, p. 358. See also Solomon, 'Emotions and Choice', p. 254.

emotion. A non-cognitive approach does not maintain its integrity or validity when it is tested logically or compared with the observed behaviour of emotion.

A cognitive theory of emotion

A cognitive theory of emotion, properly defined, fits the evidence. A non-cognitive approach promotes the separation of emotion and cognition/judgment while the cognitive approach sees these as an integrated system. If emotions are merely physiological impulses, they can be ignored, controlled or trivialized, while, if they have as their essential element thinking and judgment, they are an essential part of almost everything that we think and do.[53]

Simply put, a cognitive approach makes thought, appraisal and belief central elements in emotion.[54]

What is an emotion?

William Lyons defines emotion in the following passage.

> The evaluation central to the concept of emotion is an evaluation of some object, event or situation in the world about me in relation to me, or according to my norms. Thus my emotions reveal whether I see the world or some aspect of it as threatening or welcoming, pleasant or painful, regrettable or a solace, and so on.[55]

Arnold, the first modern psychologist who strongly advocated a cognitive approach, defines emotion 'as the felt tendency toward an object judged suitable,

---

53. At the outset of this section we must point out that some may argue that a chemical imbalance or drugs may produce emotion without cognition. All that needs to be said in response to this objection is that these physical imbalances or drugs alter cognition. For a summary of the major cognitive theorists in psychology including Arnold, Leeper and Lazarus see Strongman, *The Psychology of Emotion*, pp. 38–43.

54. Lyons, *Emotion*, pp. 33–34. It is important to note that Lyons makes a major point of differentiating belief and evaluation. Two people can believe that a situation is dangerous – one reacts with excitement and the other with fear. Or we may believe that planes are safer than cars yet still be fearful of flying and not of getting into an automobile (Lyons, *Emotion*, p. 35).

55. Lyons, *Emotion*, pp. 58–59. Arnold writes, 'It is the sequence perception-appraisal-emotion that will alone explain the conditions necessary for arousing emotion'. Arnold, *Emotion and Personality*, p. 182. See also Lazarus, 'Constructs of the Mind', pp. 10–11.

or away from an object judged unsuitable, reinforced by specific bodily changes according to the type of emotion'.[56] Although some philosophical objections may be raised to this definition, it is difficult to improve upon in clarity. The judgment differentiates the emotion.[57]

In all the varieties of a cognitive theory, belief, judgment or evaluation is the only factor that can be universally used to differentiate emotions. Let me illustrate this point. Suppose I am engaged in conversation with a man and he is very congenial and talkative. A woman walks up to us and enters the conversation and the man becomes quiet and begins to fidget. If I know that this was the man's school girlfriend I may judge that he feels awkward and embarrassed. If I know that the woman is the man's boss who has just committed to cutting her department's number of employees I may judge that the man is fearful. If I know that the woman has recently persuaded the man's wife to divorce him I may judge that the man is angry.[58] Lyons writes, 'The point is that, to work out what emotion is in question, I seek clues as to what is this person's view of the situation, that is, how he evaluates it.'[59]

Lazarus writes:

> . . . if two individuals appraise the relational meaning of an encounter in the same
> way, they will inevitably react with the same emotion; if they confront different
> environmental conditions but make the same appraisal, they will also react with
> the same emotion; and if they confront the same condition but appraise them
> differently – perhaps as a result of different goals or belief systems – they will react
> with different emotions.[60]

---

56. Arnold and Gasson, 'Feelings and Emotions', p. 203. Many cognitive theorists would deny that physiological change is a necessary element in emotion. Nussbaum writes that: 'This view holds that emotions are appraisals or value judgements, which ascribe to things and persons outside the person's own control great importance for that person's own flourishing.' (Nussbaum, *Upheavals of Thought*, p. 4.)

57. Arnold and Gasson, 'Feelings and Emotions', p. 207. There is also a strong argument to be made that some emotions require more than evaluation or belief to occur. Actual knowledge is necessary (Gordon, 'Emotions and Knowledge', pp. 408–413).

58. Lyons, *Emotion*, pp. 62–63. See also Lazarus, Averill and Opton, 'Towards a Cognitive Theory of Emotion', pp. 218–219.

59. Lyons, *Emotion*, p. 63.

60. Lazarus, 'Universal Antecedents of the Emotions', p. 165. See also Lyons, *Emotion*, pp. 65–66; Weiner and Graham, 'An Attributional Approach to Emotional Development', p. 186.

A cognitive view of emotion gives adequate reason for the differing responses of different subjects to the same situation. Arnold concurs, 'If emotions depend on appraisals there will be as many different emotions as there are different appraisals.'[61]

To conclude this section it is essential to point out that cognition can be nearly instantaneous. Associations and similarities activate memories that may produce immediate emotion.[62] It is clear that we do not think before every emotion 'I feel like this because . . .'. At the same time, an emotion can be distinguished from a reflex reaction. I may have a reflex reaction to being burned by the match that I am holding. This is purely physical and I would not say that I am angry with the match at that moment. A moment later, I may be angry at myself for my action but this anger is only produced when I realize the stupidity of my actions.

A cognitive approach succeeds in giving explanations for the operation of emotion where the non-cognitive theory failed. In the next sections we will explore some of the details and intricacies of a cognitive theory of emotion.

Objects of emotion

Emotions have objects. An object, in general, must be perceived to have some value in order to produce emotion.[63] We do not get angry when we bend a paper clip. Why? This object has no value to us. We love something, grieve over the loss of something, fear something, or hope for something. It is possible to postulate generic categories of objects (formal object) for different emotion

---

61. Arnold, 'Cognitive Theories of Emotion', p. 259.

62. Arnold, 'Cognitive Theories of Emotion', p. 259. For a similar view and specific arguments against the idea that the speed of a reaction shows a lack of cognition see Lazarus, 'Appraisal: The Long and the Short of It'. Finally, it is important to note that a cognitive theory of emotion does not preclude the subsequent influence of emotion on cognition. Lazarus writes, 'In short, feedback from the continuous interplay between the conditions causing an emotion and the effects of efforts to cope with them changes the cognition's shaping the emotional reaction'. Lazarus, Averill and Opton, 'Towards a Cognitive Theory of Emotion', p. 219. See also Lazarus, 'Constructs of the Mind in Adaptation', pp. 4–5.

63. Nussbaum perhaps does the best job in incorporating value into the fundamental nature of emotion. The depth of emotion is determined by how much value is placed in the object (Nussbaum, *Upheavals of Thought*, pp. 30–33, 55).

types.[64] For example, the formal object of fear is something that is dangerous, or the formal object of grief is the loss of something of value. Different formal objects differentiate each emotions. Thomas Aquinas wrote, 'If the object is a good not yet possessed, we have either hope or despair. If it is an evil which has not yet befallen one, we have either fear or courage.'[65] He also writes, 'joy bears upon present good, sadness upon present evil: hope upon future good, fear upon future evil'.[66]

It is not possible to remain angry when thinking about anger itself. You must focus on the object of the anger to remain in an angry state. An object can be either real or imagined. It may or may not match reality. Although the object may be an illusion, the emotion remains real.[67]

Before concluding this section it is essential to emphasize that the object of an emotion is not necessarily its cause. My anger's object may be the fact that my wife is home late but its cause may be that I am over-tired. In other words, the cause can be my mental or physical state while the emotion is still cognitively about its object. Emotions may also be caused for the purpose of the manipulation of others. Anger may be produced in order to force someone to do what you want.[68]

In summary, emotions are about something. A failure to deal adequately with this fact is one of the major failings of non-cognitive theory. The object of a specific emotion serves both to differentiate it from bodily sensation and from other emotions.

Judgments and irrationality

It is important not to equate a cognitive theory of emotions with an assertion that emotions are necessarily reasonable. Emotions are based on evaluation

---

64. Lyons, *Emotion*, p. 100. The object is present even if it is not easily identifiable by the one who feels the emotion. See also Arnold, *Emotion and Personality*, pp. 170–171; Kenny, *Action, Emotion, and Will*, pp. 60, 189–194.

65. Aquinas, *Summa Theologica*. vol. 19, 1a.2ae.23.4. See also 1a.2ae.23.1; 1a.2ae.23.2.

66. Aquinas, *Summa Theologica*. vol. 19, 1a.2ae.25.4. See also 1a.2ae.26.2.

67. Lyons, *Emotion*, p. 112. See also Arnold, *Emotion and Personality*, p. 171. Nussbaum writes: 'Hunger, to say the least, persists in the absence of food . . . Emotions, by contrast, do go away when the relevant beliefs about the object and about value alter.' She has a good section on differentiating feeling and emotion (p. 131).

68. Solomon, 'Emotions and Choice', pp. 256, 263–264. See also Ben-Ze'ev, 'The Nature of Emotions', p. 395. For a comprehensive treatment of this subject see Solomon, *The Passions*, pp. 179–191.

and not fact. The same facts can lead to different emotions in different people. An emotion can be illogical or unjustifiable because it is based on wrong judgments.[69]

People have emotions about things that they know to be false. For example, a person may know that a rope is strong enough to hold 3000 kilograms yet still fear that it may break while holding 100 kilograms. A person may construe the situation contrary to the known facts.[70] Or, I know that my parents are out of town and will not be able to be contacted for a week. I can convince myself that they have died and I will never see them again, which produces feelings of grief even when I know that there is very little chance that they are dead. A cognitive view of emotion is the only theory that is able to explain this behaviour adequately. There is no outside stimulus; the only factor in producing this emotion is my belief or construal of the situation.

Emotion and motives

There is often a link between motives and emotion. Motives can be non-emotional or emotional. I can take out the rubbish because I know it will be collected tomorrow or I can take out the rubbish because I hate the picture that I just threw away and never want to see it again. The first motive may be non-emotional while the second is highly emotional. An emotion may be a motive but a motive is not necessarily an emotion.[71]

Some motives are so strongly linked to emotion that they are difficult to separate in specific situations. It is logical to say I ran because I was afraid of the mud slide. If you did not run it would be a good reason to question if you were really afraid. However, in the definition of other emotions, such as grief, there is little or no motive for immediate action.[72]

Tomkins argues that physical feelings are not as strong a motivation as emotion. As opposed to drives or physical feelings (hunger or pain for example), emotions are versatile, varying in length and intensity, and they can be used to overcome physical sensations. Tomkins writes, 'It is the affects,

---

69. Lyons, *Emotion*, pp. 72–73. Macmurray, *Reason and Emotion*, pp. 24–25.

70. Lyons, *Emotion*, p. 77. See also Roberts' theory of emotion as construals and Ben-Ze'ev, 'The Nature of Emotions', pp. 400–401.

71. Lyons, *Emotion*, pp. 51–52; Kenny, *Action, Emotion, and Will*, pp. 71, 74; Lazarus, Coyne and Folkman, 'Cognition, Emotion and Motivation: The Doctoring of Humpty-Dumpty', pp. 233–234.

72. Lyons, *Emotion*, pp. 93–94.

rather than the drives, which are the primary human motives . . .'.[73] 'I view affects as the primary innate biological motivating mechanism, more urgent than drive deprivation and pleasure, and more urgent than even physical pain.'[74]

It is clear that emotions are not by definition motives, but they can be highly motivational. They provide the impetus for many of our actions. An emotionally motivated action is difficult to stop while a non-emotionally motivated action is difficult to continue.

Behaviour and emotion

We may say that exhibiting a certain behaviour is evidence for or against having an emotion but it is not part of the emotion itself. Where cognition is internal to emotion, behaviour is external to it. If I say I am terrified of snakes but have no (or never had) physiological feelings when I saw a snake, you may conclude that I am not afraid of snakes. However, if I say I am afraid of snakes and refuse to visit the reptile house at the zoo it is evidence that I fear snakes.[75]

Behaviour may also influence emotion. Roberts rightly points out that undertaking an action can many times bring about an appropriate emotion. Doing the right thing often leads to feeling the right thing.[76] If I am not in the mood for a party, often, having been there for a few minutes, I begin to enjoy myself. Or, compassionate feelings often come as we act compassionately. How is this explained? As we do the action it changes our thought pattern, thereby changing our emotion. However, if the behaviour fails to change our thinking, the emotion will not change. Perhaps if we think that baseball is boring, when our spouse drags us to a game we find that it is just as boring as we imagined.

Emotions are often tied to behaviours although they are not synonymous with them. Most emotions have typical behaviours that give evidence of their presence. Specific actions may influence cognition thereby changing our emotions.

---

73. Tomkins, 'Affect as the Primary Motivational System', pp. 104–105.

74. Tomkins, 'Affect Theory', pp. 163.

75. Solomon points out that it is logically impossible for the non-cognitive theorist to connect emotion and action (Solomon, 'On Emotions as Judgments', p. 190). See Frijda, 'Emotion and Recognition of Emotion', p. 242; Lyons, *Emotion*, p. 179; Peters, 'The Education of the Emotions', p. 191; Kenny, *Action, Emotion, and Will*, p. 66.

76. Roberts, 'What an Emotion Is', p. 204.

Emotion and truth

Our emotion reveals truth about ourselves and our beliefs. The emotions of others or their lack of emotion often shows us what they think, value and believe. If the emotion is missing we can make a legitimate assumption that the claimed value is not really present. If I say that I am petrified of heights and show no outward signs of fear when I stand at the edge of the Grand Canyon you may conclude that I am not really afraid of heights.

We may try to deceive ourselves in our emotional life. For example, we may convince ourselves that we are experiencing righteous indignation when in fact we are experiencing envy. However, that does not change the reality of what we are experiencing. The emotion cannot be divorced from the cause.[77] To evaluate our emotion properly, first we must acknowledge what it is. Then, we must acknowledge what it tells us about our belief. If it is a belief that we dislike or hold as morally objectionable we can begin to work to change this belief. David Pugmire writes:

> Here I refuse to identify with the verdict of my emotions . . . My emotions must be allowed to take the form they seek to take; and they must be acknowledged as authoritative expressions of part of my actual valuation attitude. A certain integrity must be granted even to 'bad' emotion. For, as we have seen, it is futile to try to redirect it . . .
>
> Does it really mean abandoning oneself to sentiment, helpless surrender in the arms of one's passions? No. I can acknowledge something as my value without affirming it as *the* value.[78]

In summary, emotion can show us the truth about our own beliefs and values and give us insight into the beliefs and values of others.

Responsibility and emotion

Can emotions be judged to be justified or unjustified? Can a person be held accountable for what they are feeling? The crux of the issue rests partially with the ability or inability to control the emotions. If you are able to control, change, or avoid having a particular damaging emotion, you may be able to be blamed for having it. This may also work in the opposite direction. Not having an emotion may be a cause for blame. Richard S. Peters argues that without a cognitive approach to emotion it is next to impossible to speak about

---

77. Pugmire, 'Real Emotion', pp. 115–116.
78. Pugmire, 'Real Emotion', pp. 118–120.

educating them. 'It is because of this central feature which they possess [appraisal] that I think there is any scope for educating the emotions.'[79]

There is an important distinction to keep in mind during this discussion. Emotions cannot be forced or had on demand. It is impossible to close your eyes, grit your teeth and say 'I will now have joy' and as a result feel joyful. However, it may be possible to sit down and think about all the good things that you have in your life while experiencing negative emotion and change some of your negative emotions to positive ones. You cannot change the emotion by dwelling on the emotion itself, but you can change the emotion by dwelling on and changing the beliefs and evaluations that lie behind it.[80]

There are a number of ways that emotions can be influenced. First, they can be changed or produced by deliberately changing your environment. If I know that I love to watch people playing football, I will probably get excited when I go to a football game. If I know that I fear heights, I will probably feel fear when I visit the observation deck of a tall building. The converse is also true. I may be able to avoid fear by avoiding the observation deck.[81]

Secondly, emotions may be changed by changing the beliefs and evaluations that cause them. This may occur in all kinds of ways. A person may talk himself into another belief. He may merely learn that he is wrong. He may face his fear (or other emotion) to prove to himself that his evaluation is wrong. For example, upon riding a roller coaster he finds that he loves it and his fear disappears or, conversely, his excitement turns to sheer terror as he experiences the ride. Anything that can change the underlying belief or evaluation may

---

79. Peters, 'The Education of the Emotions', pp. 188, 202. See also Macmurray, *Reason and Emotion*, pp. 34–35 and Strongman, *The Psychology of Emotion*, pp. 248–249. There is a very good argument to be made for the fact that emotions are no less controllable than any other action. The same arguments that can be used to assign credit and blame for actions may be equally applied to emotion. Although it is often argued that emotion is fundamentally different from action this is not a credible or logical argument (Oakley, *Morality and the Emotions*, pp. 127–131, 161–188). Further, it can be argued that even if we are not in control of our emotions we can still be held responsible for them (Schlossberger, 'Why We Are Responsible for Our Emotions', pp. 37–56).

80. See also, Lyons, *Emotion*, p. 196; Solomon, '"I Can't Get It Out of My Mind": (Augustine's Problem)', p. 405; Weiner and Graham, 'An Attributional Approach to Emotional Development', p. 186.

81. Lyons, *Emotion*, pp. 196–197. See also Gilligan and Bower, 'Cognitive Consequences of Emotional Arousal', pp. 581–582; Roberts, 'Will Power', p. 245.

change the emotion.[82] Therefore, the reasons for moral decisions become extremely important.[83] It is most effective to say, 'Do not yell *because* it is hurting my ears'. As the belief is reinforced of why it is morally wrong or unkind, an emotional disposition against the action will develop.

Emotions may be fed or fought by the one experiencing them. When faced with anger against someone, a person can choose to dwell on the words, the fears or the specific act that caused the anger; or a person may choose to dwell on the fact that the cause of the anger could have been a misunderstanding, the perception may be mistaken, or the other person may have not meant what was said. The first option strengthens the emotion while the second drains it of its veracity. Similarly, filling your short term memory with other thoughts may encourage the emotion to dissipate or even disappear.

We are responsible for our emotions because they are based on beliefs and evaluations. They provide us with a picture of our true values. We can work to change those values that do not match our stated moral beliefs. Martha C. Nussbaum concludes, 'I have spoken of truth. And it is, of course, a consequence of the view I have been developing that emotions, like other beliefs, can be true or false, and (an independent point) justified or unjustified, reasonable or unreasonable.'[84]

Emotion as a sense for perceiving objects
We have seen that emotions have objects and that they reveal truth about our own and others' beliefs and values. It seems right to ask the question, 'Can we learn something real or true about the objects of emotion from the emotion?' In other words, how much of any emotion (or emotion in general) is based on the internal subjective thinking of an individual and how much is based on the external reality of the object of that emotion? We should not assume that every emotion is internal and subjective. Many emotions are based on an objective reality that exists outside us. How closely they line up with that reality is directly proportional to how the thoughts and values behind them line up with truth.

Rick Ellrod provides us with a valuable perspective about emotion. He argues that 'in emotional response values are revealed, just as in sensation the physical qualities of things are revealed'. He is not arguing that the values of the one experiencing the emotion is revealed to others but rather that values

---

82. Lyons, *Emotion*, pp. 198–199; Peters, 'The Education of the Emotions', pp. 196–197; Ben-Ze'ev, *The Subtlety of Emotions*, pp. 221–241.

83. Peters, 'The Education of the Emotions', p. 201.

84. Nussbaum, *Upheavals of Thought*, p. 46.

embodied in the emotion's situational object are revealed *to* the one experiencing the emotion by her emotion.[85]

When thinking we think of an object. Similarly, the senses always have an object. Likewise, if emotion has an object then it can be compared with sensations or thought which also must have objects.[86] Each sense contributes something to our knowledge of an object. Emotion can act as another sense that contributes to our knowledge of an object. I feel emotional about something I perceive as real in that object. Ellrod writes: 'In some cases at least it seems to do considerable violence to our responses if we consider them *only* subjective tremors, unrelated to anything real about the thing in question.' Emotions may convey to us something true about their object.[87]

If this is correct, we can sometimes make judgments about the goodness or badness of an object based on our emotional response to it. Just as seeing something as green makes us believe that it is in fact green, seeing something as lovable presents a lovable quality to us. However, *both* our physical senses and our emotions may deceive us and must be evaluated. An object may appear black but upon examination in bright sunlight we find that it is dark blue. Similarly, an object of our love may, upon closer examination, be found not to merit love. While both sight and emotion give evidence to be evaluated, both perceptions may be accurate or inaccurate. Ellrod argues:

> Similarly, an emotion is not a judgment and cannot take the place of an abstract
> value-judgment; but it is needed to provide an appropriate basis for such judgments.
> Abstraction and generalization, judgment and inference must all go to work on the
> data of emotion before the true value-*knowledge* can be attained; but in one sense all
> evaluative knowledge begins in emotion, according to the view that I am suggesting,
> just as all factual knowledge begins in the senses.[88]

---

85. Ellrod, 'Emotion and the Good in Moral Development', pp. 465–466. See also
    Roberts, 'Emotions Among the Virtues of the Christian Life', p. 39.

86. Ellrod, 'Emotion and the Good in Moral Development', pp. 468–469.

87. Ellrod, 'Emotion and the Good in Moral Development', p. 469. For a compatible
    perspective see Solomon, *The Passions*, p. 179; Ben-Ze'ev, *The Subtlety of Emotions*,
    p. 265; Leeper, 'The Motivational and Perceptual Properties of Emotions',
    pp. 156–157. De Sousa compares emotion to a sense and believes it tells us
    something about objective reality. De Sousa, *The Rationality of Emotions*, pp. 110,
    150–158. For a refutation of this view see Kenny, *Action, Emotion, and Will*, pp. 56–57.

88. Ellrod, 'Emotion and the Good in Moral Development', p. 471.

It may be asked, 'How can emotions that are based on internal judgments be taken as a guide for finding truth?' This is the same problem we have with our senses. We cannot verify their validity except within our own perception. We must believe that what they tell us is accurate. When I see a straight stick sticking out of a pond that appears bent, I know that the water is distorting my vision. The only way that I know that my vision is distorted is by the use of my sight when the stick is out of the water. In the same way, we can use and evaluate emotion to find truth.[89] In emotion, our wonderfully complex mind is picking up clues about the true character of the object that we are perceiving.

Physiology and the cognitive theory
It is important to stress that the cognitive theory of emotion does not neglect physiological change. Physiological change remains an important part of most emotion.[90] My heart may slow or speed up and my mouth may go dry, both of which I might be aware of, or my pupils may dilate and I may blush, which I might not notice. What is clear is that the physiological change experienced in emotion is a result of cognition and evaluation and not a direct response to a stimulus. The stronger the physiological reaction usually the stronger the emotion. A person 'in the grip of an emotion' is greatly affected physiologically and may be unable to control themselves.[91] We cannot do better than the explanation of Jonathan Edwards:

> The other faculty is that by which the soul does not merely perceive and view things, but is in some way inclined toward the things it views or considers . . . The soul either views things with approval, with pleasure, and with acceptance, or it views things with opposition, with disapproval, with displeasure, and with rejection . . . [the weak outworking of this is called by Edwards 'inclination'] These are those vigorous and sensible exercises of the faculty that we call the affections . . . The body of man is not directly capable of thinking or understanding. Only the soul has ideas, and so only the soul is pleased or displeased with its ideas. Since only the soul thinks, only the soul loves or hates, rejoices or is grieved at what it thinks. The bodily effects of these emotions are not the same thing as the affections, and in no way are essential to them.[92]

---

89. Ellrod, 'Emotion and the Good in Moral Development', p. 475.

90. Physiological reactions are not a logically necessary part of emotion. Oakley, *Morality and the Emotions*, pp. 6–37; Nussbaum, *Upheavals of Thought*, pp. 58–61.

91. Lyons, *Emotion*, pp. 116–118, 123–128. For a review of the physiological aspects of emotion see Frijda, *The Emotions*.

92. Edwards, *Religious Affections*, pp. 6–7 (all quotations are from Houston's edition).

Cognitive theory reviewed

There are many strong arguments for a cognitive view of emotion. It allows us to build a workable theory which explains the operation of emotion. Emotion is always about something; it has an object. Emotion tells us about our values and beliefs. It can also tell us about the beliefs and values of others. Emotions are not necessarily rational, not because they are intrinsically irrational impulses, but because we can be irrational people. Emotions are often a powerful motivation. Just as we are held responsible for what we believe and how we act, we can be held responsible for our emotions or lack of them. Finally, it is possible that an emotion may show us objective facts about its object just as our physical senses show us objective facts about the physical word.

But it is also critical that we do not understand a cognitive view of emotions as a simple approach to the study of emotions. Emotions are highly complex phenomena that rely upon both our conscious and unconscious mind, memories, cultural factors, family upbringing and our personalities. These factors interact and respond to one another in an incredibly complex web of interdependent beliefs and values to produce particular emotions in particular circumstances.

Our summary of a cognitive approach is in sharp contrast to the results of a non-cognitive approach. In the words of Griffiths, who takes non-cognitive theory to its logical conclusion, 'The research surveyed . . . suggests that the general concept of emotion has no role in any future psychology.'[93] A cognitive view of emotion has strong implications for our view of reason, our practice of ethics, and our understanding of psychology. Some of these will be explored in the next few sections.

Emotion's effect on the mind and behaviour

Communication and social interaction

Emotions are a major way we communicate to others. Facial expressions, posture and vocalization all play a role in the communication of emotion. Emotions often precede behaviour and as such are clues to what we are likely to do. Similarly, they may act as warnings to others of danger or violent behaviour.[94]

---

93. Griffiths, *What Emotions Really Are*, p. 247.

94. Carlson, *Psychology: The Science of Behavior*, pp. 406, 412. For the role of vocalization, as well as the assertion that vocalization of emotion is well understood and universal between cultures (similar to facial expression), see Pittam and Scherer, 'Vocal Expression and Communication of Emotion'.

Facial expressions of emotion are a constant focal point in social interaction and a stimulus for others reactions.[95]

The ability to communicate emotion correctly assumes a cognitive view. To be able to recognize and understand emotion it is necessary to understand the reason and thinking behind it. Communicating what we feel to each other without a cognitive understanding of the meaning of the emotion would be impossible.[96] If we think about it, we know that emotion plays a major role in what we are saying to others. Every parent knows that there are different kinds of ways of saying 'no' to children. There is the 'No, you cannot have a cookie' and the 'No! Never run into the street without looking.' The words are similar, the emotion in our voice and body language shows the child what kind of 'no' it is.

For all the difficulty of 'experts' in defining emotions, the lay person understands what the terms mean. Joel Davitz, in his study of people's understanding of emotion terms, writes: 'Nowhere could I find adequate definitions of most of these words, yet people use these labels without obvious difficulties in communication, apparently assuming that the meaning of love, hate, joy, or sadness is so clear that they hardly need explicit definitions.'[97] In his study, people defined emotion in remarkably similar terms using similar words, experiences and analogies.

Emotion plays a major role in leadership and social interaction. For example, enthusiasm is contagious, exciting others and eliciting participation. It is probable that emotions play a larger role in successful social adjustment and popularity than does intelligence or any other single factor.[98] The intellectual understanding of a given social situation does not imply that an appropriate

---

95. Izard, *Human Emotions*, p. 73.

96. Frijda, 'Emotion and Recognition of Emotion', pp. 241–242.

97. Davitz, 'A Dictionary and Grammar of Emotion', p. 251.

98. The concept of 'Emotional Intelligence' or EQ has recently become an important topic of discussion. It takes into account both the importance of emotion in social interaction and the ability of an individual to learn to respond in an emotionally healthy way. One of the pioneers of this idea defines it: 'Emotional intelligence involves the ability to perceive accurately, appraise, and express emotion; the ability to access and/or generate feelings when they facilitate thought; the ability to understand emotion and emotional knowledge; and the ability to regulate emotions to promote emotional and intellectual growth.' (Mayer and Salovey, 'What Is Emotional Intelligence?', p. 10). Implied in this is that in some situations there are 'right' or 'wrong' emotional responses. These responses can be taught (pp. 9, 14–15).

response will follow, but an emotional understanding of the situation may be needed to have an appropriate response. Empathy for the feelings of others builds friendships while the inability to react to others' emotions often leads to rejection. The ability to display appropriate emotion and react to others' emotions appropriately is a major factor in successful relationships.[99]

Understanding our emotions and the emotions of others provides an essential tool for communication. Reading others' emotions prepares us to react and understand others, while our own emotions communicate our values to others. Emotion is a key element in making social decisions.[100] It is essential in building relationships. Gilligan and Bower conclude:

> . . . emotion can have a surpassingly strong influence on how someone thinks and acts in his social world . . . Emotion thus seems to be inextricably related to how we perceive and think, influencing them at every turn.[101]

Memory and learning

Emotion also plays a major role in memory. There is evidence to suggest that the stronger the emotion the stronger the memory will be – memories that include emotion are recalled much more easily than memories with little emotional content.[102]

People who find themselves in a happy mood remember happy memories more easily than sad memories. People in sad moods retrieve sad memories more easily than happy ones.[103] When the present emotions are the opposite of what was experienced in the learning experience, recall is negatively affected. People in a happy state tend to rate sad experiences as less sad than when in a normal state. Similarly, people in a sad state rate happy experiences as less happy than when in a neutral state. Overall there is a bias towards happy memories which are, in general, more easily recalled. In some cases, very strong negative emotions may play a role in blocking memory. For example, young children often forget instances of abuse, and depressed people's capacity for learning is seriously diminished.[104]

---

99. Sroufe *et al.*, 'The Role of Affect in Social Competence'.

100. Scherer, 'On the Nature and Function of Emotion'.

101. Gilligan and Bower, 'Cognitive Consequences of Emotional Arousal', pp. 568–569.

102. Izard, 'Emotive-Cognitive Relationships', p. 22.

103. Moore, Underwood and Rosenhan, 'Emotion, Self, and Others', p. 466.

104. Gilligan and Bower, 'Cognitive Consequences of Emotional Arousal', pp. 551–553;
     Bower, 'Some Relations Between Emotions and Memory', pp. 304–305.

Memory obviously plays a major role in learning. Yet, the role of emotion in learning is broader than affecting our memories. Bower writes:

> To summarize, emotions play three separate roles in direction learning. First, emotions frequently accompany failed expectations (or interruptions), and thus direct attention to accompanying events as important items to be learned. Second, emotions mobilize attention to those features of an external situation that learners judge to be significant or predictive of the cause of the failed expectation, and, in so doing, cause greater learning of them. Third, the inertial persistence of the emotional arousal, and its slow decay, leads to continued recycling or rehearsal of those encoded events viewed as causally belonging to the emotional reaction. All these factors promote better learning . . .[105]

So emotions play a crucial role in memory and learning. They serve to focus our attention, motivate learning, draw our attention to what is important, and aid us in recalling things that give insight into our present situation.

Work and performance

Emotions also affect our performance. Sad or depressed people are more likely to do poorly in physical or mental activities, while happy or contented feelings may aid endurance and performance. Our emotions also affect the performance of others. For example, the anger or displeasure of a boss or spouse may motivate change, action or hard work, or the happiness of a spouse or boss reinforces the behaviour that elicited that response. Emotion serves to focus our attention. Without emotion about what we are doing, our mind wanders.[106]

In children sadness slows reaction time, increases errors and increases the time it takes to learn something new, while happiness has the opposite effect in all these areas. This finding has not been duplicated with adults but some of the same results do seem to be evident. Joy has a tendency to increase altruism while sadness often decreases it. However, empathy or sadness over a friend's difficult situation serves to increase altruism and motivate compassionate action.[107] Izard writes, 'Changes in emotions can alter the appearance of our world from bright and cheerful to dark and gloomy, our thinking from creative

---

105. Bower, 'Some Relations Between Emotions and Memory', p. 304.

106. Bower, 'Some Relations Between Emotions and Memory', p. 303; Lyons, *Emotion*, p. 192; Izard, Kagan and Zajonc, introduction to *Emotions*, p. 9.

107. Moore, Underwood and Rosenhan, 'Emotion, Self, and Others', pp. 69, 477.

to morbid, and our actions from awkward and inappropriate to skillful and effective.'[108]

Similar to their role in learning, emotions serve to focus our attention on our work and motivate us to work. And perhaps most important, a positive emotional mood can add a bounce to our step that will make us more efficient and productive.

The integration of reason and emotion

A cognitive approach to emotion integrates emotion and intellect while a non-cognitive approach has a tendency to allow or promote their separation.[109] Lauritzen writes, 'embracing a non-cognitive theory leads to . . . a passive and mechanistic understanding of emotional behavior, and to a sharp dichotomy between reason and emotion.'[110] Solomon concludes, 'The wisdom of reason against the treachery and temptations of the passions has been the central theme of Western philosophy.'[111]

Many scientists see reason as being negatively influenced by emotion. Knowing is a logical concept which precludes emotion.[112] Contrary to this idea, in the romantic tradition emotion is celebrated as being irrational. In this reaction to rationalism, the evaluation of emotion is based on the same dualistic view of reason and emotion as in rationalism.[113] However, both extremes are based on the same false premise, that is, reason and emotion are two separate systems.[114]

Macmurray writes: 'the contrast we habitually draw between "reason" and "emotion" is a false one, and that error has practical consequences which have always been serious and may soon prove disastrous. For it leads to the conclusion that our emotional life is irrational, and must remain so.'[115] Leeper

---

108. Izard, *Human Emotions*, p. 18.
109. Lazarus, 'Constructs of the Mind', p. 6.
110. Paul Lauritzen, 'Emotion and Religious Ethics', p. 311.
111. Solomon, *The Passions*, p. 10.
112. Levy, 'Emotion, Knowing, and Culture', pp. 217–218.
113. Solomon, *The Passions*, p. 11.
114. A cognitive approach negates the idea that emotion provides the kind of pre-cognition knowledge advocated by Hume and Schleiermacher (Proudfoot, *Religious Experience*, pp. 344, 349).
115. Macmurray, *Reason and Emotion*, p. 5.

argues that the separation of reason and emotion has been destructive in our society:

> Hence, what has happened is that, rather than avoiding emotions (they cannot be avoided), our objectively-oriented culture has led to a very heavy use of negative emotional motives (fear of punishment, sense of shame, feelings of insecurity, and so on) and to a use of positive emotional motives of only very crude or cheap sorts, such as cravings for luxuries and special status. Out present cultural crisis illustrates the costly consequences of this.[116]

Cognitive theory offers us a healthy alternative. Reason and emotion are interdependent. Lazarus writes, 'I offer the following manifesto for cognitive theorists that sums up the issue: *Emotion and Cognition are inseparable . . .* Cognition is thus the key to emotion and integrated human functioning.'[117] Solomon writes of his theory, 'the brunt of this theory is the total demolition of the age-old distinctions between emotion and reason, passion and logic.' He continues, 'What we shall find is that emotions turn out to be far more logical, far more complex, far more sophisticated and far more a part and parcel of reason than most philosophers have ever imagined.'[118] It is time for us to realize that we naturally function as unified human beings and take advantage of the vitality and strength that this brings to our thinking.

Implications of the integration of reason and emotion
We must not emphasize the causal relationship of cognition to emotion and exclude the role that emotion plays in changing and determining cognition. Emotion serves to direct our attention and influence our thoughts. Emotion and cognition are constantly interacting. An emotion caused by a cognition will exert influence on the cognitive process, and the chain will continue.[119]

John Macmurray provides an important perspective about the integration of reason and emotion. It is obvious that our thoughts can be true or false. Those that correspond to what is real are true and those that do not correspond to reality (outside ourselves) are false. Emotions fit into this same pattern. What we feel that matches reality is true while what we feel that does

---

116. Leeper, 'The Motivational and Perceptual Properties of Emotions', p. 165.

117. Lazarus, 'Constructs of the Mind', p. 9.

118. Solomon, 'The Logic of Emotion', pp. 45, 49.

119. Derryberry and Rothbart, 'Emotion, Attention, and Temperament', pp. 138–139.

not match reality is false. Both thoughts and emotions are fallible. Morrissey writes, 'Insofar as our emotions reveal to us the really real and not just our own nature, we are feeling (and emoting) reasonably.'[120]

If our emotions are cognitive we can evaluate them and work to conform our thinking to what is true. As we have seen, emotional states may reveal to us the true state of our values and what we consider important. Morrissey writes:

> Here especially we must learn to feel what we love and love what we feel in order to fill our consciousness with the reality of what it is or who it is we love. For this reason we must educate our emotions just as we would educate our minds, so we can know truly the objective world that we confront in our daily experience . . .
>
> Therefore, just as our emotions are rational our reason is affective, being ultimately grounded in our personal, emotional life. Unless reason and emotion work in mutual harmony we cannot know reality objectively and normatively.[121]

Solomon writes, 'Emotions are not irrational; people are irrational.'[122] In other words, emotions do not promote irrationality, rather irrational emotions reflect our own irrational judgments and beliefs. Solomon continues: 'Emotional control is not learning to employ rational techniques to force into submission a brutal "it" which has victimized us but rather the willingness to become self-aware, to search out, and challenge the normative judgments embedded in every emotional response.'[123]

Ethics and emotion

If emotions are an integral part of reason they become an integral part of ethics. Emotions can be judged as right or wrong, or even judged to be missing from a person's response to a situation where emotion is appropriate.[124] Solomon writes, 'They [emotions] lie at the very heart of ethics, determining our values, focusing our vision, influencing our every judgment, giving meaning to our lives.'[125] This is in contrast to the ideas of Kant who, according to

---

120. Morrissey, 'Reason and Emotion', pp. 284–285.
121. Morrissey, 'Reason and Emotion', p. 287. See also Mandler, 'A Constructivist Theory of Emotion', pp. 22–23.
122. Solomon, 'Emotions and Choice', p. 265.
123. Solomon, 'Emotions and Choice', pp. 270–271.
124. See Taylor, 'Justifying the Emotions', p. 390.
125. Solomon, 'Some Notes on Emotion', p. 178.

Cassirer, believed: 'Morality is essentially a matter of making feelings and inclinations subservient to the principles of rational control.'[126]

Oakley writes in the introduction to his book on morality and the emotions:

> I am concerned to show the falsity of a certain popular view according to which our emotions are merely incidental events in our lives, in that they typically just 'happen to' us, and so cannot reflect well or poorly on us in any important sense. Contrary to this picture, I want to show that our emotions may actually be essential and enduring features of our moral character, and that we therefore have a fundamental reason to seek to develop our emotional capacities in ways which enrich our lives.[127]

Callahan quite rightly observes:

> In the rationalist tradition in ethics, the emotions are morally suspect. In a corrective swing of the pendulum, burgeoning philosophical interest is 'rehabilitating' the emotions in ethical decision making. The emotions and reason should be mutually correcting resources in moral reflection.[128]

The fallacy of 'purely rational' ethics

Actions that we consider ethical or unethical arouse our emotions. For example, hearing of a terrorist attack often produces anger in the hearer. What role should our emotional reaction to such an event play in determining morality? The majority of modern philosophers have held that emotions should not play a part in determining whether an act is right or wrong. In this view emotion is thought to cloud the issues. Callahan concludes: 'The idea is always to be suspicious of them [emotions], and to rely on as few as possible.'[129]

Callahan reacts against this. Determining morality should, in his view, include using information from both reason and emotion. They should be partners. 'But I would also claim that emotion should tutor reason.'[130] Ethical systems that exclude emotion presuppose a separation of emotion and cognition that is

---

126. Cassirer, *Grace and Law*, p. 58.

127. Oakley, *Morality and the Emotions*, p. 5. For a similar view see Lauritzen, 'Emotion and Religious Ethics', pp. 317–319.

128. Callahan, 'The Role of Emotion in Ethical Decisionmaking', p. 9. For documentation of the neglect of emotion in ethics and moral education see Rich, 'Moral Education and the Emotions', pp. 81–82; Oakley, *Morality and the Emotions*, p. 2.

129. Callahan, 'The Role of Emotion in Ethical Decisionmaking', p. 9.

130. Callahan, 'The Role of Emotion in Ethical Decisionmaking', p. 9.

false.[131] Robert Frank argues that conscience and emotion are key in forming a moral society.[132] Nussbaum agrees:

> If emotions are suffused with intelligence and discernment, and if they contain in themselves an awareness of value or importance, they cannot, for example, easily be sidelined in accounts of ethical judgement, as so often they have been in the history of philosophy. Instead of viewing morality as a system of principles to be grasped by the detached intellect, and emotions as motivations that either support or subvert our choice to act according to principle, we will have to consider emotions as part and parcel of the system of ethical reasoning.[133]

The function of emotion in ethics

Emotion may provide a good indication of the level of a person's moral development. John Martin Rich suggests a number of tests for determining morality:

1. Are appropriate emotions present? Does a person react with compassion in a situation where another has been maltreated?

---

131. It may seem advantageous to specifically argue against Kant and others who stress that duty is the only legitimate moral motivation. However, Kant seems to hold a non-cognitive view of emotion. It is my contention that if a cognitive view has been proved the arguments of Kantians fall. Therefore, it is not necessary to defend against this position, For this view see also Oakley, *Morality and the Emotions*, pp. 38, 94. 'Those who accord little moral significance to emotions have often based their views on inadequate accounts of the nature of emotion.' Oakley, *Morality and the Emotions*, p. 189. For an argument against Kant, in light of compassion as a motive see Blum, 'Compassion', pp. 514–515. Nussbaum concludes, 'he treats all these passions as if they derived from a prerational nature and were fundamentally impulsive and noncognitive in nature'. For Nussbaum this 'creates problems for his moral thought'. Nussbaum, *Upheavals of Thought*, p. 381. For Kant's view see Kant, *The Doctrine of Virtue*, pp. 32–33, 60; Teale, *Kantian Ethics*, pp. 50, 109–29. For a specific refutation of Kant see Oakley, *Morality and the Emotions*, pp. 86–121. Damasio points out that people who behave in a Kantian way without emotion are extremely irrational. Damasio, *Descartes' Error*, p. 172.
132. Frank, *Passion Within Reason*. Frank gives many detailed examples and philosophical proofs. See, for example, pp. 5, 35, 81, 147–158, 161, 199. Rationality fails to explain moral behaviour where emotions succeeds.
133. Nussbaum, *Upheavals of Thought*, p. 1.

2. Are appropriate emotions absent? Is guilt present after a morally wrong act?

3. Are inappropriate emotions present in situations? Is someone joyful over someone's misfortune?

Failing or passing these tests can serve to show a person's moral development or lack thereof. Emotions serve to motivate moral behaviour. Compassion may stop us from going along with our peers in teasing a handicapped person, or anger may motivate us to defend a helpless elderly person who is being assaulted.[134]

Callahan writes:

> A lack of anxiety, guilt, empathy, or love devastates moral functioning. Persons may have a high IQ and be able to articulate verbally the culture's moral rules, but if they cannot feel the emotional force of inner obligation, they can disregard all moral rules or arguments without a qualm.[135]

And Richard A. Dienstbier writes:

> Emotions influence our decisions in moral situations. When an emotion is attributable to our own internal reaction to temptation it is a crucial force in resisting temptation.[136]

The stronger the emotion the greater influence it will have. Moral lessons that are strongly taught are much more likely to be remembered and followed because of the resulting *internal* negative emotional association. If a mother says, 'No you cannot have a snack before lunch' to her toddler and later when she sees him about to touch a hot stove she yells, 'No! Get away from the stove this instant!', which command is the toddler most likely to remember? The mother has reinforced the importance of the lesson to stay away from hot stoves by her emotional reaction. In experiments it has been shown that an internal emotional response influences moral decisions. For example, when subjects are given a placebo and told that it will make them more emotional they are more likely to cheat on a test because they can attribute their emotional aversion to cheating to the placebo.[137]

---

134. Rich, 'Moral Education and the Emotions', pp. 82–84.
135. Callahan, 'The Role of Emotion in Ethical Decisionmaking', p. 10. See also Kagan, 'The Idea of Emotion', p. 69.
136. Dienstbier, 'The Role of Emotion', pp. 500–501.
137. Dienstbier, 'The Role of Emotion', pp. 504, 509–510.

Our memories are filled with emotion. We often make moral choices because we feel strongly about them. Our 'spontaneous' moral decisions are not spontaneous at all but are an informed response from emotionally triggered memories and beliefs. Reason and emotion act together in determining our ethical decision in response to a situation.

Emotions can serve as a corrective to faulty 'logical' arguments. If our emotions have been built on correct reasoning they will alert us to faulty reasoning even when we cannot immediately see the fault in logic. A very logical argument may be presented for infanticide that we cannot immediately refute, but our emotions guide us to reject it. Emotion may also push us toward new and needed moral developments in our character. We may believe that we have no moral responsibility to sufferers of AIDS but when we walk through an AIDS clinic we come to the conclusion that we must support the patients with love and care. We may have a 'logical' argument that we do not need to support famine victims but when we visit victims of famine we realize that this position is untenable. These examples show how our emotions push us towards moral growth. Reason and emotion constantly interact with one another in the process of moral development and moral decision making, each serving as a corrective for the other.[138]

The essential role of emotion in ethics is supported by experimental data. People who have had brain injuries or surgeries that have inhibited the normal function of emotion often find themselves unable to make good ethical decisions or they show a pronounced lack of moral inhibitions.[139]

Beyond this, a lack of emotion may lead to having less impact in moral action. Can we truly believe that a compassionate act out of duty will be the same as one out of love? The person who feels compassion is more likely to act and is better able to show sympathy than a person acting out of duty. Moreover, the receiver can tell if compassion is the motivation for the action and, in realizing this, they receive greater comfort than if the act was performed out of duty. The one who acts out of duty alone may be said to be detached and psychologically disjointed. Emotion is part of morality itself.[140]

Emotion and reason must be seen to function together in any viable ethical system, both serving to enhance and correct the other. Augustine writes,

---

138. Callahan, 'The Role of Emotion in Ethical Decisionmaking', pp. 11–12.

139. Carlson, *Psychology: The Science of Behavior*, p. 405. 'Emotions often provide moral barriers to many types of immoral behavior' (Ben-Ze'ev, *The Subtlety of Emotions*, p. 264).

140. Oakley, *Morality and the Emotions*, pp. 43–44.

'In our ethics, we do not so much inquire whether a pious soul is angry, as why he is angry; not whether he is sad, but what is the cause of his sadness; not whether he fears, but what he fears.'[141]

Aquinas agrees:

> All the emotions issue from certain initial ones, namely love and hatred, and finish in certain others, namely pleasure and sorrow. In like manner, all the operations that are the matter of moral virtue are related to one another, and even to the emotions.[142]

Oakley concurs:

> Emotion and reason work together within us to make moral decisions. Ethical action that is taken in concert with emotion makes it clear that the values and beliefs directing the action are held to be both true and important by the individual.[143]

Conclusion and implications for the study of the New Testament

The non-cognitive approach to emotion simplifies the academic process and may promote a feeling of rational infallibility. Therefore, it has been preferred by an academic community that has a supreme trust in the 'unbiased' rationality of man. Recently, many scholars in the disciplines of psychology, philosophy and anthropology have reacted against the idea that emotions function as an independent non-cognitive system. There are many compelling arguments for a cognitive approach. This cognitive approach understands the impossibility of 'pure reason' divorced from emotion.

The cognitive approach presents a coherent working theory of emotion where the non-cognitive approach fails to do this. It makes logical sense to understand emotion as an indicator of what we believe and value, while emotions become difficult to understand if they are only physiological responses to stimuli. If the cognitive theory is correct, emotions become an integral part

---

141. Augustine, *The City of God*, 9.5.

142. Aquinas, *Summa Theologica.*, vol. 23, 1a2ae.65.1.

143. Oakley, *Morality and the Emotions*, 55. See also Calhoun and Solomon, introduction to *What is an Emotion?*, p. 39. Ben-Ze'ev gives a good summary of emotion's function in morality, Ben-Ze'ev, *The Subtlety of Emotions*, p. 265.

of our reason and our ethics. Emotions are not primitive impulses to be controlled or ignored, but cognitive judgments or construals that tell us about ourselves and our world. In this understanding, destructive emotions can be changed, beneficial emotions can be cultivated, and emotions are a crucial part of morality. Emotions also help us to work efficiently, assist our learning, correct faulty logic and help us build relationships with others.

Holding a logical and informed theory of emotion will prove significant in the interpretation of the New Testament. First, there is a large amount of material about emotion in the New Testament. Increasing our understanding of the emotions will increase our understanding of the passages in the New Testament that emphasize emotion as well as increase our understanding of the role of emotion in the theology and ethics of the New Testament as a whole. Furthermore, a non-cognitive approach to emotion, which I believe has been used by most New Testament scholars (consciously or unconsciously), may foster mistakes in interpretation. The non-cognitive approach of an interpreter may cause him or her to de-emphasize the role of specific emotions in a passage, to interpret words for emotion in an overly theological manner, or to downplay the place of emotion in New Testament ethics and theology.

We may ask the question, 'Is there any evidence that the writers of the New Testament had a cognitive view of emotion?' (I do not imply by this that they had a well formed theory of emotion, but only that they may have had some idea that emotion is based on beliefs and values.) If the writers of the New Testament believed that emotion was cognitive it is easier to understand how it could have had a crucial and legitimate place in the faith and theology of the first-century church. In order to ascertain the answer, we may ask some key questions of the text. 'Did the writers of the New Testament separate emotion and reason or did they see them as a unified whole?' If the writers of the New Testament had a cognitive view of emotion we would expect to find that they could command emotion, were able to judge some emotions as wrong and some as right, and that they held people responsible for their emotions. Also, we might expect to find that emotion was seen as an integral part of faith and ethics. If they had a non-cognitive view of emotion we would expect to find that they did not hold people responsible for their emotions, could not command emotion and did not integrate emotion into their definition of faith and ethics. If the New Testament favours this view we might expect that believers were exhorted to exercise control over their emotions *in a general sense*.

In the following Chapters I hope to shed light on some of these issues, highlight and correct some of the mistakes that have been made in interpreting the New Testament, and provide possible answers to some of the crucial questions about the role of emotion in the New Testament that have come out of this interdisciplinary study. Oakley summarizes my own belief when he comments: 'I am suggesting that we can and ought to develop our emotional capacities so that we respond *naturally and spontaneously* with the emotions which are appropriate to various situations.'[144] The question that remains is whether this is also the goal of the New Testament.

---

144. Oakley, *Morality and the Emotions*, p. 139. See also p. 143.

2. EMOTION IN THE GRECO-ROMAN WORLD

> My own experience as a teacher tells the opposite tale. For every one pupil who needs to be guarded from a weak excess of sensibility there are three who need to be awakened from the slumber of cold vulgarity.[1]
>
> Emotional intensity is in itself no proof of spiritual depth.[2]
>
> C. S. Lewis

This Chapter has two primary objectives. First, it is important to find what ideas about emotion were present in the world of the New Testament. Were the writers of the New Testament likely to encounter a well-formed cognitive or non-cognitive theory? Second, the Chapter will present general background information in order to help us understand emotion in the New Testament. What place did emotion have in ritual and celebration? Was the free expression of emotion acceptable in society or was it repressed? What was the place of emotion in philosophy and literature?

Even the experts disagree about the precise views that are expressed in many of the ancient texts, but it may be possible to find a basic consensus about what was believed about emotion by particular groups in the ancient

---

1. Lewis, *The Abolition of Man*, p. 24. See pp. 19–25.
2. Lewis, *Letters to Malcolm*, p. 82.

world. There is strong evidence that both a cognitive and non-cognitive view were present in the world of the New Testament.

It is difficult to find good source material for the place of emotion in the Greco-Roman world outside of the writing of the philosophers. However, keep in mind that the philosophers were, in many ways, reacting to their society. For example, they talk about the need to control or eliminate emotion because they are reacting against what they see as emotional excess. The ancient writers have many insights about the nature of emotion from which we can learn. Schimmel writes: 'It is my impression that these writers anticipated and in some instances went beyond many of the insights of modern psychology into this emotion [anger]. Yet they have been ignored by most modern writers on the subject.'[3]

The Hellenistic philosophers exerted great influence on the Roman world. Their influence extended from the common man to the court of Caesar. The conquests of Alexander had set the stage for their ideas to become the dominant philosophies in the Roman world. Specifically, the Hellenistic Schools (Epicureans, Stoics and Skeptics) wanted their philosophy to impact popular culture, be practical, and help individuals live a better life. With the growth of these schools the influence of the Olympian gods declined. Plato and Aristotle, although earlier, also are relevant to our discussion. They form the background for the Hellenistic schools and their work is often both implicitly and explicitly refuted or endorsed by them. Even though Epicurus, Zeno and others taught hundreds of years before the first century AD, it is clear that their ideas and the movements that they started were the most prevalent philosophical schools in the world of the New Testament.[4] Griffin concludes, 'Philosophy supplied ethical preconceptions on which moral choices were often based even by those who neither knew nor cared much about the philosophical sects.'[5]

---

3. Schimmel, 'Anger and Its Control', p. 336.
4. See, for example, the work of Galen. Writing in the second century CE on the passions, he explicitly mentions Aristotle, Plato, Epicureans and the Stoics. Harkins, trans., *Galen on the Passions*. See also Paige, 'Philosophy'; Griffin, 'Philosophy, Politics, and Politicians at Rome' (for philosophy's influence on society see pp. 19–21).
5. Griffin, 'Philosophy, Politics, and Politicians at Rome', p. 37.

Non-cognitive theory

Plato

Plato follows the classical meaning of the word *pathos* (passion). The passions were emotional impulses that came upon a person. As in the Greek poets, emotion is something that happens to us, not something produced within ourselves. This idea was present in the vocabulary itself. In the words of Hankinson, emotion is seen as 'a compulsive, uncontrollable force'. As such, it may absolve people from responsibility for their actions.[6] Nussbaum relates that in many passages Plato treats emotions as 'irrational urges to be developed or undermined by non-cognitive strategies'.[7] Plato describes the passions thus:

> . . . passion, a contentious and combative element which frequently causes shipwreck by its headstrong violence.[8]
>
> Passion is an ill-favoured thing, and the speaker who does his wrath the favour to feast it on the poison it craves turns all the humanity education has fashioned within him into brutishness once more; persistence in his morose rancour makes him a wild beast, and that sorry return is all the return passion makes him for his favours.[9]

The passions are part of the illogical part of a divided soul. Plato argues that the soul must be divided because the passions are fundamentally different than reason.[10]

However, Plato did allow for some connection between cognition and the passions. Plato differentiated between bodily feelings and emotion; but, he did not argue for a cognitive theory of emotion.[11] Plato gave an explanation of reason and emotion's interaction in the *Phaedrus*. Fortenbaugh concludes, 'The

---

6. Hankinson, 'Actions and Passions', p. 187. See also Sherman, 'The Role of Emotion in Aristotelian Virtue', p. 3, and Dodds, *The Greeks and the Irrational*, p. 185.

7. Nussbaum, 'Poetry and the Passions', p. 105.

8. Plato, *Laws I* 863b3–5, trans. Taylor. See also Plato *Republic: I* 329c, trans. Shorey.

9. Plato, *Laws XI* 935a3–8, trans. Taylor. See also Plato *Laws IX* 866–67, trans. Taylor.

10. Plato, *Republic: IV* pp. 438–441, trans. Shorey. Plato seems to have divided emotion between two of the three parts of the tripartite soul: appetite and spirit. For some of the problems with Plato's separation of reason and passion including its faulty logic see Tiles, 'The Combat of Passion and Reason', pp. 321–330.

11. Fortenbaugh, *Aristotle on Emotion*, p. 10. Nussbaum argues that a cognitive view is present in Plato but she is effectively rebuffed by Hursthouse (see Nussbaum and Hursthouse, 'Plato on Commensurability and Desire').

Philebus certainly makes clear that Plato saw an intimate relationship between emotion and cognition. But it fails to make this relationship clear.'[12] Although Plato saw the passions as the source of disorder and suffering and the cause of war, Morrissey believes that reason was not understood to be 'abstract rationality divorced from any affective influence.'[13]

Fortenbaugh explains that in Plato, emotional appeals and persuasion were to be rejected in favour of 'truth' and 'instruction'. Plato criticized the writers of plays for 'playing upon feelings that are unintelligent and destructive of man's reasoning capacity'. Fortenbaugh continues: 'Viewed as an affliction divorced from cognition, emotion was naturally opposed to reason and conceived as something hostile to thoughtful judgment.'[14] To conclude, we should listen to Plato:

> And where there are two opposite impulses in a man at the same time about the same thing we say that there must needs be two things in him. . . .
>
> And shall we not say that the part of the us that leads us to dwell in memory on our suffering and impels us to lamentation, and cannot get enough of that sort of thing, is the irrational and idle part of us . . .? [Plato continues by critiquing poetry and its irrational exciting of the passions.]
>
> And so in regard to the emotions of sex and anger, and all the appetites and pains and pleasures of the soul which we say accompany all our actions, the effect of poetic imitation is the same. For it waters and fosters these feelings when what we ought to do is to dry them up, and it establishes them as our rulers when they ought to be ruled.[15]

Other non-cognitive philosophers

Later Stoics followed Plato, not just in their ideas, but explicitly in the division of the soul. The early Stoics (discussed later in this Chapter) received criticism from the later Stoics for their highly cognitive view of emotion. Posidonius and Panaetius argued that passions were produced in the irrational part of the

---

12. Fortenbaugh, *Aristotle on Emotion*, p. 11. See also pp. 24–25, and Plato, *Philebus* 38b8–9, trans. Hackforth.

13. Morrissey, 'Reason and Emotion', p. 277. See also de Sousa, *The Rationality of Emotions*, p. 127, and Solomon, 'The Philosophy of Emotion', p. 4.

14. Fortenbaugh, *Aristotle on Emotion*, pp. 17–18. See also Nussbaum, 'Poetry and the Passions', p. 100. Plato's perfect city was to be without the destructive emotions.

15. Plato, *Republic X* 604a10–606d7, trans. Shorey. See also Plato *Laws I*, pp. 645–646, trans. Taylor.

tripartite soul. Posidonius seems to argue that emotion is a separate system from cognition. The irrational drives and 'emotional disturbances' that corrupt us and cause us to do evil come from the irrational part of the soul.[16]

Galen explains the non-cognitive view of these later Stoics. Passions are not judgments and, specifically, are not responsive to changes in judgments. They battled against reason striving to dominate it.[17] Kidd writes about Posidonius: 'On the contrary, the psychic capacity for feeling anger, and the capacity for desire are irrational and as such quite distinct from the capacity to think . . . they [passions] were movements of irrational capacities.'[18] Therefore, passions cannot be altered by changing beliefs. These Stoics argued that they must be controlled by non-rational methods.[19] Passions are to be extirpated by reading poetry, listening to music, and using rhythm. These will appease and calm the irrational passions of the soul.[20]

Galen (writing about AD 162–166) had a similar view to Plato. Galen and Plato use the example of Medea whose passions were controlling her as she committed the great atrocity of killing her own children. Emotion short-circuits reason.[21] Galen writes, 'an error arises from false belief, while a passion results from an irrational power within us which refused to obey reason.'[22] It is interesting to observe the backlash to the highly cognitive view of the early Stoics among later philosophers: Galen, Cicero, and Plutarch all disputed this 'view'.

---

16. Kidd, 'Posidonius on Emotions', pp. 204, 206–207, 214. See also Rist, *Stoic Philosophy*, pp. 182–183 and Edelstein, *The Meaning of Stoicism*, pp. 52–53, 56–59. Marcus Aurelius also followed this scheme (Asmis, 'The Stoicism of Marcus Aurelius', pp. 2239–2241).

17. Nussbaum, 'Poetry and the Passions', p. 111. See also the writings of Arius where the passions are said to 'dominate the reason like a tyrant'. Inwood, *Ethics and Human Action in Early Stoicism*, pp. 142–143.

18. Kidd, 'Posidonius on Emotions', p. 203. See also Inwood, *Ethics and Human Action in Early Stoicism*, pp. 148–149, 158–160, 170.

19. Nussbaum, 'Poetry and the Passions', pp. 100–101, 114.

20. Nussbaum, 'Poetry and the Passions', p. 121. Here Nussbaum comments, 'The non-cognitive view yields an impoverished view of education, reducing the formation of a child's emotions to a kind of dog-training'.

21. Hankinson, 'Actions and Passions', p. 190; De Lacy, Introduction to *Galeni: De Placitis Hippocratis et Platonis*, p. 46. See also Harkins, trans., *Galen on the Passions*, pp. 31–32.

22. *Aff. Dig.* v. 2–3; cf. 7. Quoted in Hankinson, 'Actions and Passions', p. 192.

Emotion in Greco-Roman culture and literature

We will consider emotion in Greco-Roman culture and literature under the non-cognitive heading for both methodological and organizational reasons. Although it cannot be said that only a non-cognitive attitude was present in religion, society and literature, it was a prominent attitude and it seems right to deal with them in the non-cognitive section of this Chapter.

Religion

Emotion played an important part in religion, religious ritual and magic. To be emotional was an essential part of worship and the religious festivals provided a time for people to celebrate and get excited. The emotion involved in Greco-Roman religion is clearly seen in the New Testament in Acts 19 where the Ephesians feel very passionate about their god and all she represents to them.

There was an emotional element in the rituals and rites of asking the gods/spirits for healing or banishing the demons of illness.[23] Magic itself was often a mix of potions, remedies, and spells that had no cognitive basis for healing or therapy. Spells and amulets were used both to protect and curse. Even depression was sometimes treated with this kind of therapy. Magic is characterized by a manipulation of impersonal forces, is often used with unintelligible repetition of syllables, its goal is often insignificant (winning a race or lover) or negative (curse or spell), there is no overarching operative world view that motivates the act, there is no necessity of strong personal relationships, and it is surrounded by secrecy.[24]

Magic tends to have a non-cognitive emphasis.

---

23. Lloyd, *Science, Folklore, and Ideology*, pp. 168–169, 208, 214–215. For evidence of the important role of magic and superstition in daily life see Dodds, *The Greeks and the Irrational*, pp. 193–95, 248, 253. Much has been made of the decline of the gods in prominence in the later empire. This occurred especially in the higher classes but we should be careful not to underestimate the prevalence of the gods and superstitions in the daily life of the people. See Ferguson, *Backgrounds of Early Christianity*, pp. 167–170, 220–222. MacMullen writes, 'my aim is to place religion at the heart of social life as surely as it must be placed at the heart of cultural activities of every sort'. *Paganism in the Roman Empire*, p. 40.

24. Kee, *Medicine, Miracle, and Magic in New Testament Times*, pp. 54, 96–101, 107; Arnold, 'Magical Papyri', p. 667; Meier, *Mentor, Message, and Miracles*, pp. 538–552. See the good review of opinion and similar position of Theissen and Merz, *The Historical Jesus*, pp. 281–307.

Along with a fear of the unknown spiritual forces, the fear of the gods was seen as one of the bulwarks of morality.[25]

In the words of Fox:

> Like an electric current, the power of the gods had great potential for helping and harming; unlike electricity, it was unpredictable and mortals could do no more than attempt to channel its force in advance. Any account of pagan worship which minimizes the gods' uncertain anger and mortals' fear of it is an empty account.[26]

The anger of the gods was unpredictable and this was seen to account for much of the unexplained suffering in the world. They did not set a good example which made them a target for the Hellenistic philosophers. Their anger might be appeased by cultic ritual and ceremony, a non-cognitive approach.[27]

Religion provided a needed emotional outlet in society. The religious festivals and worship provided people with a time where emotions could be freely expressed.[28] The fact that the gods had human passions also allowed a level of identification of the worshipper with the deity. However, emotional excess in religion was criticized by many ancient philosophers. Religious emotion motivated people to perform acts that were foolish and extreme.[29]

This brief overview of emotion in religion brings several points to light. The belief in the gods, demons and magic created an atmosphere of superstition and fear in people's lives. These gods were capable of planting emotions in men that would lead to suffering. Emotional ecstasy was sometimes cultivated, and losing control of one's emotions in some cults was a form of worship. The gods themselves were prone to passions that raged out of control. Harmful emotions were thought by some to be cured with magic, ritual or worship.

---

25. Brunt, 'Philosophy and Religion' , pp. 179–183. See also Dodds, *The Greeks and the Irrational*, p. 44.

26. Fox, *Pagans and Christians*, p. 38.

27. Hahn, '*orgē*', p. 109; Wilson, *The Hope of Glory*, pp. 3, 159. Notice the contrast with God being unimpressed with ritual without understanding in the Old Testament.

28. Pomeroy, *Goddesses, Whores, Wives, and Slaves*, p. 217. See also Ferguson, *Backgrounds of Early Christianity*, pp. 151, 243–45.

29. Pomeroy, *Goddesses, Whores, Wives, and Slaves*, pp. 220–221; Dover, *The Greeks*, p. 65; Dover, *Greek Popular Morality*, pp. 77–79; Simon, *Mind and Madness in Ancient Greece*, p. 71.

Greco-Roman society

There are a few clues about how emotion was viewed in society and politics. Sometimes it was seen as a source of great harm and excess. Good examples of this appear in the writings of Galen where he gives specific observations of passions being the cause of violence of one individual against another (especially violence against slaves).[30] Dover writes, 'No Greek doubted that humans are easily impelled by anger, hatred or appetite (cf. III.F.2) to wrong and disastrous action.'[31]

One of the key sources about the harmful role of emotion in society is the writing of the Hellenistic philosophers. They use many examples that show the destructive force of the passions in society.[32] The Hellenistic philosophers' strong reaction against emotions that motivated harmful actions shows the strong motivating force that emotion was in the Greco-Roman world.

In one ancient tract containing advice to young women, temperance and control of the passions is seen as a primary character trait that was to be cultivated.[33] Emotion was sometimes considered a force beyond a person's control. Lenience could be granted to someone in a trial because their offence was committed under the influence of anger.[34]

Other good examples of emotion's role in society come from the life of the Caesars. It is clear, according to ancient historians, that they were often motivated by fear, jealousy, anger and pride. Their passions were seen as a source of bad leadership.[35] Sallust quotes Gaius Caesar as saying, 'Fathers of the Senate, all men who deliberate upon difficult questions ought to be free from hatred and friendship, anger and pity. When these feelings stand in the way the mind cannot easily discern the truth, and no mortal man has ever served at the same time his passions and his best interests.'[36]

---

30. Harkins, trans., *Galen on the Passions*, pp. 29–30, 38, 40–41, 46.

31. Dover, *Greek Popular Morality*, p. 81. Dover gives evidence that Greeks tended to see emotions as an outside force acting upon them to a greater degree than our culture. Dover, *Greek Popular Morality*, p. 126.

32. Nussbaum, '"By Words Not Arms"', pp. 63, 65, 69; Simon, *Mind and Madness in Ancient Greece*, p. 45.

33. Pomeroy, *Goddesses, Whores, Wives, and Slaves*, pp. 134, 136.

34. Dover, *Greek Popular Morality*, pp. 147, 153, 208.

35. Pelling, 'Plutarch: Roman Heroes and Greek Culture', pp. 205–207, 208–209, 215, 218, 221–223. See also Plutarch, *Plutarch's Moralia*, 'On Control of Anger'; Seneca, *Moral Essays*, p. 297; Rolfe, *Sallust*, p. 9.

36. Rolfe, *Sallust*, p. 89.

The attitude of Greco-Roman society towards emotion was often negative. It motivated many harmful actions. On the other hand, this may merely reflect that the history that survived reflects the mistakes that were made by people and their leaders. Emotion was considered a powerful force that could propel people towards excess and violence.

Poetry, plays and literature
As they do today, plays and poetry in the first century served to help people work through their own emotions and pain. They invited the listeners to feel with the characters and helped them realize that others struggled with the same emotions that they did.[37] Even if these writers did not have a well thought out theory of emotions, hints of their understanding of how emotion worked is often seen in their writing.

The classical poets often wrote about the destructive force of the emotions (*pathē*; 'passions'). Because of the prominent role that emotion had in their work, their stories were used by philosophers as examples of emotional excess. Writing about Greek poetry Hankinson observes: 'Passion, if it really is the uncontrollable alien force depicted in tragedy and epic, not merely diminishes responsibility it removes it altogether.'[38] Galen writes of the Illiad: 'If Homer is not clearly describing in these (verses) a battle of anger against reason in a prudent man, the victory of reason and the obedience of anger to it, then there is nothing else that anyone would concede that I understand in the poet.'[39]

Virgil takes a similar view in his plays. Anger and out of control emotion is seen as an irrational force almost forcing its victim to commit terrible and violent acts.[40]

In the play *Medea* by Euripides the main characters have some significant conversations about emotion (these are often used by later writers as source material to show the impossibility of controlling emotion). The characters of the play struggle with the battle between their will and their emotion. While Jason is motivated by reason, Medea, although she knows that reason should be her motivation, is unable to overcome her angry and

---

37. See Simon, *Mind and Madness in Ancient Greece*, pp. 78–79, 90, 144; Nussbaum, 'Tragedy and Self-Sufficiency', pp. 115–116.

38. Hankinson, 'Actions and Passions', p. 195. See also Dodds, *The Greeks and the Irrational*, pp. 3–6, 30, 41–42. Simon, *Mind and Madness in Ancient Greece*, pp. 63–97.

39. De Lacy, *Galeni: De Placitis Hippocratis et Platonis*, p. 189.

40. Putnam, 'Anger, Blindness, and Insight in Virgil's Aeneid', pp. 10, 24–30.

evil desires.[41] It is clear that emotion plays a major role in Greek literature. These plays gave their hearers the chance to express and deal with their own emotions.

In short, emotions are generally seen as a force to be wrestled with. They come upon the characters with fierce power or they may be sent like a plague by the gods to trouble their spirit. Emotion is often the motivation for harmful and immoral actions. The emotion of anger is particularly prevalent. These passions must be controlled. This emphasis is often consistent with a non-cognitive theory of the emotions. On the other hand, a careful reading shows that the complex working of cognition in emotion is not ignored by the poets.

Summary

Non-cognitive ideas about emotion had a prominent place both in philosophy and culture in the Greco-Roman world. Emotion was seen as the source of great suffering and a motivation for irrational behaviour. It was often seen as uncontrollable. The *pathē* (passions) were an irrational force in the soul. Emotion had to be calmed and controlled, reason taking the lead. Although there were hints of cognitive emotions in the writings of some of the authors that we have examined none of them saw a clear link between cognition and emotion.

Cognitive theory

Cognitive ideas about emotion were clearly present in the Greco-Roman world. The evidence for this is most prominent in the work of Aristotle and the Hellenistic philosophers. Nussbaum writes:

> The Hellenistic thinkers see the goal of philosophy as a transformation of the inner world or belief and desire through the use of rational argument. And within the inner world they focus above all on the emotions – on anger, fear, grief, love, pity, gratitude, and their many relatives and subspecies . . . Emotions are not blind animal forces, but intelligent discriminating parts of the personality, closely related to beliefs of a certain sort, and therefore responsive to cognitive modifications.[42]

---

41. Fortenbaugh, 'On the Antecedents of Aristotle's Bipartite Psychology', pp. 233–237. See also Simon, *Mind and Madness in Ancient Greece*, pp. 92–93; McDermott, *Euripides' Medea*, pp. 25, 56, 60, 109.

42. Nussbaum, *The Therapy of Desire*, p. 78.

Aristotle

Aristotle, in contrast to Plato's tripartite soul, concludes that the soul has two parts. This change is in part because he sees that Plato's theory does not deal adequately with the emotions.[43] Solomon and Calhoun write:

> Following his predecessor, Plato, Aristotle divides the human soul into a rational and an irrational part. But unlike Plato, Aristotle does not make a sharp division between the two parts. He argues that they necessarily form a unity, and this is particularly true of emotions that involve a cognitive element, including beliefs and expectations about one's situation, as well as physical sensations.[44]

While Plato thought of emotion as feeling with (*meta*) an appropriate thought (which we might compare to the ideas of Schachter and Singer), Aristotle thought that the cognition caused (*dia*) the emotion. The thought is an essential part of the definition of the emotion.[45] Aristotle writes: 'We shall define an emotion as that which leads one's condition to become so transformed that his judgment is affected, and is accompanied by pleasure or pain.' In the passage following this quote he makes it clear that emotions have objects and are based on thinking.[46]

Aristotle believed that the appetites of the physical body are subject to reason. Hunger, for example, is always directed at an object: food. The mind determines that an apple is edible and can be an object for hunger while a brick is not edible and is not an object for hunger. Even the most physical desires require the participation of reason. If this is true of the most basic physical desires, how much more will it be true of emotions. Emotions are based on beliefs and judgments.[47]

A belief that is the cause of an emotion may be correct or false and, as such, the emotion may be changed as the belief is changed. Fortenbaugh believes that an emotion was to Aristotle, 'intelligent behavior open to reasoned persuasion', not a 'totally irrational force'.[48] Beyond this, Aristotle differentiated

---

43. Fortenbaugh, 'On the Antecedents of Aristotle's Bipartite Psychology'.
44. Calhoun and Solomon, *What is an Emotion?*, p. 43.
45. Fortenbaugh, *Aristotle on Emotion*, p. 12. Fortenbaugh highlights Aristotle's ideas in opposition to James in this article.
46. Aristotle, From *Rhetoric*, pp. 44, 45.
47. Nussbaum, *The Therapy of Desire*, pp. 81–82, 86.
48. Fortenbaugh, *Aristotle on Emotion*, p. 17.

emotions on the basis of their differing cognitive content. There is a necessary physical element in all emotion.[49] Aristotle wrote:

> It therefore seems that all the affections of soul involve a body – passion, gentleness, fear, pity, courage, joy, loving, and hating; in all these there is a concurrent affection of the body . . . Consequently their definitions ought to correspond, e.g. anger should be defined as a certain mode of movement of such and such a body (or part or faculty of a body) by this or that cause or for this or that end.[50]

Incorporating another element of cognitive theory into his idea of emotion, Aristotle insists that emotion must be directed toward an object that the individual believes has innate worth. Sherman writes: 'Put briefly, emotions can register the importance of certain concerns and objects in our lives. They can be powerful modes by which we record that something is valued or not, and worth keeping or avoiding.'[51] With increased value comes increased emotion over an object's present state or its action toward us. Likewise, an object must be near in order for us to feel emotional about it. According to Aristotle, 'And even these only if they appear not remote but so near as to be imminent: we do not fear things that are a very long way off.'[52] Finally, Aristotle introduces another element in cognitive theory when he insists that certain emotions often promote typical behaviour.[53]

Aristotle aptly differentiates between simple feeling, desires and emotion so that his definition of emotion is similar to many modern cognitive definitions. Aristotle writes:

> The emotions are all those feelings that so change men as to affect their judgments, and that are also attended by pain and pleasure. Such are anger, pity, fear and the like with their opposites . . . Take, for instance, the emotion of anger: here we must discover: (1) what the state of mind of angry people is, (2) who the people are with whom they usually get angry, and (3) on what grounds they get angry with them. It is

---

49. Fortenbaugh, *Aristotle on Emotion*, p. 15. See also Arnold, *Emotion and Personality* vol. 1, p. 12; Leighton, 'Aristotle and the Emotions'.
50. Aristotle, *De Anima* 403a16–28, see Ross (ed.) *The Works of Aristotle*.
51. Sherman, 'The Role of Emotion in Aristotelian Virtue', p. 5; Nussbaum, *The Therapy of Desire*, p. 91. See also Fortenbaugh, *Aristotle on Emotion*, p. 14.
52. Aristotle, *Rhetorica* 1381a24–26, see Ross (ed.) *The Works of Aristotle*.
53. Solomon, 'The Philosophy of Emotion', p. 5; Nussbaum, 'Extirpation of the Passions', p. 141.

not enough to know one or even two of these points; unless we know all three, we shall be unable to arouse anger in any one.[54]

Pity may be defined as a feeling of pain caused by the sight of some evil, destructive or painful, which befalls one who does not deserve it, and which we might expect to befall ourselves or some friend of ours, and moreover to befall us soon.[55]

As we present Aristotle's theory of cognitive emotions, it is important to realize that the acknowledgment that the passions are in many instances predominantly based on irrationality is also present in his philosophy. Aristotle believed that emotion often alters perception thereby promoting self decep-tion and false judgments.[56] For example, Aristotle writes: 'Passion can also lead the young to neglect and misuse their study. The pursuits of the young in age or spirit are directed by their passion and not their reason.'[57]

Virtue and ethics

Aristotle used his cognitive definition of emotion to draw many of the same conclusions that we drew in Chapter one. Emotion is a vital part of a person's ethics and virtue. The proper or improper emotions in an individual's life will reveal their character or lack thereof.[58] In the words of Sherman, 'We are praised for both what we do and how we feel.'[59]

Emotions are not in themselves virtues. Rather, specific emotions can be vir-tuous or immoral. For example, anger can be felt in a legitimate or illegitimate way, toward a legitimate or illegitimate object, and for a legitimate or illegitimate reason. Emotion, when correctly guided by reason, is a valid and necessary

---

54. Aristotle, *Rhetorica* 1378a20–28, see Ross (ed.) *The Works of Aristotle*. See also Leighton, 'Aristotle and the Emotions', pp. 164–168.

55. Aristotle, *Rhetorica* 1385b12–16, see Ross (ed.) *The Works of Aristotle*.

56. Leighton, 'Aristotle and the Emotions'.

57. Aristotle, *Nicomachean Ethics*, 1095a, see Ross (ed.) *The Works of Aristotle*. See also 1179b. Aristotle may not have had a totally consistent cognitive view. Sherman, 'The Role of Emotion in Aristotelian Virtue', pp. 23–31. Rorty, 'Aristotle on the Metaphysical Status of the *Pathē*', pp. 532–537; Irwin, 'Reason and Responsibility in Aristotle', pp. 124–125. Irwin does a good job of explaining the difficult, seemingly contradictory statements in Aristotle's writings.

58. Fortenbaugh, *Aristotle on Emotion*, pp. 63–65, 73–76, 79–82. See also Sherman, 'The Role of Emotion in Aristotelian Virtue', pp. 7–8.

59. Sherman, 'The Role of Emotion in Aristotelian Virtue', p. 2.

motivation for action. Without the correct emotional motivation an action cannot be virtuous because virtue does not consist of only performing the act but also includes having correct motivation.[60]

Aristotle writes:

> . . . they are thought to be fools who fail to become angry at those matters they ought, or in the way or when at whom they ought. Such a person will appear to be without feeling or invulnerable, and in not turning to anger he will not protect himself and will slavishly have to suggest insult to himself and to those around him.
>
> The excess of angry emotions can be applied to the same parameters – becoming angry at those matters and at whom one should not, and becoming more angry than one should and more swiftly and for too long a time.[61]
>
> . . . with reference to anger we stand badly if we feel it violently or too weakly, and well if we feel it moderately; and similarly with reference to the other passions . . . (for the man who feels fear or anger is not praised, nor is the man who simply feels anger blamed, but the man who feels it in a certain way).[62]

With practice and diligence a person of good character can condition the emotions to react in correct and positive ways. Emotion and reason are both cognitive and intelligent processes.[63] Emotion may also be used, according to Aristotle, as a guide for finding value and truth. Nussbaum writes:

> The emotions recognize worth outside oneself; in so doing, they frequently recognize the truth . . .
>
> If our account has so far been correct, a detached unemotional intellectual survey of all the true opinions seems impossible: in avoiding emotion, one avoids a part of the truth. In the process of sorting beliefs and intuitions, then, Nikidion [Nussbaum's fictitious philosophy student] and her fellow students will rely on their emotional responses and on their memory of emotional experience, as guides to ethical truth . . . Her deliberation will for this reason be (according to her teacher) more and not less rational.[64]

---

60. Nussbaum, *The Therapy of Desire*, pp. 95–96. See also Solomon, 'The Philosophy of Emotion', p. 5; Roberts, 'Aristotle on Virtues and Emotions', p. 295; Fortenbaugh, 'Aristotle: Emotion and Moral Virtue', p. 171.

61. Aristotle, 'From *Nicomachean Ethics*', pp. 50–51.

62. Aristotle, *Ethica Nicomachea* 1105b28–34, see Ross (ed.) *The Works of Aristotle*.

63. Fortenbaugh, 'On the Antecedents of Aristotle's Bipartite Psychology', pp. 237–244.

64. Nussbaum, *The Therapy of Desire*, pp. 96–97.

Aristotle does not have the coherent well-defined cognitive theory of modern cognitive theorists in all his writings. However, in his philosophy we see many of the characteristics and conclusions about emotion that any coherent cognitive theory would be expected to have.

Hellenistic philosophers

It is legitimate to let Martha Nussbaum's book, *The Therapy of Desire: Theory and Practice in Hellenistic Ethics*, guide our discussion of the Hellenistic philosophers. Her stated goals align themselves with the goals of this book.[65] She provides us with conclusive evidence that the kind of philosophical questions that we are asking of the New Testament now were questions that were being considered in the world when the New Testament was written. Nussbaum writes:

> Especially where philosophical conceptions of emotion are concerned, ignoring the Hellenistic period means ignoring not only the best material in the Western tradition, but also the central influence on later philosophical developments . . .
>
> When Christian thinkers write about divine anger, or about mercy for human frailty, they owe a deep debt to the Roman Stoics . . . Thus the neglect of this period in much recent teaching of 'the Classics' and 'the Great Books' gives a very distorted picture of the philosophical tradition – and also robs the student of richly illuminating philosophical arguments.[66]

One of the distinguishing factors of Hellenistic philosophy was its commitment to increasing the quality of life of its adherents. Its goals were practical. Practical goals necessitated that the emotions were either analysed and directed toward their proper goal or subdued, for happiness and contentment is free from emotional turmoil (ataraxia).

Thus, having the right emotions or eliminating harmful emotions often proves to be one of the main objectives in achieving philosophy's practical end. Nussbaum writes, 'If passions are formed (at least in part) out of beliefs or judgements, and if socially taught beliefs are frequently unreliable, then passions need to be scrutinized.'[67] Society is a source of many false beliefs that lead to damaging emotions. The Hellenistic philosophers identified this problem and

---

65. Nussbaum, *The Therapy of Desire*, pp. 40–41.

66. Nussbaum, *The Therapy of Desire*, pp. 4–5.

67. Nussbaum, *The Therapy of Desire*, p. 9. See also p. 79. See also Striker, *Essays on Hellenistic Epistemology*, p. 183.

worked to change society. Unbridled emotion in society and among its leaders was seen by these schools as a destructive force. At the centre of much of the Hellenistic schools' analysis of emotion is the belief that emotion is capable of causing great harm.[68]

The Hellenistic schools compare destructive emotions to diseases of the soul. In order to cure the human soul of its emotional illness a number of approaches were emphasized. First, correct belief attained through philosophy can redirect the emotions. Secondly, social and political attitudes and institutions that promote wrong beliefs must be confronted and changed. Like a doctor in search of the cause of an illness, the philosopher's role is to find false belief in the individual that causes their soul to be filled with destructive passions.[69]

A search for truth is not enough; the Hellenistic philosopher who believes that philosophy's purpose is to cure the human soul realizes that truth without cure is pointless. His goal is to work toward healing.[70] We see clearly that the Hellenistic philosophers believed in the cognitive view of emotion. If this view is false their therapy for the human soul will prove useless.

Epicureans

The focus of Epicurus was obtaining a practical outcome. He argued that a philosophy that does not ease human misery and suffering is useless.[71] Right desires can be cultivated by developing good habits and learning what is truly valuable. The therapy Epicurus offered is internal, focusing on the beliefs of the individual. By changing the beliefs of the individual, Epicureanism improves the quality of their lives.[72] Epicurus is skeptical about the rational nature of man and society. Therefore, Epicureanism is more skeptical than

---

68. Nussbaum, *The Therapy of Desire*, pp. 10–26.

69. Nussbaum, *The Therapy of Desire*, pp. 12–16.

70. Nussbaum, *The Therapy of Desire*, p. 33. See also p. 35.

71. Nussbaum, *The Therapy of Desire*, p. 102.

72. Nussbaum, *The Therapy of Desire*, pp. 186–187. Changing false beliefs that do not have any practical affect on life is of little value (p. 195). The chief end is freedom from pain and not the cultivation of as many individual pleasurable experiences as possible. Striker, 'Epicurean Hedonism', pp. 10, 16–17. See also Rist, *Epicurus*, pp. 101–109. For a good summary of what is meant by the undisturbed life and the pursuit of pleasure in Epicureanism, see Purinton, 'Epicurus on the Telos'. Purinton makes it clear that the Epicurean view is often misunderstood by scholars.

Aristotle about emotions having positive value and an individual's ability to control those emotions.[73]

To the Epicurean, emotions reside in the rational part of the bipartite soul. In general, emotions are acceptable as long as they are based on correct belief. However, most emotions, according to Epicureanism, are based on false beliefs.[74] Most emotions are based on wrong desires that are not natural. Annas writes, 'Our emotions are thus dependent on our beliefs in a very direct way; changing our beliefs will change our emotions from being turbulent and a source of unhappiness . . . to being a part of the pleasant and untroubled life.'[75]

The correction of false beliefs, for Epicureans, will lead to the curtailing of strong desires that create mental turmoil (ataraxia). Harmful emotions are quieted by being self-sufficient (self-sufficiency means that the value of all that is outside of oneself is diminished). Here we see the first step toward the extirpation of emotion for which the Stoics argued. Whereas Aristotle argues for the goodness and cultivation of emotions in many situations, Epicureanism takes steps away from this view by insisting that self-sufficiency and detachment from the world is a means to control desire and harmful emotions.

The Epicurean uses her emotion to discover truth about herself and her beliefs. Their presence often serves to highlight false belief. Striker writes, 'Individual affections indicate the presence of a good or evil, and in this role they may serve, like sense impressions, as criteria of truth, providing irrefutable evidence of a rather limited range of facts.'[76] However, emotion often blinds an individual to their sickness of the soul. For example, the angry person is blinded by their anger and they are often unaware of the need to cure this emotion.[77]

Mortality and the fear of death played a major part in the arguments of Epicureans.[78] Diogenes writes: 'And what are these four troubling emotions? Fear of gods, of death, and of pains, and, besides these, desire going far beyond the natural limits. For these are the roots of all evils, and, if we cut them out,

---

73. Nussbaum, *The Therapy of Desire*, p. 103.

74. Annas, *Hellenistic Philosophy of Mind*, pp. 194, 195. See also Annas, 'Epicurean Emotions', pp. 154–159; Long, *Hellenistic Philosophy*, p. 52; Rist, *Epicurus*, p. 79.

75. Annas, *Hellenistic Philosophy of Mind*, pp. 193–194. See also Gosling and Taylor, *The Greeks on Pleasure*, pp. 348–349.

76. Striker, 'Epicurean Hedonism', p. 10.

77. Asmis, 'Philodemus' Epicureanism', pp. 2396–2399.

78. Nussbaum, *The Therapy of Desire*, pp. 193–195; Furley, 'Nothing to Us?' See also Segal, *Lucretius on Death and Anxiety*, p. 23.

none of the evils will grow up out of them.'[79] The correct belief that there is no existence after death will eliminate the fear that is based on false belief.[80]

While denying the validity of pagan religion and immortality, Epicureanism clung to a godlike self-sufficiency and 'detachment'. In contrast to the Christian and Greek concepts, the Epicurean gods are aloof with no care for human affairs. Therefore, they do not need anything from this world and their emotions are completely unaffected by what happens on earth. They are free.[81] Epicurus writes:

> For if we pay attention to these, we shall rightly trace the causes whence arose our mental disturbance and fear, and, by learning the true causes of celestial phenomena and all the other occurrences that come to pass from time to time, we shall free ourselves from all which produces the utmost fear in other men.[82]

Most forms of anger are also avoided in self-sufficiency. Nussbaum relates, 'In this way, anger is seen to rest upon a condition of exposure and weakness, in which the person, having invested a great part of herself in the vulnerable things of this world, is correspondingly subject to reversals of fortune.'[83] Avoiding this attachment greatly increases the individual's happiness.[84]

In summary, to Epicureans most negative and positive emotions have their roots in dependence and vulnerability. Because of this, anger and love are not as far apart as we would like to believe. With the cultivation of safety in love and friendship come the dangers of anger, betrayal, and violence. The greater the former virtues the greater danger there is of the latter vices. Being self-sufficient is best. Furthermore, as attachments grow so do anxiety and fear in the soul. The object of those attachments may be harmed or destroyed.[85] Yet, it is

---

79. fr. 34 Smith quoted in Purinton, 'Epicurus on the Telos', p. 299.

80. Nussbaum, *The Therapy of Desire*, pp. 201–202.

81. Nussbaum, *The Therapy of Desire*, pp. 217, 221, 251, 261.

82. Epicurus *To Herodotus*, p. 82, see Bailey, *Epicurus*. This passage refers to why men irrationally fear the stars and planets.

83. Nussbaum, *The Therapy of Desire*, p. 242. Annas points out that an Epicurean will sometimes get angry but it will be because of different reasons and beliefs than others (Annas, *Hellenistic Philosophy of Mind*, p. 192). Asmis writes, 'The Epicurean view is that anger is painful and therefore to be avoided as much as possible'. Asmis, 'Philodemus' Epicureanism', p. 2395.

84. Annas, *Hellenistic Philosophy of Mind*, pp. 196–198.

85. Nussbaum, *The Therapy of Desire*, pp. 267–269.

important not to over-argue this point. There is room in Epicureanism for concern for one's own safety and some kind of love and friendship. Therefore, the opposite dangers will also be present to some degree. In Epicureanism the control of the emotions is paramount, not their extirpation. The Epicurean will be able to control harmful emotions, while enjoying a level of love and friendship.[86]

Stoics

The Stoics went beyond the Epicureans in their analysis of the emotions. To the Stoic, reason holds the preeminent place in the human soul. People are to be evaluated in light of their reason, not their position, wealth or status.[87]

Reason shows the way towards a better society and, on a personal level, towards being a better individual. Answering questions that do not result in ethical improvements is not important to the Stoic. Good reasoning will result in good actions. When reason shines its light into the soul, goodness can be attained. You can be your own healer.[88]

People naturally seek the happy life and, if happiness is correctly defined, this is a legitimate goal. The happy life is not made possible by attaining position, wealth and emotional good feelings. It is made possible by the life of reason and virtue (almost synonymous for the Stoic). Virtue is all that is necessary for happiness (*eudaemonia*).[89] The motives for an action determine its virtue. Here we find the root of the Stoic belief that all passions must be extirpated. Wrong desires are in themselves a loss of virtue.[90] Nussbaum writes:

> A single failure in thought and passion can have, directly, the direst possible consequences for the agent's whole moral condition. If philosophy must make itself a therapy of passion, we begin to see why this should be so: the cost of failure in passion is higher here that in any other school.[91]

---

86. Nussbaum, *The Therapy of Desire*, pp. 277–279; Annas, *Hellenistic Philosophy of Mind*, p. 199.

87. Long, *Hellenistic Philosophy*, p. 108; Nussbaum, *The Therapy of Desire*, pp. 323–324.

88. Nussbaum, *The Therapy of Desire*, pp. 330, 340–341, 350; Long, *Hellenistic Philosophy*, p. 111.

89. Nussbaum, *The Therapy of Desire*, pp. 359, 362–363; Long, *Hellenistic Philosophy*, p. 173.

90. Nussbaum, *The Therapy of Desire*, pp. 356–364; Kidd, 'Moral Actions and Rules in Stoic Ethics', pp. 247–248; Edelstein, *The Meaning of Stoicism*, p. 1; Long, *Hellenistic Philosophy*, p. 173.

91. Nussbaum, *The Therapy of Desire*, p. 366; see also Inwood, *Ethics and Human Action in Early Stoicism*, pp. 139–140.

Pathē (passions) are impulses that have gone to excess that affect the movement of the heart. (Note that the Stoic concept of the *pathē* is a broader term than the English 'emotion' but would include emotions as we know the term today.) Impulses, in turn, are movements of the soul. Impulses are rational or cognitive but do not necessarily operate according to reason to the Stoics. The very definition of emotion classified them as harmful (impulses that have gone to excess). Therefore, the rational soul itself is at fault for producing emotion. For the Stoic, the soul must be cured.[92]

An overarching theme in the discussion of the emotions was the unity of the soul (in contrast to a Platonic division of the soul).[93] Rist writes: 'The emotional effects are part – and indeed an inseparable part – of the judgement itself.'[94] Inwood agrees:

> The most important feature of the passions for Seneca and for earlier Stoics as well is that they should be 'rational' in a broad sense: not in the sense that they embody or reflect correct use of reason in the guidance of human action and reaction, but in the sense that they are products of human reason and so subject to control by that reason.[95]

Therefore, the extirpation of the passions, which cause so many ills in the human soul, can be accomplished by reason through changing the judgments that are themselves the passions.[96] Here we see why the Stoics argue that a detailed analysis of emotion is necessary. The passions can only be cured if their specific cognitive nature is understood. Each emotion must be dissected into its cognitive parts and defined by its cognitive judgment in order to change the judgments that make it up. In doing this, over time, the passions can be extirpated.[97]

Stoics also acknowledge the fact that emotions may reveal the truth

---

92. Rist, *Stoic Philosophy*, pp. 39–40. See also Annas, *Hellenistic Philosophy of Mind*, pp. 104–107; Inwood, 'Seneca and Psychological Dualism', p. 170. For a definition of impulse see Inwood, *Ethics and Human Action in Early Stoicism*, p. 47.

93. Annas, *Hellenistic Philosophy of Mind*, pp. 115–117. Rist, *Stoic Philosophy*, pp. 24–26. Gould, *The Philosophy of Chrysippus*, p. 137; Inwood, 'Seneca and Psychological Dualism', pp. 170–171.

94. Rist, *Stoic Philosophy*, pp. 34–35.

95. Inwood, 'Seneca and Psychological Dualism', p. 166.

96. Nussbaum, *The Therapy of Desire*, p. 380.

97. Nussbaum, *The Therapy of Desire*, pp. 366–372, 379; Gould, *The Philosophy of Chrysippus*, pp. 162, 181–186.

about a man's moral character. They serve as a gauge to reveal the values of an individual.[98]

This thinking leads the Stoics to a very simple principle for understanding emotion. First, as we have seen in Aristotle, all emotions are based on the worth or value of an object. Second, all emotions come from good or bad conditions (either real or perceived) for the object of worth. Lastly, both negative and positive emotions can be split into present circumstances and future expectations.[99]

The Stoics believed that to be open to a positive emotion it is inevitable that you are also open to the negative emotion. Once worth is ascribed to the object, the present or future circumstances of that object will determine your positive or negative emotions. These circumstances are beyond your control so you are at their mercy. For example, if you are to get rid of fear (the negative expectation for the future of the object of worth) you must also get rid of hope (the positive expectation for the future of the object of worth). Once again the Stoics go a step beyond the other Hellenistic schools by insisting that the passions must be extirpated. Complete self-sufficiency and a complete lack of vulnerability are advocated.[100] Edelstein writes: 'They are inclined to regard even the good passions as bad soldiers, bad allies in the fight of life, because one cannot rely on their leading us in the right direction.'[101]

However, the Stoic, observes Nussbaum, is allowed an emotion-free joy (*chara*): 'There is joy here; joy without enervating uncertainty, joy without fear and grief, a joy that really does move and lift up the heart.'[102] Yet, Nussbaum concludes, 'It has no commerce with laughter and elation.'[103]

The Stoic position on anger serves as a good illustration of their theory. Anger motivates many atrocities and violent deeds. The Aristotelian would argue that not to be angry at a terrible deed is dehumanizing to the individuals against which atrocities have been committed. However, to the Stoic it is not possible to have righteous anger without opening yourself up to the anger of

---

98. Rist, *Stoic Philosophy*, p. 49.

99. Nussbaum, *The Therapy of Desire*, p. 386; Nussbaum, 'The Stoics on the Extirpation of the Passions', p. 159. See also Inwood, *Ethics and Human Action in Early Stoicism*, pp. 144–145.

100. Nussbaum, *The Therapy of Desire*, pp. 388–390.

101. Edelstein, *The Meaning of Stoicism*, p. 2.

102. Nussbaum, *The Therapy of Desire*, p. 399.

103. Nussbaum, 'The Stoics on the Extirpation of the Passions', p. 173. See also Annas, *Hellenistic Philosophy of Mind*, pp. 112, 114; Rist, *Stoic Philosophy*, p. 52.

revenge. The justifiable anger leads to unjustified anger in a manner that cannot be controlled.[104]

Anger should not play a part of justice or punishment. Punishment is only to reform the offender. Nussbaum comments:

> The Stoic views the punishment as justified, not on account of the importance of the wrong done, not on account of the pain and injustice suffered by the victim, and certainly not because he cares about what has happened in any personal way, but solely on account of the well-being of the offender.[105]

The Stoics present a unique challenge to working out the implications of a cognitive theory of the emotions. I have argued in Chapter one that a cognitive theory leads to the integration of emotion and reason and the use of both in making ethical decisions. The Stoics embraced the fact that emotion and reason cannot be separated, emotions are judgments, but they went on to argue that emotions should be eliminated. To live by virtue and reason is by necessity to live without emotion.[106]

First, we must ask if their view is logical. They did not carry their theory of cognitive emotions through to its logical conclusion. As we have seen in Chapter one, if right judgments are made right emotions will follow. The Stoic assertion that a life of emotionless reason is possible is not true. This is not the way emotion works. Furthermore, a life of radical detachment from the world that they advocate is not possible.

Most importantly, their conclusions are not based on their cognitive theory of emotion but rather on their theory about the nature of virtue. Nussbaum writes, 'So it appears that this Stoic argument, like the first, rests, after all, on the prior acceptance of a Stoic view of value, and can do little work independently of it.'[107] The Stoic ideal of the extirpation of the emotions was dictated by their definition of virtue (not to include emotion), not by the logical consequences of a cognitive theory of the emotions. These

---

104. Nussbaum, *The Therapy of Desire*, p. 403.

105. Nussbaum, *The Therapy of Desire*, p. 417.

106. See also Gould, *The Philosophy of Chrysippus*, p. 172; Annas, *Hellenistic Philosophy of Mind*, p. 113.

107. Nussbaum, 'The Stoics on the Extirpation of the Passions', p. 165. See also Inwood, *Ethics and Human Action in Early Stoicism*, p. 180; Roberts, 'Emotions Among the Virtues', p. 42.

overarching presuppositions, that virtue was independent of emotion and that emotion by its very definition was a false judgment, forced them to ignore the logical consequences of their own well-formed cognitive theory of the emotions.[108]

The Hellenistic schools: conclusion

We see in the Hellenistic schools a strong cognitive theory of the emotions. At the same time they have great skepticism about the value of emotion and they stress the harm that is caused by emotions that are out of control. To change these emotions, which are not irrational impulses but are rather based on wrong beliefs, one's belief system must be changed. In this way ataraxia can be curtailed.[109]

In formulating this ideal of the undisturbed life, they were responding to a society where they observed that people's emotions were often out of control. People lived with irrational fear of the gods, anger and sorrow because they allowed their society to determine their belief system that in turn produced these emotions. Emperors ruled according to their own selfishness and the vain pursuit of power and wealth. The belief that these things had value produced emotions in them that led them to rule in ways that were destructive. Philosophy could cure you of harmful and distressing emotions.

In the next Chapters we will be able to see the parallels between this approach and the approach of the New Testament. The New Testament also advocates a radical reorientation of the individual that will produce changed emotions. We may look for other parallels between the specific schools and the New Testament. Did the New Testament seek to extirpate the emotions like the Stoics, or to change and control them radically like the Epicureans? Or, are both of these trends evident in different books?

Conclusion

Emotions were considered a major topic of philosophical inquiry at the time of the New Testament. The emotions also had an important place in literature and society. The philosophers' rhetoric about emotion was in large measure an

---

108. For a similar view see Edelstein, *The Meaning of Stoicism*, p. 97; Annas, *Hellenistic Philosophy of Mind*, pp. 113–114. Solomon, 'The Philosophy of Emotion', p. 5; Striker, *Essays on Hellenistic Epistemology*, p. 178.

109. Nussbaum, *The Therapy of Desire*, p. 501.

attempt to correct the abuses of their society. Emotion had an important role (or non-role) in the cognitive philosophers' idea of happiness and ethics.

It is clear that both non-cognitive and cognitive beliefs were present in the ancient world. The parallels between these and the modern cognitive and non-cognitive theories, as discussed in the first Chapter, are many. There may not be the well-defined comprehensive theories that are present in the modern era, but we find the basic tenets of cognitive and non-cognitive theory very clearly in the first century. Alongside this, the two views also have similarities to their modern counterparts in their ethical and practical outlooks. The non-cognitive view stresses the unreliable nature of emotion and the need for it to be controlled by reason, while the cognitive view underscores the need to change harmful emotions by correcting false beliefs.

However, we have seen that many of the philosophers presented seemingly uncomplimentary views in different sections of their writings. Plato in a few sections leans towards a cognitive view while Aristotle in some passages seems to present a non-cognitive view. Similarly, the Stoics draw conclusions that are inconsistent with their own theory of emotion. It is legitimate to ask if these same inconsistencies are present in the New Testament.

The writers of the New Testament lived in a world where both the cognitive and non-cognitive views of emotion were present. They may have come into contact with an explicit defence of one of these views or they may have simply encountered a particular viewpoint in their culture. Philosophy often influences and reflects the views of ordinary people.

Finally, have we made progress in understanding the role of emotion in Greco-Roman culture? I believe that we can give a positive answer to this question. First and foremost we see that, just as in our culture, diversity was present and pervasive. Some institutions stressed celebration and passion, while others stressed the need for the moderation of the emotions. Secondly, it is clear that emotion was seen as a crucial part of human life and the human soul. It was a source of turmoil, suffering, motivation and pleasure. Love, fear, courage and anger were often seen as the causes of both tragedy and triumph. Finally, it is clear that a writer's theory of emotion impacts their work. This is true even if the writer could not sit down and verbalize their theory. For example, the idea that emotion came upon you as a powerful force allowed the Greeks to take anger into account when determining the penalty for a crime. The method of calming the emotions by using music was a direct result of the non-cognitive theory that was held by the philosophers who gave this advice. We cannot say that the New Testament authors' view of emotion was irrelevant because they did not have a well articulated theory of emotion. We all have ideas about emotion and these ideas impact our life.

3. EMOTION IN JEWISH CULTURE AND WRITINGS

Hear, O Israel: The Lord is our God, the Lord alone. You shall love the Lord your God with all your heart, and with all your soul, and with all your might.

Deuteronomy 6:4–5

What ideas about emotion were present in the Jewish world at the time of the New Testament? Was there a notable influence of Greek ideas on first century Judaism?

Our survey is two-pronged. First, what general ideas about emotion are present in the Old Testament itself? Although it is not possible to write a comprehensive statement here about emotion in the Old Testament, this Chapter will identify the major themes and ideas about emotion in the Old Testament that influenced the writers of the New Testament. Second, looking at the Second Temple period, we will see some of the mixing of Old Testament and Greek ideas that may have been present in the formative communities of the New Testament and we will try to discover what ideas from the Old Testament were stressed in the Second Temple period.

Emotion in the Old Testament

The emphasis in this section will be topical rather than historical. I have chosen to concentrate on a few major recurring themes in the relevant texts, concentrating on some representative texts.[1] (The vocabulary of emotion will not be a major emphasis here, which is a topic covered more adequately in the following Chapters.)

Emotions of the righteous

One way to differentiate the righteous from the wicked in the Old Testament is by how they feel. This section could be encapsulated in the phrase, 'what the godly love'. What, after all, made David a man after God's own heart? Although he did many great things, it certainly was not his perfection. He had numerous failings but David had a heart for God. He celebrated the good, felt mercy toward his enemies (Saul), loved Jonathan like a brother, and repented of sin in great sorrow. Childs writes that in the midst of David's failings: 'his final role as the ideal righteous king emerges with clarity [in Samuel]'.[2] His character shows us what godly emotions are to look like. Saul's emotions, on the other

---

1. We are not concerned with the critical or dating issues for the Old Testament texts. We are only concerned with the fact that the New Testament authors had access to them and viewed them as authoritative. These representative texts include the Shema, the Psalms and Hosea. Von Rad writes about Hosea:

    'His preaching, more than that of any other prophet, is governed by personal emotions, by love, anger, disappointment, and even by the ambivalence between two opposite sentiments. Since the prophet lends this emotional ardor to the words of God himself – or, to put it better, since Jahweh catches the prophet up into his emotions – in Hosea the divine word receives a glow and fervor the intensity of which is characteristic of the message of this prophet alone' (Von Rad, *Old Testament Theology*, p. 140). 'He saw how the struggle between wrath and love came to be resolved in God's own heart. This led him to an utterance whose daring is unparalleled in the whole of prophecy [11:8]' (p. 145). McComiskey agrees about the paramount importance of this passage in the Old Testament: 'The picture of divine love in this section is almost unparalleled in the Old Testament' (McComiskey, 'Hosea', p. 184). The Psalms proclaim the writer's emotions to a God who already knows the heart. All the joy, fear and anxiety of life are poured out. Further, as corporate songs they encompass not only the sorrow and joy of the writer but also the emotions of the entire community. Sarna, *Songs of the Heart*, pp. 205–207; Anderson, *Psalms*, p. 30.

2. Childs, *Introduction to the Old Testament*, p. 278. Note how David is held up as an example in Kings (1 Kgs 9:4, 11:4, 6; Childs, *Introduction to the Old Testament*, p. 292). See also Dillard and Longman, *An Introduction to the Old Testament*, p. 146. See Von Rad's description of David as a man 'driven by many a passion' both toward sin and toward God (Von Rad, *Old Testament Theology*, vol. 1, p. 313).

hand, tell a different story. Saul's desire was to serve himself and his emotions portray this. He hated David without cause, repented superficially, celebrated his own greatness, and his desires led him to disobedience (1 Sam. 18:8).

Important concepts and vocabulary

The righteous base their emotions on the knowledge of God.[3] It is clear that the positive emotions that Israel was to have were built on theology. They were based on the historical facts of the faith and the character of God. This applies to the meaning of the Hebrew word *yd'*. Sarna writes: 'In Hebrew, however, as in other Semitic languages, the verb 'to know' *y-d-'* possesses a rich semantic range within which the senses predominate. Emotional ties, empathy, intimacy, sexual experience, mutuality, and responsibility are all encompassed within the usage of the verbal stem.'[4]

This emphasis on the knowledge of God in the emotions of the righteous is clearly seen in the pattern of prayer in the Old Testament, especially in Psalms. It is a cognitive pattern. Emotion and thanksgiving in prayer are linked to the character of God (Ps. 51:1; 138:1–2). Praise is the result of knowing the greatness of God, contemplating his worthiness, and understanding that he has given great things to Israel. Kraus writes: 'The cult participant does not enter a sphere of ecstasy, but is asked about his everyday behavior, about his obedience to Yahweh's instructions.'[5] Beyond this, when circumstances are difficult the Psalmists turn to the eternal promises of God and reorient their thinking to dwell on the victories of the past and the salvation that is to come. This thinking changes the worshipper's sorrow to praise.[6] Similarly, repentance

---

3. Brueggemann sees that part of the essence of Old Testament faith is an acknowledgement that Yahweh has done something completely new that requires the believer to have a different orientation from what is around them. 'Israel, in voiced utterance, acknowledges in an unrestrained way that something decisive has happened that is taken to be the work of Yahweh' (Brueggemann, *Theology of the Old Testament*, pp. 128, 228).

4. Sarna, *Songs of the Heart*, p. 47. See also 32:10–11. 'To know' involves the mind, will and emotions. For a good explanation of the word *yd'* see Fretheim, '*yd'*'; Martens, *God's Design*, pp. 81–83. 'Joy and sorrow are understood from the standpoint of the reason for them' (Bultmann, '*lypē, lypeō*', p. 318).

5. Kraus, *Psalms 1–59*, p. 70. The command to rejoice is not 'a call to conjure up objectless inner feelings of elation' (Saliers, *The Soul in Paraphrase*, p. 41).

6. The very word used, 'to praise', in Hebrew has cognitive content (Von Rad, *Old Testament Theology*, vol. 1, p. 357).

in prayer is linked to a knowledge of sin and the holiness of God.[7] Prayer in the Psalms is not a ritual to conjure up emotion but, rather, a heartfelt cry based on beliefs about God and the world. Emotional prayer is no guarantee of spirituality. Instead, it is only by praying out of a theologically correct understanding that the prayer is properly felt. Kraus relates: 'The song of thanksgiving always shows a tendency to bear witness to events, to recount experiences, to teach, and to exhort.'[8] The emotion expressed in the Psalms is based in history and truth.

The emphasis on knowledge is also seen in the use of the word *lēb*. The heart in the Old Testament, writes Bauer, is the 'inward spiritual part of man'. This includes the mental, rational, intelligent, and emotional part of a man. It is the place where feelings originate and is the seat of the will. There is an integration of thinking and emotion in one faculty.[9] This diversity is also prevalent in the Greek equivalent *kardia* as it is used in the LXX. Behm concludes, '*kardia* is the true equivalent for the Hebrew *lēb*'.[10]

In the Old Testament decisions are made in the heart. It is a person's inner and unknown self, not visible to the outside world. Faith and doubt are matters of the heart.[11] God seeks those who have a heart like his own. Notice the link between knowledge and heart in Jeremiah 3:15: 'I will give you shepherds after my own heart, who will feed you with knowledge and understanding.' The wicked and godly are often differentiated by the state of their hearts.[12] Behm concludes, 'Thus the heart is supremely the one center in man to which God turns, in which the religious life is rooted, which determines moral conduct.'[13]

In both the important words *lēb* and *yd‘* there is an integration of knowledge and emotion. *yd‘* includes knowledge that is heartfelt and emotional. The idea of *lēb* includes intellectual knowledge and emotional content. In the Old Testament the ideas of emotion and reason function as an integrated whole.

---

7. Saliers, *The Soul in Paraphrase*, pp. 28, 32, 41–43, 51–58.

8. Kraus, *Psalms 1–59*, p. 364.

9. Bauer, 'Heart', pp. 360, 362. See this passage for numerous examples of feelings originating in the heart.

10. Behm, '*kardia*', pp. 609–610. There are many words that could be used for the mind or mental faculty in Greek, *nous* or *psychē*, for example. *kardia* had fallen into disuse. However, because of the influence of the Hebrew *lēb*, the LXX most often translates mental faculties as *kardia* (Silva, *Biblical Words and Their Meaning*, pp. 95–96).

11. Bauer, 'Heart', p. 362.

12. Behm, '*kardia*', pp. 606–607.

13. Behm, '*kardia*', p. 612.

The next sections will illustrate the cognitive link between knowledge and emotion in specific texts.

Love for God, delight in the Law, and joy

The righteous love God. They feel joy in God and in obeying God. They celebrate God's goodness. They desire and love to do good.

Love. We might say that all the emotional traits of the righteous are based on one basic orientation: they love God. We have seen how love is the basic emotion, and the faith of Israel is no exception to this. Love for God gives birth to the other emotions that characterize the righteous. The great text we have for the idea of Israel loving God is the 'Shema' in Deuteronomy 6. Von Rad concludes: 'In spite of this there seems to be something new in the unequivocal manner based on fundamental principles in which stress is laid on love for God as the only feeling worthy of God.'[14] The fundamental message of Deuteronomy 6 is echoed in chapter 30, where there is a definite parallel with God's presence in a person's heart (Jer. 31; Ezek. 36; and Ps. 1; and see Josh. 22:5; 1 Kgs 3:3; Ps. 5:11, 18:1, 91:4, 116:1; Isa. 56:6). God will renew Israel so they follow him with their hearts. A total heartfelt commitment to Yahweh is in view.[15] Craigie summarizes:

---

14. Von Rad, *Deuteronomy*, p. 63. Young emphasizes the requirement for genuine and passionate emotion (Young, *Jesus the Jewish Theologian*, p. 192). See Miller, *Deuteronomy*, p. vii, for a summary of Deuteronomy's paramount significance in the cannon. 'With this chapter we come to the pivot around which everything else in Deuteronomy revolves' (Miller, *Deuteronomy*, p. 97). Von Rad writes 'Rather, all commandments are simply a grand explanation of the command to love Jahweh' (Von Rad, *Old Testament Theology*, vol. 1, p. 230).

15. Von Rad, *Deuteronomy*, pp. 184–185. For a good discussion of the relation of Jer. 31 to Deuteronomy and the similar ideas which are expressed see McKane, *Jeremiah*, 8:18–27. See also Holladay, *Jeremiah*, vol. 1, pp. 181–182. For an analysis of the uses of *'āhab* for loving God see Els, "*hb*', p. 279. Els explains Deut. 11:13, 30:6 as referring to 'more than a mere feeling'. It is commanded (Els, "*hb*', pp. 279–281, 289–290). Likewise God's love is 'no mere attitude or emotion' (Els, "*hb*', p. 290). His article serves as a good catalogue of usage in different contexts but the interpretation of this usage is faulty as different contexts, in his thinking, drastically change the emotive nature of love. Instead, a cognitive understanding of love would unify the meaning in each circumstance. In fact, the diversity of love's usage reinforces its nature as the basic emotion. This article is a good illustration

The essence of the covenant, it must be stressed, lies in the relationship between God and man, and though God is the first and free mover in the establishing of that relationship, nevertheless a relationship requires a response from man. The operative principle within the relationship is that of love; God moved first toward his people in love and they must respond to him in love. The law of the covenant expresses the love of God and indicates the means by which a man must live to reflect love for God.[16]

Toombs agrees: 'True life is the consequence of a relationship with God, and, although that life is marked by obedience, its authentic, distinguishing feature is love felt in the deepest recesses of the inner being.' (Deut. 7:6–11; 6:4; 30:5.) The Hebrew '*āhab* signifies a relationship of affection apparent in the most intimate of human relationships. The use of this term is a key feature in Deuteronomy. It is used because of the intensity of feeling that it brings to these passages. God loves his people and he expects their love in return.[17]

Love is also commanded in other passages in the Old Testament, notably Hos. 3:1. It is clear that God's love for Israel in Hosea is emotional. We cannot conclude that emotion is not commanded here, as some scholars believe. Foreshadowing what we will see in New Testament studies, Andersen and Freedman write: 'Rather, Hosea is commanded to love, an instruction which people who think that love is the spontaneous expression of feeling find impossible. In Scripture love is always a command; love is action in obedience to the work of Yahweh.'[18] Notice the phrase, 'love is *action* [my italics]'. They write this in objection to the fact that Hosea could be commanded to have emotional love for Gomer. However, we have shown that emotion is cognitive in nature and therefore commanding love, the emotion, is possible.[19]

Beyond the command to love, a wholehearted all encompassing emotional devotion to God in Deuteronomy 6:5, verses 4 and 6–9 are also very significant. The command to love is framed by verses about knowledge. Verse

---

of the confusion on the matter of love in the Old Testament and the difficulty in making a logical presentation of its use without understanding the nature of emotion.

16. Craigie, *The Book of Deuteronomy*, p. 37.

17. Toombs, 'Love and Justice in Deuteronomy', p. 402.

18. Andersen and Freedman, *Hosea*, p. 297. McComiskey sees 'far more than the mere emotion of love' in this verse. McComiskey, 'Hosea', p. 156–157.

19. We will discuss what it means to command emotion more fully in Chapter five.

4 proclaims that Israel is God's people. They are given knowledge of their standing before their God.[20] Verses 7–9 go on to talk about the knowledge of God:

> Keep these words that I am commanding you today in your heart. Recite them to your children and talk about them when you are at home and when you are away, when you lie down and when you rise. Bind them as a sign on your hand, fix them as an emblem on your forehead, and write them on the doorposts of your house and on your gates.

Love is linked to knowledge. To love God you learn about him and rehearse his words constantly. This knowledge will fuel your emotions.[21] This link is echoed in chapters 29 – 30, which begin with rehearsing and meditating on the facts and history of Israel's faith. This fuels a heartfelt turning to God (30:1). A restored relationship comes from a heart that loves God and a heartfelt repentance (Deut. 30:20). The choice for God is a choice to love.[22]

The link between love and knowledge is also seen in other parts of the Old Testament. Psalm 116:1–2 reads, 'I love the LORD, because he has heard my voice and my supplications. Because he inclined his ear to me, therefore I will call on him as long as I live.'[23] Or in Psalm 18:1–3: 'I love you, O LORD, my strength. The LORD is my rock, my fortress, and my deliverer, my God, my rock in whom I take refuge, my shield, and the horn of my salvation, my stronghold. I call upon the LORD, who is worthy to be praised, so I shall be saved from my enemies.'[24] There are good reasons to love God, and the attributes of God compel the love and worship that is due to him.

In summary, the love that is in view when the Old Testament speaks of loving God is a love that is expressed by the whole person, including, heart,

---

20. Miller, *Deuteronomy*, pp. 98–99.
21. See Craigie, *The Book of Deuteronomy*, pp. 170–171. See also Josh. 1:7–8; Judg. 5:10–11. See also Brueggemann, *Theology of the Old Testament*, pp. 130, 592.
22. See Craigie, *The Book of Deuteronomy*, pp. 363–366, Miller, *Deuteronomy*, pp. 213–215. Notice also that God's response is emotional. He will delight in blessing his obedient people.
23. See Kidner, *Psalms 73–150*, p. 408.
24. Kidner writes, 'This word for *love* is an uncommon one, impulsive and emotional.' It is usually in the intensive form and denotes compassion of the stronger for the weak (Kidner, *Psalms 1–72*, p. 91).

mind and soul. Second, this emotional love is commanded.[25] It is a love that is based on the knowledge of God and strengthened by the constant rehearsal of the history of their salvation. In short, there is a strong cognitive element in the idea of loving God in the Old Testament. This understanding allows the legitimate command, 'You shall love the LORD your God with all your heart, and with all your soul, and with all your might.'

We can also briefly outline the idea of loving your neighbour. The emotional motives of empathy and compassion are operative in Israel's relationship with foreigners in their land. In Leviticus 19:34 a reason is given for loving them: 'you were like them in Egypt'.[26] Much the same can be said for Deuteronomy 10:17–19. Love for the stranger is based on the fact that God has love and compassion for them and the empathy Israel should feel because they have been in the same position themselves.

The key text about loving your neighbour is Leviticus 19:17–18. Harrison writes: 'Responsibility toward one's neighbour involves a positive attitude of heart and mind. Hatred is an emotional response which should only be employed against evil.'[27] Notice the command not to hate in verse 17. There is a coupling here: do not have the negative emotion and do have love. There is a direct command of an emotion, a cognitive basis, and an appeal to empathy.

Love for God is similar to the idea of desiring God. Love compels the lover toward an object with an almost irresistible force. This desire characterizes the love the Old Testament demands for God. Kraus writes of Psalm 42:1–4, 'The animal yearning and crying for water is an effective picture of the torment and the consuming desire with which the petitioner stretches out toward Yahweh.'[28] This is also a strong element in Jeremiah 30 – 31 and Psalm 119:2. In Psalm 40:6–8 God does not desire sacrifice, but for his followers to delight

---

25. Miller, *Deuteronomy*, pp. 101–103.

26. See Lewis, 'Jehovah's International Love'.

27. Harrison, *Leviticus*, p. 199. See also Wenham, *The Book of Leviticus*, pp. 268–269, 120–122; Morris, *Testaments of Love*, pp. 35–62. Quell presents us with a good example of exegesis controlled by a non-cognitive approach to emotions. He writes: 'Hence a statement like Lev. 19:18 . . . although couched in the legal style of the usual demand, and containing the legally very closely circumscribed term *rea'*, is not really a legal statement, because the attitude denoted by the word *'hb* is one of natural feeling and cannot be legally directed . . . It is obvious, however, that even on this side it cannot be taken seriously as a legal ordinance.' (Quell, *'agapaō, agapē, agapētos'*, p. 25.) He equates any attempt to view it as a command as a legalization of love, p. 26.

28. Kraus, *Psalms 1–59*, p. 439. See also Sir. 13:25; Warnach, 'Love', p. 525.

in doing his law (see parallels in Hosea; Jer. 31:31–34; Ps. 1).[29]

A love and desire for God will also lead to a love of the good. The right-eous will love wisdom and doing good. As evidenced in Prov. 4:1–9, Proverbs is not as concerned about a list of 'don'ts' as emphasizing how to love the good. A love of wisdom will keep the wise man on the right road.[30]

Joy and praise. The same knowledge and understanding that is linked to loving God also provides a reason to praise God. Although we might consider praise to be an action, sincere praise has a strong emotional element. The God who loves Israel, who rescued Israel in history, and who is great and awesome, is worthy of praise and adoration because of these things. Praise is linked with joy as they are both based on the same cognitive understanding. Praise and cele-bration flow out of a joyful heart. The one who loves and desires God also celebrates him.[31] It is also important to notice that in the Psalms we find no hint of an attitude where the worshipper waits to be touched by an inner experience that goes beyond reason. On the contrary, praise is based on cognitive factors.

Psalm 30 is a good example of a Hebrew praise psalm. The format of this kind of Psalm is clearly cognitive. Sarna writes, 'The structure of the psalm is typical of biblical thanksgiving psalms in general. An opening declaration of intent to extol God is followed by the immediate reason for it, and the praise is succeeded by a fuller and more specific elucidation of the occasion that prompted it (verses 2–4).'[32] Martens agrees: 'Numerous reasons are offered in the hymns for glorious praise to God.'[33]

A number of basic reasons for joy are given in the Psalms. The presence of God and the knowledge that God is with you gives joy (Ps. 16:7–10).[34] God

---

29. See Von Rad's comments about the heart of obedience in Jeremiah (31:31–34, 32:37–41) and Ezekiel (37:24–28) (Von Rad, *Old Testament Theology*, pp. 213–214, 234–235, 270–271).

30. Kidner, *The Proverbs*, p. 66.

31. Kraus, *Psalms 1–59*, p. 150. For a good summary of the uses of joy and the reasons it is felt see Grisanti, '*gîl*'.

32. Sarna, *Songs of the Heart*, p. 139. Kidner sees an 'uninhibited' celebration of jubilant praise in verse 10. See also 2 Sam. 6:14, 7:18–21; Ps. 63:1–4; Exod. 15. Kidner, *Psalms 1–72*, p. 129. Westermann comments on the cognitive nature of joy in Ps. 31 (Westermann, *The Living Psalms*, p. 175).

33. Martens, *God's Design*, p. 163.

34. Kraus, *Psalms 1–59*, p. 239. See also Brueggemann, *Theology of the Old Testament*, pp. 86, 140–141.

delivers his followers from their enemies (Ps. 18:1–3, 48–49; 103:1–5, 26). Other prominent reasons for rejoicing are the great acts of God in Israel's past history and the promise of future deliverance.[35] The fact that God loves Israel and has made a covenant with them gives reason to rejoice. In Psalm 58:10, 'The godly will rejoice when they see injustice avenged'.

Yahweh is to be served with a spirit of joy and celebration (Deut. 16:14–15: 'Rejoice during your festival'; Lev. 16:30; Ps. 81:1–4).[36] The festivals were given to Israel as a time of emotional renewal, both in rejoicing and solemn reflection and repentance. When Ezra reads the law the people mourn over their sin. However, because the day is holy to the Lord they are commanded to rejoice and celebrate. Spirituality is equated with joy. Times of repentance are followed by times of celebration as God comes to heal and forgive his people.[37]

Celebration is evident in its physical expression in Psalm 47 (notice also that there is a cognitive reason for this joy). Psalm 47:1 reads: 'Clap your hands, all you peoples; shout to God with loud songs of joy. For the LORD, the Most High, is awesome, a great king over all the earth.'[38] David gives perhaps the clearest example of the physical element of joy in 2 Samuel 6:4–5, 14–15 and he commands his readers to dance and make music in Psalm 150. The people of Israel knew how to celebrate with their whole being (Ps. 27:6, 32:11, 33:3, 66:2; 71:22; 87:7; 100:2; 149:3; Exod. 15:20; Neh. 12:43).[39]

The faith of Israel was not following laws in a sombre atmosphere. Martens writes, 'Knowing Yahweh provided for joy; festivity and celebration were integral to a life with Yahweh . . . Knowing Yahweh through the cult must be interpreted not as a dark and foreboding experience, but rather as joy-creating and joy-bringing (Lev. 23:40; Deut. 16; joy is commanded in these passages).'[40]

We should briefly mention that negative evaluations of certain kinds of joy are also present in the Old Testament. This is consistent with a cognitive interpretation of emotion. In Proverbs 24:17–18 Israel is not to rejoice over the

---

35. Kidner, *Psalms 73–150*, pp. 438–439. Kraus, *Psalms 1–59*, pp. 265. 1 Chr. 16:4–36 and Exod. 15 give good examples outside the Psalms of a number of these reasons for praising God. See also 1 Sam. 2:1 and Ps. 33:21.

36. Beilner, 'Joy', p. 438.

37. Klausner, 'The Sanctity of Yom tov and the Joy of the Festival', pp. 95–101.

38. See also Ps. 98:9; Zeph. 3:14; Zech. 9:9; Kraus, *Psalms 1–59*, p. 467.

39. See also Grisanti, 'śmḥ', p. 1251.

40. Martens, *God's Design*, p. 96.

demise of an enemy.[41] The morality of the emotion is determined by its object. There is unacceptable joy and joy that is to be encouraged.

There is a prominent place for joy in the theology of the Old Testament. Unlike the radical detachment from the world that will lead to happiness as advocated by the Stoics and Epicureans, the Old Testament's idea of happiness is rooted firmly in the things of this world and God.

We should also consider the word *makarios*, most often translated into English as 'blessed' or 'happy'. In the LXX it is most often a translation of *'ašrê*, and is often used to translate a beatitude (those sayings usually translated 'blessed are . . .'). Found predominately in wisdom literature, beatitudes often express ideas or practices that have a positive effect on earthly life (Prov. 14:21; 29:18; Ps. 1:1; Isa. 56:2).[42] The emphasis in the Old Testament's beatitudes is usually on an individual's well being, or what makes them happy.[43] The happiness described is most often earth-bound and immediate.

Although the here and now is usually the context of joy and happiness in the Old Testament, we should not neglect eschatological reasons for having joy today. Present joy can come out of the assurance or expectation of future deliverance and Israel is to wait with confidence for a future filled with great joy (Ps. 14:7; Isa. 9:2–3, 12:6, 61:9–11, 66:14; Zech. 8:19, 9:9; Zeph. 3:14–17).

In the Hebrew Bible, *'ašrê* followed by a participle, noun or pronoun, is not, as some have argued, merely a blessing formula with little emotional content. The idea of present emotional happiness is often overlooked in these passages. Vorster writes, 'Persons who abide by the rules of moral conduct are happy . . . It concerns everything that makes people happy: life, security, deliverance, posterity, military success, prosperity, and so on.'[44] Brown concurs and believes that it could be translated as 'truly happy' in these contexts.[45] God gives good gifts which will make people happy.

---

41. See Kidner, *The Proverbs*, p. 155. McKane gives a 'Stoic' interpretation that is not present in the verse: 'The absence of every trace of human feeling for the enemy who is down and out is uncanny and unpleasant' (McKane, *Proverbs*, p. 404).

42. Georg Bertram, *makarios, makarizō, makarismos*, p. 364. Unlike the Greek ideal of the happy gods, it is not a word that is used to express the state of God in the Old Testament. See also Bultmann, '*euphrainō, euphrosynē*'; Bultmann, '*hilaros, hilarotēs*'.

43. Becker, *Blessing, Blessed, Happy*, p. 216.

44. Vorster, 'Stoic and Early Christians on Blessedness', p. 46. See also Beilner, 'Joy', p. 438.

45. Brown criticizes the idea that in one context the word is said to mean blessing and in another happy, as if happy is a fleeting emotion and blessed is a spiritual state. Brown, '*'ašrê*' p. 571.

Makaristos (LXX) is used to describe man's relation to God. Proverbs 16:20 reads, 'Those who are attentive to a matter will prosper, and happy are those who trust in the LORD'. There are reasons given for being happy. Psalm 32:1 reads: 'Happy (*makarioi*) are those whose transgression is forgiven, whose sin is covered' (see also Deut. 33:29). In Psalm 2:12 we see that those who have the Lord as their refuge are happy. The election of Israel is also a great source of joy (Ps. 149:2–4, *euphranthētō*).[46]

Our analysis of happiness in the Old Testament would not be complete without mentioning its connection to obeying the law of God. Psalm 1:1–2 reads: 'Happy are those who do not follow the advice of the wicked, or take the path that sinners tread, or sit in the seat of scoffers; but their delight is in the law of the LORD, and on his law they meditate day and night.' The emphasis of 'happy' is on the present state of the one who follows God. Sarna writes, 'Happiness results from the deliberate assumption of a commitment to a certain way of life, a course that is governed by God's teaching (torah).'[47] In this theology the way to happiness is both in the knowledge of the law and the following of that law in obedience. The study of torah is delight to the godly. They find contentment in study of the law and following it leads to happiness.[48]

In summary, joy in God is at the centre of Judaism.[49] Lewis writes, 'What I see (so to speak) in the faces of these old poets tells me more about God whom they and we adore.' Praise and joy show the true nature of what we have found in God. In other words, having found an object of supreme worth it is natural that we would get excited about finding it and proclaim its attributes.[50]

It is clear that the Old Testament taught that happiness is good. Joyful celebration was to be based on good theology. The Jews encouraged celebration and festival in their religion. Festivals were based on the facts of their deliverance (Passover) or the forgiveness of God (Atonement). The idea of

---

46. Beilner, 'Joy', p. 438.

47. Sarna, *Songs of the Heart*, pp. 29–30. The preferred translation is 'happy' as opposed to 'blessed' (Kidner, *Psalms 1–72*, p. 47; Kraus, *Psalms 1–59*, p. 115). For similar thoughts see Ps. 119. See the theme of delight in 119:14–16, 103, 131. God's laws delight the writer, he longs for them, yearns for them (see Kidner, *Psalms 73–150*, p. 420).

48. Kraus specifically points to the fact that the godly react with emotion to the law. This emotional reaction is part of godly character. Kraus, *Psalms 1–59*, p. 116.

49. Hill, *Enter His Courts with Praise*, pp. 19–26.

50. Lewis, *Reflections on the Psalms*, pp. 52–53. See also pp. 95–97.

emotional ecstasy brought on by cultic ritual is unknown in Judaism. Instead they celebrated because of what they knew about God.[51]

Israel was commanded to love God and know him with their heart. A true knowledge of God would result in many different emotions: love for God, joy in God and his creation, and a great yearning for God and his law. It was understood that if the worshipper loved and knew God this would naturally result in joy and a spirit of celebration.

Have hope and do not fear

One theme that appears in many places in the Old Testament is the idea of hope for future deliverance. Israel is to be confident in the salvation of God, and the past acts of Yahweh show that he will keep his promises. These are good reasons to hope and have confidence in God.[52] It is clear in all Israel's military endeavours that their confidence is to be in God, not in military or economic strength. The story of Gideon is an excellent example of this. Hope is also part of the theme of promise and covenant. The covenant is to be a source of hope and confidence. There is a specific cognitive basis for hope. It is based on God, his acts in history and his promises.[53]

Hope in the prophets has a clear cognitive basis. People should hope because God will deliver them in the future day of salvation. Of Psalm 9, Kidner writes: 'David has firmly fixed his mind on God and the glories of the past, the future and the present, not merely as the best antidote to his suffering but as being genuinely more important than his own concerns. Consequently praise continues to mingle with his prayer.'[54] The Psalmist knows hope in hard times because he knows the character of his God.

Hope for Israel is not shifting and uncertain like the Greek idea. It is sure because God is its source (Jer. 17:7–8; 29:11; 31:17; Ps. 51:8; 90:2; 111:7). Having hope is a command of God.[55] It is a hope that dispels anxiety. Hope

---

51. Anderson presents an analysis of pagan culture that may support this conclusion (Anderson, *A Time to Mourn, A Time to Dance*).

52. See Martens, *God's Design*, pp. 20, 33, 98. Ultimate deliverance is also insured, especially in terms of the 'Day of the Lord' and the Messianic hope (Martens, *God's Design*, pp. 202–210).

53. See Hebblethwaite, *The Christian Hope*.

54. Kidner, *Psalms 1–72*, p. 70.

55. Rengstorf in '*elpis, elpizō, ap-, proelpizō*', argues that the hope in the Old Testament is generally about God and not about anything in particular. This seems to contradict his own proof texts, which talk about hope because of cognitive facts.

is based on the concrete character of God and the expectation of future deliverance that has been promised. To have hope, Israel is to dwell on their God and his promises.

Brueggemann writes:

> The amazing thing is that in the midst of the sanctions that Yahweh pronounces, in the face of guilt and in the face of mortality, in the face of both situations in which the human person is helpless, Yahweh is attentive. Full of steadfast love and compassion, Yahweh is like a father who pities, like a mother who attends. Yahweh is indeed for human persons, for them while they are in the Pit, willing and powering them to newness. It is the central conviction of Israel that human persons in the Pit may turn to this One who is powerfully sovereign and find that sovereign One passionately attentive. That is the hope of humanity and in the end its joy.[56]

Similar to the idea of having hope is the command that is often given not to fear.[57] Hope is the opposite of fear; where hope is a positive expectation for the future, fear is a negative expectation for the future. For these reasons we can logically look at the two concepts together. A classic example of a text that exhorts the follower of Yahweh not to be afraid is Psalm 27:1–3:

> The LORD is my light and my salvation; whom shall I fear? The LORD is the stronghold of my life; of whom shall I be afraid? When evildoers assail me to devour my flesh – my adversaries and foes – they shall stumble and fall. Though an army encamp against me, my heart shall not fear; though war rise up against me, yet I will be confident.

'The difference between hope and trust fades' (p. 523). Bultmann writes, 'Only where it is a matter of secular hope do we see the element of expectation characteristic of the Gk. world, and always in such a way that it is expectation of something welcome . . . However when related to persons it is like the OT – the emphasis is TRUST' (p. 530). See also Brueggemann, *Theology of the Old Testament*, pp. 446–447, 467, 476–480. These misconceptions will be dealt with at length in later sections.

56. Brueggemann, *Theology of the Old Testament*, p. 491.

57. That fear was a concrete emotional concept is evident by the fearful being excluded from combat (Deut. 20:8; Judg. 7:3). The fear of the Lord certainly contains emotional content. The fear of God is linked to the awesome nature of his deeds on earth (Ps. 111). God is beyond our grandest conceptions of his greatness. It is clear that the fear of the Lord is equated with having knowledge of him (Prov. 2:5–6, 9:10) (Kidner, *The Proverbs*, p. 33).

Just as God's character and presence in the life of Israel is a reason to hope it is also a reason not to fear (Ps. 46:1–3).[58] Wanke writes of fear in the Old Testament: 'Essential to the characterization of fear is not only a reference to its object but also a definition of the reason for it, although it is often hard to state this precisely.'[59] Fear is about specific circumstances and as such has a clear cognitive basis.

A life free of fear is part of the hope offered by Yahweh. The ideal may not come to pass in the present but it is a promise that will be fulfilled in the day of the Lord. Isaiah 54:14 reads, 'In righteousness you shall be established; you shall be far from oppression, for you shall not fear; and from terror, for it shall not come near you.'

We have seen that in the Old Testament the righteous are emotionally alive. They feel, and they feel strongly. The emotions of the righteous are based on a knowledge of God and his laws. Their emotions identify them as followers of Yahweh, for their hope centres around Yahweh and their love for him.

Anger, hate and jealousy

Loving God and loving what is true sometimes implies that an individual will be jealous for God and his commandments. It is an emotion of protecting what is rightfully God's on the behalf of God himself. The great characters of the Old Testament display this emotion: Exodus 32, David's defence of God's greatness in the story of Goliath; Psalm 69:9; 1 Kings 19:10: the reason for Elijah's actions at Mount Carmel is jealousy. In the prophets we see a healthy jealousy for God (Elijah, Jehu: Num. 25:11, 13; 1 Kgs 19:10; 2 Kgs 10:16; Sir. 45:23; Mattathias started the Jewish revolt based on jealousy for God, 1 Macc. 2:24, 26, 54, 58).[60] Further, in Numbers 5 and Proverbs 6:34 'jealousy' in the marriage relationship seems an appropriate description.[61]

There is no question that anger is seen as a destructive force in many instances in the Old Testament. This is clear at the very beginnings in Genesis 4:5–9 where anger seems to be the motivation to commit the first

---

58. Kraus, *Psalms 1–59*, p. 461.

59. Wanke, '*phobeō, phobeomai, phobos, deos*', p. 200.

60. Hezekiah and Josiah based their reforms on this positive zeal. For a good overview see Thoennes, 'Godly Human Jealousy'. See also Milne, 'Jealousy'. Peels differentiates godly human jealousy and God's jealousy in the Old Testament. He sees positive human jealousy as zeal and God's jealousy as jealousy. This, I believe, is a common over-generalization (Peels, '*qn'*').

61. Baloian, *Anger in the Old Testament*, p. 184. See also Ps. 119:139 and Num. 11:29.

murder. In Proverbs 29:11, anger is something to take very seriously and it is to be controlled: 'A fool gives full vent to anger, but the wise quietly holds it back.' The verse according to Kidner means, 'acting on the state of our feelings, not the merits of the case: cf. v. 29, which emphasizes that to see a situation calmly is to see it clearly (Prov. 14:17, 29; 16:32; 25:28; Eccl. 7:9).'[62] Anger is not forbidden, but the wise are to be very careful about how they act on it or express it. Or, is it true, as some have suggested, that Proverbs presents an injunction to never be angry under any circumstances?[63] A careful analysis of the texts will present a more balanced view than this interpretation. Proverbs 14:29, 16:32 and 25:28 speak of the wise man being slow to anger. Baloian concludes: 'The nature of human limitations warns against unleashing the powerful passion of anger. Acting without full knowledge can lead to grievous results. The OT does not encourage the elimination of human passions, but rather stresses methods of bringing them into the service of appropriate relationships.'[64]

A closer examination of the story of Cain is also informative. God asks Cain why he is angry and proceeds to explain to Cain why his anger is not justified.[65] We see a similar situation in Jonah chapter 4. God shows Jonah how confused his thinking is. Stuart translates verse four, 'What right do you have to be angry?' Is the anger of Jonah justified? No it is not.[66] Again in verse nine we see the same question. Stuart writes, 'This question about the right to be angry is central to the whole book . . . Jonah insisted in the strongest terms possible that the gourd was important to him. It was significant in his eyes! He loved it! It delighted him! Now that it is dead he is furious.' God feels for Nineveh the way Jonah felt about the plant (10–11).[67] God uses the emotion of Jonah as an illustration. Jonah is full of emotions about Nineveh and the gourd, neither of which is justified. We see clearly the cognitive nature of anger and how, in these cases, it is related to faulty reasoning on the part of Cain and Jonah. God's response is not

---

62. Kidner, *The Proverbs*, pp. 108–109. See also Baloian, 'Anger', p. 377.

63. See McKane's interpretation of Proverbs 29:11 and 14:29.

64. Baloian, 'Anger', p. 378. Baloian points out that the words used for God's anger are the same as those used for human anger (*Anger in the Old Testament*, p. 19).

65. The clear cognitive ideas in the passage are explained by Baloian, *Anger in the Old Testament*, pp. 30–31.

66. Stuart, *Hosea–Jonah*, pp. 502–504; Ogilvie, *Hosea, Joel, Amos, Obadiah, Jonah*, p. 429. See also Childs, *Introduction to the Old Testament*, pp. 423–424.

67. Stuart, *Hosea–Jonah*, pp. 506–507.

'Do not be angry' but 'Why are you angry?' Instead of just prohibiting it, God questions the cognitive basis for the anger. Hower writes, 'God did not condemn Jonah for his emotional response but rather corrected him for his faulty thinking.'[68]

The best summary of most human anger in the Old Testament is perhaps Psalm 4:4: 'Be angry, but sin not; commune with your own hearts on your beds, and be silent' (RSV). Kidner concludes, 'Ephesians 4:26, with the LXX, sees anger here, and shows that it need not and should not be sinful.' Anger should be felt and expressed in a healthy manner.[69] Baloian writes, 'In the above Psalm, the basic procedure for the control of anger is an appeal to reason . . . One cannot be wise in their choices if they are not based on a rational assessment of the positions and critical evaluation of the data.'[70]

In Proverbs anger is put in a negative light nine times and in a positive light only once.[71] Anger is an emotion that is very dangerous and must be evaluated very carefully before violent action is taken. Often the reasoning behind it is wrong and it will dissipate if this faulty thinking is corrected. This understanding of anger is consistent with a cognitive view. It is not an irrational force that comes upon one. Instead the knowledge of the wise will keep them from acting out of anger rashly and will exert a calming influence, 'Be angry, but sin not.'

If the Old Testament has a cognitive understanding of anger it is logical to assume there will be examples of positive anger that are right because anger is directed at the right objects. We find that righteous anger is a part of the Old Testament writings (Exod. 16:20; 32:19; Lev. 10:16; Num. 16:15; 31:14; Judg. 9:30; 1 Sam. 11:6; 2 Sam. 12:5; 13:21; Jer. 6:11; Neh. 5:6). Anger against sin or injustice is appropriate and praiseworthy.[72] We also see righteous anger in the character of God (which we will discuss later). As I have argued, if emotion is cognitive, the object of the emotion will determine its moral character – and this is what we find in the Old Testament. While anger is most often unjustified and harmful, the righteous have legitimate anger when it is directed against the right objects.

Close to, though not synonymous with, anger is the emotion of hatred. Ben-Ze'ev defines anger and hate in the following manner:

---

68. Hower, 'The Misunderstanding and Mishandling of Anger', p. 271.

69. Kidner, *Psalms 1–72*, p. 56.

70. Baloian, *Anger in the Old Testament*, p. 23.

71. Cerling, 'Anger: Musings of a Theologian/Psychologist', pp. 14–15.

72. See also Baloian, 'Anger', pp. 44–48, 380.

General Characterization:

Anger: A specific negative emotional attitude toward another agent who is considered to have inflicted unjustified harm upon us.

Hate: A global negative emotional attitude toward another agent who is considered to possess fundamentally negative traits . . .[73]

Foerster states that hate (*echthros*, LXX) is most often used for a national or personal enemy in the Old Testament.[74] It can also mean the hatred of sin or of the doers of sin. 'Do I not hate those who hate you, O LORD? And do I not loathe those who rise up against you?' (Ps. 139:21; see also 19–22 and Ps. 31:6). In the context of Israel being God's people it is not surprising that we find that enemies are sometimes hated. Israel's enemies are those who hate God and his people. Further, the ungodly are haters of God and righteousness. The actions of such people often mock God, are disobedient, and are directed against the righteous (Ps. 25:19).[75]

Proverbs 8:13 reads: 'The fear of the LORD is hatred of evil. Pride and arrogance and the way of evil and perverted speech I hate' (see also Prov. 15:27; 29:24). The Israelite is to hate evil as God does (Ps. 97:10; Prov. 13:5; Amos 5:15).[76] If the fear of God is largely about having a knowledge of God and his character, as McKane argues, this knowledge leads to the emotion of hating evil, a clearly cognitive connection.[77] Kidner writes of Proverbs 2: 'The process is that wisdom and knowledge, when they become your own way of

---

73. Ben-Ze'ev, 'Anger and Hate', pp. 85–86.

74. Foerster, '*echthros, echthra*', p. 812.

75. Michel, '*miseō*', p. 687. Stachowiak, 'Hatred', p. 353. Kidner, *Psalms 73–150*, p. 467. Murder committed in hatred was the criteria for capital punishment (Deut. 19:4–13, Josh. 20:5). Here we see again that emotional motive matters in the Old Testament. The emotional state and motive of the perpetrator must be considered in judgment. Michel, '*miseō*', p. 685. Here I must question Michel when he writes, 'this is not primarily an emotion of the human heart'. Similarly, he writes about the antithesis of love and hate in the wisdom literature in the Old Testament: 'What is meant is not so much an emotion as a rejection in will and deed' (Michel, '*miseō*', 687). Later we will argue that this statement is misguided.

76. Seebass, 'Enemy, Enmity, Hate', p. 555 (Num. 25:11, 13–14; 1 Kgs 19:10; 2 Kgs 10:16; 1 Macc. 2:24, 26, 50; Sir. 45:23).

77. McKane, *Proverbs*, p. 349. In Prov. 20:30 punishment causes an internal emotional aversion to the act.

thinking, and your acquired taste (10), will make the talk and interests of evil men alien to you (12–15).'[78]

Psalms also expresses strong hatred. This is often a reaction to evil or violence done to the writer. The anger/hatred shows how seriously they took sin. This is nearer to godliness than indifference.[79]

Hatred is in many instances a forbidden emotion. An injunction not to hate is found in Leviticus 19:17 (see also Prov. 24:17; 25:21). Hatred against a neighbour is not a legitimate or acceptable emotion. The definition of hatred presented above shows why hatred against a neighbour is forbidden where anger is to be slow and rare. Hatred is a characterized by a general and long standing negative evaluation of a person while anger is usually felt against a specific offence.

It is clear that anger and hatred play a significant role in the life of the righteous. The rightness or wickedness of these emotions depends on the nature of their objects. Anger against your fellow man is very dangerous and should not be acted upon in a rash moment, where hatred for sin is appropriate and right. In fact, an identifying mark of the righteous is the fact that they hate sin. The assertion that this hate is emotional will be, perhaps, the most contested point of this Chapter because many scholars have classified this kind of hatred as non-emotional rejection. We can ask two questions: first, is this assertion a result of their own presupposition about the nature of emotion? Second, is a belief that hate is not emotional consistent with the meaning of knowledge and heart in the Hebrew Old Testament? We contend that an accurate understanding of the true nature of evil will naturally lead to hating it. If this hatred of evil is not present, it is a sign that the love of the good is not truly present.

Sorrow and the lament

As they do with anger and hate, the righteous have particular emotional dispositions when it comes to grief and sorrow.

Sorrow is encouraged in a number of circumstances in the Old Testament. First, unlike the Hellenistic philosophers' belief, it is right and proper to feel sorrow over trouble, death and destruction in this world. Sorrow is often shown in a very visible and physical way. Just as joy often involves shouting, dancing and playing music, sorrow often involves weeping, loud wailing, the tearing of clothes and periods of mourning. This is especially true at the

---

78. Kidner, *The Proverbs*, p. 62.

79. Lewis, *Reflections on the Psalms*, pp. 23–33.

death of a loved one. The emotion was displayed by a very active experience. The use of professional mourners in the Old Testament may have acted to help free the grieving to express their emotion (2 Chr. 32:25; Amos 5:16; Jer. 9:17; see also David's response to the death of Saul and Jonathan in 2 Sam. 1).[80] Collective grieving allowed the expression of emotion so that healing could begin. Walters writes of grief in the Pentateuch, 'Grief is described in terms totally consistent with the circumstances in which the death is seen to occur.'[81] He continues, 'In all of the stories [of the Old Testament], written by a variety of authors at different times and it different political and religious contexts, the reality of grief is fully acknowledged. The need to grieve is never denied.'[82]

Sorrow is also appropriate in repentance. One of the things that differentiates genuine repentance from that which is superficial is the presence of genuine sorrow (Isa. 22:12–13). The book of Lamentations is a good example of corporate grief over sin. Sullender writes, 'The primary aim of the poems is the catharsis of grief emotions leading to repentance.'[83] Our own experience of offering and receiving forgiveness confirms the need for a genuine feeling of sorrow in repentance. A person who says they are sorry and does not express appropriate emotions is not taken seriously. The emotion shows that the repentance is genuine and the lack of emotion proves it false.[84]

Contrition involves an element of self examination and brokeness about one's character that is not present in other similar emotions (Ps. 51:4–6).[85] The emotional nature of true repentance is frequently seen in the Old Testament narrative. It is not only a feature of the narrative but it is explicitly mentioned as a requirement for God hearing the prayer of repentance. God forgives people who repent with their hearts (2 Chr. 6:36–39).

A survey of the history of repentance shows that when God's people repent with their full hearts Yahweh forgives (1 Kgs 8:46–48; 21:22–29; Ezra

---

80. Sullender, 'Saint Paul's Approach to Grief', pp. 63–64. See also Bultmann, *'penthos', pentheō'*, p. 41. For an excellent survey of lamenting over personal loss in the Old Testament, see Moberly, 'Lament'; 2 Sam. 3:31–35, 18:33; Gen. 50:3; Jer. 34:5. For the emotional meaning of the vocabulary of grief see Oliver, *''bl'*.

81. Walters, *Why Do Christians Find It Hard to Grieve?*, p. 16.

82. Walters, *Why Do Christians Find It Hard to Grieve?*, pp. 23–24.

83. Sullender, 'Saint Paul's Approach to Grief', p. 64. See also Hill, *Enter His Courts with Praise*, p. 129.

84. Matthews, 'Ritual and the Religious Feelings', pp. 345–346.

85. Roberts, 'The Logic and Lyric of Contrition', pp. 194–197.

9:2–12; Isa. 22:12–13; Jer. 50:4–5; Joel 2:12–13). Further, we see isolated examples of non-genuine repentance that is rejected. This fits with our earlier analyses of God answering heartfelt prayer. Prayers of repentance or for help in the Old Testament generally have a sense of spontaneity. According to Martens, 'they hardly follow a rigid or prescribed form. They represent intense emotional involvement.'[86] Prayer is not a repeated formula to get God's attention. Instead, the prayer of repentance is often a gut-wrenching cry for help from the heart. The desperate prayer for help and the prayer of repentance is with the whole heart, mind, soul and emotion (Ps. 78:34; Isa. 1:27; Jer. 8:6; 9:5; 31:19; Ezek. 14:6; 18:30; Dan. 9:3–20; 1 Kgs 22:27–29; 2 Kgs 19:1–7, 20; 22:11–20; Neh. 1:4–11; Ezra 9:10; Amos 5). When emotion drives genuine repentance, God hears and forgives.

The community of Israel moved between the moods of deep anguish and misery to profound joy and celebration. The lament presents a pattern for expressing sorrow and grief to God and receiving his restoration.[87] This restoration most often came in the form of a rehearsal of knowledge about God. The facts of Israel's history, God's acts of deliverance, and remembering the great character and love of God changed mourning to joy.

The lament gave expression to the inner thoughts and struggles of the community. Brueggemann writes: 'Israel knows that one need not fake it or be polite and pretend in his presence, nor need one face the hurts alone.' Anger, hurt, fear, and resentment are all part of the dialog with Yahweh. The lament assumes that God is listening and is able to change circumstances or personal attitudes.[88] Moberly concludes: 'Moreover they show that the experience of anguish and puzzlement in the life of faith is not a sign of deficient faith, something to be outgrown or put behind one, but rather intrinsic to the very nature of faith.'[89]

Psalm 77 begins with sorrow and lament. The author then specifically calls upon his knowledge of God to lift his spirits: 'I will call to mind the deeds of the LORD; I will remember your wonders of old. I will meditate on all your work, and muse on your mighty deeds. Your way, O God, is holy. What god

---

86. Martens, *God's Design*, p. 225. See also Konkel, '*ṣʿq*'. Konkel gives a good summation of God's response to the repentant cry from the heart.

87. Brueggemann, 'From Hurt to Joy', p. 3.

88. Brueggemann, 'From Hurt to Joy', p. 4. See also Kraus, *Psalms 1–59*, pp. 48–49; Dillard and Longman, *An Introduction to the Old Testament*, pp. 200–222; Von Rad, *Old Testament Theology*, vol. 1, pp. 401–402.

89. Moberly, 'Lament', p. 879.

is so great as our God? (11–13).' Dwelling on God's saving acts and the character of God are clearly prescribed as a remedy for discouragement. The NLT translates Psalm 103:1: 'Praise the Lord, I tell myself'. Again in this Psalm the writer is discouraged and begins to rehearse facts about God to encourage his heart. Perhaps the greatest agony in the Old Testament is the feeling of abandonment by God. The writer's grief is dealt with by repeating the certainty of covenant, God's promise of love, and God's past acts of blessing (Ps. 113).[90]

The widely recognized, formal structure of the Lament Psalms, according to Brueggemann, is 'address, complaint, petition, motivation, vow of offering, assurance of being heard'. In the address God is expected to intervene on the sufferer's behalf because of a previous commitment.[91] The complaint details the suffering or trouble that is being experienced. The petition asks for a change in circumstances in order to rectify the suffering or trouble. God is able to change the situation and the one who petitions is willing to put it in God's care. This petition often includes a reason or motivation for God to act on the behalf of the sufferer. While the speaker is helpless, God can transform the situation. Finally, there is an expression of assurance that God has heard. The mere knowledge that God has heard is in itself an assurance that transformation has or will happen.[92] Notice the clear cognitive progression and emphasis of the pattern.

There is clearly an emotional transformation in many of these Psalms. The writer starts honestly expressing pain and emotional agony and ends with praise. Two factors seem to be evident in this change of emotions. First, the expression of deeply felt, honest emotions to God frees the writer. Second, the rational confirmation that God hears and is able to act reassures the writer. Even if God does not act, emotions are changed by the realization that God is in control and is able to act.[93] Brueggemann continues, 'Thus

---

90. Kidner, *Psalms 1–72*, pp. 78, 86; Kidner, *Psalms 73–150*, p. 364; Kraus, *Psalms 1–59*, pp. 215–216. Kraus emphasizes that the change of emotion in 113 verse 5 is due to a new knowledge. See also Psalms 13 and 22; Martens, *God's Design*, p. 160.

91. Brueggemann, 'From Hurt to Joy', p. 6. See also Moberly, 'Lament'.

92. Brueggemann, 'From Hurt to Joy', pp. 6–8; Kraus, *Psalms 1–59*, pp. 78–81.

93. Brueggemann, 'From Hurt to Joy', p. 8. Brueggemann wonders what transforms the writer's mood. He surveys the major theories of Old Testament scholars to explain the transformation concluding that the reason for transformation cannot be known definitively. We can argue that a cognitive view of emotions may explain the mood change. It is very difficult to explain the change in

we suggest that the lament form, as contrasted with the funeral song, gives expression to Israel's most fundamental conviction, namely that Yahweh is sovereign over the present situation and can work good out of it.' A new perspective makes the worshipper realize that their God is bigger than their problem. As the writer re-affirms these beliefs, their emotions change and they are reassured.[94]

The pattern of lament carries beyond the Psalms. For example, we see a similar pattern in the exodus event (Exod. 2–15), in the wanderings in the wilderness, in the pattern of the judges (Judg. 6:3; 8:22; 13:15), in the deliverance of Jerusalem under Hezekiah and in the lives of the prophets. In each of these situations the characters in history cry out to God in great trouble and he delivers them. The pattern of the lament is lived out.[95] The strong acts of God in past history serve to give confidence and faith in the present.

In the lament the emotional resolution is linked to the fact that Yahweh is the God who hears and responds. Unlike the pagan deities that are only stone idols, Yahweh acts for his people (Isa. 41:7; 44:18; Jer. 10:5). Therefore, Israel can be confident while the nations fear.[96] In summary, the lament shows a strong cognitive pattern. It is good to express sorrow, but this sorrow will pass as the theology of Israel is rehearsed in the believers' hearts and minds.

The patterns we see in the emotions of anger, hate and sorrow in the lives

---

emotion without understanding the function of emotion. From a cognitive perspective, we understand that as the writer expresses emotion and reconfirms what he believes about God, his emotions change. Here Brueggemann answers his own question without realizing that he has. 'And that is a central conviction of Israel about the structure of reality. Life is transformed, health is restored, enemies are resisted and destroyed, death is averted, *shalom* is given again.' It is precisely the reaffirmation of the fact that God does these things that changes the writer's mood (Brueggemann, 'From Hurt to Joy', pp. 8–10). Westermann agrees that there is no clear reason for the change in emotion (Westermann, *The Psalms*, pp. 60–61).

94. Brueggemann, 'From Hurt to Joy', p. 13.

95. Brueggemann, 'From Hurt to Joy', pp. 13–18; Westermann, *The Psalms*, pp. 52–53. Westermann gives a list of many passages of lament outside the Psalms. Westermann, *The Living Psalms*, p. 21. See also the laments in Jeremiah (Moberly, 'Lament', p. 878).

96. Brueggemann, 'From Hurt to Joy', p. 19.

of the righteous are similar to those we considered in the positive emotions. There is a freedom of expression for emotion coupled with the expectation that the emotions of the righteous will be based on the theology of Israel. Even anger can be expressed legitimately for righteous reasons: the righteous are to hate evil. The righteous repent in sorrow. Finally, when sorrow overwhelms the people of Israel they are to think about their God and his work for them. This will strengthen them in hard times. In each of these areas there are strong cognitive links; Israel will feel the right way when they know the right things in their hearts.

Emotions of the wicked: what they love and what they hate

Just as the righteous have certain emotional characteristics, so do the wicked. Here are just a few key concepts.

First and foremost, whereas the righteous love God and desire the good, the wicked love evil and desire to do wrong. Their basic emotional disposition is fundamentally opposite from the righteous. As with the righteous' love of Yahweh, this desire has a link with knowledge and understanding. For the wicked, it is a lack of knowledge or no desire to obtain right knowledge that leads them to ruin. Hosea 4:6 reads: 'My people are destroyed for lack of knowledge; because you have rejected knowledge, I reject you from being a priest to me. And since you have forgotten the law of your God, I also will forget your children.' The wicked hate instruction (Prov. 5:12; 1:22).[97]

Hosea 4:8 reads: 'Sin was their sustenance, the object of their delight and satisfaction.' The people of Israel sat under judgment because they delighted in the doing of evil (Ps. 35:15; Ezek. 36:5; Obad. 12; Mic. 7:8).[98] The wicked love evil and rejoice in doing it (Isa. 57:8; Jer. 5:31; 14:10; Amos 5:15; Mic. 3:2; 6:8; Prov. 2:14; 24:17; Hab. 1:15). Hosea 9:1 relates that the Israelites were rejoicing in a pagan festival as if it were to the true God. They took delight in the wrong thing.[99] Hosea 7:3 is difficult to translate but it may be another passage that condemns Israel because of its positive emotional attitude towards what is wicked. It reads: 'By their wickedness they make the king glad.'

---

97. Notice that the love of the righteous is for a personal God where the love of the wicked is for impersonal objects or evil itself. See also Grisanti, 'šwš', p. 1224.

98. McComiskey, 'Hosea', p. 63. See also 4:18 and the comments of Stuart, Hosea–Jonah, p. 86 and Grisanti, 'śmḥ', pp. 1252–1253.

99. Stuart, Hosea–Jonah, p. 142.

McComiskey emphasizes the emotion in his translation and comments that the king and court delighted in their sin.[100]

This message is further emphasized by Hosea 7:14. The emotions pictured here are probably not genuine. Ritual alone does not get God's attention especially if it is based on faulty understanding. This verse seems to have in mind pagan rites like those of the prophets of Baal cutting themselves before Elijah. If this is correct it fits with our analysis of emotion in the Old Testament. Their desire was to placate God in rites and ceremony. God desires heart-felt knowledge based repentance, 'crying from the heart' of the first phrase, not ritualistic display.[101] Hosea 6:6 confirms this message. Perhaps the best translation is 'rather than' sacrifice. It is not against sacrifice but rather it is a condemnation of where their heart is. Again the message is that ritual with no heartfelt allegiance is empty. Notice also the link with knowledge in this passage. They had knowledge of the ways of sacrifice but no knowledge of what God really wanted from them. The knowledge God required was not simply the facts about how to sacrifice but a broken heart over sin and a love for God.[102]

Evil desires are a general characteristic of the evil man in the Old Testament (Prov. 11:6; 21:25; Gen. 6:5).[103] Psalm 52:3–4 reads: 'You love evil more than good, and lying more than speaking the truth. You love all words that devour, O deceitful tongue.' (See also Isa. 5:20.)

We can say that a love or desire for evil or sin is a prevalent theme in Old Testament and Jewish theology. Israel would not sin if they did not desire it, they sin because their heart is drawn toward evil instead of good. Sin is driven by an emotional disposition that loves and desires evil.

It is also clear that that negative or inappropriate emotions are often forces that lead characters in the Old Testament toward sin (Gen. 30:1; Judg. 16:16; 2 Sam. 13:2). There are particular emotions that characterize the wicked. We have already mentioned the propensity to become angry quickly. This often results in violence and destruction.[104] Another charac-

---

100. McComiskey, 'Hosea', pp. 101–102; McKeating, *Amos, Hosea, Micah*, p. 114. See also the translation of Macintosh, *Hosea*.

101. McComiskey, 'Hosea', p. 115. See also Andersen and Freedman, *Hosea*, pp. 474–475; Stuart, *Hosea–Jonah*, p. 123.

102. McComiskey, 'Hosea', pp. 92–93. Inadequate knowledge of God is a regular theme in Hosea.

103. Gamberoni, 'Desire', p. 206. See also Kidner, *The Proverbs*, p. 145.

104. Baloian, 'Anger', p. 379. Some of his examples for this are misplaced.

teristic emotion is jealousy (*zēlos* in the LXX) over the wrong objects. This is an emotion that, like anger, is often destructive.[105] Although it is easily based on the wrong objects and abused, from our previous discussion we see that the emotion itself is neutral. One reason that jealousy is too often seen in a negative light is the fact that it is confused with envy. Envy, as we see in the seventh commandment (Exod. 20:17), has as part of its very definition desiring something that is not yours. This is not the case with jealousy.

The wicked can be seen clearly for what they are by observing their emotions. They love and delight in evil and they despise wisdom and the knowledge of God. Beyond this, their actions are often motivated by destructive, self-centred and strongly felt jealousy, hatred, anger, base desire and envy.

Emotions of God

It is clear that the Old Testament presents Yahweh as an emotional God. He loves Israel, desires their obedience, delights in those who follow him, hates wickedness, is angered by disobedience and is jealous for Israel's loyalty. These emotions of God have been seen as metaphorical by many, starting with the church fathers. We see the same arguments in Philo. I reply to these in other sections.

Some false ideas about the emotions of God seem to have their roots in Platonic philosophy and the desire for Yahweh not to appear like the pagan gods who were driven by irrational passions. However, I find no evidence in the Old Testament to support this contention. God is presented as emotional and he should be studied in this context without reading the text through philosophical constructs.[106] God's emotions play a key role in many texts, as God feels with intensity.[107]

---

105. Stumpff, '*zēlos, zēloō, zēlōtēs, parazēloō*', p. 877.

106. Anderson says of the Psalms, 'these anthropomorphic descriptions of God express the belief that the Almighty is able to share in human feelings'. Anderson, *Psalms*, p. 66. More correctly, we can say people's emotions are made in the image of God.

107. Exodus 34:6–7, a key text in the Old Testament about God's character, refers to his major emotional traits. He is merciful, slow to anger, and full of steadfast love. See Brueggemann, *Theology of the Old Testament*, pp. 215–217. This list of attributes is often repeated (Ps. 145:8, 86; John 4:2; Lam. 3:21–24; Isa. 54:9–10). The use of *lēb* for the emotions of God reinforces the idea of an emotional God (Luc, '*lēb*', p. 750). See Gen. 6:6.

God's love

Once again love is the best place to start. God has chosen and loves Israel. Can we say that God's love is love as we know it if it contains no element of emotion? Would we react strongly to God loving us if we knew that God's love was without emotion? Hill writes, 'It is this persistent love that is introduced as the basis for Yahweh's dealings with Israel, and it is in the book of Hosea that one finds for the first time the notion that the relationship between Yahweh and Israel is founded on his love.'[108] The three major themes in Hosea according to Helfin are 'God suffers exceedingly because of human rebellion against him; second, that God loves unconditionally; and third, that God forgives completely.'[109]

God's love is like a parent's love for their child. Is there any stronger emotion? Hosea gives a beautiful picture of this in chapter 11. Ogilvie writes, 'Yahweh gave Ephraim compassionate attention and provision. And as He reflected on the past, the heart of God was stirred with loneliness. It could not be otherwise. To love that deeply and have that love rejected is loneliness with an aching sob in it.'[110] We see in verses eight and nine that this father-love influences Yahweh's decision not to execute his anger against Israel. 'How can I give you up, Ephraim? How can I hand you over, O Israel? How can I make you like Admah? How can I treat you like Zeboiim? My heart recoils within me; my compassion grows warm and tender. I will not execute my fierce anger.' (Jer. 3:19; Isa. 49:15; 63:16; 66:13; Ps. 103:9–14).[111]

Andersen and Freedman write of 11:8: 'we glimpse the agony in the mind of God'. They continue to emphasize the emotional struggle within the mind

---

108. Hill, 'Hosea 11: Yahweh's Persistent Love', p. 27. For comments on God's free choice to love Israel see Brueggemann, *Theology of the Old Testament*, pp. 410–411, 415–416. See also Baer and Gordon, '*ḥsd*'. They believe God's love functions in very similar terms to this thesis (Neh. 13:22; Ps. 6:4, 13:5, 26:1–3, 36:7, 147:11). It should be dwelt on for comfort and security (Ps. 40:10, 48:9, 106:7). It is also regularly included in descriptions of God's character (Exod. 34:6, Num. 14:8, Neh. 9:17, Ps. 86:15, Joel 2:13). Els insists that '*'hb*' is emotional when used of God loving his people. (Jer. 31:20). Els, '*'hb*', pp. 279–281.

109. Heflin, 'Hosea 1–3: Love Triumphant', p. 9.

110. Ogilvie, *Hosea, Joel, Amos, Obadiah, Jonah*, p. 158. See also pp. 162–163 on 11:8.

111. For a good summary of God's strong love in Jeremiah see Morris, *Testaments of Love*, pp. 10–11. It is God's great motivation in the midst of Israel's unfaithfulness.

of God: 'a tumult of emotions is occurring, not just a clash of ideas'.[112]
McComiskey writes:

> The drastic change of emotion that takes place between this verse and the previous
> context is one of the most significant aspects of Hosea's prophetic message. We feel
> Yahweh's deep emotions welling up within his heart. He looks at his erring child and
> is overwhelmed by love . . . We see the grace of God here as we have not yet seen in
> the whole of prophecy . . . The intensity of emotion is underscored by the word
> *yahad* (together). This appears as 'all' in the Author's translation. It pictures all the
> emotions of tenderness and love in Yahweh as burning within his heart.[113]

Hosea 2:16–20 uses the relationship of a husband to a wife to illustrate the relationship that God desires with Israel.[114] In Hosea we see the most emotional
relationships in human experience used to illustrate God's feelings about Israel.

God's covenant love may form the basis for many Psalms (Ps. 44:26; 92:1–2;
106:44–45; 103:17–18; 143:12). Leonard believes that the most repeated
phrases used in praising God – 'his steadfast love endures forever' – includes
the idea of covenant (Ps. 92:1–2; 106:1; 107:1; 118:1, 29; 136:1–26; 1 Chr. 16:34;
2 Chr. 20:21). Leonard writes, 'In many respects "covenant love" is the key
word or concept in the book of Psalms; it pervades all that is said to, or about,
Yahweh, whether the word *ḥesed* is present or not. In its praise of the Lord,
Israel joyfully celebrates his covenant love.'[115] What better reason for Israel to
praise God than that promise of enduring love. The foundation of Israel's
faith is God's enduring love for Israel.[116]

God's love moves him to compassion and pity. These turn away his anger
and wrath from the sinner (Hos. 1:6–7).[117] Similarly, God's act of returning

---

112. Andersen and Freedman, *Hosea*, pp. 587, 588–589. See also Ps. 105:25; 1 Sam. 4:19;
     Lam. 1:20; Zech. 1:13. See also Stott, *The Cross of Christ*, p. 130.

113. McComiskey, 'Hosea', p. 191. Like Von Rad, McComiskey notes the parallel with
     Lam. 1:20 in this verse.

114. The word for love used here, *ḥesed*, signifies parental love, tenderness and
     unshakable attachment (McKeating, *Amos, Hosea, Micah*, p. 88; Andersen and
     Freedman, *Hosea*, p. 430).

115. Leonard, 'Psalms in Biblical Worship', p. 248.

116. Martens, *God's Design*, p. 43. See also Exod. 15:13; 20:6.

117. McComiskey, 'Hosea', p. 25. According to Dillard and Longman the book of
     Judges is a historical witness to this kind of compassion (*An Introduction to the Old
     Testament*, p. 119).

Israel from exile is motivated by the love and compassion God has for
his people. He is motivated by the fact that he feels their suffering (Jer. 30; 31;
Isa. 14:1; 49:14–16; 54:7–8). Israel's grief and repentance motivate Yahweh to
change his anger to compassion.[118] Hosea is a book of great emotion, namely
the emotion of God for a wayward people. The people were religious in practice but their hearts were not God's. Their religion was outward or they mixed
Yawhehism with the worship of Baal. God's response to this is great heart-
break and grief. Yahweh's love for Israel led him to grief over Israel's sin. It
could also lead him to rejoicing as we read in Zephaniah 3:17: 'he will rejoice
over you with gladness, he will renew you in his love; he will exult over you
with loud singing' (Isa. 62:5; 65:19; Jer. 32:41; Deut. 30:9).[119]

God's jealousy and wrath

God's love and personal nature also imply that he will be jealous for his people.
According to Von Rad and Eichrodt, God's jealousy is central to God's moral
character. It is the reason behind the second commandment where God's name
is said to be jealous (Exod. 34:14). God is jealous for a personal and exclusive
relationship with his people because this is his right.[120]

God loves the good and hates sin. Therefore, God pours his wrath out on
the wicked. Kidner writes about Proverbs 15:8–9: 'The pair of sayings show
how intensely our regular behavior matters to God.'[121] In other words, God
has an emotional reaction to the path that a man chooses. God hates the
worship of idols, immorality and improper or insincere worship (Isa. 61:8;
Deut. 16:22; Prov. 6; Ps. 5:6; 11:5).[122] God's anger is typically a response
to unrighteousness. God's anger is for a constructive purpose, that is, to bring

---

118. Martens, *God's Design*, pp. 240–241; Brueggemann, *Theology of the Old Testament*,
pp. 278, 299–300, 436–437, 441. Compassion in the Old Testament clearly 'signifies
emotion'. (Butterworth, '*rḥm*', p. 1094).

119. Kent, 'Hosea: Man, Times and Material'; Grisanti, '*śwś*', pp. 1223–1224.

120. Thoennes, 'Godly Human Jealousy'. 'Hosea clearly perceives at the depth of the
thought of the election and the covenant the spontaneous love of the acting God.'
(Quell, '*agapaō, agapē, agapētos*', p. 31). Brueggemann defines Yahweh's jealousy as
'strong emotional response to any affront against Yahweh's prerogative, privilege,
ascendancy, or sovereignty' (Brueggemann, *Theology of the Old Testament*, p. 293).
Theissen points out that pagan gods are not jealous for exclusive devotion
(Theissen, *The Shadow of the Galilean*, p. 64).

121. Kidner, *The Proverbs*, p. 113.

122. Seebass, 'Enemy, Enmity, Hate', p. 556. See also Struthers, '*ʾnp*'; Grisanti, '*ḥdh*'.

repentance or to judge sin. It is also important to note that God's anger can be directed against his own servants (Exod. 4:14; Num. 12:9; Jon. 1:4).[123]

Some theologians argue that emotional anger is not consistent with Yahweh's character. Stachowiak writes, 'This way of speaking is, of course, metaphorical; it would be quite impossible in view of the loving assent of Yahweh to his creation to transfer to him human hatred in the real sense of the term.'[124] How can God be both angry with sinners and love mankind? God does not love the sinner and is angry at the sin. Rather, God loves the sinner and he is angry at the sinner when he sins, just as I may love my wife and still be angry at her. Anger and love are not incompatible. In fact, we are often most angry with those we love, because we care most about what happens to them. I am angry with my son for disobedience because he is my son and I care deeply about what kind of man he will become. Thus our emotions are like God's. We are able to show both anger and love toward the same individual (Ps. 95:10).[125] Pedersen writes:

> Through the ages men have viewed and even now continue to view God as a being with very depersonalized emotions. There is a biblical alternative to this view in seeing God as moved personally by the actions of his creatures. He cares for them and is angry at them personally because of their response to Him. This is only possible if God can be allowed to have both anger and love for a person with neither emotion ruling out the other.[126]

Anger is often part of God's punishment of sin. Cerling writes:

> God is angry at sin and at human oppression, a result of sin. Therefore, if we are going to say that anger is justifiable, we must make that qualification of the object of anger. Anger is not justifiable if it is a response to personal offense . . . Anger is justifiable as a response to sin and human oppression.[127]

---

123. Hower, 'The Misunderstanding and Mishandling of Anger', p. 270. See also Struthers, *"br"*.

124. Stachowiak, 'Hatred', p. 352. See also Hanson, *The Wrath of the Lamb*, p. 24.

125. Pedersen, 'Some Thoughts on a Biblical View of Anger', pp. 210–212. See also Cassirer, *Grace and Law*, pp. 101, 106–107, 115. The vocabulary in Ps. 95 can mean loathed, disgusted or angry (Kidner. *Psalms 73–150*, p. 346).

126. Pedersen, 'Some Thoughts on a Biblical View of Anger', p. 212.

127. Cerling, 'Anger: Musings of a Theologian/Psychologist', p. 15.

God's anger is always legitimate because he is holy and just. An offended person may or may not be angry at sin. Their anger may or may not be justified. An offence against God is sin by definition. Therefore, an offence against God is always a cause for anger while an offence against another person is not.[128] Baloian presents a good summary:

> Yahweh can be angry solely because of human cruelty, or He can be angry exclusively because of the idolatry, rebellion or pride of human beings. That Yahweh can be angry because of humans disregarding their common sense of justice demonstrates that he cares about how human treat humans. He is not only concerned about His cult and its maintenance. He is concerned about the lives of human beings and whether justice takes place among them. This concern is not merely a passive interest.[129]

Hosea presents us with good illustrative passages concerning God's hatred. In Hosea 9:15 the word *śn'* probably means strong hatred. McComiskey writes, 'Here, however, the hatred is intense.'[130] God hates because 'of the wickedness of their deeds'. There is a good reason for this hatred. Hosea 10 continues to illustrate this point. Their promises to Yahweh are not kept in their hearts and their ritual is meaningless. God hates the divided heart and has no place for competing loyalties.

At the same time, Yahweh is characterized by being slow to anger (Exod. 34:6; Num. 14:18; Neh. 9:17; Ps. 86:15; 103:9–14; 145:8; Isa. 48:9; Joel 2:13; Jon. 4:2; Nah. 1:3); notice also that this attribute is attributed to the wise man in Proverbs (14:29; 15:18; 16:32; 19:11).[131] God does not act on his anger without thought and reference to his own compassion. God's anger or wrath has an understandable motivation that is made clear to the reader. This encouraged morality and did not leave in confusion those with whom God was angry. They

---

128. Cerling, 'Some Thoughts on a Biblical View of Anger: A Response', pp. 266–267; Baloian, *Anger in the Old Testament*, pp. 71–76. God's anger in the Old Testament is 'both just and rational'. Unlike pagan gods, we do not find God being angry when he does not have a good reason for it. Anderson, *Psalms*, p. 88.

129. Baloian, *Anger in the Old Testament*, p. 73. He also writes, 'The wrath of Yahweh is different in one respect from human wrath. Anger in God is always more than just emotion.' It takes action. Baloian, *Anger in the Old Testament*, pp. 98, 165. We might rather say that God's anger is always acted on because it is always justified.

130. McComiskey, 'Hosea'. See also Ogilvie, *Hosea, Joel, Amos, Obadiah, Jonah*, p. 140.

131. See Brueggemann, *Theology of the Old Testament*, p. 488; Baloian, *Anger in the Old Testament*, p. 70.

were responsible for God's anger against them and it was justified. Baloian concludes his study on anger, 'Hence, Israel's encounter with the burning wrath of Yahweh can not only be understood as just . . ., but it was also understood as an expression of his love. When Israel committed idolatry, she was killing herself, and Yahweh become passionately involved when those he loved were moving toward death.'[132]

In summary, God, in the theology of Israel, is a person. He reacts and is moved by human events. Heschel writes, 'This notion that God can be intimately affected, that he possesses not merely intelligence and will, but also feeling and pathos, basically defines the prophetic consciousness of God.' Often his anger serves to bring Israel back into fellowship with Yahweh. They are his children and that is his goal. Yahweh's anger is produced by his character, which is just. Beyond anger, God actually suffers for his people.[133] God desires to be loved by Israel. His loves drives him toward reconciliation and faithfulness in the midst of Israel's disobedience and idolatry. Brueggemann writes: 'But the way to healing is not an easy one for Yahweh; Yahweh goes through loss, anguish, rage, and humiliation. The healing costs the healer a great deal.'[134]

To postulate a God without passion is to take the heart out of Jewish worship. God's emotions are not like the self-centred, irrational passions of the pagan gods, nor is he the Epicurean god that feels no passion.[135] Baloian concludes: 'The Bible speaks unashamedly of Yahweh's passion, presenting him as an intense and passionate Being, fervently interested in the world of humans.'[136] Yahweh has emotion; he cares for Israel. All the emotions that flow naturally out of this love are appropriate for him. God's emotions are always in line with his holiness and moral character. God's emotions are always correct, righteous and moral because he is always correct, righteous and moral. Further, human emotions are part of man being made in the image of God. Emotions are a good and legitimate part of man's character because they are clearly part of God's character. We have often been told that God's emotions were 'anthropomorphisms', described like those of humans. In reality, human emotions are in the image of God himself.

---

132. Baloian, 'Anger', pp. 380–384; Baloian, *Anger in the Old Testament*, pp. 109–112, 178.

133. Heschel, 'The Divine Pathos: The Basic Category of Prophetic Theology', p. 33. See also pp. 34–36.

134. Brueggemann, *Theology of the Old Testament*, p. 254.

135. Heschel, 'The Divine Pathos: the Basic Category of Prophetic Theology', pp. 38–39.

136. Baloian, 'Anger', p. 380. See also Cassirer, *Grace and Law*, p. 99.

Emotion in the Old Testament: conclusion

Although this has been a brief and rudimentary analysis of emotion in the Old Testament, I know of no other source that attempts a survey of this kind. I hope that it at least gives an overview that will bring up important issues and show the crucial importance of emotion in Old Testament theology. Perhaps the ideas that I have presented can be a starting point for competent Old Testament scholars to explore these issues more thoroughly. I have also made no attempt to differentiate various understandings of emotions that may be present between different books. My only concern has been to identify some major themes and strands of thinking about emotion. It seems difficult to deny that strong cognitive links between emotion and knowledge are present in many places in the Old Testament. An analysis of texts about emotion that passes lightly over the emotional vocabulary or stresses that this vocabulary is symbolic and metaphorical and has little or no emotional content must be questioned closely.

The Psalms are cognitive and emotive in nature. They are about the stuff of history and the character of God. Childs writes, 'Israel's prayers are not simply spontaneous musing or uncontrolled aspirations, but rather an answer to God's word which continues to address Israel in his Torah.'[137] In this we see the coming together of the cognitive theological truths of Israel's faith with an emotional response to that faith. As such, they provide evidence that a cognitive understanding of emotion was dominant. We have also seen this link between theology and emotion in many texts from other parts of the Old Testament. The righteous are known by how they feel.

Perhaps one of the best summaries of this is found in Joel 2:13–14:

> Yet even now, says the LORD, return to me with all your heart, with fasting, with weeping, and with mourning; rend your hearts and not your clothing. Return to the LORD, your God, for he is gracious and merciful, slow to anger, and abounding in steadfast love, and relents from punishing.

Here we see an emotional God responding to the emotions of his people linked with theology about who God is. (See also Jer. 9:24; Isa. 66.)

A rehearsal of knowledge is stressed throughout the Old Testament. The festivals remind the worshipper of who God is and what he has done (Deut. 26). In the prophets God is shown to love Israel like a son.[138] The facts about God's acts in history and his laws are to be rehearsed and repeated. Such

---

137. Childs, *Introduction to the Old Testament*, p. 513. See also p. 522.

138. Martens, *God's Design*, p. 114.

practices laid the foundation for the emotional life of Israel. Emotion in the faith of Israel was God-centred. There was truth to rejoice in and a God who deserved their love.

Judaism at the time of the New Testament

As well as the Old Testament exerting influence on how the Jews of the New Testament era viewed emotion, we must ask what other influences and practices may have helped to form the Jewish communities' ideas about emotion. This section is an attempt to round out the picture of the ideas about emotion that were present in the Jewish world that may have influenced the writers of the New Testament.

There are two major areas that we will concentrate on. First, specific areas of emphasis, belief or practice that may aid our understanding of how emotion was viewed at the time of the New Testament in the Jewish community will be considered. Second, we will endeavor to analyse Judaism's contact with Greek ideas about emotion and discuss how these ideas may have influenced Jewish thinking. We cannot come to any firm conclusions about how a diverse and segmented Judaism may have viewed emotion. The best that we can do is to identify how particular writers viewed emotion and review some general trends that may have influenced the culture's ideas.

The practices of Judaism

The family unit was Torah-centred in daily ritual and observance. They strove to put the law of God at the centre of their thinking, especially on the Sabbath. The pre-eminence of the study and knowledge of the Torah is well attested. This centrality of the law in Jewish life obviously had an impact on the emotions. Since their culture and their faith were intertwined, it is safe to assume that they were emotional about their faith. Many passages attest to this in Second Temple literature, both pagan and Jewish. They vigorously fought for the right to practise their beliefs to the point of enduring persecution and martyrdom. Sacrifice for law and country, often viewed as almost one and the same, was advocated by nationalistic groups.[139]

We also see their hate for Samaritans and those who did not worship God as the law prescribed. Their heartfelt knowledge and understanding of their

---

139. Schürer, *The History of the Jewish People*, vol. 2, pp. 415–416, 605–606; Scott, *Customs and Controversies*, pp. 251–253.

faith insured that they would be emotional about fulfilling its requirements and remaining distinctly Jewish both in the nation of Israel and in the Diaspora. Sanders insists that this kind of passion for their religion was widespread. It was part of their culture and national identity.[140]

Loyalty to the cult and practices of Judaism was shown in the keeping of the festivals as commanded in the Torah. These were deeply emotional times for the community in celebration, solemn repentance and corporate prayer. Sanders estimates that 300,000–500,000 people attended Passover. He continues:

> The Jewish festivals were like Christmas: a blend of piety, good cheer, hearty eating, making music, chatting with friends, drinking and dancing. While the festive atmosphere started on the road, the true feast came in Jerusalem. We recall that pilgrims had their 'second tithe' money to spend. According to Deuteronomy, as long as the money was spent in Jerusalem it could be spent [Deut. 14:26] . . . We may accept that the pilgrim families followed this advice; their trip to the temple was their main feast of the year and was an occasion for 'splurging'.[141]

The Jews were not sombre in their worship. The great national celebration of Passover was a very emotional experience. Hundreds of thousands of people gathered with thousands of lambs slaughtered, great choirs sang, and worshippers participated in temple ceremonies. The form of the feasts them-selves elicited emotion. From the spreading of blood at the Passover over the doorpost to the making of shelters at the feast of booths, the rituals caused the people to remember their history and their God with their hearts. They were the people of Yahweh![142]

Beyond the major festivals of the Jewish calendar, the Sabbath was a weekly celebration and day of refreshing the knowledge of their faith. A special meal was in order as well as sharing friendship with neighbours.[143] The Sabbath served as a weekly reminder to celebrate the faith of Israel, show solidarity and reinforce the basic doctrines of the faith of Israel.

---

140. Sanders, *Judaism: Practice and Belief*, p. 141.

141. Sanders, *Judaism: Practice and Belief*, pp. 128–129. See also pp. 130–136. See also Scott, *Customs and Controversies*, p. 69.

142. Sanders, *Judaism: Practice and Belief*, pp. 139, 256–257. In contrast, the Day of Atonement was a day of solemn remembering of sins (Sanders, *Judaism: Practice and Belief*, p. 144).

143. Sanders, *Judaism: Practice and Belief*, p. 210; Scott, *Customs and Controversies*, pp. 252–253.

In the festivals and the observance of Sabbath we see celebration combined with a rehearsal of the knowledge of the Jewish faith. All of life was centred around law and Yahweh. In Judaism religion was central to all of life and was the foundation of the emotional life.

In Second Temple Judaism we see a number of theological emphases that contribute to our understanding of emotion in Jewish culture during this time. The Shema, writes Sanders, was 'Fundamental to Jewish life and worship'.[144] As we have seen, this text is crucial both in terms of loving God and the knowledge that was behind this love. The Jews recited it twice a day and many literally hung it on their door-posts and on their bodies in small containers. The Jews were constantly reminding themselves that they were to love God. Beyond the Shema and reading of the Old Testament in the synagogue, prayer was an important part of Jewish practice. The individual was encouraged to communicate to God. We see examples of both ritual prayer and personal, emotional repentance from sin (at Qumran) in this period.[145]

Religion to the Jews was concerned with all areas of life. The correct practice of their religion, orthopraxy, was an emphasis of Second Temple Judaism. All of life was religious and as such many of their emotions were based on their religion.[146] Schürer writes, 'The whole purpose of education in family, school and synagogue was to transform the Jewish people into "disciples of the Lord". The ordinary man was to know, and do, what the Torah asked of him.'[147] Emotions would be based on the truth of Torah. In Judaism emotion was a good thing; they were to feel their faith. It was good to have zeal over the law, to celebrate God, to love one's neighbour, to repent in sorrow, and to worship with the heart.

Greek influence on Jewish culture

There were many forces that shaped Second Temple Judaism. In addition to the influence of Torah and Jewish tradition, there was the influence of Hellenization. After Alexander conquered Palestine it became a battle ground between the Seleucid and Ptolemaic empires. Much of this time the Jews willingly coexisted with Greek culture. When the Seleucids took over Palestine

---

144. Sanders, *Judaism: Practice and Belief*, p. 195; Schürer, *The History of the Jewish People*, vol. 2, pp. 457–459. Charlesworth writes, 'New Testament scholars must put aside the old view that Jewish liturgy in Jesus' time was cold and concretized' (Charlesworth, 'Jewish Hymns, Odes, and Prayers', p. 425).

145. Sanders, *Judaism: Practice and Belief*, pp. 196, 202–206.

146. Sanders, *Judaism: Practice and Belief*, p. 191.

147. Schürer, *The History of the Jewish People*, vol. 2, p. 464.

for the final time before independence they began to force Greek culture on the Jews in a more radical way. This culminated in the reign of Antiochus IV Epiphanes (175–163 BC). During this time lines were drawn between those groups which accepted Hellenism and those groups that violently opposed it. A growing animosity toward Hellenism and foreign rule soon led to the Maccabean revolt.

In general, there is good evidence to suggest that during its early contact with Judaism Hellenism was not violently opposed by the Jews. We know of some later sources that believe the Jewish religion to be a legitimate philosophy.[148] Pagans could not worship their gods on Jewish soil but this was one of only a few major restrictions. Goldstein concludes, 'As for Jewish participation in other aspects, God had shown no opposition either in Judea or in the Diaspora, and we find Jews throughout regarding them as permitted.'[149]

We see that the reaction to Hellenism was mixed depending on the time, the sect and the violence of the Greek rulers of Palestine in forcing it upon the Jews. Hellenism had many well-defined ideas about emotion both from their philosophers and from their poets, myths and gods. These ideas were so prevalent that we can assume that educated Jews came into contact with them. What was the Jewish reaction to these ideas, many of which were foreign to the ideas found in the Old Testament?

Studying the reaction to Hellenistic ideas about emotion in contemporary Jewish writings will give us a good point of comparison for the New Testament. The reaction to Hellenistic ideas about emotion in Jewish literature of the time is a valuable source of information about how the New Testament authors might have viewed these ideas and a valuable yardstick with which to compare the New Testament.

The penetration of Jewish thought and culture by Hellenism was by no means complete. Judaism clearly remained the controlling theology. Although there are many allusions to Hellenistic philosophy in contemporary Jewish writings, Schürer writes:

> However, the Jewish features of much Hellenistic philosophy remain so patent that it is also possible to argue that such fusion was very rare indeed and that, like Jewish

---

148. Walzer, *Galen on Jews and Christians*, p. 15. See also Josephus, *J.W.* 2.8; Mack and Murphy, 'Wisdom Literature'; Hengel, *Judaism and Hellenism*, pp. 159–160, 166–168, 170, 310, 253–258.

149. Goldstein, 'Jewish Acceptance and Rejection of Hellenism', p. 86. See also pp. 72–74; Hengel, *Judaism and Hellenism*, p. 56.

history and poetry, the use of Greek had only a marginal effect on the content of what was written . . . But even those most deeply penetrated by them are essentially rooted in Judaism.[150]

The Jews had no explicit philosophical ideas about emotion. Regardless of the cognitive leaning and positive view that we have argued is implicit in the Old Testament, in the Old Testament we find no philosophical explanation of how emotion functions. It is easy to see how well-thought-out Greek philosophical ideas might simply be taken as correct by an educated Jew. In many Jewish writings we see a blending of Old Testament and Greek ideas about emotion.

We can take a brief look at the major works of Jewish literature from close to the time of the New Testament in order to understand some of the contemporary ideas about emotion that were prevelant. Philo believes many of the ideas about the destructive nature of the passions of the Hellenistic philosophers, yet he rejects the Stoic idea of extirpating them. They are to be subjugated not extirpated.[151] Showing Greek influence, Philo writes:

> The passions he likens to wild beasts and birds, because, savage and untamed as they are, they tear the soul to pieces, and because like winged things they light upon the understanding; for the assault of the passions is violent and irresistible [*Leg. All.* 2.4–5].[152]
>
> Because the perfect wise man can, by wholly renouncing anger, utterly avert and drive off the uprising of the spirited element in him [*Leg. All.* 3.51].[153]

To Philo, the Jews are a people who are known for controlling their passions and their sacred Torah advocates this. When it comes to emotion, Philo sees the Old Testament largely through Hellenistic philosophy. A good example of this is that Philo takes the Stoic view of *lypē*, the righteous simply do not feel it.[154] Similarly, in Philo we see that a trust in God overcomes fear in the absolute

---

150. Schürer, *The History of the Jewish People*, vol. 3, pp. 567–568.

151. *Introduction to Philo*, Colson and Whitaker, trans. vol. 1, pp. xviii–xix. See also Schürer, *The History of the Jewish People*, vol. 3, p. 887.

152. Philo, vol. 1, pp. 231–233. For other strong statements see *Omn. Prob. Lib.* 7, 22; Philo, vol. 9, pp. 37, 101. See *Leg. All.* 2.2; Philo, vol. 1, pp. 228–230 for Philo's idea of what passions are. The passions must be mastered like a wild horse. *Leg. All.* 2.25; 287–288.

153. Philo, vol. 1, p. 401. See also *Leg. All.* 3.60; Philo, vol. 1, p. 417.

154. Bultmann, '*lypē, lypeō*', p. 319. See also Sandmel, *Philo of Alexandria*, p. 55.

sense of the Hellenistic philosophers.[155] Philo struggled with the anthropomorphic attributes of God as described in the Old Testament. His belief about
the passions derived from Hellenistic philosophy would not allow God to have
'destructive' passions.[156] Philo writes:

> Again, some on hearing these words suppose that the Existent feels wrath and anger,
> whereas He is not susceptible to any passion at all. For disquiet is peculiar to human
> weakness, but neither the unreasoning passions of the soul, nor the parts and
> members of the body in general, have any relation to God [*Deus Imm.* 11.52].[157]

It is clear that the Greek philosophers greatly influenced his ideas and he often
interpreted Jewish theology through this Hellenistic construct.[158]

Josephus makes few if any direct statements about the nature of emotion.
The best we can do is to get some idea about what he thought by looking at
passages where the characters act emotionally and analysing Josephus' interpretation of these feelings. He sees that emotion has a good and legitimate
place in people's lives. For example, the anger of Pompey is seen as appropriate and justified. Josephus also outlines a 'just anger' that is present in the
Old Testament. The good leader Vespasian is empathetic toward his troops
and is level headed. Vespasian is not driven by self-centred passions.[159]

At the same time, he often sees anger as a very destructive passion. It is the
motivation of awful and senseless acts of violence and slaughter. This is especially true in the character of Herod the Great.[160] Of Herod, Josephus writes,
'His passions also made him stark mad.'[161] Similar to the actions of Herod,

155. Balz, '*phobeō, phobeomai, phobos, deos*', p. 207.

156. Hengel, *Judaism and Hellenism*, pp. 164–167. This was a particular concern of
Aristobulus. Schürer, *The History of the Jewish People in the Age of Jesus Christ*, vol. 3,
pp. 582–586; Philo, *Introduction to The Unchangeableness of God*, Colson and Whitaker,
trans., vol. 3, p. 5.

157. Philo, vol. 3, p. 37. See also God *Deus Imm.* 11.70; Philo, vol. 3, pp. 45–47. God *Deus Imm.*
34.137–167; 181–183; Philo, vol. 3, pp. 94, 99–101; *Ebr.* 25; Philo, vol. 3, pp. 369–371.

158. Schürer, *The History of the Jewish People*, vol. 3, p. 876.

159. Whiston, *The Works of Flavius Josephus*, vol. 1, p. 182, *J.W.* 4.1, vol. 1, pp. 27–28,
J.W. 1.6, vol. 2, p. 311, *Ant.* 2.5.

160. Whiston, *The Works of Flavius Josephus*, vol. 1, p. 61, *J.W.* 1.16.

161. Whiston, *The Works of Flavius Josephus*, vol. 1, pp. 84–85, *J.W.* 1.22–23. See also
Whiston, *The Works of Flavius Josephus*, vol. 1, pp. 105, 108, 123, *J.W.* 1.28–29, 33 and
vol. 3, pp. 361, 380, 382, 442, 446, 467, *Ant.* 15.3, 7, 16.3, 8, 11.

Josephus relates that atrocities were committed against the Jews as the perpetrators 'could not refrain their passions'. In this situation the hero Titus, like Vespasian, had a reasoned and controlled response.[162]

Similarly, he extols the virtues of the Pharisees because they control their passions: 'Now, for the Pharisees, they live meanly, and despise delicacies in diet; and they follow the conduct of reason; and what that prescribes to them as good for them, they do; and they think they ought earnestly to strive to observe reason's dictates for practice.' We see links with Hellenistic philosophy both in simplicity of lifestyle and the emphasis on reason.[163]

Josephus sees some positive place for the emotions even to the point of there being justifiable anger. We see that in much of his writings his thoughts about emotion are strongly coloured by Greek ideals. Heroes control their passions with reason and act in moderation, while villains are controlled by their unruly and out of control emotions.

4 Maccabees, probably written in the first century CE, is a treatise about how reason should rule over the passions. Its original title was, 'On the Sovereignty of Reason'.[164]

Klauck describes this book as, 'a witness of that Hellenistic Judaism that in many ways served as a bridge between the Greco-Roman world and early Christianity.'[165] The following passages clearly illustrate the book's dependence on Greek philosophy; 4 Maccabees 1:1–4 reads:

> The subject that I am about to discuss is most philosophical, that is, whether devout reason is sovereign over the emotions. So it is right for me to advise you to pay

---

162. Whiston, *The Works of Flavius Josephus*, vol. 1, pp. 479, 486, *J.W.* 7.3, 5. See also vol. 4, pp. 40–41, 47, 86, *Ant.* 18.8, 19.3 where the emperor Caius, of whom Josephus had a very low opinion, is portrayed as man who was enslaved to his passions. The people of Masada set their grim course due to Eleazer's logic in spite of their passionate love for one another (Whiston, *The Works of Flavius Josephus*, vol. 1, pp. 508, 514, *J.W.* 7.8, 9).

163. Whiston, *The Works of Flavius Josephus*, vol. 4, p. 3, *Ant.* 18.1.

164. Schürer, *The History of the Jewish People in the Age of Jesus Christ*, vol. 3, pp. 589–592; Hadas, *The Third and Fourth Books of Maccabees*, p. 114. *Pathos* is used 63 times in 4 Maccabees to refer to harmful impulses (Michaelis, '*paschō, pathētos*', p. 927).

165. Klauck, 'Brotherly Love in Plutarch and in 4th Maccabees', p. 145. See also Hadas, *The Third and Fourth Books of Maccabees*, p. 91; deSilva, *4 Maccabees*, p. 74; *The Third and Fourth Books of Maccabees*, pp. 97, 100–101, 106, 113, 115.

earnest attention to philosophy. For the subject is essential to everyone who is seeking knowledge, and in addition it includes the praise of the highest virtue – I mean, of course, rational judgement. If, then, it is evident that reason rules over those emotions that hinder self-control, namely, gluttony and lust, it is also clear that it masters the emotions that hinder one from justice, such as malice, and those that stand in the way of courage, namely anger, fear, and pain.

4 Maccabees does not advocate the extirpation of the emotions but believes that the good man will have control over these passions. This is only possible by following the law that God gave to guide reason.[166] 4 Maccabees 1:6 reads: 'For reason does not rule its own emotions, but those that are opposed to justice, courage, and self-control; and it is not for the purpose of destroying them, but so that one may not give way to them.'

4 Maccabees 7:17 concurs: 'Some perhaps might say, "Not all have full command of their emotions, because not all have prudent reason". But as many as attend to religion with a whole heart, these alone are able to control the passions of the flesh.' (See also 11:21–27.)

In summary, we see that religion gives reason its power, not right thinking as in Hellenistic philosophy. The ideas expressed in 4 Maccabees, although they have the similar goal of controlling the emotions as Hellenistic Philosophy, in truth are very different from the Greek ideal. The writer of 4 Maccabees believes that following God and knowing the law will enable the Jews to control their emotions. DeSilva concludes, '4 Maccabees is valuable not only as a rapprochement between Jewish faith and Hellenistic philosophy . . . it is also remarkable as an expression of Hellenistic Jewish theology.'[167] The Greek influence is also evident in Ben Sira. Ben Sira borrowed Greek ideas and language if he believed it coalesced with Jewish thought.

The author sees ultimate answers as being based on the fear of Yahweh and following the law (Sir. 19:20, 1:10).[168] Those who fear the Lord will be happy and have joy (Sir. 1:12–13). Sirach 21:11 concludes, 'Whoever keeps the law controls his thoughts, and wisdom is the fulfillment of the fear of the Lord.' This has the ring of Hellenistic influence with wisdom playing the part of reason. The Wisdom of Solomon shows some of the same tendencies as Ben Sira.

---

166. Ferguson, *Backgrounds of Early Christianity*, pp. 424–425; deSilva, *4 Maccabees*, p. 131; Hadas, *The Third and Fourth Books of Maccabees*, pp. 146, 151. See also 4 Macc. 1:19, 29, 35; 3:2–4 where this is expressly stated.

167. DeSilva, *4 Maccabees*, p. 127.

168. See Di Lella, *The Wisdom of Ben Sira*, pp. 76, 79.

There is a Hellenistic influence. However, in this book we see again that the ultimate source of knowledge and wisdom is God.[169]

The rage of Cain is blamed for his sin. His anger led him to reject wisdom (10:3). Similarly, 'Fear is nothing but the abandonment of reason's aid' (17:12). This shows Hellenistic influence; knowledge has the power to erase fear.[170] In Wisdom, we see the fusion of Greek and Jewish ideas.

In each of these books there is an integration of Greek ideas about the nature of emotion with a Jewish world view. They are very informative when it comes to understanding how Hellenistic ideas were affecting the Jewish culture at the time of the New Testament. In 4 Maccabees the triumph of reason, even though it looks very Hellenistic at the outset, is based on Jewish theology. Reason can only be obtained by following the law and fearing God. Life is firmly rooted in this world and there is no sense of being able to achieve happiness by radically detaching yourself from this physical world. The foundational ideas in Judaism and Greek philosophy are so diametrically opposed that a full integration is not possible. Hellenistic ideas about emotion have an uneasy coexistence with the Old Testament's ideas.

Emotion in Judaism: conclusion

Jews had contact with Hellenism and pagan culture and much of this was not antagonistic. They lived in the world where the ideas of Greek philosophical schools dominated academia and learned Jews were exposed to this. As a result we see a sometimes subtle and sometimes blatant integration of Jewish and Hellenistic ideas about emotion in Second Temple Jewish writings. Even though the thinkers we have examined were first and foremost Jews, often devout Jews, when it came to emotion the ideas from Greek philosophy often influence their outlook. They took the well-thought-out ideas from the philosophers as a matter of course and integrated them with their Jewish beliefs. Most often, this was not a good match and their writings on the matter were not logically consistent with the Old Testament.

The people lived out their faith with intense emotion. They celebrated God with joy and repented from sin in sorrow. The great festivals of the

---

169. Winston, *The Wisdom of Solomon*, p. 6. See also Nickelsburg, *Jewish Literature*, p. 178. *Wisdom* has been dated between 200 BC to AD 50. A likely date is AD 37–41 (Winston, *The Wisdom of Solomon*, p. 23). For a summary of the Greek influence seen in the book see Winston, *The Wisdom of Solomon*, pp. 29, 51–58, 61–62.

170. Winston, *The Wisdom of Solomon*, pp. 210, 213, 302, 308. See also Kolarcik, 'Book of Wisdom', pp. 438–441.

Jewish calendar were times of remembering who God was and what he had done for Israel and this stirred the heart. They were an emotional people whose feelings revolved around their faith because their faith encompassed all of life.

These two strands went on together: Hellenistic ideas about emotion, and the Jewish idea of an emotional faith. There is no way to put this puzzle together. Second Temple Judaism does not have a unified or consistent view about the nature of emotion. Simply put, educated Jews did not, in general, choose between the conflicting views of the Old Testament and Greek philosophy. Instead, they made an unhappy union of the two.

Jewish backgrounds and emotion in the New Testament

With the end of this Chapter the stage is finally set to evaluate emotion's role in the New Testament. We have looked at the true nature of emotion. We have seen what the Greco-Roman world thought about it. And now we have examined the role emotion played in the Old Testament and in Second Temple Judaism. In the words of Wright, 'The history we have already sketched, and the worldview we have now outlined, formed the context for and indeed helped to generate a passionately held theology, and a hope that refused to die.'[171]

Do we see the same mixing of Greek and Jewish ideas in the New Testament that we see in many Second Temple writings? Does the New Testament have the same belief that the emotions of the righteous should be based on the knowledge of and love for God that is prevalent in the Old Testament? Are the passions seen as a source of danger and sin in the New Testament, a force to be controlled, as they were in some Second Temple literature?

The Old Testament may have agreed with the Hellenistic philosophers in the assertion that emotion was cognitive. However, to the Jews, both in the Old Testament and in the Diaspora, having the proper emotions comes from having a knowledge of God, not a knowledge of how to reason. Even in the most Hellenized Jewish thinkers it was right to have positive emotions about their faith and it was good to be happy about the material world. We might say that in Judaism the ultimate measure of happiness was not the lack of damaging emotions but rather the love of God and obedience to him. Ultimately, however strongly they believed Hellenistic ideas about the nature of emotion, the Old Testament remained the foundation of their world-view.

---

171. Wright, *The New Testament and the People of God*, p. 243.

Finally, unlike the Greco-Roman deities or pagan gods of the Canaanites, who often demanded appeasement through ecstatic ritual and were emotionally volatile, Israel's God was emotionally stable. Their God's emotions were based on his perfect character. He loved Israel and was slow to anger. God's emotions flowed naturally and reasonably out of both his love and holiness. Israel was to return this love with all their heart, soul and mind.

One of the best summaries of emotion that we find in the Old Testament comes from Ecclesiastes 3. Emotion is seen as an integral part of life and it is naturally integrated into the theology of the Old Testament.

> For everything there is a season, and a time for every matter under heaven:
> a time to be born, and a time to die;
> a time to plant, and a time to pluck up what is planted;
> a time to kill, and a time to heal;
> a time to break down, and a time to build up;
> a time to weep, and a time to laugh;
> a time to mourn, and a time to dance;
> a time to throw away stones, and a time to gather stones together;
> a time to embrace, and a time to refrain from embracing;
> a time to seek, and a time to lose;
> a time to keep, and a time to throw away;
> a time to tear, and a time to sew;
> a time to keep silence, and a time to speak;
> a time to love, and a time to hate;
> a time for war, and a time for peace.

4. EMOTION IN THE NEW TESTAMENT: GENERAL ANALYSIS, LOVE, JOY AND HOPE

#277 The heart has its reasons, which reason does not know.

#278 It is the heart which experiences God, and not the reason. This then is faith: God felt by the heart, not by the reason.

#280 The knowledge of God is very far from the Love of him.

#282 We know truth, not only by the reason, but also by the heart, and it is in this last way that we know first principles; and reason, which has no part in it, tries in vain to impugn them. The skeptics, who have only this for their object, labour to no purpose.

Blaise Pascal, *Pensées*[1]

As we have seen, emotion is an often misunderstood and mishandled subject in academic studies. New Testament studies are not immune from this. Very rarely has there been a deliberate attempt to understand emotion in its own right before exploring emotion in the New Testament. The analysis of emotion has rarely been seen as an important element in understanding a text.

It is time to take a different approach. We must begin to interpret emotion in the New Testament in light of a thorough understanding of what it is and how it was perceived in the first century. Understanding the true nature of emotion can make a significant impact on how we interpret a particular text.

---

1. Pascal, *Pensées*, pp. 95–96.

Many academic disciplines have added to our understanding of the New Testament in recent years: literary criticism, sociology and linguistics, to name a few. It is time to give the same consideration to modern studies of emotion.

In Chapters four and five we examine particular emotions, their meaning and their use in the New Testament in order to study the role of emotion in the New Testament. In the final Chapter we will look at how a proper understanding of emotion should impact our theology and ethics.

This and the next Chapter will emphasize what I believe to be some of the major and consistent mistakes that have been made when it comes to interpreting emotion in the New Testament. These can be divided into several major categories:

1. mistakes in interpreting vocabulary or emotion words;
2. mistakes made in exegesis due to misinterpretation of emotion;
3. a general neglect of emotion in New Testament studies;
4. a pervasive non-cognitive understanding of the emotions.

The philosophical misinterpretation of what emotion is has led many scholars to misinterpret emotion in specific texts and in the broader discipline of New Testament theology.

Through the centuries many Christian scholars have written on emotion, some with profound insight. My desire is to bring the insights of Aquinas, Calvin, Edwards and others up to date. Taking the insight we have gained from psychology and philosophy we will be able to have a better understanding of emotion in the New Testament.

Vocabulary of emotion and lexicography

It is logical to centre our study in this and the next Chapter on the vocabulary of emotion. It is what most of us think about when we think of the meaning of emotion in the text. However, we should not presume that word meanings are the only element to use in discovering the emotional content of the New Testament. Emotion may be detected in texts where emotional vocabulary is not used. This is clearly evident in the parable of the Good Samaritan that nowhere mentions love. These kinds of texts may be crucial to our understanding. Studies of emotion in the New Testament over the last hundred years have been predominantly the study of emotion words and their use in different contexts. This is a mistake to be avoided.

In general, New Testament studies have not hitherto emphasized the emotional content in the New Testament. This is particularly evident in the lack of emotional content that is given to key emotion words. The tendency has been to de-emphasize, trivialize or delete these words' emotional content. It is an important aim of this book to bring some balance into understanding the definition of these important words. But it is not an attempt at a word study in the tradition of the *Theological Dictionary of the New Testament* (*TDNT*). The goal is not to create a catalogue of emotion words and their precise meanings but rather to consider the place of emotion in the world view of the early church and highlight potential mistakes in biblical interpretation in the light of this.

Method and mistakes to be avoided

For our purposes the *Greek–English Lexicon of the New Testament: Based on Semantic Domains* is especially useful.[2] Its arrangement allows us to examine the words that contain similar emotional content together and its insistence on defining words without adding theological meaning allows us to concentrate on the emotional content of the word. Louw and Nida stress that in many New Testament lexicons words are defined on the basis of theology instead of lexicography. As this has been a particularly pronounced problem in dealing with words that express emotion it is hoped that the use of Louw and Nida's work will help to eliminate confusion between theological or philosophical content that is given to a word by a scholar and the definition of the word itself.[3]

We can begin our critique of New Testament studies' view of emotion with observations about the lexicon's definition of emotion words. Louw and Nida have erred in putting some negative emotional words under the heading of 'Moral and Ethical Qualities' rather than in the category 'Attitudes and Emotions'. Hatred, Anger and Jealousy are listed along with Holy, Evil, Sin and 'Sexual Misbehaviour'. The words listed for 'Sexual Misbehaviour', for example, refer to sexual sin where the words that denote the physiological aspects of sex are listed under the morally neutral 'Physiological Processes and States'.

---

2. *BDAG* is still necessary as it gives more linguistic information and examples than do Louw and Nida (*Greek–English Lexicon*). See Grayston, 'Review of *Greek–English Lexicon of the New Testament based on Semantic Domains*', pp. 200–201. Louw and Nida is a 'corrective' and not a 'substitute'. Marshall, 'Review of *Greek–English Lexicon of the New Testament based on Semantic Domains*', pp. 184–186.

3. 'One problem is the tendency to divide not along semantic lines but along theological lines.' (Louw and Nida, *Greek–English Lexicon*, 1: xi). See also Silva, *Biblical Words and Their Meaning*, pp. 172–174.

This implies that the emotions listed in this category are not neutral but inherently immoral and destructive. Louw and Nida seem to assume that the New Testament sometimes perceives these words as generally immoral, like the Stoics.

A good example of this is the word *zēloō*. They list *zēloō* under emotion ('Love, Affection, Compassion') as 'to have a deep concern for' and under 'Moral and Ethical Qualities' as 'a particularly strong feeling of resentment and jealousy against someone'. They imply that one use of the word is a morally neutral emotion and the other is an impious vice. Arndt and Gingrich and Aland and Aland also follow this dichotomy with their analysis of *zēloō* saying that it is 'in a good sense zeal' and 'in a bad sense jealousy, envy'. Similarly, both lexicons differentiate secular and Christian hope, and human anger (*orgē*) and the wrath of God, implying that these terms have different meanings in different contexts.[4] As we will see, this is clearly not the case; these are morally neutral emotions sometimes to be praised and sometimes to be condemned.

In modern lexicography, decisions have been made on the basis of a faulty view of what emotion is or a misunderstanding of its use in the New Testament. We have a difficult task when it comes to interpreting emotion in the New Testament, a road that must be travelled carefully at every step.

As mentioned, there has been a tendency to define words in terms of theology instead of lexicography. Attributing theological meaning to individual words that is not present in the vocabulary itself is a pitfall that has been especially prevalent in interpreting emotion words.[5] Silva writes (about the *TDNT*):

> To use a different sort of example: if the word we are interested in is *hamartia* it must be clear in our minds whether we want to know all that the Bible teaches concerning the doctrine of sin (the 'concept'), or the range of meaning covered by the specific word *hamartia*. But these two things are constantly confused. Indeed, the confusion may be inherent in the nature of *TDNT*, which seeks to deal with conceptual history (*Begriffsgeschichte*) in the form of a dictionary of words.[6]

The specific meaning of the vocabulary of emotion is not equivalent to analysing

---

4. Aland and Aland, *Griechisch-deutsches Wörterbuch*, and *BDAG*. Arndt and Gingrich's discussion of *orgē*, specifically talks about God not having emotions like people.

5. Silva, *Biblical Words and Their Meaning*, pp. 22–23. See also Nida and Louw, *Lexical Semantics of the Greek New Testament*; Barr, *The Semantics of Biblical Language*, pp. 212, 219, 255–256, 261.

6. Silva, *Biblical Words and Their Meaning*, pp. 26–27.

emotion in a passage. It is my contention that because of the anti-emotion bias in modern scholarship and the misunderstanding of the nature of emotion, this mistake is magnified in the interpretation of emotional vocabulary.

Some words that have been defined as non-emotional in certain contexts may actually be emotional in those contexts. Louw and Nida write, 'In the classification of meanings the most difficult distinction to make is the one between attitudes and emotions, which include such positive emotions as desire, love, hope, contentment, and joy, as well as negative emotions such as shame, astonishment, worry, fear, sorrow, and discouragement.'[7] It may also be difficult to determine the emotional content of words that are not specific emotions but have significant emotional meaning, e.g. forgive, faith and compassion. In general, these words will not be a major focus of our discussion.

Culture and individual personality may have a great influence on a particular word's emotional meaning. Ullmann argues that a basic method for determining meaning is the overall emotional content of a word or passage. This includes any figure of speech, description or other examples that convey emotion.[8]

It is my contention that many New Testament scholars have taken their theology and defined emotion words by drawing on these beliefs. In other words, emotional vocabulary has often been redefined to mean a theological concept devoid of its emotional meaning. This method is the wrong way around; the cart is before the horse! Instead, we must understand the emotion word and then see where emotion fits into the theology of the passage.

Looking at individual emotions is the tool we will use to determine how the New Testament looked at emotion in general and how the discipline of New Testament studies has treated emotion in the text.

Before we begin to examine the New Testament in this way we should briefly look at one other issue. How are we to know that the New Testament's idea of emotion is the same as our own? In other words, if we give love our own definition from the modern era, how are we to know that this is what

---

7. Nida and Louw, *Lexical Semantics of the Greek New Testament*, p. 102; for other cautions see Nida, 'Analysis of Meaning and Dictionary Making', pp. 281–282, 283, 288–290; Silva, *Biblical Words and Their Meaning*, pp. 34–44, 48.

8. Ullmann, *The Principles of Semantics*, pp. 96–98. Ullmann argues that emotive meaning is more difficult to ascertain than intellectual meaning. Words can have emotional overtones that are '*variable* and unstable' (Ullmann, *The Principles of Semantics*, p. 104).

was meant in the time of the New Testament? Or, more generally, would the writers have defined love, joy, hope, fear, anger, jealousy, and sorrow as emotions? Would they have understood the basic category of human function we call emotion? Let us give several answers to this possible objection. First, the seven basic emotions we will discuss have been carefully chosen as those that are the most basic of human feelings. All other feelings are combinations or variations of these most basic emotions, which have been demonstrated to exist in all cultures. We can insist that regardless of how feelings are fit or not fit into a logical systems, these basic emotions exist in all people. They are part of our internal make up. As such, it is difficult to conclude that the vocabulary used for these key concepts did not have similar meaning to what we use today. Emotion vocabulary is only the means of communicating a universally felt human experience.

Further, as we will point out repeatedly, where positive emotions in the New Testament text are often redefined by interpreters, negative emotions are easily understood with their present day meaning. Any interpreter that wishes to conclude that love, joy and hope had a significantly different meaning than in our culture, must then explain why sorrow, anger and jealousy did not or they must also redefine the negative emotions. This has never been attempted to my knowledge. If you cannot define anger or hatred without reference to emotion, you cannot then insist that its logical opposite, love, can be defined without reference to emotion. We might say that we are using modern categories to describe a universal understanding of emotion, categories that are derived from research indicating the shared nature of emotional experience. Our analysis will use the modern context and categories to analyse our shared emotional experience written about in the New Testament. Even when our view of what constitutes emotional language in the text goes beyond some other interpreter's understanding, we will find many passages where we all can agree that the text is full of emotional emphasis and meaning.

Important words with strong emotional content

There are a number of words that have general emotional content in the New Testament that are not specific emotions.

Heart and knowledge

First among this vocabulary is *kardia*. We could analyse a number of other words in this section such as *ho esō* (inmost being), *psychē* (psyche), *splanchna* (spleen) and *koilia* (belly, womb).[9] We will concentrate on *kardia* as it is used most often (over 150 times) and its meaning is similar to *lēb* in the Old Testament.

We have seen that the idea of the heart in the Old Testament includes emotion. Seeing the Greek and Hebrew terms as similar, the translators of the LXX translated *lēb* most often as *kardia*. The New Testament reflects much of the emphasis of the Hebrew.[10] Behm writes, 'In the LXX "*kardia*" is the true equivalent for the Hebrew *lb*.'[11] In short, it connotes the integration of mind, will and emotion. A particular context may emphasize one of these concepts over another.[12] This full meaning is demonstrated by Louw and Nida placing it in a number of different domains. However, a closer look at the specific contexts of their examples reveals that it has often been placed in a particular domain as a result of contextual clues. When it is found in an emotional context *kardia* has an emotional meaning, when *kardia* is found in a thinking context it has an intellectual meaning. This is also seen in Friberg's definition: 'viewed as the innermost man, the source and seat of functions of soul and spirit in the emotional life (Acts 2:26), the volitional life (2 Cor. 9:7), the rational life (Acts 7:23)'. Clearly Acts 7:23 could be just as emotional in meaning as Acts 2:26. Both stand for the whole person rather than one having an emotional meaning and one having rational content. In most contexts *kardia* will contain some emotional content. We should not assume that we can clearly separate its rational and emotional meanings.

---

9. See Louw and Nida, *Greek–English Lexicon*, 26.1–16. Some of these terms denoted organs, innards, stomach or womb. We often feel emotion in our gut so these words came to connote an inner emotional feeling. *splanchna* is most notable for strong emotional content. It may mean love and compassion (Matt. 18:27; Luke 15:20; Esser, '*splanchna*', p. 599). For Paul it was the 'centre of loving action' (2 Cor. 7:15; Esser, '*splanchna*', p. 600). Friberg defines it as '(2) fig. (a) the deep, inner seat of tender emotions in the whole personality, in differing cultures it is conceived to be heart, stomach, bowels (2 Cor. 7.15); (b) the heartfelt emotion itself translated to fit the context affection, love, deep feeling, compassion (Phil. 1.8).' Louw and Nida stresses that *psychē* is the seat of the feelings (Louw and Nida, *Greek–English Lexicon*, 26.4).

10. Silva, *Biblical Words and Their Meaning*, pp. 95–96; Behm, '*kardia*', pp. 606–607; Schnelle, *Neutestamentliche Anthropologie*, pp. 120–122.

11. Behm, '*kardia*', pp. 609–610.

12. Bauer, 'Heart', pp. 360, 362; Sorg, '*kardia*', p. 181. See Sorg for numerous examples of feelings originating in the heart. See also Gnilka, *Theologie des Neuen Testaments*, pp. 54–55; Berger, *Theologiegeschechte des Urchristentums*, pp. 501–502.

Decisions are made in the heart. It is also a person's inner self which is not readily known by others.[13] In the New Testament God makes himself known in the heart. Bultmann writes: 'Like *nous*, "heart" is a man's self, and in most cases where it is used it performs the service of a personal pronoun. For the "heart" is the subject that desires (Rom. 10:1), lusts (Rom. 1:24), purposes (1 Cor. 4:5), decides (1 Cor. 7:37; 8:16; Phil. 1:7).'[14] Behm concludes, 'Thus the heart is supremely the one center in man to which God turns, in which the religious life is rooted, which determines moral conduct.'[15] The heart is the place where faith takes root in both mind and emotion.

Perhaps most informative are the words of Jesus. The righteous can be identified by looking at the condition of their hearts. The ethics of the kingdom are concerned with a person's heart.[16] Jesus' parables are also informative. The father of the prodigal son is driven by his emotion for his son (Luke 15:20). This is how God feels for us. The Pharisees, on the other hand, are characterized by the feelings of the older brother. The person with a hard heart has closed their emotions to God.[17]

We see a similar trend in other parts of the New Testament. Paul was not shy in making his strong feelings known for those he loved. This is a confirmation of the positive role he saw for the emotions (2 Cor. 6:12; 7:15; Phil. 1:7, 8, 12). This is especially clear in these passages because of the use of *splanchna* (great or deep affection and compassion). Romans 10:6–10 shows clearly the emphasis that Paul put on having the right heart (2 Cor. 3:14; Heb. 10:22).[18]

The meaning of heart and its importance in New Testament theology is clear. Why then do many scholars, who would affirm this, go on to misunderstand and play down the importance of specific emotions? If the *kardia* of a person includes their emotions, it is clear that emotion must have a prominent place in the theology of the New Testament.

---

13. Bauer, 'Heart', p. 362; Sorg, '*kardia*', pp. 181–183; Bultmann, *Theology*, vol. 1, p. 226.

14. Bultmann, *Theology*, vol. 1, p. 221. Behm, '*kardia*', p. 612.

15. Behm, '*kardia*', p. 612. See also Dunn, *The Theology of Paul the Apostle*, pp. 74–75.

16. Ladd, *A Theology of the New Testament*, p. 129.

17. Blomberg, *Interpreting the Parables*, pp. 174–175, 179. See also Snodgrass, 'Parable', p. 591. Stuhlmacher emphasizes the idea of God as father, father love motivates the joy (*Grundlegung Von Jesus zu Paulus*, pp. 88–89). Young emphasizes the state of the hearts of the individuals in the parable of the Pharisee and the tax collector. Both are loved by God but only one has a clean and sincere heart (pp. 192–193).

18. For a categorization of Paul's usage see Ladd, *A Theology of the New Testament*, p. 475; Stuhlmacher *Grundlegung Von Jesus zu Paulus*, p. 278. Defined in Louw-Nida 25.49.

The vocabulary of mind and knowledge is also important for our study. *Nous*, *phrēn*, *phroneō* and *ginōskō* deserve a brief analysis. *Nous* in Greek philosophy came to mean reason, representing the intellectual side of a person. This, however, is not what the translators of the LXX wanted to convey in many contexts. They rarely use the word because this limited understanding of reason is not what the Old Testament meant when it referred to the mind. Similarly, it is not used frequently in the New Testament. This seems to be an indication of the influence of Hebrew thought and the LXX.[19] We see in Rom. 1:28 that Paul's idea of knowledge includes more than rational knowledge. Having a debased mind (*nous*) is linked to evil acts.[20] The uses of the word indicate that *nous* when used did not connote the faculty of pure reason in the New Testament as it did in Greek philosophy.

Phrēn in 4 Maccabees 1:2, as it was for the Stoics, is the ruling virtue (4 Macc. 7:17).[21] It was the intellectual force that stood against the emotions. Similar to *nous*, this is not its meaning in the New Testament. The New Testament has a more holistic view of the word, which in many cases is similar to the idea of wisdom in the Old Testament.[22]

Like *lēb* and *kardia*, *yd'* and *ginōskō* share similar meanings in the view of the New Testament. This is clear, for example, in the first chapter of Romans where Paul rejects the Greek idea that knowing God is synonymous with knowing only intellectually. Knowledge of God is a full faceted heart knowledge and acceptance of him.[23]

At this point it is important to make some comments about emotion and cognition. What is the relation in the New Testament between emotion and mind? In Romans 12:2 most commentators argue that a transformation of the whole person is in view. In a theory of cognitive emotions this makes sense (Eph. 4:23: *nous*, Rom. 8:5: *phroneō*; Col. 3:2: *phroneō*). To transform your values, beliefs and knowledge will naturally lead to a new emotional outlook. These verses are not speaking of getting facts straight but of a change of orientation of the entire individual. Similarily, to be of the same mind is to have the same values and beliefs. These common values will lead to emotional solidarity.

---

19. Harder, '*nous*', pp. 122, 124, 127. See also Louw and Nida, 30.5; Schnelle, *Neutestamentliche Anthropologie*, pp. 123–126.

20. See Ladd, *A Theology of the New Testament*, p. 476; Dunn, *The Theology of Paul the Apostle*, p. 75.

21. Bertram, '*phrēn*, *aphrōn*', p. 228. See also Goetzmann, '*phronēsis*'.

22. Goetzmann, '*phronēsis*', p. 617. See also Louw and Nida, 26.15.

23. Schmitz, '*ginōskō*', pp. 396–400.

People in the community will care about the same things (1 Cor. 1:10: *nous*; Phil. 2:5, 3:15, 4:2: *phroneō*). Bertram writes, 'The fundamental demand of Pauline exhortation is a uniform direction, a common mind, and unity of thought and will' (Phil. 1:7; 2:2–5; 4:2, 10; Gal. 5:10; 2 Cor. 13:11; Rom. 15:5).[24] This is the opposite of the ungodly who set their minds on earthly things (Phil. 3:19). Similar things are meant by putting on the mind of Christ (1 Cor. 2:16). The correction of Peter's thinking in Matthew 16:23 and Mark 8:33 is also informative. Peter is emotional about the wrong things. Jesus' reply is to say his thinking is not correct. These texts point to the fact that a reorientation of thinking will result in a reorientation of the emotions.

We should also point out that in this passage (Mark 8:33) it seems that Jesus is choosing what he sets his mind upon. By choosing to dwell on the greater goal, his primary mission, or the good that will come from his mission, the severe negative emotions that would be felt as a result of thinking about his future suffering are not predominant. Instead, his emotions are set upon accomplishing his task.

In some texts we see clearly the interplay of heart and mind. Heart, knowledge and hope are put together in Ephesians 1:18 (Phil. 1:7; 2 Cor. 4:6; Rom. 1:21; Rev. 2:23). The heart and mind are to be guarded in Philippians 4:7. These are examples of contexts where the whole person is in view: mind, emotion, thoughts and will. Hebrews 3:10 is also a good example. Israel does not obey in their hearts because they do not have the true knowledge of God (1 John 3:19). Both the vocabulary of heart and mind have a holistic view of humans and the interaction of the vocabulary of mind and heart further illustrates the interdependence of emotion and reason.

These important concepts in the New Testament have strong emotional content as they did in the Old Testament. Knowing God and knowing the truth is not a purely factual intellectual knowledge as many tend to think of it today. Instead, to know is to know with heart, mind and soul.[25] The condition of the heart determines a person's standing before God. A person's emotions are an essential element in their righteousness or rebellion against God, i.e. the state of their heart. This interplay of mind and heart and the holistic meaning of each that we see in the New Testament is how emotion functions in a cognitive view.

Knowledge of a thing is greater than belief in its existence. To believe the Grand Canyon exists is not the same as seeing it, knowing it. To know that Jesus died for your sins, writes Roberts, 'is to feel gratitude and peace and other

---

24. Bertram, '*phrēn, aphrōn*', p. 233. See also Goetzmann, '*phronēsis*' (Col. 3:2).

25. Frankemölle, *Der Brief des Jakobus: Kapitel 2–5*, pp. 540–541.

emotions'.[26] Whereas to read facts about the Grand Canyon in a book may produce no emotion, to have seen the Grand Canyon is to feel its majestic awesome spectacle.

As we conclude we should note that we have largely agreed with the analysis of works like *TDNT* and the opinion of most scholars about these concepts. Why are these words understood correctly by these sources and, at the same time, they make significant mistakes in interpreting specific emotion words? If they were consistent they would not neglect the emotional content of words like love, hope and joy.

The passions

We have seen that the word *pathos* is often used by the Hellenistic philosophers to designate emotion in a generic sense. It is also used extensively in 4 Maccabees for the emotions, including love, fear and anger. Philo uses it 400 times for the emotions; as we saw in the previous Chapter he usually sees *pathos* as a destructive force that must be overcome.[27]

This usage is very different from how the word is used in the New Testament, where it is used for both suffering and strong evil desire. Louw and Nida write that it means 'to experience strong physical desires, particularly of a sexual nature'.[28] Friberg agrees: '(1) as an experience suffering, misfortune; (2) as a strong emotion of desire or craving passion; in the NT, only in a bad sense uncontrolled sexual passion, lustful desire, evil craving (Col. 3:5).'

Having strong emotion is not generically condemned in the passages that use *pathos*.[29] All of these uses are Pauline (Rom. 1:26, 7:5; Gal. 5:24; Col. 3:5; 1 Thess. 4:5). In each of these contexts it is clear that *pathos* refers specifically to evil, lustful desire and is not used as a generic term for emotion.[30]

---

26. Roberts, 'Emotions as Access to Religious Truths', p. 84.
27. Michaelis, '*paschō, pathētos*', pp. 904–907, 910–911, 927. Suffering and the emotions were both thought to come upon the individual. There was little you could do about them. This is their relation to one another. See also Gärtner, '*paschō*', p. 719.
28. Louw and Nida, 25.30. See also *BDAG*.
29. Michaelis, '*paschō, pathētos*', pp. 928–929; Pokorny, *Colossians*, p. 106; Dunn, *Epistles to the Colossians and to Philemon*, p. 215; Louw and Nida, 25.30. Bultmann, *Theology*, vol. 1, p. 239. Martin's general condemnation of desire is not supported by the texts. Martin, 'Paul Without Passion', pp. 201–203, 205, 207–211.
30. Bruce, *The Epistles to the Colossians, to Philemon, and to the Ephesians*, p. 143; Lindemann, *Der Kollosserbrief*, 56; Longenecker, *Galatians*, p. 254; Lohse, *Colossians and Philemon*, p. 138; Patzia, *Ephesians, Colossians, Philemon*, p. 73.

Love

Love: an introduction

The most basic understanding of love has been largely misunderstood or ignored. Many of the misconceptions about emotion in New Testament studies are clearly seen in the study of love. Most scholars have asked, 'What is love in the New Testament?' I wish to begin with the more general question of 'What is love?' After a thorough survey of theological philosophy on the subject of love, Outka concludes: 'The meaning ascribed in the literature to love in general and to *agapē* in particular is often characterized by both variance and ambiguity.' She gives two reasons for this: first, love is often defined in light of the author's theological beliefs and second, 'it is unrealistic to suppose that all of the characteristic meanings could be absorbed into some single point of identity'. Love's meaning is too broad to define precisely.[31] We must agree with the first point and, as we will see, dispute the second.

What is love? I agree with Aquinas, Arnold and other leading theorists that love is most generally an attraction towards an object.[32] This attraction is the result of seeing a quality in an object that is good, valuable, or desirable. This definition is the only definition which will allow love to function as the root of all other emotions (see Chapter one). This is not to say that love as seen in the New Testament would be fully defined as such. However, it is to say that without this central core anything that we label as 'love' is not love. I affirm that love is necessarily emotional in that it involves at its heart an attraction that is produced by a cognitive evaluation of the objects as valuable.

At this point you may already see objections to this idea. It does not seem to agree with the unconditional nature of *agapē* love. We must be careful not to oppose cognition, the fact that love is necessarily about something, and unconditional love. Love for good reasons may be without conditions. You may see few lovable qualities in a person but there may still be good reason for loving them. Love for that person is based on cognition but not on their good character, fun personality, or good looks. As we will see, the New Testament provides us with reasons for loving others, reasons that differ from those of the world.

A brief survey of love in the New Testament shows clearly that 'love' is used for all kinds of things, as it is in English. You can love an object, sin, praise, another person, or God. The understanding of love prevalent in New

---

31. Outka, *Agape*, pp. 257–258.
32. Love is an 'Over-all admiration for the other', Solomon, *The Passions*, p. 338.

Testament studies cannot account for this variety of usage. Instead of defending this definition of love more fully, it is better to examine the other definitions of love seen in New Testament studies and explain why they are not adequate.

Phileō and agapaō
To do this, we need to look briefly at the vocabulary of love. As recent research has shown, the common interpretation of *agapaō* as being a term the translators of the LXX infused with noble and divine meaning while avoiding the more secular meaning of *phileō* is unfounded. This does not fit the usage of the LXX which, for example, uses *agapaō* for immorality and other godless loves. Further, the use of *agapaō* is well attested in Hellenism.[33]

Butler traces the history of New Testament scholarship about the two words and highlights confusion and inconsistencies that are often witnessed in scholars' definitions. Butler clearly shows the tangle that scholars have created by trying to maintain that the words have distinct meanings. Often they end up contradicting themselves.[34] Butler puts together the most common definitions of the two words when he writes:

> *Agapao* is defined to mean: an unselfish and reverential love, or spiritual; affection, which values and esteems; a love without coldness, deeper than *phileo*, using reason in selecting its proper objects, which themselves are worthy of it; a love that expresses the essential nature of God: . . . *Phileo* is defined to mean: a friendly affection, liking, or caring; a more personal and human love than *agapao*, more instinctive and passionate; a love from which a man can excuse himself, not an irresistible urge.[35]

These kinds of distinctions are not fully accurate as clearly shown by the actual usage of the words in the New Testament. Like Silva, his conclusion is that *agapaō* has taken much of the meaning of *phileō* in the natural development of the language. They are both, '*a love of any kind whatever.* In this respect both

---

33. Silva, *Biblical Words and Their Meaning*, p. 96. The difference between the two words has often been stressed in John 21. The arguments that are made for this are not convincing. A classic example of this faulty interpretation is found in the Easton Bible dictionary, *Love*.

34. Butler, *The Meaning of 'Agapao' and 'Phileo'*, pp. 9–14. For agreement with Butler see Turner, 'Modern Linguistics and the New Testament', pp. 154–155.

35. Butler, *The Meaning of 'Agapao' and 'Phileo'*, p. 18.

words correspond exactly to the English word *love*.'[36] They are both used in similar contexts and for loving the same kinds of objects.[37]

We should also make clear that the misinterpretation of these words is often linked to a non-cognitive understanding of the emotions. Warnach writes about *agapaō*: 'it should be noticed that these latter words are less emotionally charged than those previously mentioned. As used outside the Bible they designate a sober kind of love in the sense of placing a high value upon some person or thing.'[38] He continues that the English word 'love' is not always a good translation for the Biblical concept: 'for the kind of love that is meant in the Bible is no merely instinctive or purely emotional impulse . . . It is to be understood, rather, as constituting from the outset a movement of the whole being, . . . and in which all man's powers are engaged, including, precisely, the cognitive faculties.'[39] Friberg's analysis is similar. *Agapaō* is 'love; esp. of love as based on evaluation and choice, a matter of will and action', and *phileō* is 'love; as devotion based in the emotions, distinguished fr. *agapaō*, which is devotion based in the will like, feel affection for'.[40] Here we see a clear misunderstanding of emotion. The cognitive traits that, in Warnach's view, preclude love from being an 'emotional impulse' are what emotion is all about.

What are the actual differences in meaning between the two terms? Louw and Nida write that *phileō* is: 'to have love or affection for someone or something based on association'.[41] After emphasizing the similarity of the terms and the fact that there are no clear distinctions between them, they write, 'that is to say, *phileō* and *philia* are likely to focus upon love or affection based on

---

36. Butler, *The Meaning of 'Agapao' and 'Phileo'*, p. 72. Morris concludes that the words are used very similarly in the LXX. Morris, *Testaments of Love*, pp. 102, 111. Even with his limited use of the methods of modern linguistics, Butler's arguments are sound.

37. Butler, *The Meaning of 'Agapao' and 'Phileo'*, pp. 49–53. Butler gives a good catalogue of usage for both words. In specific contexts many of the 'unique' meanings for the words are contradicted. The so-called spiritual meaning of *agapaō* quickly breaks down in contexts like Luke 11:43, and the interpersonal nature of *phileō* is not evident in contexts like 1 Tim. 6:10.

38. Warnach, 'Love', p. 518. Later he writes that the love of God for his people is greater than the love of a parent for their child. How is this a 'sober kind of love?' Is there a more emotional love that the love of parent for child? Warnach, 'Love', p. 521. See also Vine, *Love*, p. 382; Bornkamm, *Jesus of Nazareth*, pp. 115–116.

39. Warnach, 'Love', p. 526.

40. *ANLEX*.

41. Louw and Nida, 25.33. *BDAG* gives a similar definition.

interpersonal association, while *agapaō* and *agapē* focus on love and affection based on deep appreciation and high regard'.[42] Their distinction is not as strong as the earlier works. Suffice it to say that although the words may have slightly different emphasis in particular contexts, great care should be taken before placing great significance in these differences. For this study, it is clear that they both can be used as we use the English word 'love'.

Theological interpretation

There are two basic approaches that have been taken to interpreting love in the New Testament by philosophers and theologians. First, following Kant, it is argued that love in many theological contexts is not an emotion. Kant writes:

> In this context, however, *love* is not to be taken as a *feeling* (aesthetic love), i.e. pleasure in the perfection of other men; it does not mean *emotional* love (for others cannot oblige us to have feelings) . . . According to the ethical law of perfection 'love your neighbour as yourself', every man has a duty to others of adopting the maxim of benevolence (practical love of man), whether or not he finds them lovable.[43]

Kant believed that the emotion of love toward a neighbour cannot be demanded. Therefore this love must mean something other than emotion. As we saw in Chapter one, Kant's non-cognitive view of the emotions led him to consider them irrational forces that are below reason.

C. H. Dodd is a good example of a scholar who follows Kant in this assertion. He writes: 'It is not primarily an emotion or an affection; it is primarily an active determination of the will. That is why it can be commanded as feelings cannot.'[44] Many others have agreed by defining love in non-emotional terms. This has often been in response to trying to answer the question of how love can be commanded.[45] Most scholars try to define love in non-emotional terms, as an inner inclination of the heart. It is more than action

---

42. Louw and Nida, 25.43. Notice the strong cognitive element. *BDAG*'s definition of 'to have a warm regard for and interest in another' falls short of properly defining the word.

43. Kant, *The Doctrine of Virtue*, pp. 116–118. See also Cassirer, *Grace and Law*, pp. 16–17.

44. Dodd, *Gospel and Law*, p. 42. See also p. 44.

45. Outka, *Agape*, pp. 125–127. This is also a prevalent misconception on Old Testament studies. Els concludes: 'The fact that love could be commanded indicates that *'hb* in Deut. 6:5; 10:12; 11:1, 13, 22; 19:9; 30:15, 16, 19–20; Josh. 22:5; 23:10–11 expresses not primarily feeling, but rather a certain behavioural pattern, i.e. obedience

but not an emotion. Usually, it is difficult to understand what love actually is from this perspective as its meaning vacillates between being an action and an inner disposition. Schnackenburg writes: 'we can say that love for God, as Jesus understood it, above all means fulfilling in faith and obedience all the requirements that God has made known through Jesus as conditions for entering the kingdom of God . . . and that this love implies quite concrete guiding principles'.[46] Yet, to Schnackenburg, love is not synonymous with obedience and is an 'interior disposition'. 'Love is not primarily moral effort but an inner transformation.'[47] We are left with no understanding of what the essence of love is. Furnish concludes, 'So love is an act of the will, not just some vague and generalized "disposition of the soul", feeling, or attitude.'[48]

A second major emphasis in New Testament studies is that love is in an unearned gift given for no reason. Nygren's work *Agape and Eros* laid the foundation for much of this understanding of love in the New Testament. Watson writes that Nygren's goal is to find, 'not how the Greeks or the primitive Christians actually loved, but what they thought about love, their ideas or theories of love'.[49] In this goal it is similar to the present work. Nygren argued that the *Agape* of the New Testament was a very different concept than the *Eros* of the Greeks. (Nygren uses *Eros* and *Agape* as philosophical terms and they do not have a one to one correlation with the definition of the Greek words.)[50] Nygren writes, 'When we seek to analyse the structure of the idea of *Agape*, what first attracts our attention is its spontaneous and unmotivated character . . . *Agape* has nothing to do with the kind of love that depends on the recognition of a valuable quality in its object; *Agape* does not

---

(in gratitude) to Yahweh's conventional commandments and faithful and total commitment to him' (Els, "*ḥb*', p. 287).

46. Schnackenburg, *The Moral Teaching of the New Testament*, p. 99. He continues: 'Love for God is very far, therefore, from being a weekly attitude; . . . Jesus embodied this love which is obedience and readiness for death itself' (Schnackenburg, *The Moral Teaching of the New Testament*, p. 100). Palmer concludes about man's love for God, 'This obedience is more fundamental to the nature of love for God than any feeling' (Palmer, 'Love', p. 711).

47. Schnackenburg, *The Moral Teaching of the New Testament*, p. 220.

48. Furnish, *The Love Command in the New Testament*, pp. 199–202.

49. Watson, Translator's Preface to *Agape and Eros* by Nygren, p. viii.

50. Nygren, *Agape and Eros*, p. 54. Carson presents an excellent summary of the arguments against the ideas of Nygren. Carson, *The Difficult Doctrine of the Love of God*, pp. 26–29.

recognize value, but creates it . . . The man who is loved by God has no value in himself; what gives him value is precisely the fact that God loves him.'[51] He also contends that '*Agape* is "indifferent to value".'[52] Love has no cognitive content; in fact its lack of cognitive content is what makes it the pure love of God.

Eros, according to Nygren, is the opposite of *Agape*. It is based on the desire for an object because of its value and as such it is self-centred.[53] *Eros* is of Man, *Agape* of God. *Eros* is about self and *Agape* is about others. *Agape* is spontaneous; *Eros* is about seeing the thing as valuable.[54]

If this is the nature of *Agape* then this love can only be felt toward other individuals. It excludes loving objects. Quell emphasizes that love's true character is only present when loving another person. This interpretation has fostered the redefinition of love. It is also clear that these ideas about the nature of love have a non-cognitive emphasis. He emphasizes the spontaneous and irrational nature of love as a feeling that wells up from personality.[55] Nygren's ideas about the meaning of love can lead to the glorification of love as an irrational force. Quell insists that love's essence is found in its irrational nature.[56]

In response to Nygren's idea that Christian love is 'spontaneous and unmotivated', without cause or reason, I would ask the simple question, 'Does God love trees and plants as he loves people?' Obviously he does not. God loves people in a special way because there is something unique and lovable about them. They are his special creation, made in his image. As we will see later in this section, God, Jesus and Christians have a special love for certain groups of people for specific reasons. Further, it is clear that people have many good reasons for loving God.[57] What determines the depth and nature of love someone has for a particular individual is something that they believe about that individual. Nygren's hypothesis, that the major feature of *Agape* is its lack of cognitive content, is directly contradicted by both a proper understanding of

---

51. Nygren, *Agape and Eros*, p. 78. See also pp. 85, 152. 'The phenomenon of love in the OT is experienced as a spontaneous force which drives one to something or someone over against itself' (Günther and Link, '*agapaō*', p. 540; see also p. 542).

52. Nygren, *Agape and Eros*, p. 77.

53. Nygren, *Agape and Eros*, pp. 175–176, 179.

54. Nygren, *Agape and Eros*, p. 210.

55. Quell, '*agapaō, agapē, agapētos*', pp. 22–24. His comments centre on the Old Testament.

56. Quell, '*agapaō, agapē, agapētos*', p. 29.

57. Edwards, *Religious Affections*, pp. 89–91.

love and the New Testament itself.[58] It leaves us with no concrete understanding of love's fundamental nature.

We see that mistakes are made by both views due to an adherence to a non-cognitive theory of the emotions. On the one hand, love is exalted by some because it is spontaneous, unearned and about nothing, while it is seen by others as action not emotion. If emotion is cognitive, love is about something, can be commanded and is emotional.

Commanding emotion

Jesus commands in Mark 12:31: 'You shall love your neighbour as yourself'. This is the command in the New Testament that is most often cited as an example of the fact that 'you cannot command emotion'. We have already observed that in the Old Testament there are many commands to have or not to have particular emotions in particular contexts. This pattern continues in the New Testament. But because we will argue that these kinds of statements are commands of emotion, it is important that this objection is answered more fully. The fact that these things are commanded is not disputed. What is at issue is: (1) are emotions actually commanded in these passages, and; (2) what do these commands mean in practice?

The burden of proof is upon those who would argue that these are not commands of emotion. The meaning seems very straightforward. Whether or not we believe it is logical to command emotion, the simplest interpretation of these passages is that the biblical writers do, in fact, command emotion. Although I have never run across this, the most straightforward argument for the proponents of the position that emotion cannot be commanded would be to say that the writer who commands emotion holds a false premise – what the writer commands is not possible. However, what is usually argued is that the emotion word in this context does not imply an emotional state. As we will argue in the following sections, there is no evidence from the texts themselves that these terms have been redefined by the writers as theological concepts that do not contain an emotional core. On the contrary, the evidence points to these words retaining their usual meanings of simple emotions. The arguments of those who deny that emotion can be commanded seem to come from a desire to be consistent with their own philosophical understanding of emotion and, at the same time, maintain

---

58. See Schrage, *Der erste Brief an die Korinther*, p. 322. A combination of these two major views (Kant and Nygren) is also possible; they are not mutually exclusive. Allender and Longman, *Bold Love*, p. 32; Vine, *Love*, pp. 381–382.

the integrity of the writers of the New Testament. We must challenge the tenability of this position.

Further, negative emotions, as prohibited by particular texts (do not be angry or do not fear), are rarely if ever defined as not being emotion by commentators. There is no hesitancy to believe that the New Testament prohibits feeling a negative emotion. Often, the same commentator will then go on to argue that it is not logical to command positive emotions. We see in this the logical inconsistency of their argument. Again, we must emphasize that it is never disputed that these passages do in fact contain commands.

This leads into our argument for the legitimacy and logic of issuing commands to have or not to have emotion in particular circumstances. It is perhaps easier to understand the command to stop having destructive emotions. It is clear, for example, that people who are controlled by rage must learn to limit or eliminate this emotion in most circumstances to become a healthy person. Since both anger and love are based on cognition, both are equally controllable. In as much as we can learn not to have damaging anger, we can also learn to have love. Chapter one has already argued the following: that because emotions are cognitive, people can be held responsible for having particular emotions; that you can blame someone for having destructive emotions; that it can be morally wrong not to have a particular emotion in a particular situation; that it is possible to educate the emotions; and that there are many methods that can be used to change harmful emotions or produce healthy emotions. If these things are true, it is a logical step to assume that emotions are able to be commanded. If a cognitive understanding of emotion is correct, and this perspective logically implies that people can be held responsible for their emotions, then emotions can be legitimately commanded.[59]

---

59. It is argued that emotion cannot be commanded because the reader is not able to carry out the command. It is assumed that a command that cannot be followed is logically impossible. However, even if the command is impossible this does not imply that it cannot be commanded. In philosophical terms, 'ought' does not imply 'can' in this instance. In other words, if the idea that you cannot be held responsible for something that it is not in your power to do is proved false in this case, emotions may be commanded. Most proponents of the view that emotion cannot be commanded would agree that having the emotion of love and acting as love dictates is a higher good than only action. If that is the case it may follow that the command in the New Testament reflects this truth. There are three levels of argument that 'ought' does not imply 'can' and if any of them is true it disproves that emotion cannot be commanded in the New Testament. There is not the space

Chapter one also argued that emotions cannot be forced or had on demand – one cannot change the emotion by dwelling on the emotion itself, but one can change the emotion by dwelling on and changing the beliefs and evaluations that lie behind it. The New Testament's commands of emotion can be placed in this context. The command of emotion is not identical to a command of simple action. To say 'love your neighbour' is not the same thing as to say 'go to the store and get a loaf of bread'. The fact that the command of emotion cannot be followed immediately is not to say that it cannot be commanded. In fact, a command of emotion (according to Mark Talbot) may be the paradigm of a command that cannot be acted on immediately.[60] We might say that the command of emotion is indirect.[61] That is, the cognition behind the emotion must be changed to change the emotion. Since these cognitions are under our control, emotion can be commanded.

Emotions tell us the truth about what we believe and what we value. When the New Testament commands emotion it is exhorting the believer to have the values and beliefs out of which godly emotions flow. If you are not joyful in trials, the biblical command is an exhortation to bring to mind the truths that will produce joy even in trying circumstances, as is clear in the passages that command this. If love of an enemy is commanded, it is linked with the cognitive understanding that will produce this love. If hatred of a brother is prohibited, it is a command for the person to examine themselves and change the beliefs that have produced the hatred.

---

to relate these arguments but we can refer to proponents of them for further study. First, this can be proved for the specific command of emotions in the New Testament. This is well argued by Schlossberger who concludes, 'my argument that we are responsible for our emotions does not depend in any way upon our being able to control our emotions' (Schlossberger, 'Why We Are Responsible for Our Emotions', p. 48). Second, we can argue that the logic of 'ought' implies 'can' is fundamentally flawed. This is argued convincingly by Pigden in his article 'Ought-Implies-Can: Erasmus, Luther, and R. M. Hare'. Finally, it can be argued that the 'ought' implies 'can' 'gap' can be bridged by the active power of God in a believer's life. The Holy Spirit is able to give the believer the ability to bridge this otherwise impossible gap. This argument is made by Hare who concludes, 'there is a God who loves us enough both to demand a high standard from us and to help us meet it' (Hare, *The Moral Gap*, p. 275).

60. I am indebted to Mark Talbot, professor of philosophy at Wheaton College, for helping me to think through the argument in this section.

61. See Ben-Ze'ev, *The Subtlety of Emotions*, p. 246.

Generally we do not see commands of emotion in the New Testament as commands to engage in immediate action. They are commands to have the beliefs and values that will produce the commanded emotion. In commanding the emotion, the writer puts their finger on the true indicator of *whether* these beliefs and values are *genuinely* held by the believer. There can be no self deception or hiding behind simple intellectual assent when emotions are commanded. That said, we should not discount an immediate change in emotion that is the result of a command. For example, the command not to be angry at a person because the offense is clearly not their fault may lead to a quick change in emotion. In contrast, loving an enemy may necessitate a persistent, targeted and deliberate reorientation of beliefs and values. This may include identifying, facing and working to change long held cultural norms and values or working through past experiences of great pain and suffering.

Love in the Synoptic Gospels and Johannine writings

Thus far we have examined the vocabulary used for love in the New Testament and the philosophical attitudes of some New Testament scholars towards love. We now move forward into the New Testament material itself. What ideas about the nature of love do we find in the text? It is not my intention to do in depth exegesis of particular passages. Instead, this section and the similar sections later in this book will do two things. First, it will survey important literature and draw conclusions about the validity of their conclusions. Second, it will draw conclusions about particular emotions and emotion in general in the New Testament.

The Synoptic Gospels

The most familiar passages about love are found in the Synoptic Gospels on the lips of Jesus. The discussions of the greatest commandment (Matt. 22:34–40; Mark 12:28–34; Luke 10:25–28) and the command to love your enemies (Matt. 5:43–48; Luke 6:27–28, 32–36) are most prominent.[62] There is

---

62. Luz concludes, 'for Matthew, *love* is the foremost commandment, and hence the *guiding precept* by which Jesus' other commandments are to be interpreted' (Luz, *The Theology of the Gospel of Matthew*, p. 52. See also Luz, *Das Evangelium nach Matthäus*, vol. 3, pp. 124, 126; Gnilka, *Das Matthäusevangelium*, vol. 2, p. 167, Gnilka, *Das Evangelium nach Markus*, p. 165; Schnackenburg, *Jesus in the Gospels*, p. 123). See also Stuhlmacher, *Grundlegung Von Jesus zu Paulus*, pp. 98–101; Pesch, *Das Markusevangelium*, vol. 2, pp. 243–247.

no command in the New Testament to love God except for Jesus' quotation of the Old Testament in these passages.

The love commandment is introduced by questions about the law. Jesus says this is the primary moral requirement of the law. We find that to Jesus, having the right emotion is at the core of obeying the law. The key question according to Chilton and McDonald is 'how can love (*agape*) be commanded?'[63] They go on to circle around this question but never face it head on. In a cognitive framework, as we have seen, the question is easily answered. Luz seems to argue that due to the fact that love of God is based on knowledge it is not an emotion.'[64] We have found the opposite to be true – love is emotional because it is based on what you value and knowledge.

We must also disagree with Davies and Allison when they write, 'Love of God like love of neighbour, is not firstly an attitude or affection but – as the example of Jesus shows – a way of life. . . . This is why, unlike an emotion, it can be commanded.'[65]

Love for one's neighbour is illustrated by the story of the Good Samaritan. The parable has been interpreted to mean that love is not an emotion; for example, Schrage writes of the Good Samaritan: 'His actions make it unmistakably clear that his actions cannot be identified with feelings and emotions. Love means active and concrete involvement on behalf of those who suffer.'[66] Is this what love means or did emotion motivate these actions? Would the Samaritan have taken these actions without feeling in his heart? The difference of the Samaritan from the other characters is his loving heart which motivated radical action.

The command to love your enemies has a clear cognitive foundation. The coming reward and the example of love from the Father to the wicked give

---

63. Chilton and McDonald, *Jesus and the Ethics of the Kingdom*, p. 93. Morris has some of the same difficulties and concludes, 'In understanding this response, we must not confuse love with passion or with sentimentality' (Morris, *Testaments of Love*, p. 187).

64. Luz, *Das Evangelium nach Matthäus*, vol. 3, p. 279.

65. Davies and Allison, *Matthew*, vol. 3, p. 241. Hagner agrees: 'In neither case is love construed as an emotion.' Hagner, *Matthew 14–28*, p. 648. See also Cranfield, *Mark*, p. 378; Ladd, *A Theology of the New Testament*, p. 132; Ernst, *Das Evangelium nach Lukas*, 265. To Furnish, Mark does not emphasize emotion but obedience to the 'moral law' (Furnish, *The Love Command in the New Testament*, p. 30).

66. Schrage, *The Ethics of the New Testament*, p. 78. See also Furnish, *The Love Command in the New Testament*, pp. 43–45, 60. Stauffer, '*agapaō, agapē, agapētos*', p. 46.

good reasons to love your enemy (Luke 6:35–36).[67] Theissen and Merz summarize the reasons that are given to love an enemy:

(1) A *comparison* with an attitude of mutuality;
(2) The *promise* of being a child of God;
(3) A *foundation* in the behaviour of God;
(4) A direct *call* to imitate God.[68]

Scholars again argue about the difficulty in commanding emotional love for your enemy. Lutzer relates: '*Divine love is based on and dependent on the lover* [an idea from Nygren]. It is not a feeling, for with it we can even love our enemies. Clearly, if love were a feeling, God would be putting a burden on us that we could not possibly bear.'[69] Hagner writes of the command to love your enemies, 'The love he describes, of course, is not an emotion . . . but volitional acts.'[70] Luz emphasizes, 'It is correct that that one must think not primarily of friendly feelings but of concrete deeds; but it is still more important that "love" is a behaviour of the *entire* person which does not exclude feelings.'[71] Luke 6:27–28 shows Schrage that love is not about finding something to love in the other.[72] In the interpretation of this command we continue to see the hesitancy of scholars to classify love as an emotion and their faulty idea about the nature of love in the New Testament.

Scholars often argue that this love is an inner deep disposition but not an emotion. Furnish emphasizes action but believes there is also 'something deeper' involved.[73] Piper, to his credit, argues strongly that this love is far more

---

67. See Minear, *The Commands of Christ*, p. 71; Gnilka, *Das Matthäusevangelium*, vol. 1,
      p. 197; Ernst, *Das Evangelium nach Lukas*, p. 173; Schürmann, *Das Lukasevangelium*,
      vol. 1, p. 342.
68. Theissen and Merz, *The Historical Jesus*, p. 391. See also Wolbert, 'Die Liebe zum
      Nächsten, zum Feind and zum Sünder', pp. 276–279; Schnackenburg,
      Matthäusevangelium: 1, 1–16, 20, pp. 60–61; Ernst, *Das Evangelium nach Lukas*, p. 175.
69. Lutzer, *Managing Your Emotions*, p. 38. He contrasts this with human love which, he
      argues, is about something in the other person. See also Bruce, *The Hard Sayings of
      Jesus*, pp. 72–73.
70. Hagner, *Matthew 1–13*, p. 136.
71. Luz, *Matthew 1–7*, p. 341.
72. Schrage, *The Ethics of the New Testament*, p. 77. He differentiates between *Agape* and
      Eros.
73. Furnish, *The Love Command in the New Testament*, p. 66. See similar comments in

than action. It is a matter of the heart. It 'is an obedience which consists in a radical transformation of the deepest spring of man's being, even the depth over which he has no control.'[74] This deep 'inner' disposition, this matter of heart, would be much more easily explained if scholars simply understood that love is an emotion.

Piper comments with a strong exegetical analysis. 'But prior to the act comes that change of heart.'[75] Piper points to strong cognitive motivation in the text of Luke for this love. He concludes his book by listing the cognitive features that motivate the love of enemy in each of the gospels: the mercy of God; being God's children (father love of God); eschatological blessing, which 'is in some sense dependent upon one's obedience to the command of enemy love'; fear of judgment; the presence of the new kingdom with new values, and the need for a renewed mind.[76]

In addition to these key passages we can draw a number of conclusions from the use of love in other instances. It is clear that Jesus uses love in a very typical way (Matt. 5:46, 6:24; Luke 6:32, 7:5). We have no hint of a unique idea of Christian love in these passages.[77] In Luke 11:43 *agapaō* is used of a thing. Günther and Link insist that this is an exception to the relational meaning of the word while *phileō* is used more regularly for objects (Matt. 23:6; Luke 20:46). This conclusion, we contend, is based on the fact that they want to redefine love as a theological concept. Instead, these passages make it clear that the gospel writers' idea of love was similar to our own.[78]

In Luke 7:47 a knowledge that one has been forgiven gives good reason to love.[79] We also observe a unique love between Father and Son. In the

---

Nolland, *Luke 9:21–18:34*, 585; Bovon, *Das Evangelium nach Lukas*, vol 1,
pp. 316–318; Mann, *Mark*, pp. 479–481; Mounce, *Matthew*, p. 210. Marshall says it
is 'inner disposition', a 'way of life,' and 'undivided loyalty'. Marshall, *Luke*,
pp. 442–443. This love is 'that inner commitment to God for his own sake'
(Lane, *Mark*, p. 434).

74. Piper, *Love Your Enemies*, pp. 144–145, 150.

75. Piper, *Love Your Enemies*, p. 161. Blomberg rightly sees the actions as serving 'only
to underline the extent of the Samaritan's love' (Blomberg, *Interpreting the Parables*,
p. 230).

76. Piper, *Love Your Enemies*, pp. 168–69, 173–174.

77. See Morris, 'Love', in *DJG*, pp. 492–493.

78. Günther and Link, '*agapaō*', p. 543. See similar comments in Brown, '*phileō*', p. 548.

79. Stauffer believes that the fact that this love has no object is significant; it is free
('*agapaō, agapē, agapētos*', p. 47). However, the object is implied.

synoptics God loves Jesus in a special way for the simple reason that he is his son (Matt. 3:17; 17:5; Mark 12:6). Further, Jesus was touched by love for certain individuals (Mark 10:2–22). Jesus' action and speech was motivated by his love (Mark 10:21).[80]

A difficult saying of Jesus is found in Matthew 10:37. The general feeling about the passage is that the meaning of love is 'to prefer' or 'to place above' with little emotional content.[81] Yet, this robs the expression of its impact. If we redefine the word to mean 'to prefer' we loose Jesus' sharp point. Matthew 24:12 states that 'the love [*agapē*] of many will grow cold'. This is a reason for judgment. Not only does this show that emotion is a state for which people can be held morally accountable, but it also seems to imply that love is an emotion. Emotional love is what can grow cold.[82]

An indicator of which people are wicked or hypocritical is that they love the wrong things, their love is misplaced. For example, they love to impress others (Matt. 6:5, 23:6; Luke 11:43, 20:46; Mark 12:38). Jesus also highlights the emotion of loving wealth or the world. Those who love these things cannot love God (Matt. 6:24, 19:16–22; Mark 10:17–22; Luke 16:13, 18:18–23). If emotions are cognitive this misplaced emotion is showing the truth of what the ungodly value. Their emotional love is Jesus' point – it reveals their true belief about what is important.

Conclusions about the character of Jesus have often been faulty. Morris writes: 'For him love depends on the nature of the lover rather than that of the beloved. Jesus loved because he was a loving person, not because he found attractive qualities in those he loved.'[83] Here we see the influence of Nygren. To Hansen, 'Love is an unshakable commitment of the will. Love transcends feeling and keeps on going when feelings falter or vanish.' It is 'much more than emotion.'[84] It is true that people do not deserve the love of Jesus but he does give it for good reason. These are people, loved by God, made unique and special by God in his image. Is our special love for our children solely based on our own character, because we are 'loving people?' No, we love them

---

80. See Gnilka, *Das Matthäusevangelium*, vol. 1, p. 192.

81. Stählin, '*phileō*', p. 129.

82. See France, *Matthew*, pp. 338–339; Gnilka, *Das Matthäusevangelium*, vol. 2.

83. Morris, 'Love', in *DJG*, p. 492. Morris points to their being no object for the love of the woman in Luke 7:47, but the implied object as the NRSV translates is probably Jesus Himself (p. 495). I would say an object is there by necessity; the point is to become a lover of specific people with whom you have contact.

84. Hansen, 'The Emotions of Jesus', p. 45. Ironically, here in an article about emotion, love is not seen to be an emotion.

because of our special relationship with them. No matter what they do they are ours. God loves us in a similar way.[85]

We have seen that while many scholars believe that love is with the whole heart or a deep inner disposition they often insist that it is specifically *not* an emotion. We must ask what exactly this means, if not emotion. No scholar we have examined attempts to answer this question. Bultmann emphasizes that the love that Jesus talks of is without legalistic boundary or limit.[86] We should ask, what but emotion motivates like this?

Johannine literature

John has a unique emphasis and some key insights into what love is. His approach is different from the synoptics. Further, the letters of John have a similar emphasis to the gospel of John. Due to this commonality we will consider the perspective of these writings on love together.[87]

It is clear in John's Gospel that there is a special relationship between the Father and the Son. There is a unique bond of love (John 3:35, 5:20, 14:31). There are good reasons for this (John 10:17, 15:9–11).[88] We must contest the opinion of Schnackenburg, 'The bond of love embraces Father and Son not as feeling but in mutual devotion in activity.'[89] But surely this is a deeply emotional relationship. It is also clear that there is a special relationship of love between God/Jesus and those who love and obey him (John 14:23). John 16:27 gives a good reason as to why the Father has a special love for believers, 'because you have loved me [Jesus]' (1 John 4:19). Beyond this, Jesus had a special relationship with certain individuals like Lazarus and his sisters and John the disciple.[90] In John 11:33–38 the vocabulary reflects the intense

---

85. Ernst, *Das Evangelium nach Lukas*, p. 261.

86. Bultmann, *Theology*, vol. 1, pp. 18–19.

87. Matera, *New Testament Ethics*, pp. 105–106; Berger, *Theologiegeschechte des Urchristentums*, p. 665.

88. Carson, *The Difficult Doctrine of the Love of God*, pp. 16, 35; Schnackenburg, *John*, vol. 1, pp. 388, 400; Becker, *Das Evangelium nach Johannes: Kapitel 11–21*, p. 455. The use of different vocabulary in 3:35 and 5:20 reinforces the similarity of *agapaō* and *phileō*. Bruce, *John*, pp. 97, 310–311.

89. Schnackenburg, *Jesus in the Gospels*, p. 254. This perspective leaves us little desire to emulate the relationship.

90. Ridderbos, *John*, p. 388; Gnilka, *Theologie des Neuen Testaments*, pp. 316–357; Berger, *Theologiegeschichte des Urchristentums*, p. 240. For a summary of Jesus' love for special individuals in John see Morris, *Testaments of Love*, p. 147.

emotion of Jesus.[91] In short, he had special emotional bonds with certain individuals, as all of us do (11:3, 5, 36; 13:23; 19:26).[92] This has been taken by Morris to mean that: 'The Father's love is not to be thought of as some lofty and ethereal emotion; it has its effects on earth and the continual presence of the divine with the believer.'[93] Instead, we conclude that it indicates a cognitive understanding of emotion. Jesus' love is like ours.

Believers are to have a special relationship to and love for one another (John 14:23). These unique bonds of love in John make sense in a cognitive framework. Love is about something, and special bonds of love are about something about the other person. In the context of John, we love other believers because they are part of the family of God.[94] We must disagree with Witherington when he writes, 'Notice here that love is commanded. Jesus is not referring to a warm mushy feeling; he is referring to an action.'[95] The warm feelings believers have for one another is a sure sign of their discipleship (John 13:34–35).

John 3:19 and 12:43 speak of loving the wrong things. What people love shows who they really are. Love as cognitive emotion is the only interpretation that makes good sense of these statements. A person's beliefs can be evaluated by what they love. 1 John 2:15–16 is similar to the idea of hating sin. We are not to love the world. According to Ladd, not loving the world in 1 John tells the Christian that, 'He is to set his affections upon an entirely different set of values.'[96] Ladd briefly outlines one of the major themes of this book. What the New Testament has in view is a radical transformation of the emotions due to a radical reorientation of people's thinking.

Love in John's epistles is equally important. It is the sign of new life (1 John 3:14), love for one another is commanded (1 John 3:23; 4:21; 2 John 6), and it is the will of God (1 John 2:7–8, 24; 2 John 5). We know love because Christ died

---

91. Hansen, 'The Emotions of Jesus', p. 45.

92. See Barrett, *John*, p. 377. Some interpreters take this emphasis to mean that love is only for other believers and John's emphasis is therefore deficient. Hays summarizes this position and argues against it. Hays, *The Moral Vision of the New Testament*, pp. 139–140, 144–147.

93. Morris, 'Love', in *DJG*, p. 493; see also Warfield, 'The Emotional Life of Our Lord', pp. 103–106.

94. Hays, *The Moral Vision of the New Testament*, pp. 144–147.

95. Witherington, *John's Wisdom*, pp. 247–248.

96. Ladd, *A Theology of the New Testament*, p. 613. See also Burge, 'John, Letters of', p. 595; Bultmann, *Johannine Epistles*, p. 55.

for us (1 John 3:16; 4:1–21). Many commentators on these verses take them to mean that love is in fact the action. Johnson writes, 'love is primarily, not an interior state of the heart, but the visible commitment in action . . . The love is in the deed'.[97] Bruce concurs, 'When John speaks of love (*agape*), it is no sentimental emotion he has in mind, but something intensely practical.'[98] Let us offer an alternative conclusion. We can say that the cognition behind the action should match the cognition behind the emotion. These actions are expressions of love, not love itself.[99] The emotion of love even motivated the cross (John 15:12–13). We see clearly that emotion takes centre stage in John's theology. Love shines as a beacon affirming the genuine belief.

Christian love is not different because of its unique definition of love. What sets Christian love apart is the belief that the other person's value is so high they are worth the ultimate sacrifice. Marshall concludes of 3:18, 'Their love is to be demonstrated "in truth", which is a call not just for actions to prove the reality of their inward feeling but also for a love which is in accord with the divine revelation of reality in the love shown by Jesus.'[100]

Clearly, love is also a motivation for action in John 3:16; God's love is the motivating force behind sending the Son. Notice also the relational emphasis of the verse. Further, John emphasizes the love of the world; God loves those outside the family.[101] As John 3:16 shows, Love is not synonymous with the action as some would like to argue.[102] The evidence does not clearly point in this direction, for if this were true John would be advocating a form of legalism. Love is the motivation behind the service and this is an important distinction. A similar argument can be made about 1 John 4:20. If love is not an

---

97. Johnson, *1, 2, and 3 John*, p. 118. Hays agrees, *The Moral Vision of the New Testament*, pp. 145, 155; Klauck, *Der erste Johannesbrief*, pp. 217, 247–248.

98. Bruce, *Epistles of John*, p. 96.

99. Verhey, 'Ethics', p. 351. This understanding is not contradicted by 3:18. Words do not necessarily show emotion for they can be false. See Kruse, *Letters of John*, p. 138; Smalley, *1, 2, 3 John*, p. 198.

100. Marshall, *The Epistles of John*, p. 196. See also pp. 192, 213–214.

101. Bultmann, *Theology*, vol. 2, p. 82. See the excellent comments of Carson on this verse. Love in John does not mean, 'spontaneous, self generated, without reference to the loved one'. Carson, *John*, p. 204. See also Guthrie, *New Testament Theology*, pp. 909, 932, 917; Beasley-Murray, *John*, p. 51; Ridderbos, *John*, p. 138; Carson, *The Difficult Doctrine of the Love of God*, p. 16.

102. Ladd, *A Theology of the New Testament*, p. 280; Günther and Link, '*agapaō*', p. 546; Schrage, *The Ethics of the New Testament*, pp. 307, 314–315.

emotion, just action, it would be possible to love God and hate your brother. Emotional love must be in view here. This passage is true because the cognition that lies behind loving God is not compatible with hating a brother.[103] It is only when both loves are based on Christian truth that loving God and hating brother are incompatible. A cognitive understanding of love makes sense of the passage.

In 1 John the love for individuals and God are dependent on love from God. Morris writes, 'indeed, love to God and love to men and the keeping of God's commandments are all wrapped up together (1 John 5:12)'.[104] The emotion shows what beliefs are held in the heart and it becomes an indication of genuine faith. Kruse writes, 'the nature of the true experience of God is such that it cannot exist without manifesting itself in love for God's people'.[105] We also see in John 17:26 that believers' love is to be a reflection of God's love for the Son (John 15:9). If one is emotional the other one will also be emotional. In 1 John 3:14 love is a sign of salvation. Those who set their minds on God will learn to love – it is a natural by-product of the new way of thinking.[106]

There is an emphasis on love and knowledge in these writings. Love is the proof that believers abide in him and have true knowledge of God (1 John 3:14, 4:7, 8, 12, 16). 1 John 4:8 reads, 'He who does not love does not know God; for God is love' (RSV). An intimate knowledge of God naturally results in love, and the lack of love may show a conversion to be false (1 John 4:7).[107] The fact that living in love is 'walking in the light' to John further enhances the link between love and knowledge. In 1 John 4:12 love shows God's presence. This also seems to speak of knowledge resulting in love. Brown writes, 'The secessionists claim to know God; but since they do not love, their claim is false.'[108] We have seen in cognitive theory that the presence or lack of an emotion may prove the authenticity or falsehood of the assertion that a certain belief is held. This comes across strongly in these

---

103. Marshall makes similar comments. Marshall, *The Epistles of John*, pp. 225–226. Stott emphasizes the cognitive content in this statement in a good summary (Stott, *The Letters of John*, p. 173).

104. Morris, *Testaments of Love*, p. 172. See also Culpepper, *The Gospel and Letters of John*, pp. 269–271.

105. Kruse, *Letters of John*, p. 170.

106. Matera, *New Testament Ethics*, p. 112.

107. Ladd, *A Theology of the New Testament*, p. 616; Smalley, *1, 2, 3 John*, pp. 238, 239.

108. Brown, *John*, p. 549.

passages. If you know him you will love (1 John 2:9–10; 4:20; 3:14–15; 4:8–10).[109]

In John 15 the interrelationship of knowledge of God, love of God for the Son and the love of the Son for believers is powerfully evident. A similar interrelation is seen between abiding in God, knowledge, belief and love in 1 John 4:16.[110] 'So we have known and believe the love that God has for us. God is love, and those who abide in love abide in God, and God abides in them.' It is a good summary of this section.

Furnish summarizes the predominant idea of what love is to Jesus in the gospels:

> It means the compassionate serving of whoever stands in need, active 'doing good' even to one's enemies, restraint in judging others, forgiveness, reconciliation, and sharing one's resources with all the brethren in the Christian *koinonia*.[111]

We have found a different emphasis in the gospels. We have found a Jesus who loves with a full and bursting heart. A Jesus whose great understanding of the character of God and understanding of men and women as made in the image of God motivates a depth of love that cannot be contained but must be shared and expressed. This love, in turn, naturally motivates the actions that Furnish rightly emphasizes. Young concludes of Jesus, 'The foundation of his ministry was healing love for others. The sacrificial love of Jesus was deeply rooted in the Jewish understanding of divine compassion for people created in the image of God.'[112] This love was not a formless love for humanity – it was a love of the individuals that Jesus met. Love saw a person who had great value in the mind of God, love had compassion for a person who has needs and struggles and took radical action on behalf of this neighbour.[113]

---

109. Burge, 'John, Letters of', pp. 592–594; Kruse, *Letters of John*, p. 136; Bruce, *Epistles of John*, p. 56.

110. Morris, *The Cross of Jesus*, p. 61. See Schnackenburg, *John*, vol. 3, p. 109; Becker, *Das Evangelium nach Johannes: Kapitel 11–21*, p. 486; Stuhlmacher, *Von der Paulusschule bis zur Johannesoffenbarung*, pp. 257–258; Carson, *John*, p. 521. Morris presents a good survey of love in John which supports my major points. Morris, *Testaments of Love*. See also Guthrie, *New Testament Theology*, pp. 104–105, 663–664; Barrett, *John*, p. 180.

111. Furnish, *The Love Command in the New Testament*, p. 90.

112. Young, *Jesus the Jewish Theologian*, p. 238.

113. Barclay, *The Mind of Jesus*, pp. 110–112, 124.

Love in Pauline literature

Do we see the same patterns and uses of the word in Paul that we saw in the Gospels? Does a cognitive understanding of love help make sense of Paul's use of the word?

We find many of the same misconceptions about love in Paul as we found in the Gospels. Schrage writes of Paul:

> It has often been emphasized that love cannot be subsumed in ethics; it refers in the first instance to what we are, not what we do. But it is surely of equal importance for Paul that love finds expression in specific types of conduct and ways of life (cf. the variety of verbs in 1 Cor. 13:4ff.). Love must not be confused with a vague feeling of good will or a conformist pragmatism . . . Human love, like God's love is not an attitude or an emotion but an act (cf. 'labour of love' in 1 Thess. 1:3.).[114]

Matera agrees, 'Love is not a sentiment or emotion, although it does not necessarily exclude these.'[115] Bultmann emphasizes that although *agapē* has some connotation of 'sentiment' it is primarily the language of God's action. In Paul it is the action of redemption in Christ (Rom. 5:8). Romans 8:35 is about the Christ event, this is the 'love' mentioned. Of 2 Corinthians 13:14 he writes: 'In such cases, *agape* like *charis* means all that God has done or bestowed for salvation.'[116] Käsemann concurs, 'Characteristically he usually inverts it, speaking of God's love for us [Rom. 8:28], not in an emotional sense, but in the sense of his "being for us".'[117] We disagree – the text itself does not point to these conclusions, rather the scholar's bias is at work. As we will see, when Paul expounds on love in 1 Corinthians 13, love is necessarily emotion.

Cranfield, following Nygren, writes of Romans 5:5, that it draws 'out the nature of God's love for us as altogether undeserved and spontaneous'.[118] Stauffer writes, 'As for Jesus, so for Paul *agapē* is the only vital force which has a future in the aeon of death.'[119] Love seems to be seen in these passages as

---

114. Schrage, *The Ethics of the New Testament*, pp. 211–212. See also Schmithals, *Der Römerbrief: Ein Kommentar*, pp. 318, 472.

115. Matera, *New Testament Ethics*, p. 255.

116. Bultmann, *Theology*, vol. 1, p. 292.

117. Käsemann, *Romans*, p. 243. Moo writes, 'God's love for us is not simply an "emotion" but his gracious action on our behalf' (Moo, *Romans*, p. 543). See similar comments in Zeller, *Der Brief an die Römer*, pp. 167–169.

118. Cranfield, *Romans*, p. 257. See the similar comments of Edwards, *Romans*, p. 138.

119. Stauffer, '*agapaō, agapē, agapētos*', p. 51. Dunn writes of Rom. 5:5, 'Paul uses vivid

a spontaneous and irrational force that has no cognitive cause. This conclusion also has no base in Paul's writings.

The fact that God loves men is at the heart of Paul's gospel. It is clear to Paul that God's love is expressed in Christ's death (Rom. 5:8; Eph. 2:4–5; 2 Thess. 2:16; Gal. 2:20). Paul is driven by this understanding of the love of God which motivated the cross (2 Cor. 5:14–15).[120] Ladd concludes that for Paul love is the great motivation for Christian action (Rom. 5:5, 15:30; Gal. 5:22; Col. 3:14).[121] Love plays the major role in Paul's ethical system. Like Jesus, for Paul, love of God and neighbour is the summation of the law (Gal. 5:14; Rom. 13:8–10).[122] Murray writes of Romans 13, 'Love is emotive, motive, and expulsive. It is emotive and therefore creates affinity with and affection for the object. It is motive in that impels action. It is expulsive because it expels what is alien to the interests which love seeks to promote.'[123] Paul is ready to command love. In this he echoes the words of Jesus (Rom. 13:8–10; Gal. 5:14).[124] Another command to love is given in Titus 2:4. Love of husbands (*philandros*) and children (*philoteknos*) can be taught to the young women. Love of husbands for wives, *agapate*, is commanded in Col. 3:19 and Eph. 5:25. This is logical in a cognitive view. As you cultivate right thinking about spouse and children and as you value them as you should love will naturally be the result.

"Pentecostal" language ("poured out in our hearts"), and obviously recalls his readers to deep emotional experiences' (Dunn, *Romans 1–8*, p. 265). He continues by emphasizing the great power that is given to be believer in realizing that they are loved. Dunn, *Romans 1–8*, p. 512.

120. Bassler, 'Centering the Argument', pp. 167–168.

121. Ladd, *A Theology of the New Testament*, p. 522. See also Martin, *2 Corinthians*, pp. 128, 133; Matera, *New Testament Ethics*, pp. 254–255; Wolff, *Der erste Brief des Paulus an die Korinther*, p. 325. The consensus is that this is Christ's love for us (subjective genitive) in 2 Cor. 5:14.

122. Lohse, 'The Church in Everyday Life', p. 252; Schnabel, 'How Paul Developed His Ethics', pp. 271–273, 276–277; Fung, *Galatians*, pp. 246–247; Furnish, *Theology and Ethics in Paul*, pp. 64, 199; Fitzmyer, *Paul and His Theology*, p. 98; Schrage, *The Ethics of the New Testament*, pp. 213, 216; Cassirer, *Grace and Law*, p. 155. Ridderbos explains, 'the law does not find its criterion in love, but just the reverse, the requirement of love is so imperative because in it lies the summary of the law' (Ridderbos, *Paul: An Outline of His Theology*, p. 282).

123. Murray, *Romans*, vol. 2, p. 161. See also Schmithals, *Der Römerbrief: Ein Kommentar*, pp. 474–477.

124. Dunn, *The Theology of Paul the Apostle*, p. 655.

Love for people is commanded while love for the wrong things is a sign that people are not following God. In 2 Timothy 3:2–4 one of the chief identifying marks of the ungodly is what they love: themselves, money, pleasure (2 Tim. 4:10). The fact that this list of vices begins with love of self shows that the other vices flow from this emotion. The list is bracketed by similar phrases.[125] Conversely, the bishop is to be 'a lover of goodness' (Titus 1:8).[126]

Paul assumes that believers love God. Paul does not often mention a love for God but it seems clear that he believes that the church is a community of those who love God (Rom. 8:28; 1 Cor. 2:9, 8:3; 16:22; Eph. 6:24; 2 Tim. 3:4). Furnish summarizes, 'The Christian is summoned to love in a double sense: to be loved and to be loving. Within the precincts of Pauline theology these two are not separable.'[127] Paul is strongly motivated by his love for others (1 Thess. 2:8). Paul's attitude of love and strong affection toward his co-workers and the churches are clear. This is perhaps best illustrated by 2 Corinthians. Evans writes, 'The feeling between them was not limited by Paul's lack of love for them but by the restriction of their affections for him (6:11–13).'[128] His emotions are tied up in the relationship. In 2 Corinthians 2:4 Paul's strong emotions and grief are a sign of his great love. Here we see both love as the primary emotion, as it causes the grief, and Paul's willingness to share and show emotion (2 Cor. 7:3; 11:11; 12:15). 'For I wrote you out of much distress and anguish of heart and with many tears, not to cause you pain, but to let you know the abundant love that I have for you.' The request of Paul for them to open their hearts in 7:2 is highly emotional.[129] Paul longs for others to return his affection; their love for him is a source of comfort and joy (2 Cor. 7:6–7; 1 Thess. 3:6–10).

In 2 Corinthians 12:14–16 Paul writes as a parent to a child. This emphasized the depth of feeling Paul has for the Corinthians. Yet, not everyone in the community returns his affection. Carson writes, 'Grace gives, what more can we do than give thanks? What response to grace could be more vile than ingratitude?'[130] Their lack of emotion toward Paul defines their character. It is

---

125. Marshall, *The Pastoral Epistles*, pp. 771–775; Guthrie, *The Pastoral Epistles*, p. 157; Knight, *The Pastoral Epistles*, pp. 430–432.

126. See Grudem, *Systematic Theology*, p. 748; Fee, *1 and 2 Timothy, Titus*, p. 270.

127. Furnish, *Theology and Ethics in Paul*, p. 202.

128. Evans, 'Interpretation of 2 Corinthians', p. 26. See also Thrall, *Second Epistle to the Corinthians*, pp. 165–169, 469; Furnish, *2 Corinthians*, pp. 140, 153. For a good summary of 'brotherly love' in Paul see Morris, *Testaments of Love*, pp. 203–206.

129. Evans, 'Interpretation of 2 Corinthians', p. 27.

130. Carson, *From Triumphalism to Maturity*, p. 160.

only in a cognitive framework that Paul would be able to chastise the Corinthians for their lack of gratitude. In 2 Corinthians 2:8 the repentant is to be restored through a visible display of affection.

We see signs in 2 Corinthians of Paul's special relationship with this church. Like Jesus, Paul had those he had a special love for (Phil. 1:7).[131]

As in John, it is clear that the love between believers is a special bond of affection (Rom. 9:13–15; Gal. 6:10; Col. 2:2; 1 Cor. 13; 2 Cor. 8:16; 1 Thess. 4:9).[132] The reference of the Last Supper as a 'Love Feast' emphasizes believers' unity and visible affection for one another.[133] Paul is prone to speak of his affection for others and urge affection in the beginning and end of his letters (Eph. 5:23; Rom. 16:16; 1 Cor. 16:20, 24; 2 Cor. 13:12; 1 Thess. 5:26; Phlm. 1:7–8).[134] The reasons for loving change from being in the same social class or ethnic group to being in the family of God.[135] Certainly many of our churches would be embarrassed by the strong emotional love that Paul advocates. How many of us would write: 'Therefore, my brothers and sisters, whom I love and long for, my joy and crown, stand firm in the Lord in this way, my beloved.' (Phil. 4:1)?

In Romans 12:9–10 Paul insists that love for one another must be genuine. It must also be based on the right things: 'hate what is evil' and 'hold fast to what is good'.[136] Moo comments, 'Paul is warning about making our love a mere pretense, an outward display or emotion . . .'[137] In fact, the opposite it true, genuine emotion will show the truth of the love. If love was action how could it be judged as insincere? This would make action not out of love to be genuine love. This cannot be true.

We see a strong link in Paul between love and knowledge (Phil. 1:9): 'be of the same mind, having the same love, being in full accord and of one mind'

131. See Barrett, *The Second Epistle to the Corinthians*, pp. 89, 191, 204; Martin, *2 Corinthians*, p. 185; O'Brien, *Philippians*, p. 68; Ernst, *Die Brief an die Philipper, an Philemon, an die Kolosser, an die Epheser*, p. 40; Gnilka, *Der Philipperbrief*, p. 50.

132. Mohrlang, 'Love', pp. 575, 77; Engberg-Pedersen, *Paul and the Stoics*, pp. 276–277.

133. Marshall, *Last Supper and Lord's Supper*, pp. 110, 154; Schrage, *Der erste Brief an die Korinther*, vol. 2, pp. 454–457.

134. Patzia, *Ephesians, Colossians, Philemon*, p. 109.

135. Theissen, *The Social Setting of Pauline Christianity*, pp. 108–109, 140.

136. Günther and Link, '*agapaō*', p. 542; Cranfield, *Romans*, 630. Dunn's analysis of *agapē* in this verse leaves little doubt that the traditional understanding of love is still prevalent. Dunn, *Romans 9–16*, p. 739.

137. Moo, *Romans*, p. 775.

(Phil. 2:2). Friedrich draws the conclusion that the link between knowledge and love implies that love is not an emotion. This is clearly based on a misunderstanding of emotion as emotion, in fact, is based on understanding.[138]

Morris sees evidence of a link between knowledge and love in Paul. Paul links love and knowledge in Phil. 1:9, and 1 Cor. 13:12 ends the great love chapter with a statement about knowledge (Rom. 5:8). Morris concludes, 'For both writers [Paul and John] love is more than sentimentality and is linked with knowledge.'[139] In Eph. 4:32–5:2 the life of love is lived because 'Christ has forgiven you' and because of the example of Christ. There is good reason to love one another. Being chosen by God and the forgiveness of sins is reason to love in Colossians 3:12–15. Love is also often linked to faith in Paul (Gal. 5:6; 1 Tim. 1:14; 2 Tim. 1:13, 3:10). If faith includes a knowledge of what Christ has done for men, then love would naturally flow out of this knowledge. Notice also the listing of love, faith and knowledge together (2 Cor. 8:7–9). In this context, we should not neglect the role of the Holy Spirit in enabling the believer to love in Paul's writings (Rom. 5:5, 15:30; Gal. 5:22).[140] In as much as the Holy Spirit gives knowledge and faith, he empowers the believer with love.

We have saved an analysis of 1 Corinthians 13 to finish our study of love in Paul. The passage shows Christians how they are to love one another. Christian love is not identical to the love of the world, it has unique characteristics. This is not to say that the emotion is different, but rather that the reasons it is felt and the actions it motivates are uniquely Christian. Carson writes, 'In these verses, love is not so much defined as described; and even this description is not so much theoretical as practical.'[141] In contrast to a Greek idea of passionless virtue, he continues, 'here we find the apostle Paul insisting that the indispensable proof of authentic Christianity is a life characterized by love, that is, by a "passionate" existence'.[142]

---

138. Friedrich, 'Der Brief an die Philipper', p. 140. See also Ernst, *Die Brief an die Philipper, an Philemon, an die Kolosser, an die Epheser*, p. 41.

139. Morris, *The Cross of Jesus*, p. 61. See also Bruce, *Philippians*, p. 36; Hawthorne, *Philippians*, pp. 26–27; Bockmuehl, *Philippians*, p. 67; Furnish, *Theology and Ethics in Paul*, pp. 235–236.

140. Ladd, *A Theology of the New Testament*, p. 491; Zeisler, *Pauline Christianity*, pp. 116–117; Mohrlang, 'Love', pp. 576–577.

141. Carson, *Showing the Spirit*, p. 61. See also pp. 62–63. See also Hays, *The Moral Vision of the New Testament*, p. 35; Schrage, *Der erste Brief an die Korinther*, pp. 319–320, 327–333, 359; Dunn, *The Theology of Paul the Apostle*, p. 596.

142. Carson, *Showing the Spirit*, p. 65.

The characteristic actions of love in this passage have been taken by some scholars to mean that love is these actions. Günther and Link, suggest that 'In place of the word "love" we can put the name of Jesus Christ.' They continue, 'God's action can be defined as love.'[143] Fee agrees, 'Love is not an idea for Paul, not even a "motivating factor" for behaviour. It *is* behaviour.'[144] It is ironic that the passage itself insists that action without the emotion is useless. Fee's statement directly contradicts 13:1–3. It is clear from the passage that love is the motive, not the action itself.[145] Dunn writes, 'And without love even the most self-sacrificing, spiritual, and even faithful acts can be worth nothing.'[146] In 1 Corinthians 13 love is by definition emotional.[147] As we would expect in a cognitive framework, in 13:6–7 love is defined by the presence of other feelings. Christian love rejoices in truth and 'hopes all things' (1 Cor. 1:23–2:4). We should also not neglect the emphasis of 13:11–13. The climax of the chapter is about knowledge. As Christian knowledge increases so will Christian love.[148]

In Paul we meet a man who knows how to love and what to love. Paul is consumed by his love for God, his love for his brothers and sisters in Christ, and his love for those who have not heard the good news. This is his great motivation for ministry. He demands no less from his converts.

Love in the general epistles and Revelation

In specific passages, the same misconceptions of scholars about love are evident as we have seen elsewhere. Furnish writes: 'As in 1 Peter and Revelation so in Hebrews Christian love is viewed in terms of its visible deeds within the community.'[149]

---

143. Günther and Link, '*agapaō*', p. 544.

144. Fee, *Corinthians*, p. 628. Thiselton agrees that it is not emotive and is 'above all a *stance* or *attitude* which shows itself *in acts of will . . .*' (Thiselton, *The First Epistle to the Corinthians*, pp. 1034–1035).

145. See Barrett, *The First Epistle to the Corinthians*, p. 301 He goes on to follow Nygren in answering the question, 'what is love?' It is 'without motivation'. Notice also that love and conduct are differentiated in 1 Tim. 4:12. Bornkamm gives a good summary of the passage that supports this view (Bornkamm, *Paul*, pp. 218–219).

146. Dunn, *The Theology of Paul the Apostle*, p. 669.

147. Mohrlang, 'Love', pp. 577–578.

148. Thiselton, *The First Epistle to the Corinthians*, pp. 1069–1070.

149. Furnish, *The Love Command in the New Testament*, p. 171. See also Stauffer, '*agapaō, agapē, agapētos*', p. 52.

Love, as in the other parts of the New Testament, can be used in a generic way. In 1 Peter 3:10 the love of life is expressed. The consistent use of love referring to objects and ideals points away from Nygren's ideas and toward a cognitive theory of the emotions. The righteous are to love the good while the wicked love evil (2 Pet. 2:15; Rev. 22:15).[150] In Hebrews 1:9 a characteristic of Christ was his love for good and hatred of evil (Ps. 45:7). Morris writes, 'The love for what is right runs through the whole of Scripture, and it is one of the important things about God.'[151]

The condemnation of the loss of love is seen in Revelation 2:4. This loss of emotion is seen as a moral lapse.[152] Some commentators have construed this to mean that love is theological understanding or action (2:5).[153] These ideas are interesting in light of the fact that he knows 'your works, your toil and your patient endurance' (2:2). Good works and theological discernment are present in the church at Ephesus (2:6). If love is by definition actions or theology then the lack of love could not be condemned. This is parallel to 1 Cor. 13 where, even though Paul says that works are not love, some commentators define love as action. Revelation 2:2–6 presents strong evidence that love is emotion.

God loves his people (Rev. 1:5; Heb. 12:6). He has a special love for believers, even when they disobey (Rev. 3:19).[154] One of only a few references that believers should love God is found in 1 Peter 1:8–9. However, similar to the writings of Paul, this is often assumed. Love for fellow believers is expressed in the list of virtues in 1 Peter 3:8. 2 Peter emphasizes the link between this love and knowledge (2 Pet. 1:5–7).[155]

The paramount importance of loving fellow believers is seen in 1 Peter 1:22 (and see also 2 Pet. 1:7; 1 Pet. 2:17; 3:8, 4:8; 5:14; Heb. 13:1; Jude 2; Jas 2:5). According to Michaels this is in a cognitive context. 'The single command of

150. See Bauckham, *Jude, 2 Peter*, p. 268.

151. Morris, 'Love', in *DLNT*, p. 694.

152. Beasley-Murray, *Revelation*, p. 75; Morris, *Revelation*, p. 60; Kraft, *Die Offenbarung des Johannes*, pp. 57–58.

153. Wall, *Revelation*, p. 71; Beale, *Revelation*, p. 230. If love is about a lack of Christian action as Lohse insists, how does it grow cold? (*Die Offenbarung des Johannes*, p. 22). Ladd writes, 'Doctrinal purity and loyalty can never be a substitute for love' (*Revelation*, p. 39).

154. Morris, 'Love', in *DLNT*, pp. 694–695.

155. Davids, *Peter*, pp. 124–125. Note also the emphasis on unity of mind in 1 Pet. 3:8. Charles gives a good summary of the importance of knowledge in 2 Peter (Charles, 'Virtue Amidst Vice', pp. 132–134).

vv. 22–25 to "love one another unremittingly from the heart", is set in a strongly theological context: a reminder of the assured realities of spiritual purification and the new birth.'[156] This special love for others in the church was, according to Morris, 'because they themselves were now loving people'.[157] There is no reason for it, as believers can be fallible and hard to love. But Morris misses the point – there is reason to love other believers; they are family, loved and chosen by God. Best argues that, 'the total phrase implies a steady resolve to love with the whole being involved; love can be no passing emotion'.[158] This is an interesting comment in view of the command to love 'deeply from the heart' and his own contention that it means with the 'whole being'. Does emotion imply that love is short lived? From our analysis it does not. The duration and intensity of the emotion has everything to do with the cognition behind it and nothing to do with the emotion itself.

Love in the New Testament

Love is an emotion. As with any emotion, a Christian world view will have unique reasons for love and distinct ideas about what action and behaviour it should motivate. With Carson, we must also refute the argument that God's love must be fundamentally different from ours, that the only similarity between God's love and our love is self-communication, not emotion or feeling. Emotional love is fundamental in God and people.[159] Our goal is to bring out the ideas about love found in the New Testament that tell us about emotion and to ascertain how it was perceived by the writers. There are a number of recurring themes.

Loving God is related to knowing God. If you do not love God you do not truly believe. The Bible does not require blind love; love is based on

---

156. Michaels, *1 Peter*, p. 80. See also Morris, 'Love', in *DLNT*, p. 696; Goppelt, *Der Erste Petrusbrief*, pp. 129–134; Brox, *Die erste Petrusbrief*, p. 86; Grudem, *1 Peter*, p. 89.

157. Morris, 'Love', in *DLNT*, pp. 694, 697. See his similar comments about Jas 2:8. See also Furnish, *The Love Command in the New Testament*, pp. 163–166. The vice list that follows is an illustration of what people who love each other do not do (Best, *1 Peter*, p. 96).

158. Best, *1 Peter*, p. 94. Cranfield agrees that it 'is not just a matter of the emotions, whether warm feeling for the brethren in general or even for particular brothers, but involves the will and work of strenuous effort'. We can agree that it involves effort, but this does not preclude emotion in a cognitive understanding. Cranfield, *1 and 2 Peter and Jude*, p. 58.

159. Carson, *The Difficult Doctrine of the Love of God*, p. 29. See also pp. 46–47.

knowledge.[160] Love for even the vilest of people is possible because of the truths expressed in the New Testament. Love is felt because they are made in the image of God, God values them, and in reality each of us is guilty. Knowing that God loved us 'while we were still sinners' gives us reason to love the worst sinners around us. Solomon, an important cognitive theorist, writes that a universal love requires a 'radical overhaul' of our values.[161] The New Testament agrees. A radical transformation of the believer's values will lead to genuine love for neighbour.

Schrage writes: 'it is impossible to overlook the high value New Testament ethics itself places on reason and rational knowledge'.[162] In looking at love in the New Testament we find a repeated appeal to knowledge, reason and wisdom. The cognitive nature of love is also apparent in the special relationships of love that are present throughout the New Testament: God loves the son in a special way, Jesus has a special relationship and love for his disciples, Jesus even has a disciple 'whom he loves', and members of the church are to have a unique love for one another.[163] These significant relationships are based on cognitive features: Jesus is God's son; Jesus chose the disciples; the church is the believer's family.

Most experts do not give any reason for why God loves or why people are to love each other. Although many of his points are disputed, Nygren's idea that New Testament love is always spontaneous and for no reason is still widely accepted. Some of the worst abuses of Nygren and *TDNT* are corrected in recent literature, but nowhere do we find an informed view of love as a cognitive emotion as a prerequisite for understanding the texts. Love is never adequately defined in its most basic sense. Nygren's misunderstanding centres around not understanding the distinction between love that is deserved and love for a reason.[164] Certainly the wayward son may not deserve or merit the love of the parent, but regardless of this, the son has immeasurable value, for he is a son. This is good reason to love, even to motivate the cross.[165]

---

160. Bornkamm, *Paul*, p. 152.

161. Solomon, *The Passions*, p. 339.

162. Schrage, *The Ethics of the New Testament*, p. 6.

163. For a summary of God's special love for his people see Carson, *The Difficult Doctrine of the Love of God*, pp. 18–19.

164. Furnish, *Theology and Ethics in Paul*, pp. 128–129.

165. See Stuhlmacher *Grundlegung Von Jesus zu Paulus*, p. 160; Nussbaum, *Upheavals of Thought*, p. 51.

Love is prominent as a motivation for action both for God and men. Often this has been interpreted as love being synonymous to the action itself. However, a cognitive understanding of love allows it to be seen in its proper light; as emotion that is separate from action. Those authors who make love synonymous with action reduce morality to a code of duty. Calvin writes, 'Those duties, however, are not fulfilled by the mere discharge of them, though none be omitted, unless it is done from a pure feeling of love.'[166] As the story of the woman who anointed Jesus' feet shows, he is moved by full, extravagant, and wholehearted love that motivates radical action.[167]

Perhaps the most meaningful conclusion I can bring to the discussion beyond identifying major areas of misinterpretation is the unifying element that a cognitive understanding of love brings to our theology. Love as a cognitive emotion fits with all the uses in the New Testament. There is no need to formulate a special definition of love when it is used in theological contexts. Although love may have different objects and intensity, the most basic concept remains the same.

The New Testament uses the word 'love' in much the same way that we do. It is used to refer to all manner of objects, good and bad. Unfortunately, many scholars have strongly disputed this point. They have redefined love in ways that may lead to misunderstanding many of the important texts. After a good discussion of 14 texts that do not match his definition of love, Morris writes:

> Such passages show common usages of the term love, references that anyone might make. They would be significant if they comprised the major usage of the New Testament, because they would show that the New Testament sees love in much the same way as do other writings. But such references are few, and do not suggest the distinctively Christian concept of love.[168]

In other words, any mention of love in a theological context means one thing, and any mention of love in a non-theological context means another. Morris' view is the view of many other scholars and is flavoured by his misunderstanding of the nature of emotion. Specifically, *agapē* love cannot be commanded and

---

166. Calvin, *Institutes*, translated by Beveridge, 3.7.7.

167. Barclay, *The Mind of Jesus*, pp. 198–199; Berger, *Theologiegeschechte des Urchristentums*, p. 323.

168. Morris, *Testaments of Love*, p. 225. See also pp. 275–276.

is totally uncaused. These positions are not supported by any textual evidence but are based on false philosophical presuppositions. Can we say that God expects less than the passionate love we naturally give our spouse or our children? A cognitive understanding of emotion quickly lets us dispose of this unproductive distinction and allows us to interpret the texts correctly. God requires a full and passionate love for him and for others. While this point is understood, we should not neglect the distinction that is clearly seen in the objects of love that are characteristic of the believer and the unbeliever. The believer may legitimately love strawberries or race cars but he is characterized by his love for God and his love for people. These great loves, if properly felt and based on good theology, will lead to righteous action. The wicked are characterized by their love for objects such as acclaim, money, or sin itself. Their love is impersonal and selfish and will lead to sinful action and feelings.

Love as the greatest commandment is also seen more clearly within a cognitive understanding. Love is the most basic emotion and Jesus proclaims that it is the cornerstone on which Christian ethics are built. Only love can be the centre of Christian ethics both internally and as a motivation for action. Love is central to joy, hope, anger at sin, sorrow over sin, being slow to anger against others and the whole range of righteous emotion. In short, the New Testament view of love matches up well with modern cognitive definitions.[169]

In speaking of Peter's conversation with Christ after the denial Morris aptly writes: 'But in doing so Jesus does not ask him about his faith or his courage or his ability to lead or anything of the sort. The one question that matters in this situation in the question of love.'[170] In reinstating Peter to leadership, Jesus' priority is finding the emotional state of his heart, 'Do you love me?' In asking this question there can be no self-deception – Jesus is known as Lord and Saviour. A new heart has been birthed within. The disciples' love will motivate the passionate proclamation of the gospel in both word and deed. It would change their world.

---

169. Pavelsky, 'The Commandment of Love', pp. 418–442. Stuhlmacher emphasizes the emotional nature of the command. Stuhlmacher, *Grundlegung Von Jesus zu Paulus*, p. 101. We have not dealt with the idea of self love in the New Testament. It does not figure prominently in the texts. It is assumed that people love themselves. Morris gives a good defence of this position. Morris, *Testaments of Love*, pp. 199–203. See also Moo, *Romans*, p. 816; Tannehill, *Luke*, p. 182; Luz, *Das Evangelium nach Matthäus*, vol. 3, p. 281.

170. Morris, *Testaments of Love*, p. 181.

Joy

The section on love has set the stage for much of what we will find in study-ing other emotions. In joy we find many of the same patterns in the New Testament that we observed in the Old Testament. Joy is felt for good reason, often over those people and things that we love. Those who love God will take joy in him and praise him because of who he is and what he has done.

There is a diverse vocabulary of joy which could take many pages to analyse and differentiate. For this task I must refer you to others (Louw and Nida, *TDNT*, *NIDNTT*, and Morrice, 'Joy'). There are distinctions between the words, but, as these sources confirm, we may say that they all have similar positive content. It may be advantageous to differentiate joy and happiness at some points but we too easily forget that they have many of the same char-acteristics. It is not my intention to unwind the separate meanings of different words but only to demonstrate the emotional character of joy as a concept in the New Testament. In the LXX words are often used interchangeably.[171] The context must be studied carefully to differentiate specific meanings. We must confirm that all cognates have a basic emotional content.

Typical mistakes in dealing with vocabulary were outlined early in this Chapter. These mistakes are often made when defining the words used for joy. Words are given theological content, secular and spiritual meanings are distin-guished, and emotional content is often downplayed. Hauck writes, 'In the New Testament *makarios, makarizō, makarismos* refers overwhelmingly to the distinctive religious joy which accrues to man from his share in the salvation of the kingdom of God.'[172] The word itself does not have this special meaning as we could prove by its usage in the New Testament. Instead, its objects in certain contexts may give this meaning to a particular passage. In New Testament studies, the emotion of joy in the New Testament is not often seen as significant. Theological 'joy' is held to be important while the significance of how a Christian should feel is rarely mentioned.

Morrice writes in his conclusion to discussing the vocabulary of joy: 'Life in Christ and the hope of glory beyond this present world of time and space both bring this inward state of joy to the Christian.'[173] The often used cliché of 'inner' joy gives the idea that the joy of faith can dwell inside without outward

---

171. Beyreuther and Finkenrath, '*chairō*', p. 357.

172. Hauck, '*makarios, makarizō, makarismos*', p. 367. Warfield also differentiates spiritual joy from secular. Warfield, 'The Emotional Life of Our Lord', p. 126.

173. Morrice, *Joy in the New Testament*, p. 75.

expression (the specific meaning of this is seldom explained). The word 'inner' provides a way to assert that it is not an emotion while maintaining the claim that joy is present. Where does the New Testament speak of this 'inner' joy? I will argue that the predominant meaning in the New Testament is emotion plain and simple. Joy experienced by Christians was something to be seen by the world and drew people to Christ.

A prevalent definition of joy is expressed in popular form by Calvin Miller:

> Many Christians confuse happiness with joy, as did I. Happiness is about a buoyant emotion that results from the momentary plateaus of well-being that characterize our lives. Joy is bedrock stuff, on the other hand. Joy is a confidence that operates irrespective of our moods. Joy is the certainty that all is well, however we feel.[174]

Parallel ideas can be found in many standard reference works. Another characteristic of these accounts is that joy is given by God and is not based on circumstance.[175]

According to this definition, it would seem that a very sombre theology professor, rarely smiling, could be said to be the most joyful person you know. After all, she knows the contents of the gospel better than anyone you know. Would we want to have this kind of joy? The joy we desire is full of life and vitality. Joy is not confidence, it is emotion, it is a bounce in our step and a smile. As we grow to understand the worldview of the gospel we will increase our joy. The reason that Christian joy is above circumstance is not because it is present 'however we feel' but because it is based on unchangeable facts.

Morrice presents the most thorough analysis of joy in the New Testament and he also makes many of the same mistakes as Miller in defining joy. He follows the method of *TDNT* and does not attempt to analyse the words' emotional content but rather gives a thorough catalogue of their usage in the Old and New Testaments. From this, the reader is meant to understand the words' meanings. He emphasizes that if we understand the theological content of the words we will understand joy. Unfortunately, it would seem to be possible to read his book and come away not having a good idea of what joy is.[176] Yet, it is clear from Morrice's analysis that the source of Christian's joy is holding Christian beliefs. We affirm that the most basic definition of joy is the feeling that comes from something good happening to an object you love.

---

174. Miller, *Joy*, pp. 10–11.
175. Davis, 'Joy', p. 588.
176. Morrice, *We Joy in God*, p. 86. See also Beck, *Jesus and Personality Theory*, pp. 45–62.

Joy in the Gospels

Joy was the hallmark of the coming of Jesus. The Magi, his parents, angels, shepherds, Anna, and Simeon, rejoiced at his coming. Jesus' first advent of preaching was an occasion for joy. The Holy Spirit's ministry is linked to joy. People who are filled with the Holy Spirit have great joy. The new faith found joy in celebrating their God and his worship. The presence of Jesus on earth gave reason to rejoice.[177] Beilner attempts to differentiate a believer's joy from emotional experience in Luke. He writes: 'the highly emotional joy of the disciples even constitutes an obstacle to their believing in the resurrection (Luke 24:41).'[178] In our view the verse's meaning is more accurately about the fact that their joy was so great, they could hardly believe it was real. The emotion was joy of utter amazement that Jesus was actually alive. The joy was confirmation of unbelievable truth, not obstacle to belief.

Luke has been called the gospel of joy and it gives many reasons why joy is felt. In some places it is felt for very normal, non-theological, reasons (Luke 23:8). Beyreuther and Finkenrath outline the prevalent reasons for joy in the text of Luke/Acts: (1) the coming of John the Baptist, the coming of Jesus, and the new age of salvation that their ministry inaugurates (Luke 1:14, 44, 68; 2:11); (2) the miracles of Jesus and the manifest power of God (Luke 13:17, 10:17); (3) 'God's electing love' (10:20); (4) the mercy and grace of God (Luke 15:7, 10, 23) and the repentance and restoration of lost sinners (Luke 15:6, 9, 32); (5) suffering for the sake of Christ (Acts 5:41); (6) the salvation of the Gentiles (Acts 11:23, 13:48, 15:3, 8:8, 39, 15:31). The gospel ends on a note of great joy (Luke 24:11, 41, 52).[179]

Jesus specifically shows people the reasons to rejoice that the kingdom provides. He teaches, do not be happy (*makarios*) about the things of this world, instead be happy about kingdom values. The switching of the object on which the emotion is based points to a cognitive understanding of emotion. An intellectual change of thought patterns is in view and it assumes that happiness is linked to what the mind concentrates on (Luke 11:27–28, 10:20: *chara*). He gives general reasons for being happy (Matt. 13:16; 16:17; 24:46; Luke 7:23; 10:23; 12:37, 43; 14:14–15).[180] In Luke 10:20–21 joy is

---

177. Schillebeeckx, *Jesus: An Experiment in Christology*, p. 203; Morrice, *We Joy in God*, pp. 80, 15, 17, 36–46.

178. Beilner, 'Joy', p. 440.

179. Beyreuther and Finkenrath, '*chairō*', pp. 358–359. See also Morrice, *Joy in the New Testament*, p. 367; Ernst, *Das Evangelium nach Lukas*, p. 317.

180. See Garland, 'Blessing and Woe', p. 79.

clearly based on eternal reality – it is based on membership in a new community.

Joy in the parables of Jesus is also informative. The kingdom of God is something in which to rejoice (Matt. 13:44, 25:21). Jeremias concludes in Matthew 13:44, 'When that great joy, beyond measure, seizes a man, it caries him away, penetrates his inmost being, subjugates his mind. All else seems valueless compared with that surpassing worth.'[181] Luke 15 is an especially powerful example. In summing up the message of these parables Jeremias uses joy at least nine times. The emphasis of the chapter is God's joy at people's redemption. He concludes that the point is 'simply and solely the joy of finding what was lost'. We might conclude that these parables show the value of the object that was recovered. The great emotion is a direct reflection of the value given to the object.[182] Linnemann speaks not only of the joy of finding but 'emotion felt over a loss'.[183] Unfortunately, Jeremias also writes that this emotion must 'not be ascribed to God'.[184] These parables have a central place in the book of Luke. The mercy, love, and joy of God are paramount.[185]

By telling these stories, Jesus criticizes the Pharisees' reaction to sinners. Their negative emotion portrays the state of their heart. In contrast, God rejoices over the salvation of sinners (Luke 15:7–10; 15:31–32). A similar illustration is found in Luke 19. Zacchaeus receives Jesus with great joy while the religious leaders felt disturbed that Jesus would associate with Zacchaeus. As we saw in Chapter one, this is one of the major implications of a cognitive theory of emotions. A person's emotional state will betray their moral character. Jesus uses this principle to illustrate the differences between the heart of the unrighteous Pharisees and the heart of God. Morrice points out that the

---

181. Jeremias, *Rediscovering the Parables*, p. 158. See also Wenham, *The Parables of Jesus*, pp. 105, 201–209; Schnackenburg, *Matthäusevangelium: 1, 1–16, 20*, p. 128; Young, *Jesus the Jewish Theologian*, pp. 158–159.

182. Jeremias, *Rediscovering the Parables*, p. 107. See also Blomberg, *Interpreting the Parables*, pp. 180–181; Marshall, *Luke*, pp. 597–611. 'Whatever else may be true in the parable of the lost sheep, the focus is on the joy' (Snodgrass, 'Parable', p. 599).

183. Linnemann, *Parables of Jesus*, p. 66.

184. Jeremias, *The Parables of Jesus*, p. 135.

185. Fitzmyer, *Luke*, p. 1071. 'The point of the parable is not only the shepherd's gracious willingness and initiative to seek out the lost, but also to celebrate its finding with joy' (p. 1075). See also Scott, *Hear Then the Parables*, pp. 101–103, 118; Becker, *Jesus of Nazareth*, pp. 141, 238–241. Theissen and Merz, *The Historical Jesus*, p. 265. True acceptance of the kingdom requires emotional response.

joy of the Father is the root of the believer's joy. The fact that God feels like this, his love, and forgiveness is a reason for their own joy.[186]

The gospels also relate instances of people rejoicing over evil. This is further evidence that joy is a morally neutral cognitive emotion (Mark 14:11 *chara*). *Chara* is used in John 16:20, 22 for both rejoicing over evil and good.[187] Those who are evil rejoice over evil. Beyond this, those who pursue hedonistic joy for its own sake are not wise and their actions are condemned (Luke 12:19; 16:19).

The beatitudes are particularly important for our study. The emphasis of the New Testament beatitudes is usually eschatological. Hauk observes, 'In keeping with the tension into which the dawn of the age of salvation sets the soul, the NT beatitudes have great emotional force (Matt. 13:16; Rev. 19:9).'[188] They are often used to contrast the state of the believer with the state of those who do not believe. The usual formula used for a beatitude in the New Testament, *makarios hos*, does not parallel normal Greek usage but instead follows the LXX. This points to the New Testament's independence from Greek ideas. In the beatitudes of Jesus there is a reversal of 'all human values'. The humble, weak and poor are those who are happy.[189] How is this possible? Contentment is not found in material things but in following Christ. The Synoptics see the blessing or happiness in this life as having a direct correlation to the disciples' status in the coming kingdom.[190]

How much emotional content is in the word *makarios*? Although the beatitudes of Jesus are the central text in this discussion, we will not limit our discussion to the gospels. We have seen in the Old Testament that a good case can be made that beatitudes have significant emotional content. Louw and Nida present the word under 'Attitudes and Emotions: Happy, Glad, Joyful'. Both Friberg and Louw and Nida define it as an emotional state that is due to 'favourable circumstances'.[191] When it comes to beatitudes of eschatological blessing, Revelation is of special interest. Those who persevere will receive a reward. The attainment of the kingdom *is makarios*.[192]

---

186. Morrice, *We Joy in God*, pp. 80, 5–8, 11; Bornkamm, *Jesus of Nazareth*, pp. 84–85.

187. Mann, *Mark*, p. 560. Witherington gives a good summary. *John's Wisdom*, p. 265.

188. Hauk, *'makarios, makarizō, makarismos'*, p. 368.

189. Hauk, *'makarios, makarizō, makarismos'*, pp. 367–368. See also Ernst, *Das Evangelium nach Lukas*, p. 169.

190. Hauk, *'makarios, makarizō, makarismos'*, pp. 369.

191. Louw and Nida, 25.118; Friberg, *makarios*.

192. Hauk, *'makarios, makarizō, makarismos'*, p. 369; Becker, *Blessing, Blessed, Happy*, p. 216; Betz, *The Sermon on the Mount*, p. 93.

A few comments about *makarios* in the Pauline corpus are appropriate. Passages in Timothy are the only ones in the Bible that associate *makarios* with God (1 Tim. 1:11; 6:15; see also Titus 2:13). Romans 4:7 and 14:22 parallel the ideas expressed in the Old Testament. It makes sense that emotional happiness would be the state of the man who is at peace with his own conscience and free from sin. Finally, 1 Corinthians 7:40 seems to imply a state of contentment or emotional happiness.

Many commentators wish to see the content of the word as a non-emotional idea of blessing. Hawthorne writes: 'the translation "happy"/"count happy" is hardly the best, for "happy" suggests an emotional reaction based on circumstances, while in fact *makarios*/*makarizo* suggests rather a reaction to whatever life may bring based on the faithfulness of God.'[193] Carson agrees that happy is not a good translation of the beatitudes. 'Blessedness cannot be reduced to happiness.'[194] In Hawthorne's own definition, the fact that happiness is based on the unchangeable faithfulness of God is a way to describe a cognitive emotion. (Matt. 25:34; Mark 11:9).

Garland writes that in the gospels *makarios* 'indicates a state of happiness or joy associated with the eschatological new day occasioned by the presence and activity of Jesus'. Hagner is among those who emphasize the meaning as emotional. He also emphasizes the cognitive nature of the beatitudes; there are good reasons given for this happiness.[195] Garland continues by saying that Jesus' beatitudes ascribe happiness based on the new eschatological reality. Disciples are happy because of the new reality of the kingdom.[196] In both Luke and Matthew persecution and future reward are good reasons for joy (*chairō*) at the end of the beatitudes (Matt. 5:12; Luke 6:23).[197] Betz writes: 'As the second part makes clear (vv. 12b–c), gladness and jubilation are called for at the present time, not only in the eschatological future.' He continues: 'The faithful disciple can justifiably be joyful even now, because they can be sure that their reward is awaiting them in heaven and that God himself as the guarantor of justice is guarding the treas-

---

193. Hawthorne, *Joy*, p. 602.

194. Carson, *The Sermon on the Mount*, p. 18. See also Grudem, *Systematic Theology*, p. 218.

195. Garland, 'Blessing and Woe', p. 78. Hagner, *Matthew 1–13*, pp. 88, 92. He writes, 'it is confidence about the future that can and should produce joy in the present' (p. 95). This is a 'deep inner joy' (p. 91). Luz agrees that the primary meaning is happy. Luz, *Matthew 1–7*, p. 232. See also Davies and Allison, *Matthew*, vol. 1, p. 434.

196. Garland, 'Blessing and Woe', p. 78. See also Luz, *Matthew 1–7*, p. 242.

197. Marshall, *Luke*, p. 254; Evans, *Luke*, p. 108.

ure.'[198] Some have emphasized that the reason for this happiness is a hope of the afterlife, while others have emphasized the future coming of the kingdom.[199] The important thing to realize is that both are cognitive reasons to be happy now. In formal beatitudes we cannot insist that *makarios* has an exclusive emotional meaning as it is part of a pronouncement of blessing and well-being, but we should not easily pass over the idea of emotional joy that is also present.

The emphasis of John in his presentation of joy is usually said to be eschatological. Bultmann insists that joy in John is different from the world's joy for this reason. 'But this joy, although a gift of the Revealer, is never a definitely realized state, but always lies ahead of the believer as something to be realized' (John 15:11).[200] The eschatological emphasis is important but we need to be careful that this is not allowed to rob joy of present emotion, which is also clear: we feel joy now because we believe things about the future. A cognitive theory of emotions shows us how present emotional joy could be based on future events (John 16:33). Joy will not be complete until the coming age at which time it will come into fullness.[201]

Bultmann disagrees with this ideal of joy by writing 'it has no describable object in which it rejoices' (John 16:22–23).[202] Conzelmann agrees: 'The presupposition of its perfection is the very fact that it has no perceptible basis.'[203] This contention seems to come from Bultmann's own ideas and not from the text. It is similar to the tendency we saw in love, where *agapē* love was to be for no reason. The text itself refutes this non-cognitive idea. It is clear that joy in John has good reasons. In the verse Bultmann cites it is because they will see Jesus again.

The presence of Jesus and his ministry in John have special emphasis as reason for joy (John 3:29; 4:36; 8:56). The fact that Jesus is going to prepare a place for us, that he will be with the Father, that he will return, and the Holy Spirit's presence in a believer's life are good reasons to have joy. Smith writes about 20:21, 26: 'Joy and peace, unlike life or eternal life, are not the subject of

---

198. Betz, *The Sermon on the Mount*, pp. 151–152.

199. Vorster, 'Stoic and Early Christians on Blessedness', p. 48.

200. Bultmann, *Theology*, vol. 2, p. 83. See also Bultmann, *Theology*, vol. 1, p. 339; Beyreuther and Finkenrath, *'chairō'*, p. 359.

201. Morrice, *Joy in the New Testament*, pp. 105–110; Becker, *Das Evangelium nach Johannes: Kapitel 11–21*, p. 502.

202. Bultmann, *Theology*, vol. 2, p. 84.

203. Conzelmann, *'chairō, chara, synchairō'*, p. 371. Schnackenburg points to the presence of Christ and promise for the future as reason for the change from sorrow to joy (*The Gospel According to St John*, vol. 3, pp. 157–159).

theological reflection, but are simply spoken of as if the hearer, or reader, would immediately understand.'[204]

Jesus drew people to himself. Some of this was due to the presence of joy in his life and ministry. John 15:11 makes it clear that the joy of Jesus was also to be experienced by his disciples.[205] Beyond this, it shows that one of the reasons for the coming of Christ was to bring joy (John 16:24; 17:13). In John 15 a believer's relation to God and the assurance of God's love is to bring joy as it brought joy to Jesus. Love for Christ is also linked with joy (John 14:28).

The gospel of joy was born into a world that was difficult, sullen and without purpose. The prevalent philosophies of the day did not aim at producing a joyful life. The joy of Christianity was a radical departure from the spirit of the age.[206] The gospels radiate joy as the story of salvation is good news, a reason to rejoice.

Joy in Pauline literature

Joy is an important concept in the Pauline corpus. According to Morrice, 40 per cent of the uses of joy in the New Testament are found in these books. It is something that the Christian is to feel consistently and it is prevalent in the apostle's own life. (Rom. 14:17).[207] Morrice summarizes:

> Paul proceeds to point out that since 'the sacrifice is offered Christ himself', we ought to do away with all corruption and wickedness and live true and sincere Christian lives in a continual festival of joy (1 Cor. 5:7f.) . . . the Christian ought to aim at purity and sincerity and to make his whole life a festival celebration.[208]

Paul is encouraged in hard times as he thinks of the glory that is to come. In fact, the future glory is tied to the present suffering (2 Cor. 4:17; see also Acts 5:41).[209] Strong reasons for perseverance and having positive emotions in suffering are given in Romans 8:12–39. There is a purpose for it. 'God is for us . . . Who will separate us from the love of Christ?' (1 Cor. 15:55–58; 2 Cor.

---

204. Smith, *The Theology of John*, pp. 150–151.

205. Morrice, *Joy in the New Testament*, pp. 85–90. See also Conzelmann, '*chairō, chara, synchairō*', p. 370. Conzelmann believes that joy in this verse 'is lifted up to the theological plane'. We must instead emphasize that the truths expressed bring great joy *down* into the fabric of life.

206. Morrice, *Joy in the New Testament*, pp. 11–14.

207. Morrice, 'Joy'. Notice the context of knowledge in this passage.

208. Morrice, *Joy in the New Testament*, pp. 116–117.

209. Pesch, *Die Apostelgeschichte*, vol. 1, p. 221.

4:14–18; 8:1–2; 1 Thess. 1:2–7; 2 Thess. 1:3–5).[210] Paul presents an excellent summary of his reasons for having positive emotion in hard times:

> . . .because we know that the one who raised the Lord Jesus will raise us also with Jesus, and will bring us with you into his presence. Yes, everything is for your sake, so that grace, as it extends to more and more people, may increase thanksgiving, to the glory of God. So we do not lose heart. Even though our outer nature is wasting away, our inner nature is being renewed day by day. For this slight momentary affliction is preparing us for an eternal weight of glory beyond all measure, because we look not at what can be seen but at what cannot be seen; for what can be seen is temporary, but what cannot be seen is eternal. (2 Cor. 4:14–18)

Philippians is an illustration of joy in the midst of suffering as it is an epistle that is written from prison and is full of joy. Morrice writes, 'The joy of Paul comes to its climax in the letter to the Philippians.' There are 19 uses of joy in this letter. The Philippian church is a great source of joy for Paul.[211] Paul takes joy in the Philippians themselves, their salvation, and their partnership with him (1:4–5; 4:1; Rom. 16:19; Col. 2:5; 1 Thess. 2:17; 3:9).[212] Similarly, Bruce writes of the Thessalonians, 'But nothing can disguise the pride and delight which they take in their converts themselves, who have become so dear to them (v. 8). As parents rejoice in their children and cherish high hopes for them, so is it with the writers and their converts.'[213] Paul takes joy in good relationships and mutual fellowship (1 Cor. 16:17; 2 Cor. 2:2; 7:6; Phil. 2:28).[214] Believers are to feel with the joyful and the hurting (Rom. 12:15).

---

210. Wanamaker writes, 'The joy of the early Christians was based on their certainty of future salvation regardless of what happened to them in the present' (1 Thess. 2:19) (Wanamaker, *Thessalonians*).

211. Morrice, *Joy in the New Testament*, p. 126.

212. These are reasons for thanks in 1:4–6 and also seem linked to Paul's joy. See O'Brien, *Philippians*, pp. 58–63, 66. The language of 1 Thess. 2:19 is highly emotional which shows Paul's care for his converts. Morris, *Thessalonians*, p. 67. See also Marshall, *Thessalonians*, p. 87.

213. Bruce, *Thessalonians*, p. 56.

214. Hughes, *Second Epistle to the Corinthians*, pp. 262–263; Bruce, *The Epistles to the Colossians, to Philemon, and to the Ephesians*, pp. 210, 214. Paul's feeling for Onesimus is deeply emotional. Martin emphasizes that Paul's joy in 2 Corinthians 7 is not only about seeing Titus but about the message he brings. The passage presents many good reasons for joy. Martin, *2 Corinthians*, pp. 225, 229, 246.

Paul rejoices in the proclamation of Christ (1:18), the unity of the body, and the Philippians' renewed concern for him (4:10). Even as Paul's body is failing, his joy is great (1:14–18). The Philippians are commanded to rejoice in God himself (3:1; 4:4).[215] After a good paragraph on how cognitive factors were behind Paul's joy in Philippians, Hawthorne writes, 'They thus came to realize that when he talked of joy he was, in reality describing a settled state of mind characterized by *eirēnē* ("peace"), an attitude that viewed the world with all of its ups and downs with equanimity, a confident way of looking at life that was rooted in faith.'[216] This statement seems to portray a strong misunderstanding of joy as emotion. However, Hawthorne himself clearly explains the strong emotions of Paul that are based on his relationship with the church.[217] We must also take issue with Bockmuehl's statement, 'Joy in the Lord is not a feeling but an attitude, and as such it can be positively commanded.'[218] A good summary of the reason for Christian joy is found in 3:20: 'But our citizenship is in heaven, and it is from there that we are expecting a Saviour, the Lord Jesus Christ.'

Moving beyond Philippians, we find good reason to rejoice in Romans 12:12: 'Rejoice in hope.' There is often a relationship in Paul between joy, faith, hope and grace.[219] This is logical if joy is a cognitive emotion. They are based on the same basic understanding of the gospel. Unfortunately, some scholars have taken this relationship as meaning that joy has essentially the same meaning as these words instead of joy being based on similar theological concepts.[220]

In Galatians the church is to rejoice over their freedom as Sarah rejoiced over the birth of Isaac (4:27). Morrice writes, 'Christians should be able to rejoice in their new-found freedom no matter what the circumstances are.'[221] In Colossians 1 there is also a good example of joy based on cognitive reasons. In 1:9–14, there is an emphasis on knowledge and the work of Christ in redemption. Morrice refers to this as 'inward joy' implying that it is not highly emotional. He goes on to rightly say, 'All these blessings ought to make us joyful in spite of any trials that we are called upon to endure patiently.'[222]

---

215. Notice the emotional and cognitive context of 4:4. See also Bruce, *Philippians*, p. 31; Beyreuther and Finkenrath, *'chairō'*, p. 360; O'Brien. *Philippians*, p. 486.

216. Hawthorne, *Philippians*, p. 18. See also Friedrich, 'Der Brief an die Philipper', p. 158.

217. See Hawthorne, *Philippians*, pp. 18, 22–25.

218. Bockmuehl, *Philippians*, p. 59. See also Cousar, *The Letters of Paul*, pp. 131–132.

219. Morrice, 'Joy'.

220. Beilner takes joy in Phil. 1:25 as almost identical to faith. Beilner, 'Joy', pp. 441.

221. Morrice, *Joy in the New Testament*, p. 114.

222. Morrice, *Joy in the New Testament*, p. 125.

Christian joy, as we found in the Gospels, is often based on eschatology. Joy in Romans 15:10 and Galatians 4:27 are to Bultmann exclusively about eschatology. While the eschatological emphasis is clear, certainly the emotion is very real in these texts. These verses present a situation where emotional joy is the right response.[223]

In 2 Corinthians 9:6–7 giving is blessed by God when it is characterized by positive emotion while God is not pleased with reluctant giving (Prov. 22:9). Joyful giving is the signature of authenticity (2 Cor. 8:2–3).[224] Paul's appeal for funds is couched in emotion. This emotional evaluation of giving makes sense in a cognitive framework. A cheerful gift portrays the right understanding of the believer while a reluctant gift portrays the stinginess of the person's heart (Rom. 12:8, contrast Phil. 2:14).[225]

1 Corinthians 13:6 is an important verse for our study: 'it [love] does not rejoice [chara] in wrongdoing, but rejoices in the truth'. The virtue of joy is determined by its object and what gives a person joy shows the reality of their love. Finally, love as the basic emotion is linked to joy.[226]

Joy is found in doing the work of Christ. Paul was joyful over the growth of the church and the love of friends. Thinking about kingdom truths made him happy, even in the midst of pain and difficulty.[227] Paul's view of joy is well summarized in Romans 5:1–11 (this assumes we can take kauchaomai to mean joy as the NIV and NLT translate). Here we find a powerful mix of theology and emotion. The theological truths give Paul reason to rejoice at all times.[228]

Joy in the general epistles and Revelation

We have seen similar cognitive patterns in Paul and the gospels. These are also seen clearly in the later New Testament. There are also some areas of emphasis that are notable in Peter and Revelation.

---

223. Bultmann, 'euphrainō, euphrosynē', p. 772. See also Conzelmann, 'chairō, chara, synchairō', p. 369.

224. Piper, Desiring God, pp. 93–98; Hafemann, 2 Corinthians, p. 332. See also Sir. 35:8. We see in this passage that Paul is willing to use high emotional pressure to promote right action.

225. Martin, 2 Corinthians, p. 253.

226. See Thiselton, The First Epistle to the Corinthians, pp. 1055–1056.

227. Morrice, We Joy in God, pp. 54–60.

228. Robinson, 'The Priesthood of Paul in the Gospel of Hope', p. 240. F. F. Bruce sees three good reasons for joy in Romans 5: the hope of glory; suffering; in God himself (Bruce, Romans, pp. 114–115).

First, there is a clear emphasis on joy being based firmly in eschatology and the coming kingdom. Of 1 Peter, Morrice writes, 'The thought of the future inheritance kept for them in heaven can bring joy in the present world' (1 Pet. 1:6).[229] Numerous reasons are given for having joy in these books. These are summarized by Hawthorne: redemption (Acts 2:46; 3:39; 1 Pet. 1:5–8); future glory (1 Pet. 4:13; Rev. 19:6–7); 'attainment of his purpose' (Jude 24); the presence of God (Acts 2:28); rain and provision (Acts 14:17); growth of the church (Acts 11:23; 13:48); an invitation to the wedding feast of the Lamb (Rev. 19:9); participation in the resurrection (Rev. 20:6).[230]

In 1 Peter 5:2 the minister of God is to have positive emotions about doing ministry. In 3 John 3–4 the author's greatest joy is that his readers are following the truth. Joy was one of the reasons for the writing of 1 John (1:4). In some contexts we see two different words used for emphasis. This may emphasize joy's emotional character and celebration (Acts 2:26; 1 Pet. 1:8; 4:13; Rev. 11:10; 19:7).

There is also an emphasis on joy in suffering in James and Peter. Both books clearly emphasize a cognitive basis for this joy. In 1 Peter 1:6–7 they are to rejoice in their salvation and in the fact that suffering will prove the validity of their faith that brings glory to God. In 1 Peter 4:13–14 they are to rejoice that they share Christ's suffering and in the glory that is to come. James 1:2–4 shows how joy comes in trials due to the knowledge (*ginōskō*) that testing brings endurance and a mature faith. In the context of James, what awaits them is reward and victory at the end of the age. All these instances provide strong cognitive reasons for why there is joy in suffering (Acts 5:41; Heb. 10:32–34). Further, this joy is strongly commanded.[231] Conzelmann recognizes the reality of joy in suffering but has no explanation for it. Without a

---

229. Morrice, *Joy in the New Testament*, p. 139. Davids gives an excellent summary of the cognitive reasons for joy that are presented in the New Testament (Davids, *Peter*, p. 55). See also Grudem, *1 Peter*, pp. 60–61.

230. Hawthorne, *Joy*, pp. 601, 604. Revelation 19 gives strong cognitive reasons for praise and joy. Beasley-Murray, *Revelation*, pp. 271–272.

231. Chester, 'The Theology of James', p. 17; Mußner, *Der Jakobusbrief*, p. 65. Moo, *James*, in *TNTC*, pp. 59–60. 'This is not a surface happiness.' Davids, *James*, in *NIBC*, p. 26. Moo rightly emphasizes 'intense' joy and writes, 'James does not, then, suggest that Christians facing trials will have no response other than joy, as if we were commanded never to be saddened by difficulties. His point, rather, is that trials should be an occasion for genuine rejoicing. Why is this so, he will explain in vv. 3–4' (Moo, *James*, PNTC, p. 53).

cognitive understanding of emotion it is difficult for commentators to explain how this is possible.[232]

The wicked rejoice (*chara*) and celebrate about the wrong things, even the killing of the godly (Rev. 11:10).[233] *Euphrainō* (festival celebration) is used in Acts 2:26, 28; 14:17 and in Revelation 11:10 for the joy of the wicked. Finally, we should not neglect that there are a number of passages where the saints rejoice that the wicked will face judgment (Rev. 11:18; 18:20). In Revelation we have clear examples of the wicked rejoicing over and loving evil and the right-eous rejoicing over the good and the downfall of the wicked.[234]

Worship

In the believer's life joy often overflows into worship for God. The act of worship is most often a joyful emotional experience. The pattern is similar to what we saw in the Old Testament. Worship is about something. It is not medi-tation, mindless ceremony, or working oneself into a religious frenzy. We should also point out Jesus' introduction to the Lord's prayer, 'And when you pray, do not keep on babbling [*battalogeō*] like pagans, for they think they will be heard because of their many words' (Matt. 6:7, NIV). Instead, it is thanks-giving and praise that is based on who God is, what He has done for his people, and the great privilege of being chosen by God.[235]

Although worship is not exclusively emotional, it is often an emotional response to a cognitive understanding. Ephesians 1:1–14 presents us with an excellent list of reasons to praise God (Phil. 2:6–11; Col. 1:12–20; 1 Tim. 3:16). Prayer, knowledge, and praise are linked (Col. 3:16; Eph. 5:17–20).[236] Those who feel thankful should worship (Jas 5:13). Beale writes of Rev. 19:2, 'Verse 2 makes it explicit that the judgement of Babylon in ch. 18 is the ground (*hoti*) for the outburst of praise in v. 1. The praise is based on God's "judgements" being "true and just".'[237] Heaven is filled with the reality of God's presence; therefore we see constant and full worship.[238] Martin concludes: 'Because of what God

---

232. Conzelmann, '*chairō, chara, synchairō*', p. 368.

233. Beasley-Murray, *Revelation*, p. 186; Ladd, *Revelation*, p. 158; Mounce, *Revelation*, p. 227.

234. Keener, *Revelation*, p. 449.

235. Martin, *Worship in the Early Church*, p. 9.

236. Peterson, 'Worship in the New Testament', p. 80; Lincoln, *The Theology of the Later Pauline Letters*, pp. 121, 144. See also Revelation 11:10. Mounce, *Revelation*, pp. 372–373.

237. Beale, *Revelation*, p. 926.

238. Peterson, 'Worship in the New Testament', pp. 87, 90. Martin outlines the reasons that God is given praise (Martin, *The Worship of God*, pp. 24–29).

has done for us – He has loved us, saved us, blessed us, kept us – and is still doing, we owe it to him to offer our tributes of corporate praise and prayer.'[239]

In some traditions the role of emotion in worship is routinely trivialized and downplayed. This may be due to a number of factors including a non-cognitive understanding of emotion, a desire to make worship a purely theological exercise, and a desire to distinguish Christian worship from other religious forms of worship or meditation. However, it seems clear that emotion was an important element in New Testament worship. In fact, right theology believed in the heart will mandate emotional praise.

Some scholars take the opposite approach. To them worship is an experience that is not encumbered by rational thought. The misunderstanding of worship as an internal state that is not based on cognition is epitomized by Leonard. He writes, 'The confrontation with the numinous is a direct apprehension in the inward being of the worshiper; the intellectual, moral, and even psychological categories that describe and define it are secondary to this intuitive encounter. Awareness of the numinous issues from the deepest level of apprehension in the human soul, transcending the rational mind.'[240]

A cognitive view of emotion can bring these two extremes into balance. Worship includes genuine emotion based on genuine understanding.

Joy in the New Testament

I have found no better way to describe joy in the New Testament than a quote from a young theologian. Janet, 19, says 'Joy is that happy exultation when we jump up and down and yell, "yippee!" and the world smiles.' The Christian view is similar to the Stoics in that it is the belief system that determines the person's happiness. Vorster writes, 'To be happy is to become wise in the eyes of both Stoics and early Christians.'[241] However, instead of cultivating detachment from the world as the primary means to achieve happiness, Christian happiness is gained by adopting Christian beliefs and attitudes. Vorster writes: 'After the death of Jesus, happiness was motivated Christologically. His complete life was seen as the sole basis for happiness.'[242] Christian joy is intimately tied to the past, present and future work and person of Christ. In short, both Stoics and Christians were concerned about living in joy. For Stoics it was their pursuit, for Christians a

---

239. Martin, *Worship in the Early Church*, p. 17.

240. Leonard, 'The Numinous Aspect of Biblical Worship', p. 72.

241. Vorster, 'Stoic and Early Christians on Blessedness', p. 51.

242. Vorster, 'Stoic and Early Christians on Blessedness', p. 44. See also Schlatter, *Die Christliche Ethik*, p. 348.

byproduct of their faith. Obviously the idea of joy was also different. For the Christian, joy was the unabashed emotion, not the Stoic idea of *eudaimonia*.

Morrice has a number of great strengths in his book *We Joy in God*. He outlines a list of cognitive reasons why we are to be joyful. We are to have joy because God has loved us as a Father, because God sent Christ, because Christ is risen, because we have the Holy Spirit, because we have an important commission, because our sins are forgiven, and because we have the hope of future glory. However, in the midst of these good points Morrice never puts the pieces together with an informed understanding of what joy is. He ends his study by writing, 'Such joy, as Paul Tillich realized so well, is not something emotional and superficial.'[243] But, as we have seen, emotional joy is anything but superficial and surface level. It is rooted in our beliefs and in our values. Instead, a lack of emotion in our joy would prove us to be superficial.

Many scholars emphasize the eschatological content of joy in the New Testament. The age of salvation has come with Christ and he is coming again.[244] But in emphasizing eschatology, they often blatantly dismiss the possibility that Christian joy is a present emotional experience. Beilner writes: 'In fact earthly joy remains generally in the background in the scriptures. Joy as a religious possession is in every respect bound up with the person of Jesus Christ and the salvation which is given through him.'[245] Yes and no. Yes, our joy can be based on future reality or spiritual knowledge but, no, this does not imply that it is not emotion felt in the present. Calvin insists, 'Let us, however, consider this settled: that no one has made progress in the school of Christ who does not joyfully await that day of death and final resurrection.'[246]

The same mistake is sometime made when it comes to joy in suffering. Scholars argue that joy is not emotional in these passages but rather theological and eschatological. However, the reality of joy in suffering is explained in cognitive terms by the same scholars. Beyreuther writes about joy in suffering: 'For even while they weigh heavily upon us we have paradoxically good reason to rejoice. Such rejoicing is grounded entirely in the person of Christ. The Lord himself, risen, present, and returning, is the basis for all our joy.'[247] The good reasons for having joy that are presented in the New Testament are not tied to this earth. Therefore, joy is possible when things on earth are difficult, even

---

243. Morrice, *We Joy in God*, p. 80. See also p. 20.

244. See Bultmann in *TDNT and* Beyreuther, '*agalliaomai*', p. 353.

245. Beilner, 'Joy', p. 439.

246. Calvin, *Institutes*, vol. 1, translated by Battles, 3.9.5 (Titus 2:23; 2 Tim. 44:8).

247. Beyreuther, '*agalliaomai*', p. 354.

in persecution. We do not need to redefine joy in order to have it in hard times. We should not rob the church of the joy of Christian faith by arguing that it is not emotional. To the contrary, it is emotional at its core.[248]

Hawthorne summarizes: 'It is a word with great theological significance, because everywhere in these documents joy in the true sense, both individual and corporate, is rooted in an unshakable faith in God and originates in a realization that God has acted and is acting to save those who put their trust in him.'[249] He concludes:

> What then is joy? One begins to suspect that for most of these Christian writers joy was more than a happy feeling, a pleasing mood or a sense of overflowing jubilation, although it might include these. Rather, by joy they seem to have been referring to something more profound, something more difficult to define yet real. Joy seems not be laughter, gaiety, lightheartedness, and dance and song (at least in this present world) but something more akin to faith, more akin to a settled state of mind marked by peace. Joy is fundamentally an attitude toward life that views and accepts the world with equanimity, a confident way of looking at life that is rooted deep in faith, in a keen awareness of and trust in the sovereign God who has revealed himself in Jesus Christ and his death and resurrection.[250]

Here we see the best and the worst of a typical understanding of joy in the New Testament. It is cognitive, and it is about the values and beliefs of the kingdom, but this does not imply that it is not emotional celebration and jubilation. Joy was singing in prison and the thrill of salvation. It is theological because it is cognitive, full of content about God and his acts in history. Christian joy may well include dance, song, and laughter.

The sources that deal with joy get many things right. Generally, they give good reasons for Christian joy. These lists are complete and I can add little insight. However, what is missing is the answer to what is joy. Too often the good reasons for joy are seen as good reasons for an inner theological state rather than good reasons for jubilant celebration and joyful emotion. A cognitive perspective brings these things together.

A study of joy in the New Testament quickly reveals that it was often spontaneous in nature. People rejoiced in a moment when something good

---

248. See Allender and Longman, *The Cry of the Soul*, pp. 256–257.

249. Hawthorne, *Joy*, pp. 600–601. See also Morrice, *Joy in the New Testament*, p. 153.

250. Hawthorne, *Joy*, p. 604. His ideas seem guided by a mistaken view that God could not demand emotional joy in suffering rather by the New Testament itself.

happened. This certainly speaks of its essential cognitive emotional nature. Joy can be felt in hard times because of what has been done for the Christian in Christ and the future triumph of the kingdom of God and coming glory. Morrice concludes, 'And why can we rejoice in the present? We can do so because of our sure and certain hope of further fulfillment and realization of our exultant joy in God in the future world.'[251] A desire for joy and happiness is God-given according to the New Testament. It is assumed and expected. This desire is fulfilled in Christ. Piper writes, 'The pursuit of pleasure is a necessary part of all worship and virtue.'[252]

Lewis writes:

> It is only in our 'hours-off', only in our moments of permitted festivity, that we find an analogy. Dance and game are frivolous, unimportant down here; for 'down here' is not their natural place. Here, they are moment's rest from the life we are placed here to live. But in this world everything is upside-down. That which, if it could be prolonged here, would be a truancy, is like that which in a better country is the End of ends. Joy is the serious business of heaven.[253]

Hope

The emotion of hope

Hope is a positive expectation for something in the future. Or, the emotion that comes from believing that something good might/will happen to something you love in the future.[254] It is one of the most misunderstood emotions in the New Testament. Characteristically in New Testament studies hope is seen primarily in an eschatological light and is perceived as fundamentally different from the hope we encounter in everyday life. To most scholars, hope is sure eschatological truth. It is not the fleeting emotional expectation of the world. When defining Christian hope, little or nothing is said about emotion in the life of the believer.[255]

I was told by an eminent New Testament scholar that the idea that hope was an emotion was 'highly controversial and novel'. Similarly, I had to defend the

251. Morrice, *Joy in the New Testament*, p. 24.

252. Piper, *Desiring God*, p. 19.

253. Lewis, *Letters to Malcolm*, pp. 92–93.

254. For a detailed analysis see Ben-Ze'ev, *The Subtlety of Emotions*, pp. 474–478.

255. For example, see Ladd, *A Theology of the New Testament*, pp. 555–556; Bultmann, '*elpis, elpizō, ap-, proelpizō*', p. 532.

idea of hope being an emotion to both my father and my advisor. With these kinds of reservations, it is essential that we first consider the question: 'Is hope an emotion?' Having based this study upon research into the nature of emotion, this question did not initially come to mind. From the review of the literature on emotion in psychology and philosophy, we find that it is assumed that hope is an emotion. For example, the writings of Aquinas, Frijda, Ben-Ze'ev, Izard, Solomon, Nussbaum, and Arnold define hope as an emotion.[256] We need to answer two questions: Why is hope assumed to be an emotion by leading experts on emotion? And what are some possible reasons that many theologians do not consider hope an emotion?

First, most basic emotions, as we have seen, have opposites. Love has the opposite definition of hate, joy has the opposite definition of sorrow, and hope has the opposite definition of fear. Where fear is the future expectation of pain or hardship, hope is the future expectation of a positive event.[257] Fear is assumed to be emotional by theologians (although this is not always the case when it comes to the fear of the Lord, a concept we will deal with in a later section). If hope is not emotional, we must question if fear is an emotion. However, you only have to remember the last time you were afraid to know that fear is clearly an emotion.

Hope, like fear, has all the characteristics of an emotion. It has an object, its intensity is dependent upon the worth or value that is placed on an object, and it is often accompanied by a physical feeling. It is possible to hold a belief about a future outcome without having hope. I may believe that the Boston Red Sox will win the World Series but since I live in Chicago I really do not care. When it comes to the Chicago Cubs, I really hope they win the World Series. Their success is important to me. What differentiates hope from a simple belief about the future is the value that the one who hopes places in this outcome. Just as joy comes when something good happens to something you love, or sadness comes when something bad happens to something you love, our very definition of hope is a clear definition of an emotional state. Ben-Ze'ev writes, 'whereas happiness and sadness are concerned with our present fortune, hope and fear are concerned with future fortune.'[258]

---

256. Solomon, *The Passions*, p. 328; Arnold, *Emotion and Personality*, vol. 1, pp. 194–196; Izard, *Human Emotion*, p. 204; Ben-Ze'ev, *The Subtlety of Emotions*, pp. 473–478; Frijda, *The Emotions*, p. 280; Nussbaum, *Upheavals of Thought*, p. 28; Aquinas, *Summa Theologica*, vol. 21, 1a2ae.40.

257. See Arnold, *Emotion and Personality*, vol. 1, p. 196; Frijda, *The Emotions*, p. 280; Solomon, *The Passions*, pp. 312, 328.

258. Ben-Ze'ev, *The Subtlety of Emotions*, p. 473.

Now we come to the question of why many theologians do not consider hope an emotion. For some, it is a simple misunderstanding of what emotion is. As we will see, often they define hope in a similar way to the emotion of hope, but they still insist that it is not an emotion. I have, in fact, been in a discussion where the other party conceded that my definition of hope was correct but disputed that hope was an emotion. In this context, you would need to deny that love, joy, fear, sorrow and anger were emotions as they are defined in the same terms. It is also significant to note that Louw and Nida place *elpizō* in the domain 'Attitudes and Emotions' and define it in a way that is similar to our understanding: 'to look forward with confidence to that which is good and beneficial.'[259]

Another reason that hope is not considered an emotion is that it is often less intense than some of the other basic emotions. We cannot do better than the explanation of Ben-Ze'ev:

> As an acute emotion, hope is not as intense as most other typical emotions. Consequently, some people have claimed that hope is not an emotion since it lacks an intense feeling dimension and hence does not involve any behavioral or physical symptoms . . .
>
>   Hope is not as intense as other typical emotions because of the temporal distance between us and the emotional object. When the emotional object of hope is not so far away in the future, hope may be intense and could have all emotional characteristics, including intense feelings. It is interesting to note that although fear is also directed at a future situation, no one has claimed that fear is not an emotion; on the contrary, fear is often described as the most basic and typical emotion. This difference expresses the greater emotional impact we attach to negative events as compared with positive ones.[260]

General discussion

Moule reminds us of Nygren's work on love when he claims that true biblical hope is not based on anything.

> Accordingly, and lastly, hope is not a calculated security. On the contrary, the first requisite if we are to possess hope is that we should be dispossessed of security, and instead should daringly and at absolute risk cast ourselves trustfully into the deep

---

259. Louw and Nida 25.59.
260. Ben-Ze'ev, *The Subtlety of Emotions*, pp. 474–475.

which is God's character. To hug the shore is to cherish a disappointing hope; really to let myself go and to swim is to have discovered the buoyancy of hope.[261]

We, however, understand that 'hope' without cognitive basis is not in fact hope: this makes no logical sense.

Bultmann summarizes major points about Biblical hope. It is an expectation of the future, is connected to trust and faith, and involves patient waiting. Unfortunately, this is the full essence of hope to Bultmann. There seems to be little or no emotional content for hope in the New Testament. He writes, 'it cannot count on controllable factors'.[262]

It can be difficult to understand what some scholars mean by hope. Rengstorf does a poor job of relaying a coherent definition of what hope is. The best summary statement he writes is, 'Here it is everywhere regarded as self-evident that hope is simply man's projection of the future.'[263] In this Rengstorf captures only one aspect of hope. Hope is the emotion that comes from the belief; it is the feeling that is produced from the expectation of future good.

Moule comments that with only a few exceptions hope in the Bible is not applied to things that are uncertain. Therefore, he reasons, Biblical hope is fundamentally different from secular hope.[264] It is true that secular hope, from the perspective of the New Testament, is temporary and often ill-founded. Tasker comments, 'The majority of secular thinkers in the ancient world did not regard hope as a virtue, but merely as a temporary illusion.' According to the New Testament itself pagans do not have true hope (Eph. 2:12; 1 Thess. 4:13). The biblical idea of hope because it is sure and solid 'is scarcely recognizable as hope'.[265] Bultmann agrees, 'Only where it is a matter of secular hope do we see the element of expectation characteristic of the Gk world, and always in

---

261. Moule, *The Meaning of Hope*, p. 19.

262. Bultmann, *'elpis, elpizō, ap-, proelpizō'*, p. 531. See also Conzelmann, *An Outline of the Theology of the New Testament*, p. 185.

263. Rengstorf, *'elpis, elpizō, ap-, proelpizō'*, p. 521.

264. Moule, *The Meaning of Hope*, pp. 1–2. He defines hope as: 'a wish strongly tinged with doubt; and even the more positive use – for expectation of something yet to be realized in the future – has to be greatly deepened, and augmented, and made more personal before it becomes really characteristic of the Bible' (p. 4).

265. Tasker, 'Hope', p. 489. See also Barr, ' "Hope" (*ELPIS, ELPIZŌ*) in the New Testament', p. 70. Barr argues against the fact that Christian hope and the concepts behind it are 'at best an emotional stimulus' (p. 76). Dunn, *Romans 1–8*, p. 219.

such a way that it is expectation of something welcome, with no differentiation between *agathē* and *ponēra elpis.*' (Luke 6:34; 1 Cor. 9:10; 2 Cor. 8:5; 1 Tim. 3:14; Phil. 2:19).[266]

In this view the definition of hope in the New Testament differs from its generic equivalent. In many biblical dictionaries secular and spiritual hope is differentiated. Hope when it is used in theological contexts is made synonymous with the theological concepts on which it is based. 'The difference between hope and trust fades', writes Rengstorf.[267] Little or no mention is made of hope as an emotion. After a good definition of secular hope Hoffmann writes about biblical hope, 'In formal structure it resembles secular hope (see above), but is essentially different in content, basis and effects.'[268] So instead of saying hope is emotion and the Christian can feel this way for the following reasons, hope is by definition the knowledge that these things will happen in the future, or the future events themselves.[269] In the New Testament hope had power to uplift and encourage in the present because it was based on sure future expectations. Hope in the New Testament is the same emotion that is found in the world. The difference in Christian hope is not the nature of the emotion, or the fact that it is not an emotion, but the object of the emotion.

Some practical examples may clarify the point that hope in the New Testament is not differentiated by its fundamental nature but by the nature of its object. I may hope that my team wins the big game tomorrow. We all know that this is not a sure prospect. A man lost in the woods in the middle of the night may hope that the sun will soon appear and he will be able to find the path to safety. Both emotions may be defined in the same manner. They are both the positive expectation of a future event. What differs between these different hopes is the nature of their object. No one can tell who will win a sports event in the future; everyone knows that the sun will come up tomorrow. One hope is tentative and one sure. The difference in New Testament hope is the sure and solid nature of its object, not the nature of the emotion.[270]

---

266. Bultmann, '*elpis, elpizō, ap-, proelpizō*', p. 530.

267. Rengstorf, '*elpis, elpizō, ap-, proelpizō*', p. 523.

268. Hoffmann, 'Hope', p. 239.

269. See *Hope*, in *The Eerdmans Bible Dictionary*, pp. 500–501.

270. As we begin our study of specific texts we should keep in mind that the noun might be used as a simple object in some passages (Gal. 5:5). See Hoffmann, 'Hope', p. 241. Even in Gal. 5:5 it is not sure that hope is the object itself. While the NRSV translates 'the hope of righteousness', the NIV says 'righteousness for which we hope'.

Hope in Pauline literature, the general epistles and Revelation

The Greek word for hope (*elpizō*) is seldom used in the gospels. When it is used it is consistent with normal usage. For example, Herod hoped to see Jesus (Matt. 12:21; Luke 6:34, 23:8, 24:21; John 5:45). Its absence from John and revelation is also notable. The concept of hope is not absent from these texts as they present abundant reasons to hope. However, the word is not emphasized.[271]

The word is most often used by Paul who sees it as one of the essential three elements of the 'primitive Christian triad: faith, hope, and love', according to Hoffmann (1 Cor. 13:13; 1 Thess. 1:3, 5:8). It is also paired with faith alone on a number of occasions (Heb. 11:1; Rom. 4:18, 15:13; Gal. 5:5; Col. 1:23; 1 Tim. 4:10; 1 Pet. 1:21).[272] It is important that it is paired with faith, for faith fuels hope. Paul gives good reasons for the Christian to hope. Hoffmann writes:

> In the realm of the word *elpis* [hope], its content is defined as: salvation (1 Thess. 5:8), righteousness (Gal. 5:5), resurrection in an incorruptible body (1 Cor. 15:52 ff.; Acts 23:6; 24:15), eternal life (Tit. 1:2; 3:7), seeing God and being conformed to his likeness (1 John 3:2 f.; *image*), the glory of God (Rom. 5:2) or simply *doxa* [glory] (Col. 1:27; cf. 2 Cor. 3:12, the abiding *doxa* of NT service).[273]

Everts summarizes: 'Every statement Paul makes about Christian hope is also a statement about what God has given the believer in Christ. In his letters, especially the letter to the Romans, Paul explores the ground of Christian hope, what it means to live in hope and the Christian hope for the future.'[274] However, to Everts hope is about theology, the fundamental emotional nature of hope is never mentioned. This implies that hope is the object itself. But hope is not the object – it is the emotion which is based on these things. Beker writes, 'Faith, hope, and trust are all synonyms in the Old Testament (*batah; kawah; aman*) and

---

271. Bultmann, '*elpis, elpizō, ap-, proelpizō*', p. 532. John is full of hope for the future and 'eternal life'. Hebblethwaite gives a good summary, *The Christian Hope*, pp. 31–32. See also Davies, 'Eschatological Hope in the Early Christian Community', pp. 109–110, 112; Barr, '"Hope" (*ELPIS, ELPIZŌ*) in the New Testament', p. 68; Becker, *Das Evangelium nach Johannes: Kapitel 11–21*, pp. 360–362. Fulfilled hope is central to the preaching of Jesus (Wright, *Jesus and the Victory of God*, pp. 622–624).

272. Hoffmann, 'Hope', p. 242. See also p. 243.

273. Hoffmann, 'Hope', p. 242. See also Zeller, *Der Brief an die Römer*, pp. 232–233.

274. Everts, 'Hope', p. 415. See also Conzelmann, 'Der Brief an die Epheser', p. 94; Barr, '"Hope" (*ELPIS, ELPIZŌ*) in the New Testament', pp. 72–73.

this meaning persists in Paul in the New Testament.' Faith and trust are not emotions, so we can conclude that neither is hope an emotion to Beker. Again, hope is seen as a theological concept rather than an emotional attitude.[275] However, Beker goes on to describe hope as a cognitive emotion, 'so hope in its relation to glory (Rom. 5:2) is not just the posture of faith but is directed toward a specific object, time, and place: the time and place of the *Parousia* and the glory to come.'[276] The New Testament, we believe, has an emotion in view. The believer is to live in expectant hope that does the heart good.

In Romans, hope is a major theme. Speaking of the hope expressed in chapter 8, Robinson writes: 'The language in this chapter – of election, of calling, of justification, of glorification, of the saints, of God's foreknowledge, of his purpose, of redemption, of sonship, of inheritance – all belonged to the theology, and specifically to the eschatology, of Israel.'[277] The hope of glory is central. The final victory over death is also an emphasis. In this chapter, Paul presents significant reasons to hope.[278]

Romans 8:23–25 is informative in discovering how Paul defines hope: 'and not only the creation, but we ourselves, who have the first fruits of the Spirit, groan inwardly as we wait for adoption as sons, the redemption of our bodies. For in this hope we were saved. Now hope that is seen is not hope. For who hopes for what he sees? But if we hope for what we do not see, we wait for it with patience.' Here hope is definitely based on future events.[279] The events are hoped for, they are not hope itself. Christian hope is based on

---

275. Beker, *Paul the Apostle*, p. 147. Beker does a good job in describing the object of hope and its strong cognitive content. Martin agrees, 'for Peter, the two terms, hope and faith, overlap (1.21). The letter concentrates on hope as the incentive needed to carry them through their trials to hope's ultimate reward' (1:3, 8, 13; 3:5, 15; 5:10; Martin, 'The Theology of Jude, 1 Peter, and 2 Peter', pp. 88–89).

276. Beker, *Paul the Apostle*, p. 148. For a summary of the passages that see future glory as a source of hope and motivation, see Ridderbos, *Paul: An Outline of His Theology*, pp. 488–489.

277. Robinson, 'The Priesthood of Paul in the Gospel of Hope', p. 234. See also Barr, '"Hope" (*ELPIS, ELPIZŌ*) in the New Testament', p. 74; Cranfield, *Romans*, pp. 407–415.

278. Robinson, 'The Priesthood of Paul in the Gospel of Hope', pp. 235, 244–245; Dunn, *Romans 1–8*, p. 264; McCaughey, 'The Death of Death (1 Corinthians 15:26)'.

279. See Hebblethwaite, *The Christian Hope*, p. 28; Gnilka, *Theologie des Neuen Testaments*, p. 348; Cranfield, *Romans*, p. 420; Zeller, *Der Brief an die Römer*, p. 169; Moo, *Romans*, p. 522.

a sure confidence for the future in the midst of hard times. This passage gives a list of the major reasons to have hope and is similar to Hebrews 11:1.[280]

Romans 5 is also a key passage. The hope of verses 2–4 is explained in the rest of the Chapter. It is based on a certainty that Christ has given life just as surely as Adam brought death, that God loves people, and that 'we were reconciled to God'.[281] Moo writes, 'Verses 5–8 set Christian hope on the unshakable foundation of the love of God revealed in the cross . . . Paul invites believers to take joyful pride in what God had given them.'[282] Paul makes it clear that patient endurance is possible because of sure hope (1 Thess. 1:3; Rom. 5:3–5).[283] God's love 'provides the grounds for hope', writes Cousar.[284] Again, the very basic truths of the Christian faith are the basis of hope, most notably the central emotion of love. Romans ends with a call to hope which produces great joy.[285]

Ephesians 1 is another important passage. In the midst of an excellent discussion of the firm cognitive foundation for Christian hope, Best writes, 'In v. 18 the emphasis does not lie primarily on the expectant hoping of believers for, as Eadie comments, it would not require enlightened lives to produce the emotion of hoping. Instead the emphasis lies on the content of what is hoped for . . . The actual content of the hope is not spelt out and has to be gleaned from the rest of the letter.'[286] Pokorny emphasizes the fundamental difference of Christian hope from its secular counterpart.[287] We have seen, however, that hope without future expectation is not in fact hope. Patzia writes, 'Hope, here, is not some sub-

---

280. Bruce, *Hebrews*, p. 278; Zeller, *Der Brief an die Römer*, p. 163. There is some debate over the translation of *hypostasis*. The best translation seems to be assurance (subjective) as opposed to substance (objective) (Attridge, *Hebrews*, pp. 306–311). See the comprehensive discussion of Ellingworth, *Hebrews*, pp. 566.

281. Bultmann, *Theology*, vol. 1, pp. 252, 336, 347; Schmithals, *Der Römerbrief: Ein Kommentar*, pp. 156–157.

282. Moo, *Romans*, p. 298. Dunn differentiates the fading hope of the Greeks and the sure idea of hope of the Hebrews when he analyses these passages (Dunn, *The Theology of Paul the Apostle*, p. 438).

283. Tasker, 'Hope', p. 489. Furnish does a good job in connecting present and future in Christian hope (Furnish, *Theology and Ethics in Paul*, pp. 126–127, 132, 175).

284. Cousar, *The Letters of Paul*, p. 107.

285. See Beker, *Paul the Apostle*, pp. 92–93; Hays, *Adam, Israel, Christ*, p. 85; Gnilka, *Theologie des Neuen Testaments*, p. 390.

286. Best, *Ephesians*, p. 166. O' Brien agrees (O'Brien, *Ephesians*, pp. 134–135). See also Schnackenburg, *Ephesians*, p. 75.

287. Pokorny, *Der Brief des Paulus an die Epheser*, p. 80.

jective feeling … Rather, it is an objective element that belongs to the believer.'[288] These are surprising statements in several areas. First, the passage is filled with good reasons to hope. Second, the fact that the hope is clearly cognitive gives Best reason to pronounce that hope as not emotional. The truth is that the cognitive content of the hope (1:17–18) is a clear basis for the emotion which Christians are to feel. Finally, to think that Paul is writing this great list of reasons to hope to a Christian community without the goal of producing a positive emotional hope in them seems difficult to defend. He desired to lift their spirits.

Davids rightly concentrates on the object of the hope in Peter rather than differentiating Christian and secular hope, 'They are to hope totally in their reward at the return of Christ instead of setting their hope on the transitory and corrupt.'[289] Cranfield gives a good summary, 'In the first place get down to some hard thinking!' He continues, 'Two things are vital here – that the object of our hope be the right one and that we hope for it unreservedly, wholeheartedly.'[290] Hope is a characterization of believers (1 Pet. 3:15).[291] This cognitive reality has led some to the conclusion that the hope is the facts themselves. Best writes, 'in this letter "hope" is used almost as an equivalent for faith . . . the Christians have thus to explain their faith.'[292] However, the command is to build your emotional hope upon a cognitive reality. Hope in the present hard times is made possible by the promises for the future.[293]

1 Peter has a particular emphasis on hope in the midst of trial.[294] Like joy in trials, hope in hard times is based on good theology.[295] Martin concludes, 'Hope is much more than that vague optimism that "all shall be well and all manner of things shall be well"; rather it is that virtue, along with faith (1.21), that pins us to the living Christ who is the same in every age.'[296] 1 Peter 1:13 brings the

---

288. Patzia, *Ephesians, Colossians, Philemon*, p. 167. Lincoln gives a good summary of the centrality of the idea of hope in Ephesians. Lincoln, *The Theology of the Later Pauline Letters*, pp. 117–119.

289. Davids, *Peter*, p. 65.

290. Cranfield, *1 and 2 Peter and Jude*, pp. 47–48.

291. Hillyer, *1 and 2 Peter, Jude*, p. 109.

292. Best, *1 Peter*, p. 134.

293. Ladd, *A Theology of the New Testament*, p. 596.

294. Martin, 'The Theology of Jude, 1 Peter, and 2 Peter', pp. 102–106. Martin argues that 1 Peter is oriented around the concept of hope (Martin, 'The Theology of Jude, 1 Peter, and 2 Peter', pp. 123–124).

295. Piper, 'Hope as the Motivation of Love: 1 Peter 3:9–12', p. 215.

296. Martin, 'The Theology of Jude, 1 Peter, and 2 Peter', p. 132.

mind, grace, and hope together. Hope is a natural result of setting your mind on grace.

Part of what makes Christians unique is their hope in the resurrection of the dead (Acts 23:6; 24:15; 26:7; 28:20). The idea of hope for the future may also be rooted in the past. Believers can hope for the future because God has proved faithful (Heb. 10:23; 3:6; 6:15).[297] In Romans 15:4 we see that the truth of the Old Testament gives good reason to hope. Because God is the one who will make these things come to pass, or because the hope is in him directly, Christian hope is certain, as made clear in Hebrews 6:13–20. To Lane, the hope of Hebrews has little or no emotional content. He writes, 'Both in 6:18 and 10:23a the "hope" to which the writer refers is an objective reality related to the priestly activity of Jesus. In Hebrews the term "hope" always describes the objective content of hope, consisting of present and future salvation.'[298] Certainly some objective meaning of hope may be present in Hebrews, but the writer was concerned that a community have a positive outlook to sustain them. The objective facts about the future will give the strength to feel hope.

C. S. Lewis writes about future glory:

> If there lurks in most modern minds the notion that to desire our own good and earnestly to hope for the enjoyment of it is a bad thing, I submit that this notion has crept in from Kant and the Stoics and is no part of the Christian Faith. Indeed, if we consider the unblushing promises of reward and the staggering nature of the rewards promised in the Gospels, it would seem that Our Lord finds our desires not too strong, but too weak. We are half-hearted creatures, fooling about with drink and sex and ambition when infinite joy is offered us, like an ignorant child who wants to go on making mud pies in a slum because he cannot imagine what is meant by the offer of a holiday at the sea. We are far too easily pleased.[299]

Finally we should consider that hope is used in many non-theological contexts. Paul uses the word when referring to others. He has hope that they will endure in the faith (1 Thess. 2:19; 2 Cor. 1:7; 10:15). He hopes to see others or to accomplish a task (Rom. 15:24; 1 Cor. 16:7; Phil. 2:19; 1 Tim. 3:14; see also 2 John 12; 3 John 14). All lose hope in the great storm of Acts 27 (see also Luke 6:34; Acts 16:19). In simple terms, hope is used in a very generic non-theological manner

---

297. Eastman, 'Hope', p. 500. Ellingworth believes this is objective, or what is hoped for (Ellingworth, *Hebrews*, p. 525); Weiß, *Der Brief an die Hebräer*, pp. 528–531.

298. Lane, *Hebrews 9–13*, p. 288. See also pp. 321, 328–329, 394.

299. Lewis, *The Weight of Glory*, pp. 1–2.

numerous times. This points to it being a generic emotion rather than a theological concept. Unfortunately, these passages have often been used as examples of secular hope that is then strongly differentiated from the meaning of Christian hope.[300] False hope also plays a role in the New Testament. What differentiates Christian hope and false hope? It is the object. Pagans put their hope in their possessions (Matt. 6), their gods, or their position. Christians put their hope in Christ.

We should not confine our discussion to those passages that use hope explicitly. In 1 Thessalonians 4:13–18 believers are to encourage one another with the facts of their faith. Part of the Christian hope is the hope of rewards (Matt. 10:42; Luke 6:35; 1 Cor. 3:12–15; 9:24–27; Col. 3:22–24; Heb. 4:1; 6:4–6; 10:35–36; 11:6; Jas 1:12; 4:8; Rev. 2:7–10; 3:5; 21:3).[301] In 2 Cor. 4:17–5:6, why is Paul able to continue in confidence and hope? Because of the assurance of the glory that is to come.[302] These passages do not specifically use the word but they certainly emphasize the hope of the believer (Phil. 1:6; 3:14; 1 Cor. 9:24; 1 Thess. 1:10; 2:19; 5:23–24).

Romans 15:13 makes hope clearly a major part of the Christian's emotional disposition: 'May the God of hope fill you with all joy and peace in believing, so that you may abound in hope by the power of the Holy Spirit' (Rom. 12:11–12).[303] The Christian is to be full of hope, a hope that gives confidence in hard times, a hope that fills the heart with gladness, a hope that brings joy and peace.

Hope in the New Testament
The man who believes that the Chicago Bulls will win the NBA championship but has no feeling associated with that belief does not have hope. He only has a belief about the future with no personal value attached to it. In leaving out emotion from their definition of hope scholars alter the very nature of hope. A hope without emotion signifies that what is believed about the future is not very important to the individual. Hope is, by definition, emotion. Christian hope requires passionate faith in Christ and valuing this relationship above all else. Hope is distinguished from simple belief about what will happen in the future by its emotional core.[304]

Eastman writes, 'The meaning of "hope" and its cognates in the NT is

300. Barr, '"Hope" (*ELPIS, ELPIZŌ*) in the New Testament', pp. 69–70.

301. Williams, *1 and 2 Thessalonians*, p. 86. See Fuller, 'Rewards'; Friedrich, 'Der Brief an die Thessalonicher', p. 243.

302. See Barrett, *The Second Epistle to the Corinthians*, pp. 143–146; Hafemann, *2 Corinthians*, pp. 188–189, 194, 204.

303. See Zeller, *Der Brief an die Römer*, pp. 232–233.

304. See Cousar, *The Letters of Paul*, p. 133.

radically different from that of the English word hope. Rather than expressing the desire for a particular outcome that is uncertain, hope in the NT by definition is characterized by certainty.'[305] This is a good example of the general feeling about hope in the New Testament among New Testament scholars. They fail to show what makes hope in the New Testament 'radically different' from its secular counterpart. Further, most authors use this to downplay the emotional element in Biblical hope.[306] We have also seen that it is inaccurate to interpret hope as a concept that is specifically not about anything concrete (Bultmann). This parallels the idea of love found in Nygren. New Testament usage is very similar to what we know as hope. It is used of normal circumstances as 'I hope to see you soon' or 'whoever plows should plow in hope' (see 1 Cor. 9:10) and it clearly contains a strong emotional element. Hope is to encourage and strengthen the community of believers in a very tangible and emotional way. What is unique in Christian hope is not 'the meaning' of hope itself but the nature of what is hoped for.

The lonely spouse's hope may be that his wife is coming home in a week because that is the return date on her ticket. This is relatively sure. The businessman's hope may be that he will get a cheque from a particular customer on Friday because he knows that they sent it on Monday. Or we have hope that the sun will be up in the morning. The besieged soldier may hope that his army will relieve him, or the child of separated parents may hope that they will get back together. These last hopes are much less certain. Hope has many different levels of certainty. The object of hope may be valued to a greater or lesser degree and it may therefore vary in intensity. Yet, each one is felt as hope. In the New Testament hope is sure, for God is behind the promise. Hope is also pervasive and strong as what is hoped for is of supreme value. Therefore, the fundamental nature of hope is not different in the New Testament as many contend, but rather the one behind the promise is unique, God Himself. We may conclude with the words of Furnish:

> The believer who has been baptized into Christ's death and has therefore died to his own past does not stand in some shadowy limbo waiting for the resurrection life. He now stands 'in' and 'under' grace (Rom. 5:2; 6:14) which gives his hope a special character (Rom. 5:2, 5). While the object of his hope is not yet 'seen' (Rom. 8:24–25), its power is already operative through the spirit (Rom. 5:5) which gives life to those in whom it dwells (Rom. 8:9 ff.).[307]

---

305. Eastman, 'Hope', p. 499.

306. See Moule, *The Meaning of Hope.*

307. Furnish, *Theology and Ethics in Paul,* p. 195.

5. EMOTION IN THE NEW TESTAMENT: JEALOUSY, FEAR, SORROW AND ANGER

I have always, even as a boy, been engrossed in the philosophical problem of the relation between emotion and reason. Certain truths originate in feelings, others in the mind. Those truths that we derive from our emotions are of a moral kind – compassion, kindness, forgiveness, love for our neighbour. Reason, on the other hand, teaches us the truths that come from reflection.

But with the great spirits of our world – the Hebrew prophets, Christ, Zoroaster, the Buddha, and others – feeling is always paramount. In them emotion holds its ground against reason, and all of us have an inner assurance that the truth of emotion that these great spiritual figures reveal to us the most profound and important truth.[1]

Albert Schweitzer

Zeal, jealousy and envy

Vocabulary

We begin our analysis of negative emotions with jealousy. We may place zeal or jealousy between those emotions which we have just covered that have a

---

1. Albert Schweitzer, in an interview with Radio Brazzaville, 1953.

positive feeling and those emotions that have a prevailing negative feeling associated with them. Defending the perceived rightful place of an object in a person's life is at the core of this emotion. In the case of zeal for God, jealousy is being protective of his glory and dominion, which is rightly his. In the case of being envious of your neighbour's car, the car is rightfully your neighbour's and you want it. Therefore, jealousy and envy are neither wholly negative nor positive as there are both positive and negative evaluations that are at the core of the emotions. The possession of the object is seen as positive while the emotion felt toward the one currently in possession of the object or trying to gain possession of the object is negative.

Envy and jealousy can be easily confused. Ben-Ze'ev writes:

Envy: The emotional attitude of wishing to have what someone else has and which is important for the subject's Self-definition.

Jealousy: The emotional attitude of wishing not to lose something (typically, a favorable human relationship), which is important for the subject's self-definition, to someone else.[2]

He continues by arguing that an individual's exclusive relationship is often a factor in jealousy. The object of jealousy cannot be generically replaced. 'Hence, jealousy is often concerned with exclusiveness. Envy, on the other hand, is concerned with inequality.'[3] Jealousy is concerned with rivalry while envy is concerned with inferiority. Romantic love, therefore, always *may* produce jealousy. The jealous person is often interested in maintaining the present situation while the envious person often desires something new. Envy is almost always considered a moral flaw while jealousy can be legitimate.[4]

---

2. Ben-Ze'ev, 'Envy and Jealousy', pp. 489–490. See also Ben-Ze'ev, *The Subtlety of Emotions*, pp. 282–283.

3. Ben-Ze'ev, 'Envy and Jealousy', p. 493. See also Berenson, 'What Is This Thing Called "Love"', p. 75. He observes that envy is likely to be over things and qualities while jealousy involves the fear of losing one you love. See also Solomon, *The Passions*, pp. 334–335. Jealousy is more likely to be over one object where envy is more likely to be all encompassing.

4. Ben-Ze'ev, 'Envy and Jealousy', 'In summary, envy and jealousy have an important common feature: the wish to have something. They differ in our relation toward this thing: in envy we wish to gain it and in jealousy not to lose it.' Ben-Ze'ev, *The Subtlety of Emotions*, p. 326; Solomon, *The Passions*, p. 306.

Louw and Nida put *zēlos* in three different domains and five different subject headings.[5] The translation of the term in the NRSV follows closely the differentiation of Louw and Nida. A brief analysis shows that it is translated as 'jealous' 13 times, 'zeal' 10 times, 'eager/strive/make much of' 7 times and 'envy' 3 times. Each of these translations, excluding envy, is used in both positive and negative contexts.[6] We may be able to eliminate some of these 'different' meanings with a better understanding of jealousy as an emotion. Although there are different emphases, an understanding of the core meaning of *zēlos* serves to unite a majority of the usage.

The most common mistake in interpreting *zēlos* in the New Testament is to classify it as 'jealousy' when it is generally negative, while using the English 'zeal' when it is seen as generally positive. Hahn writes in *NIDNTT*, 'Where the goal is good, *zēlos* means eager striving, competition, enthusiasm, admiration . . . In a bad sense, the zeal has had a wrong goal and has become a defect; it then means jealousy, ill-will, envy.'[7] Davis writes that *zēlos* is, 'An intense emotion which may be seen in a positive light as zeal or in a negative light as envy. It is a single-minded devotion which, when turned inward to one's self, produces hatred and envy of others or, when turned beyond one's self, produces intense zeal leading to total selflessness.'[8] This is echoed in Louw and Nida who define *zēlos* as: 'to set one's heart on something that belongs to someone else' in domain 88.[9] The positive meaning of *zēlos* is said to be 'to be deeply committed to something' in 25.46 (25.76). *BDAG* makes a similar distinction: (1) 'intense positive interest' and (2) 'intense negative feelings over another's achievements or success'.

Stumpff declares that 'personal emotion . . . is the true and probably the original core of the meaning'.[10] Bultmann agrees: 'ultimately both [jealousy and zeal] are the same word . . . But the fact that *zēlos*, 'jealousy', can be directed toward either right or wrong ends indicates that its basic meaning is that of a non-qualified striving.'[11] Most commentators agree that strong emotion or zeal

---

5. Louw and Nida list it in 25.21, 46, 76; 78.25; 88.162.

6. See the good discussion of Longenecker, *Galatians*, p. 256. For *parazēlouē* see Bell, 'Provoked to Jealousy', pp. 39–42.

7. Hahn, 'Zeal', p. 1166.

8. Davis, 'Jealousy', p. 576.

9. Louw and Nida, 25.21, 88.162. See also Luter, 'Jealousy, Zeal', p. 461.

10. Stumpff, '*zēlos, zēloō, zēlōtēs, parazēloō*', p. 882. Stumpff emphasizes the difference in God's and people's zeal, a faulty distinction in our view. (Stumpff, '*zēlos, zēloō, zēlōtēs, parazēloō*', p. 884). It is 'no mere mood' (p. 888).

11. Bultmann, *Theology*, vol. 1, pp. 225–226.

is the core meaning of the word. As Bultmann explicitly states, this tendency seems to come from a desire to understand the positive uses of the word without any connotations of 'negative' jealousy.[12]

We concur that the word is highly emotional but raw emotion or 'striving' is not the core meaning. There seems to be little room for positive jealousy in this framework. If jealousy is negative and zeal denotes only strong emotion and does not entail defending the proper place of someone or something, we loose the understanding of proper jealousy. For example, a wife has every right to be jealous of her husband if another woman is seriously flirting with him. It is not difficult to see how the English zeal, which has come to mean unbridled enthusiasm, has some of the same meaning as jealous. They both involve placing high value in an object and pursuing that object with a high degree of enthusiasm. To see two distinct meanings in the Greek term is misleading and it should not be used to whitewash the meaning of legitimate jealousy in positive contexts.

We must also consider *phthonos*. This is translated by the NRSV seven times as 'envy' and three as 'jealousy' while the NIV uses 'envy' in each context. It is used in a negative sense nine of those times while it seems positive only in James 4:5. The human spirit may be the subject of James 4:5 (NIV) or it may be better translated as jealousy in the tradition of the Old Testament's conception of God as jealous as in the NLT.[13] The evidence in the text itself seems to stand for the latter. It is possible that James wishes to avoid the negative connotations that *zēlos* has in 3:14–16 when he used *phthonos* in 4:5.[14] Even in light of James 4:5, we can say that *phthonos* is similar to the English 'envy'.

Jealousy in the New Testament

A brief survey of its usage makes clear that the predominant meaning of jealousy in the New Testament involves the proper ownership or place of something in an individual's life. When this is challenged a strong emotional reaction is felt. We can use Louw and Nida's examples of being zealous in Gal. 4:17; Romans 10:2; 1 Corinthians 12:31 and Revelation 3:19 to guide our discussion. These are classified as strong desire or deep commitment as opposed to jealousy.

---

12. Stumpff, '*zēlos, zēloō, zēlōtēs, parazēloō*', p. 880.

13. 'Jas 4:5 is one of the most difficult verses in the NT [to translate]' (Moo, *James, TNTC*, p. 188).

14. Field, 'Envy'. See Laws, *James*, pp. 175–178; Moo, *James, TNTC*, pp. 144–146; Moo, *James*, PNTC, pp. 188–190; Davids, *James, NIGTC*, pp. 164–165; Martin, *James*, pp. 149–151 for a strong defence of God as the subject.

Yet in each case the meaning of jealousy is evident. Romans 10:2 is about the Jews being passionate for God to have his rightful place; in 1 Corinthians 12:31 Christians are to desire what is rightfully theirs, the greater gifts; Galatians 4:17 is about exclusive relationship; and Revelation 3:19 pertains to God having his rightful place in a believer's life. Clearly, the separation between jealous and zealous is not so obvious. We have not mentioned the clear instances of positive jealousy (2 Cor. 11:2; Rom. 11:14; John 2:17; Titus 2:14).[15] In these passages it seems apparent that positive jealousy is in view, not raw emotional enthusiasm.

The idea of God's jealousy is rare in the New Testament but we do find it in 1 Corinthians 10:22.[16] In 2 Corinthians 11:2 Paul feels this same kind jealousy.[17] The evidence for the purity of his actions and motives is emotional. He was motivated by love, concern and compassion (11:28–29). Notice that the justification of actions based on emotional motives is only possible in a cognitive framework. Paul feels legitimate godly jealousy (Exod. 20:4–5). They owe their devotion to God and Paul and are not giving it.[18]

In James 3:14–16, jealousy (*zēlos*) clearly has a negative object and in 4:5, God's righteous jealousy (*phthonos*) is for the good of his people. As in 1 Corinthians 10:22 and 12:20, in close context we have both positive and

---

15. Boice rightly recognizes that the motive behind the zeal and anger determine its morality. Boice, 'Galatians', pp. 479, 496. On the positive use of jealousy in Rom. 11, see Bell, 'Provoked to Jealousy', p. 156. He writes 'Deut. 32 was the one source, and as I will argue, the primary source for his theology of jealousy', p. 285.

16. See Fee, *Corinthians*, p. 474. Mare describes this as highly emotional. Mare, '1 Corinthians', p. 252. Rosner presents an excellent case for the strong Old Testament background of this statement. This along with our analysis of God's jealousy in the Old Testament reinforces the emotional content in this passage. Rosner, *Paul, Scripture, and Ethics*, pp. 195–203.

17. We should also point out that the passage speaks of the legitimate jealousy in marriage for the affection of a spouse. God's and Paul's jealousy is legitimate just as it is legitimate in the marriage relationship. See Barrett, *The Second Epistle to the Corinthians*, p. 272; Hughes, *Second Epistle to the Corinthians*, p. 373; Martin, *2 Corinthians*, p. 332. Harris writes, 'Human Jealousy is a vice, but to share divine jealousy is a virtue. It is the motive and object of the jealousy that is all-important.' As we have often observed, he is right and wrong. The object does determine the morality of the jealousy, bur we cannot say that divine jealousy is the only appropriate jealousy (Harris, '2 Corinthians', p. 385).

18. Evans, 'Interpretation of 2 Corinthians', p. 29; Carson, *From Triumphalism to Maturity*, pp. 84–87; Grudem, *Systematic Theology*, p. 205.

negative uses of the concept. The vocabulary is used in the opposite manner than is normal; *phthonos* conveys a positive jealousy. This fact reinforces the idea that it is the object that determines the emotion's morality. We should also point out the highly cognitive context of 3:14–16. Heavenly wisdom does not produce the harmful emotion.[19]

Paul's pre-Christian jealousy is misplaced. Acts 22:3 and Galatians 1:13–14 speak of Paul being zealous in the tradition of Phineas according to Luter (Num. 25). It is jealousy for what he perceives to be rightly God's (Phil. 3:6; Rom. 10:2–3).[20] Unfortunately Luter classifies this as zeal as opposed to jealousy. However, Paul's jealousy was not just intense emotion. It was the desire to defend God and the law against Christians that he believed were intent on robbing them of their proper place in Jewish society and religion. Jealousy for God is good. However, when it is based on wrong knowledge, like the pre-conversion jealousy of Paul and his Jewish counterparts, it is destructive. In Romans 10:2 we see clearly that jealousy itself is not the problem. However, jealousy for God based on the wrong facts is destructive, it is 'not based on knowledge' (NIV).[21] Luke 13:34 may hint at the jealousy of Jesus over Israel. These passages fit with our analysis of emotion as cognitive. Dunn presents an excellent defence of zeal as understood in this book:

> There are three striking features of 'zeal' thus understood. First, in each case the zeal was an unconditional commitment to maintain Israel's distinctiveness, to prevent the purity of its covenant set-apartness to God from being adulterated or defiled, to defend its religious and national boundaries. Second, a readiness to do this by force. In each case it is the thoroughgoing commitment expressed precisely in the slaughter of those who threatened Israel's distinctive covenant status which merited the description 'zeal' or 'zealot.' And third, the fact that this zeal was directed not only against Gentiles who threatened Israel's boundaries, but against fellow Jews too.[22]

We should not neglect the clear negative usages of jealousy. These reinforce the previous analysis. The word in these passages is clearly negative because of

---

19. See Moo, *James*, *TNTC*, pp. 132–134. The emphasis in 3:16 is the destruction of relationship (Frankemölle, *Der Brief des Jakobus: Kapitel 2–5*, p. 548).

20. Luter, 'Jealousy, Zeal', p. 461. See also Conzelmann, *Acts*, p. 186; Bell, 'Provoked to Jealousy', pp. 301–306, 360; Barrett, *Paul*, pp. 47, 82; Fitzmyer, *Paul and His Theology*, p. 80.

21. Cranfield, *Romans*, p. 514; Dunn, *Romans 9–16*, pp. 586, 594; Murray, *Romans*, vol. 2, p. 48.

22. Dunn, *The Theology of Paul the Apostle*, p. 351.

the object of the jealousy. It is the desire for possession of a wrong object or an attitude of desiring that which is the rightful possession of someone else. The attitude of the religious leaders against Jesus and his followers is characterized by jealousy over their perceived rightful place before God and the people (Matt. 27:18; Mark 15:10; Acts 5:17; 13:45; 17:5).[23] Similarly, the instances of jealousy being named as a general vice are clearly instances of people desiring what is not rightfully theirs. They envy others' position or possessions (*phthonos* in Rom. 1:29; 13:13; Gal. 5:21; 1 Tim. 6:4; 1 Pet. 2:1; and *zēlos* in 2 Cor. 12:20, Gal. 5:20, Jas 3:14).[24] Sinful jealousy of someone or envy is in view. It is clear in these contexts that the object of jealousy is not right.

God deserves his rightful place and his followers should feel jealousy when this is not given to him. When jealousy is wrong it is over something that is not rightfully the possession of the one who is jealous. Jealousy over one's own husband or wife is the natural and right reaction to certain situations. However, jealousy of a neighbour's possession, wife, or position is universally condemned (Exod. 20:17; Rom. 7:7; 13:9). The broad condemnation of jealousy that we find in some passages is a function of the fact that this is jealousy for the wrong objects, and it brings strife and discord.

In our analysis of jealousy a cognitive understanding of emotion makes sense of New Testament usage. Further, it greatly simplifies the work of scholars who have endeavored to draw artificial lines between jealousy and zeal, lines that are often not as clear as they insist. If jealousy is understood as a morally neutral cognitive emotion these kinds of distinctions are not necessary.

Fear

Fear is the negative expectation of something in the future.[25] In examining fear there are several points to highlight. First, fear is usually accepted as an emotion by New Testament scholars. Second, the fear of the Lord is usually

---

23. See Luter, 'Jealousy, Zeal', p. 462; Pesch, *Das Markusevangelium*, vol. 2, pp. 464–465; Williams, *Acts*, pp. 105–106; Marshall, *Acts*, p. 117.

24. We should point out that the link between faulty theological knowledge and beliefs and envy is very strong in 1 Tim. 6. See Fee, *1 and 2 Timothy, Titus*, pp. 141–142; Quinn and Wacker, *The First and Second Letters to Timothy*, pp. 487–489. See also Bruce, *Galatians*, p. 248; Betz, *Galatians*, p. 229.

25. For a more detailed analysis see Ben-Ze'ev, *The Subtlety of Emotions*, pp. 478–481.

seen as non-emotional. Louw and Nida gives a good cognitive definition of fear: 'a state of severe distress, aroused by intense concern for impending pain, danger, evil, etc.'[26] In a characteristic dichotomy of emotional and less emotional uses of emotional vocabulary, *BDAG* gives two definitions of *phobos*: (1) 'be afraid' and (2) 'reverence, respect'. In our view, fear is the feeling which comes from the anticipation of something bad happening in the future to an object you love.

Fear in the New Testament

One of the key clues to the fact that the New Testament has a cognitive understanding of fear is how it tells the Christian to deal with the emotion. Christians are given good reasons not to fear. There is no ceremony, ritual or prescription provided to clear the mind of the believer. Rather, there are good reasons why a Christian does not need to fear. Carson sees five good reasons not to fear that Jesus gives in Matthew 10: (1) persecution is to be expected (24–25); (2) God will give help at crucial times (19–20); (3) someday all will be revealed (26–27); (4) God's wrath is more to be feared than man's (28); (5) God cares about the details of his children's life (29–31; see also Luke 12; John 14; Heb. 11:23).[27] France writes, 'There are right and wrong fears for the disciples of Jesus, and true discipleship depends on distinguishing them.' He continues, 'Two types of *fear* are here contrasted: fear of men is a self-interested cowardice, but fear of God is a healthy response of awe and obedience.'[28]

The New Testament also emphasizes the idea that there is no longer reason for Christians to fear death (Heb. 2:15; Rev. 2:10).[29] Fear that is condemned in the New Testament is usually fear of death or fear of men (Matt. 8:12; Mark 11:32; John 9:22; 12:42). The love of God in the believer will overcome fear

---

26. 25.251. Gavin De Becker, a crime expert, concludes that sometimes fear is based on mental clues about things that are strange and out of place. The victim of crime often feels afraid before an act of violence but does not know why. After the fact, when the situation is gone over in detail, the victim recognizes the objects in the situation that triggered their fear. He concludes, 'True fear is based on perceptions from your environment. Unwarranted fear is based on your imagination or memory' (De Becker, 'Listen to Your Fear', p. 133).

27. Carson, *When Jesus Confronts the World*, pp. 144–149. See also Hagner, *Matthew 1–13*, p. 286. See also Cranfield on Romans 8:15 (Cranfield, *Romans*, p. 396). On John see Smith, *The Theology of John*, p. 39.

28. France, *Matthew*, pp. 185–186. See also Goppelt, *Der Erste Petrusbrief*, p. 235.

29. Mundle, 'Fear', p. 623.

(1 John 4:17–18; 2 Tim. 1:7). Fear is also conquered by thinking about the promises of God.[30] A knowledge of God's protection and final judgment will ease fear.

This should not be taken to mean that there is no place for fear in the Christian's life. Fear of frightening circumstances is not condemned and is seen as a normal response (Matt. 17:6; Luke 1:13; 5:10; 8:25, 35, 37; Heb. 12:21; Rev. 1:17).[31] The New Testament does not rob the believer of this natural defence mechanism. It is a prolonged state of fearfulness that is not to be felt. The apostles feared Saul (Acts 9:26). Fear and awe were a regular reactions to Jesus (Matt. 14:26; Luke 5:26). In Matthew 28:8, fear is the reaction to seeing the resurrected Jesus. Mark's gospel ends with fear at seeing the risen Lord. Certainly to see Jesus alive was an awesome thing and fear was part of the natural response.

Paul is told twice in visions not to fear (Acts 18:9; 27:24). In Acts 18 this is followed by a threefold cognitive response to fear: 'that the Lord would be with him'; 'that none would harm him'; and that God had many people in this city.[32] In Acts 27 fear is the response to a great storm. Paul writes: 'For even when we came into Macedonia, our bodies had no rest, but we were afflicted in every way – disputes without and fears within' (2 Cor. 7:5; see also 2:4).[33] In this case Paul is comforted by the coming of Titus and the good news that he brings.[34] Paul was not immune from feeling fear, but he was comforted by the truths of the gospel and the warmth of Christian fellowship. We should also note that Paul naturally talked about his fears, a response we would not see from a Hellenistic philosopher.

The emotion of fear or worry over the state of his converts is also a legitimate emotion of Paul (Gal. 4:11; 1 Thess. 3:5). The phrase used by Paul, 'fear and trembling', which is used in positive contexts, is an interesting study (1 Cor.

---

30. Balz, 'phobeō, phobeomai, phobos, deos', p. 216; Morris, *Testaments of Love*, p. 192; Lutzer, *Managing Your Emotions*, pp. 75–81.

31. Balz, 'phobeō, phobeomai, phobos, deos', pp. 209–210; Hagner, *Hebrews*, p. 225; Ellingworth, *Hebrews*, pp. 675–676.

32. Williams, *Acts*, p. 316. See also Bruce, *Acts*, p. 372; Marshall, *Acts*, p. 296.

33. Thrall argues for Paul referring to the 'whole person' rather than just physical difficulties (Thrall, *Second Epistle to the Corinthians*, p. 487). 2 Cor. 12:21 gives cognitive reasons for Paul's fear of how the Corinthians may respond to him (Harris, '2 Corinthians', p. 401).

34. Barrett, *The Second Epistle to the Corinthians*, p. 207; Furnish, *2 Corinthians*, p. 395; Hafemann, *2 Corinthians*, pp. 310, 320.

2:3; 2 Cor. 7:15; Phil. 2:12; Eph. 6:5). Many commentators have downplayed the emotional content of the phrase, instead emphasizing respect or obedience.[35] Why is this necessary? The use of trembling certainly gives an emotional emphasis. It seems that scholars' tendency to play down the emotion in this phrase is driven more by their misunderstanding of the emotion of fear than by the text itself.

In the context of legitimate reasons to fear it is important to note that Jesus is never said to fear. Although he experiences grief, sorrow and anger, he does not fear. This would seem to be due to his superior authority, understanding of the future, and knowledge of God's provision and power. This is a powerful argument that in the New Testament emotions are cognitive. Jesus has no need to fear anything – he is the Son of God.

The New Testament also emphasizes the fear of God, or the awe and reverence that are due to him (Acts 9:31; 13:26; Rom. 3:18; 2 Cor. 5:11; 7:1; Eph. 5:21 [of Christ]; 1 Pet. 2:17; Rev. 14:7; 15:4; 19:5). This fear is clearly cognitive. That which is known to be true of God causes the believer to fear God. The Lord has power over us, we are in awe of him, he is our judge, and he is able to determine the future. In the tradition of the Old Testament (Deut. 13:11) the fear of God is motivational (Matt. 10:28; Luke 18:2; Acts 9:31; 2 Cor. 7:11; 1 Pet. 2:17). Matthew 10:28 clearly links the fear of God with future judgement (Heb. 10:31; Phil. 2:12; 1 Pet. 2:17). Hagner writes, 'The thought of the judgement of the living God is something that can only fill the heart with fear.'[36] 2 Corinthians 5 presents an interesting case. Paul gives reasons not to fear, followed by the fact that he fears God (v. 11). The proper fear of God helps to overcome the fear of death.

Scholars have often argued for a definitive separation of the fear of God from general fear.[37] For believers, the assurance that they do not sit under the judgment of God, like unbelievers, changes the fundamental character of the fear of the Lord. Like fear of earthly authorities, the fear of punishment keeps

---

35. Bruce, *Philippians*, pp. 82–83. For Porter it has little emotional content (Porter, 'Fear, Reverence', p. 293). It 'may have meant something far less forceful than what one might expect from considering separately each word of which it is composed' (Hawthorne, *Philippians*, p. 100). Bockmuehl downplays the emotional content (*Philippians*, p. 153). See also Gnilka, *Der Philipperbrief*, p. 149; O'Brien, *Philippians*, pp. 282–284.

36. Hagner, *Hebrews*, p. 170. See also Ellingworth, *Hebrews*, p. 543; Luz, *Matthew 8–20*, pp. 102–103.

37. Balz, '*phobeō, phobeomai, phobos, deos*', pp. 197, 258.

a person from doing wrong, but if no crime has been committed there is no reason to fear. At the same time, the knowledge of their position and authority does impart a general fear.

The fear of the Lord also has some affinity to the fear that slaves are to have for their masters (Eph. 6:5; 1 Pet. 2:18). This fear should be a motivation to do good.[38] Paul is also not afraid to use a strong rebuke, to put a healthy fear of sinning into the church (1 Tim. 5:20; Rom. 11:19–22). In 2 Peter 2:10 the wicked are characterized by their lack of fear for heavenly beings. Although there is a different emphasis and spirit from general fear for the believer, there are good reasons to fear God. To clearly differentiate this fear as meaning awe, as opposed to emotional fear, is misguided.

Do not worry

Worry, like fear, is the opposite of hope. Where hope is based on a positive expectation of the future, worry is the negative expectation of the future with an emphasis on the fact that the future outcome is not sure. Where fear is most often an intense feeling about a specific future event, worry is most often a general pervasive anxiety. Worry is often prohibited in the New Testament. Betz writes of Matthew 6: 'The prohibitive imperative "Do not worry" (*mē merimnate*) is meant to be categorical with no exception allowed; it is repeated in 28, 31 and 34, and thus constitutes the major exhortation of the passage.'[39]

Worry is predominantly seen in a negative light in the New Testament but it is not condemned universally. For example, Paul uses terms for worry, anxiety or care about himself where it is not condemned (2 Cor. 11:28; 12:25; Phil. 2:20, 28),[40] However, worry is most often felt over things of this world which the Christian is not to value. Following Paul's example, anxiety over the state of a specific person or church is sometimes legitimate, where a pervasive attitude is not.

This is well illustrated by the command of Jesus in Matthew 6:25–34 (Luke 12:22–34). Do not worry about what you will wear or what you will eat. Jesus emphasizes the sovereignty of God in response to worrying about the daily

---

38. Stein, 'The Argument of Romans 13:1–7', pp. 332–333.

39. Betz, *The Sermon on the Mount*, p. 469.

40. Hay presents a good summary of the doubts and anxiety that Paul expresses in 2 Cor. and the part this plays in the writing of the book (Hay, 'The Shaping of Theology in 2 Corinthians', pp. 144–146). For an analysis of the vocabulary see Goetzmann, 'Care, Anxiety'. He notes that it can be used in both a positive and negative sense. On Phil. 2:20 see O'Brien, *Philippians*, p. 319.

cares of life.[41] The major point for us is the clear cognitive basis for not worrying. When believers are told not to worry about these things there are good reasons for it. For example, believers are not to worry about what to say in their defence because God will provide them with what to say (Matt. 10:19; Mark 13:11; Luke 12:11–12). The cares of this life are not worth worrying about in light of future glory or judgment (Luke 21:34). Paul also presents a reason for not worrying in Philippians 4:6. The believer, instead of worrying, is to make prayers to a faithful God (Rom. 8:38–39). In 1 Peter 5:7 Christians can cast their worry on God with the assurance that he is concerned about them, a response similar to that of Jesus in Matthew 6.[42] A belief in God, his care for his people, and his activity in history on behalf of his people give freedom from worry.

We have seen that to the Hellenistic philosophers fear was universally harmful and was to be overcome with right thinking. The New Testament has both similarities to and differences from this view. Fear is not seen as a universal enemy. Instead, it is often a natural reaction to an event or is felt for those that are loved. God would not rob us of a needed defence mechanism that often protects both our body and spirit from harm. Fear of God, of earthly leaders, of angels and concern over the welfare of others are often seen as appropriate. In some of these cases the fear is to be quickly dispelled with knowledge. Both the Hellenistic philosophers and the New Testament used knowledge to overcome fear. Christians are not to live in a state of fear or worry and they are not to fear the future or the powers of this world.

Grief and sorrow

Solomon writes, 'Sadness, sorrow, grief, and mourning are, like fear, extremely simple emotions, judgements of loss. The difference between them is mainly the severity and scope of the loss and its relative place in our world.'[43] Many Hellenistic writers agree with the Stoics that grief is usually negative. To Philo being without sorrow is an attribute of God. This was also taught by some church fathers (2 Clem. 19:4).[44] In contrast, in the New Testament sorrow and

---

41. Carson, *The Sermon on the Mount*, pp. 89–105; France, *Matthew*, pp. 141–142; Betz, *The Sermon on the Mount*, p. 475.

42. See Minear, *The Commands of Christ*, p. 139.

43. Solomon, *The Passions*, p. 359. See also Ben-Ze'ev, *The Subtlety of Emotions*, pp. 466–467.

44. Bultmann, '*lypē, lypeō*', pp. 319, 323.

grief are profound human emotions that help us come to grips with tragedy. When something of great value is lost, our hearts express sorrow. Jesus and Paul weep over those who have not listened to their message (Phil. 3:18). Paul grieves over the sin of his converts (2 Cor. 2:1). Grief and sadness is a sign of true repentance (Jas 4:8–9). Grief is felt by the community over death and loss (John 11:33–36; Acts 8:2; 9:39; Rom. 12:15). Calvin writes:

> You see that to bear the cross patiently is not to have your feelings altogether blunted, and to be absolutely insensible to pain, according to the absurd description which the Stoics of old gave of their hero as one who, divested of humanity, was affected in the same way by adversity and prosperity, grief and joy; or rather, like a stone, was not affected by anything.[45]

Sorrow in the Gospels

Jesus was a man of sorrows. This is readily evident in the Synoptic Gospel's passion narrative with the use of *perilypos* (deeply sad or distressed) (Matt. 26:38; Mark 14:34).[46] The strong language in these passages, commentators agree, is emotionally intense.[47] Jesus' full understanding of the suffering before him was the reason for the overwhelming nature of this sorrow.[48] It is interesting to note that many commentators see this sorrow as evidence of the humanity of Jesus. Yet, we have seen that the sorrow of God plays a major role in the Old Testament. The sorrow of Jesus, therefore, is not necessarily a special sign of the humanity of Jesus. This implication seems to show a belief in the impassibility of God.[49]

Warfield writes of the passion, 'In the presence of this mental anguish the physical tortures of the crucifixion retire into the background, and we may well believe that our Lord, though he died on the cross, yet died not of the

---

45. Calvin, *Institutes*, translated by Beveridge, 3.8.9. Here he cites the examples of Paul and Jesus.

46. Bultmann, '*lypē, lypeō*', p. 323.

47. Davies and Allison, *Matthew*, vol. 3, p. 496; Hagner, *Matthew 14–28*, p. 782; Pesch, *Das Markusevangelium*, vol. 2, p. 392; Mann, *Mark*, pp. 479–481.

48. Cranfield, *Mark*, pp. 431–432; Lane, *Mark*, p. 516. Several commentators contrast this to rejoicing in tribulations and Stephen's attitude in facing death. In the case of Stephen, he had knowledge of the glory that awaited him while Jesus concentrated on the pain that he was about to face. The contrasting emotions are based on contrasting thinking.

49. For example, Hurtado, *Mark*, p. 242.

cross, but, as we commonly say, of a broken heart, that is to say, of the strain of his mental suffering.'[50] This passage also presents us with a good opportunity for further analysis. Before and after the agony of the garden, Jesus appears to set his mind and will upon the task and goes forward towards the cross with great determination. As we have seen, our emotions can be changed by what we choose to dwell upon, or what thoughts we choose not to dwell upon. However, even Jesus must allow the thoughts of the future suffering to be at the forefront of his mind for a time. He does not deny these thoughts but gives himself the freedom to experience a time of deep emotional pain. This seems similar to the pattern we see with the death of Lazarus. As we all have experienced with great grief, there are times we choose to dwell on other things and go on with life, and times we must just let it flow out of our hearts.

Jesus was grieved for other's pain or over their condition. Mark 3:5 relates: 'And he looked around at them with anger, grieved at their hardness of heart, and said to the man, "Stretch out your hand". He stretched it out, and his hand was restored.' To Warfield the sigh of Jesus speaks of his sorrow (Mark 7:34; 8:12).[51] Likewise Jesus grieves over Jerusalem. His love compels his grief (Matt. 23:37).[52] Jesus' sorrow is like the sorrow of the prophets over Israel. It is sorrow over rebellion against God and as such clearly cognitive.[53] As one who grieves, Jesus also knows how to give comfort to those who weep. This may take the form of a miracle of healing or the presentation of good reasons not to be troubled (Luke 7:13). The exhortation is not a Stoic exhortation never to grieve, but rather, comfort given in specific circumstances.

John does not mention Jesus' agony of soul in the garden but he does mention it in 12:27.[54] To Robinson this agony is part of the background and setting of the passion (John 12:27; Matt. 26:37; Mark 14:34).[55] In John 16:6, 20–22 it is clear that Jesus expects the events of his death to bring great grief and sorrow to his disciples. This is not something that he is protecting them from or forbidding them. He sees it as a natural consequence of the events

---

50. Warfield, 'The Emotional Life of Our Lord', p. 133.

51. Warfield, 'The Emotional Life of Our Lord', p. 100. Notice that in 8:12 this sorrow is over sin.

52. Davies and Allison, *Matthew*, vol. 3, pp. 319–320.

53. Guelich, *Mark 1–8:26*, p. 137.

54. Carson, *John*, pp. 439–440. See also Witherington, *John's Wisdom*, p. 224; Beasley-Murray, *John*, p. 212; Bruce, *John*, pp. 265–266.

55. Robinson, 'Gethsemane'. See Schnackenburg, *John*, vol. 2, p. 387.

that will follow. Schnackenburg believes that the point of the teaching is for the disciples to be able to overcome this sorrow because of their knowledge of 'the joy which has [will] been given to them since Easter and which cannot pass away.'[56] The knowledge of the risen Lord will wipe away the sorrow felt over the loss of Jesus. Jesus also offers a cognitive way of dealing with sorrow in John 14:1–3 (Rom. 8:18). Sorrow is only temporary.[57]

John 11 is perhaps the most controversial passage about grief in the gospels. Jesus' weeping in John 11 is not universally accepted as grief over the death of Lazarus. To Haarbeck it is 'because of the faithless and hopeless lamentation for the dead with which he finds himself surrounded . . . His saving life giving work puts an end to lamentation for the dead (Luke 7:13) . . . All natural mourning for those who have fallen asleep is now eradicated by the living hope of the resurrection (Rom. 8:17, 18).'[58] This approach to grief is certainly not what we see in the New Testament. Luke 7:13, his example, is a comfort for grief, not an exhortation not to grieve.

Schnackenburg finds that the weeping is for 'the darkness and inevitability of death' and expressly argues that it is not about the death of Lazarus.[59] Beasley-Murray writes, 'How, then, are the tears of Jesus to be interpreted? Certainly not through grief for Lazarus: his illness and death had been stated to be for the glory of God (v. 4), and Jesus was now advancing to his tomb to call him from it, not to weep beside it.'[60] These interpretations make one wonder if attributing the emotion of genuine grief to Jesus is what is in reality difficult for these scholars.

Walters agrees that many scholars have a predisposition to deny the deep grief of Jesus. He argues strongly that every evidence in the passage points to Jesus' tears being shed in grief over the death of Lazarus. 'The language used in this rare cameo of Jesus' feelings is extremely graphic and vivid . . . So far, there would seem to be nothing in the words used to indicate that Jesus was suffering anything other than grief for a dead friend.' Further, anger and grief often go hand in hand, making the argument of many commentaries that grief

---

56. Schnackenburg, *John*, vol. 3, p. 127. See also the excellent discussion in vol. 3, p. 159; Beasley-Murray, *John*, p. 285; Bruce, *John*, pp. 322–323.

57. Lutzer, *Managing Your Emotions*, p. 169.

58. Haarbeck, '*klaiō, koptō*', pp. 418–419. See also Becker, *Das Evangelium nach Johannes: Kapitel 11–21*, p. 354.

59. Schnackenburg, *John*, vol. 2, p. 337. See also Schnackenburg, *Jesus in the Gospels*, p. 241; Becker, *Das Evangelium nach Johannes: Kapitel 11–21*, p. 363.

60. Beasley-Murray, *John*, p. 193. See the similar comments of Carson, *John*, p. 416.

cannot closely follow the anger in 11:33 untenable.[61] Bruce also presents an excellent summary of the passage. 'Some commentators have found it difficult to suppose that he who is presented in this Gospel as the incarnate Word, knowing what he was going to do, should be genuinely moved by sorrow and sympathy . . . and have put his tears down to some other cause – anger and frustration, perhaps . . . But the friends and neighbours who were there had no doubt about the cause of his tears: he was weeping for a dearly loved friend.'[62]

Walters also points out that the grief in Acts 8:2, over the death of Stephen, is proof of the legitimate place of grief in the New Testament. Stephen was assured of eternal reward and believers grieved over his death.[63] This example parallels our analysis of John 11 and refutes the argument that Jesus would not have grieved because of his knowledge of the future.

We should not neglect the fact that in the synoptic Gospels there are also a number of reasons why the unbeliever grieves. The rich ruler in Luke 18 is grieved over the possible loss of possessions which shows the condition of his heart (Rev. 18:7–11).[64] The wicked weep in anguish after death (Matt. 8:12; 13:42; Luke 6:25).[65] The second coming will be a time of sorrow for those who do not believe (Matt. 24:30). Sorrow for the unbeliever is great as they love those things that will perish.

Sorrow in Pauline literature and the later New Testament

2 Corinthians has an especially high number of references to sorrow and grief. A key text is 7:8–11. What is the difference between godly and worldly grief

---

61. Walters, *Why Do Christians Find It Hard to Grieve?*, pp. 28–29. 'We find the evangelist teaching us the surprising reality that grief is a valid response to death, even for those who hope for the resurrection beyond death' (p. 30). A number of commentators point out that the genuine nature of Jesus' sorrow is emphasized by the fact that Jesus is said to *dakryō* while the other mourners *klaiō* (Michaels, *John*, p. 206). See also Barrett, *John*, p. 334; Tenney, 'John', p. 119.

62. Bruce, *John*, p. 246. Ridderbos gives a good summary arguing against a 'forced interpretation' (Ridderbos, *John*, pp. 401–403).

63. Some insist that this was grief of non-believing Jews. Walters rightly points out that grief is felt even when hope in the resurrection is part of the mourners' faith. Walters, *Why Do Christians Find It Hard to Grieve?*, p. 33. See Haenchen, *The Acts of the Apostles*, p. 294; Pesch, *Die Apostelgeschichte*, vol. 1, p. 265.

64. Sadness is the result of love for the world. Gnilka, *Das Matthäusevangelium*, vol. 2, p. 316.

65. Bovon, *Das Evangelium nach Lukas*, vol. 1, pp. 302–303.

(*lypē*)? Simply put, what is the object of the grief? Grief which is felt over the values of this world is worldly, that which is felt over God's values is godly. Godly grief leads to spiritual renewal.[66] In this context, we should also mention the sorrow in repentance expressed in James 4:9. This is reminiscent of the sorrow over sin that is seen in the Old Testament.[67] Moo writes: 'What men will do when God's judgement overtakes them can be avoided if they mourn and weep for sin now.'[68] Davids concludes, 'Grieving is so natural that any other response would be inappropriate.'[69] True remorse for sin will be expressed in emotional grief.

We also see Paul grieving over the Corinthians' sin (2 Cor. 12:21; see also 1 Cor. 5:2). In 1 Corinthians 5:2, instead of seeing sorrow in repentance, Conzelmann writes, 'Sorrow is not primarily a feeling, but likewise a judgment – a judgment on sin.'[70] Bultmann writes that 1 Corinthians 5:2 'is not a sorrowful expression of repentance' and about Matthew 5:4 'Hence the sorrow referred to here is not to be regarded too narrowly as penitent sorrow for sin.'[71] To the contrary, feeling counts in repentance. The person who says they are sorry and does not feel sorry is not repentant. An insincere apology does little good to the one who was wronged. The emotion says that the repentance is true and the lack of emotion proves it false.[72] Fee counters that the verse refers to 'that deep anguish of soul frequently related to true repentance'.[73] This agrees with our conclusions from the Old Testament, where grief is a sign of true repentance.

In Ephesians 4:30 Paul commands not to grieve (*lypeō*) the Holy Spirit. Bultmann believes this is to insult, not to produce emotional grief in the Holy

---

66. See Thrall, *Second Epistle to the Corinthians*, p. 492; Bultmann, *Theology*, vol. 1, p. 226; Hughes; *Second Epistle to the Corinthians*, p. 273; Wolff, *Der zweite Brief des Paulus an die Korinther*, p. 157.

67. Laws, *James*, p. 184; Moo, *James, TNTC*, pp. 148–150; Mußner, *Der Jakobusbrief*, p. 186; Moo, *James*, PNTC, p. 195.

68. Moo, *James, TNTC*, p. 150. See also Davids, *James, NIGTC*, p. 167.

69. Davids, *James, NIBC*, p. 103.

70. Conzelmann, *1 Corinthians*, p. 96.

71. Bultmann, '*penthos, pentheō*', p. 43. The use of the same word for both grief over sin and grief over death speaks to the similarity of the emotional experience.

72. Matthews, 'Ritual and the Religious Feelings', pp. 345–346.

73. Fee, *Corinthians*, p. 202. See also Thiselton, *The First Epistle to the Corinthians*, p. 388; Schrage, *Der erste Brief an die Korinther*, vol. 1, p. 372.

74. Bultmann, '*lypē, lypeō*', p. 322.

Spirit.[74] However, if God feels emotion there seems to be no need for this interpretation. Louw and Nida do not acknowledge the definition of 'to insult' for the
word. The Holy Spirit feels grief over believers' sin.

Christians are to share each other's sorrows and burdens. Michaelis argues
that the use of 'suffer' (*sympaschō*) in 1 Corinthians 12:26, 'When applied to the
community 12:26a does not mean that when a member suffers harm all the
members share the loss emotionally' (Rom. 8:17; 12:15).[75] However, suffering
is part of the Christian life and is to be shared by the community. When we
grieve with another we show our love and care for them. What hurts them
hurts us. To limit this to non-emotional sharing in suffering is to rob bearing
one another's burdens of its positive impact.

In 2 Corinthians 6:3–10 it is clear that grief is part of Paul's ministry (John
16:20–22). Romans 9:2–3 shows Paul experiencing grief and mental anguish
over the unbelief of Israel. The tears of Paul are a sign of 'the abundant love
that I have for you' (2 Cor. 2:4).[76] Paul both acknowledges the grief in his own
life and the life of others while insisting that grief and sorrow can be tempered
and healed with a knowledge of eschatology and Christian truth. Hawthorne
writes of Philippians 2:27, 'In the final analysis even for Paul death is an enemy
(cf. 1 Cor. 15:26), and sickness and death are bearers of pain and grief which
are not at all anticipated or endured with joy.'[77]

Paul puts together lists of afflictions like the Hellenistic moralists. Instead of
showing himself as a model of endurance and staying power, Paul was a model
of God's sustaining grace in weakness (2 Cor. 1:8, 9). Thus we see both similarity and great differences between the two.[78] To Paul there are good reasons
for endurance in suffering. It produces fruit in the believer's life, increases
reliance on God, and it shows us how to comfort others (Rom. 5:3–4; 2 Cor.
1:3–9).

According to Sullender, Paul combined elements from the Greco-Roman
philosophical school, Hebrew traditions and his own Christian perspective
when he dealt with grief. Grief is natural when you encounter loss, but it is to
be tempered by the knowledge of Christ and the resurrection. The loss is temporary. Unlike the Greek philosophers, the knowledge that softens the blow is
eschatological, not philosophical. A major theme in Paul is the comfort of the
saints. He provides this comfort by speaking about the truths of the gospel

---

75. Michaelis, '*paschō, pathētos*', p. 925.

76. See Bultmann, '*lypē, lypeō*', p. 320; Hughes, *Second Epistle to the Corinthians*, p. 54.

77. Hawthorne, *Philippians*, p. 118.

78. Kruse, 'Afflictions, Trials, Hardships', pp. 19–20; Martin, *2 Corinthians*, pp. 14, 36.

(1 Cor. 12:26).[79] Personally, comfort came to Paul from both spiritual knowledge and human companionship (2 Cor. 7:6; Rom. 5:3–5; 8:25; 2 Cor. 5:6–8; 4:1, 16; 1 Cor. 13:7). These methods of dealing with sorrow seem to imply that Paul held a cognitive view of the emotions. Paul believed that loving one another will naturally result in a community that comforts those who grieve.[80]

In 1 Corinthians 7:30 it may seem that Paul advocates the idea of avoiding mourning and grief. This is not the case. Barrett summarizes, 'The point is that neither laughter not tears is the last word; a man should never allow himself to be lost in either.'[81] Sorrow is not to be exalted or celebrated – it is part of a fallen world. Paul is glad that he is spared the sorrow of Epaphroditus' death (Phil. 2:27).[82]

As we have seen, grief of the Christian is tempered by future hope. 1 Thessalonians 4:13–18[83] is well worth reading as it presents an excellent summary.

Sorrow in the New Testament

Grief is not a sinful emotion but it is a result of sin. God and his people have legitimate grief because of sin and the pain it brings (Acts 8:2; 20:37–38; Phil. 2:27). At the same time, the Christian has different reasons for sorrow than the world. The Christian is not to feel overwhelming grief over the loss of goods, fortune or position. Sorrow over our own sin or over others being lost is a sign of our love for God and other people. Believers look towards a day when grief will be banished (Rev. 7:17; 21:4).[84] Even in facing the death of another person, Christians have a hope that allows them not to 'grieve as others do who have no hope' (1 Thess. 4:13; see also 5:10; 1 Cor. 15:55–57). The wicked's eternal state, however, will be characterized by sorrow and pain. Luke uses the expression 'there will be weeping and gnashing of teeth' to describe their future torment (Luke 13:28).

---

79. Sullender, 'Saint Paul's Approach to Grief', pp. 66–67.

80. Sullender, 'Saint Paul's Approach to Grief', pp. 68–69. When we do not grieve we do not heal and our grief will often work its way out physically in some other way (Sullender, 'Saint Paul's Approach to Grief', pp. 69–73).

81. Barrett, *The First Epistle to the Corinthians*, p. 178.

82. O'Brien, *Philippians*, pp. 340–341.

83. See Harris, '2 Corinthians', pp. 344–345; Holtz, *Der erste Brief an die Thessalonicher*, pp. 204–208; Marshall, *Thessalonians*, p. 120; Bruce, *Thessalonians*, pp. 96, 103–105.

84. This has strong cognitive content in Revelation. Aune, *Revelation 17–22*, pp. 1124–1125; Caird, *Revelation of St John*, p. 265; Keener, *Revelation*, pp. 503–509; Ladd, *Revelation*, pp. 277–278; Morris, *Revelation*, p. 238; Beale, *Revelation*, p. 1049.

Finally, sorrow is a part of true repentance. Roberts writes:

> the feeling of emotion, however finely tuned it is in itself, and however dramatic may
> be the actions that issue from it, is no guarantee of genuine penitence. And yet an
> emotion (I call it contrition) is the centerpiece and moving force of the process of
> repentance and the formation of a new self.[85]

The relation of repentance to the love of God is revealed in the parables of
Luke 15. The characters understand the immensity of their sin before God.
This is in opposition to the pride of the Pharisees in their own righteousness
(Luke 18:13).[86] Grief shows that the gravity of the sin is understood and the
desire to repent is present.

Anger and hatred

Stauffer believes that a child of God birthed by love 'renounces all hatred'.[87]
Kant also presented objections to hatred.[88] Generally, in Christian circles anger
is seen as destructive and sinful. Psychologists, on the other hand, have often
argued for a healthy release of anger in many circumstances. To them, feeling
anger is not a reason to feel guilty. What is the position of the New Testament?
    Ben-Ze'ev defines anger and hate in the following manner:

> General Characterization:
> *Anger*: A specific negative emotional attitude toward another agent who is considered
> to have inflicted unjustified harm upon us.
> *Hate*: A global negative emotional attitude toward another agent who is considered to
> possess fundamentally negative traits . . .
> Beliefs:
> *Anger*:
> (1) A belief that the object has committed a blameworthy act;

---

85. Roberts, 'The Logic and Lyric of Contrition', p. 194.
86. Schnackenburg, *The Moral Teaching of the New Testament*, pp. 28–29, 32. With
    increased joy in God there will be increased sorrow over sin (Schlatter, *Die
    Christliche Ethik*, pp. 322–323).
87. Stauffer, '*agapaō, agapē, agapētos*', p. 48.
88. Murphy and Hampton, *Forgiveness and Mercy*, pp. 100–101.

(2) A perceived threat to something of value to the subject;

(3) A belief that the object's act has undesirable consequences for the subject;

(4) A belief that the object deserves to be punished.

Hate:

(1) A belief that the object has some fundamentally negative traits;

(2) A perceived threat to something of fundamental value to the subject;

(3) A belief that the object's fundamental traits oppose the subject's basic standards;

(4) A belief that the object deserves to be avoided or even eliminated.[89]

In general, hate is more universal and continues through time, where anger is usually about an individual's situation and is short-term.[90] With the exception of hating evil, a failure to feel hatred is rarely a character flaw. Not feeling anger often indicates a character flaw. For example, not being angry at the holocaust shows the moral depravity of the person.[91]

In this section we will consider hatred and anger together as they have many of the same characteristics. When discussing them we should remember the differences outlined above. We will concentrate on *orgē* (anger), *thymos* (wrath) and *miseō* (to hate).[92]

---

89. Ben-Ze'ev, 'Anger and Hate', pp. 85–86. He also emphasizes the overlap in meaning. 'The borderline between anger and hate is not always clear' (Ben-Ze'ev, *The Subtlety of Emotions*, p. 383). See also Taylor, 'Justifying the Emotions'; Solomon, *The Passions*, pp. 283–286.

90. Ben-Ze'ev, 'Anger and Hate'; Ben-Ze'ev, *The Subtlety of Emotions*, pp. 380–382.

91. Taylor, 'Justifying the Emotions', p. 401.

92. The definitions of Greek lexicons are not particularly helpful for this discussion as they use the English equivalents of anger and hate. It is clear that these terms had emotional content. *Orgē* and *thymos* are similar and both are similar to the Hebrew terms (Schönweiss, '*thymos*', p. 106; Hahn, '*orgē*', p. 108). Many writers classify *orgē* as a more settled disposition that is more likely to be used of the wrath of God and *thymos* as a hot passion that is more likely to be used of the sinful anger of man. However, both are used for both ideas. See also Longenecker, *Galatians*, p. 256. Chambers argues extensively that *lypeō* can also contain the idea of anger. If this is true, the case for moral cognitive anger as presented in this thesis of both God and man becomes even stronger (Matt. 19:22; John 16; Eph. 4:30; 2 Cor. 7:8–11) (Chambers, 'Godly Human Anger', pp. 78, 81, 85, 90, 103, 109–113).

Anger in the Gospels

Anger

Mark 3:5 is the only passage in the gospels where Jesus is clearly said to be angry. Jesus' anger in Mark 3:5, according to Cerling, was because of an 'unmet or violated human need'.[93] Compassion fueled it. He was both angry at the Jewish leaders' hypocrisy and grieved at their hardness of heart (Mark 11:17). His anger shows the character of God.[94] The reason for anger in this situation fits the pattern for God's anger, i.e. anger at 'sin, oppression, and injustice'.[95]

In Mark 10:14 Jesus was indignant (*aganakteō*) with the disciples. The disciples' emotions came from their misplaced values and Jesus responded in anger. Mann writes, 'this verse enshrines the whole point of the periscope'. Jesus' emotion shows the importance of the lesson.[96] The aim of Jesus' anger was to set things right, it had a constructive purpose. We should also highlight the fact that Jesus was sometimes angry with his disciples, his friends. This fits a cognitive framework. He placed great value in them and therefore their wrong actions hurt. In John 11 many commentators take the language of verses 33 and 38 to speak of the anger of Jesus.[97]

Even when anger vocabulary is not used, anger is sometimes implied in Jesus' words (Matt. 3:7; 16:23; 21:12; 23:13–17; Mark 8:33; 11:15; 12:24–27; Luke 19:45; John 2:14–17).[98] In these passages it would be hard to picture Jesus without anger. This is especially true of the cleansing of the temple. It is clear

---

93. Cerling, 'Anger: Musings of a Theologian/Psychologist', pp. 12–13.

94. Cranfield, *Mark*, p. 121. See also Lane, *Mark*, p. 123.

95. Cerling, 'Anger: Musings of a Theologian/Psychologist', p. 13. See also Tasker, *The Biblical Doctrine of the Wrath of God*, p. 30; Warfield, 'The Emotional Life of Our Lord', pp. 107–108, 122; Pesch, *Das Markusevangelium*, vol. 1, p. 193; Gnilka, *Das Evangelium nach Markus*, vol. 2, p. 128.

96. Mann, *Mark*, p. 396. See also Gnilka, *Das Evangelium nach Markus*, p. 81.

97. Schnackenburg, *John*, vol. 2, pp. 336–338; Beasley-Murray, *John*, pp. 192–194; Carson, *John*, pp. 415–416. Carson writes, 'With most of us, to be angry with someone is inconsistent with being loving.' This statement is clearly not true. Love often drives anger; we are much more likely to be angry with our own child for their lack of discipline than someone else's.

98. See Chambers, 'Godly Human Anger', pp. 184–186.

that Jesus took this dramatic action for good reason. His anger was fuelled by an understanding of the true role of the temple.[99] Warfield gives a good summary of Jesus' 'anger' in passages where anger is not mentioned. His rebuke of evil spirits seems to contain anger. He also uses harsh names for the enemies of God (Matt. 7:6, 15; 12:34; Mark 7:33; Luke 13:32; John 8:44).[100] Morris points to Jesus' many sayings of judgment and being in danger of hell as clear words of personal wrath against sin.[101] God is also seen to be angry at sin in the Gospels (John 3:36). Carson writes, 'God's wrath is not some impersonal principle of retribution, but the personal response of a holy God who comes to his own world, sadly fallen into rebellion, and finds few who want anything to do with him.'[102]

Jesus also tells stories where anger seems to be legitimate (Matt. 18:34; 22:7; Luke 14:21). Hahn explains these by saying: 'Yet it has to be asked whether in these cases anger is not to be understood as participation by men in the anger of God.'[103] He implies that anger is legitimate for God and not for man. A cognitive understanding of anger quickly makes this kind of explanation unnecessary. Anger felt by God or man for the right reasons is legitimate. The important factor is not who is feeling the anger but why it is felt. In the parable in Luke 14:21 a strong word for anger is used, *orgizomai*). The word is meant to express passion and deep feeling.[104]

The teaching of Jesus elicited violent anger in some of his hearers (Luke 4:28). Here we see a cognitive reason for anger, they were angry at the content of his teaching. The enemies of Jesus are not passive; their anger against Jesus' message is intense and motivates their vicious attacks.[105]

Jesus offers a cognitive solution to wrong anger. In John 7:23–24 Jesus attacks the thinking behind the anger in order to show that their anger with

99. Lane, *Mark*, p. 406; Hurtado, *Mark*, p. 55; Tenney, 'John', p. 44; Witherington, *John's Wisdom*, p. 87. 'His anger was kindled to a white heat at the site of simple people cheated. (Barclay, *The Mind of Jesus*, p. 191).

100. Warfield, 'The Emotional Life of Our Lord', pp. 119–121; Schnackenburg, *Jesus in the Gospels*, p. 34.

101. Morris, *The Apostolic Preaching of the Cross*, p. 181. See also Tasker, *The Biblical Doctrine of the Wrath of God*, pp. 28, 36.

102. Carson, *John*, p. 214.

103. Hahn, '*orgē*', p. 111.

104. Denney, 'The Word "Hate" in Luke 14:26', p. 41.

105. Barclay, *The Mind of Jesus*, pp. 160–161. See also Ridderbos, *John*, pp. 116–117; Becker, *Jesus of Nazareth*, pp. 60–62.

him is not right (Matt. 21:15–16). We must carefully analyse Jesus' prohibition of anger directed towards a brother (Matt. 5:22). Anger in this case is subject to judgment; people are held accountable for it. This is only possible in a cognitive framework. Scholars are quick to make this a blanket prohibition of anger while making no reference to the object of that anger.[106] Davies and Allison write: 'They must go to the source and root out all anger.'[107] Becker agrees: 'The focus is not on the issue of justified or unjustified anger, but on anger itself as a possibility for human existence . . . Every angry person stands completely under God's wrath.'[108]

Carson disagrees: 'Jesus forbids not all anger but the anger that arises out of personal relationships.' This is clear in the idea of murder and the examples of Jesus.[109] Keener agrees, 'Jesus' prohibition of acting in anger is a general principle. As in each of his six examples, Jesus graphically portrays a general principle . . . Most people understood that such general principles expressed in proverbs and similar sayings sometimes needed to be qualified in specific situations.'[110] Our anger all too easily revolves around ourselves, even when it seems to be about injustice. We must also ask if Jesus' command points toward a cognitive view of anger. The reason that anger can be compared to murder is because the thoughts and values that are behind it are similar or identical. Anger can be a sin in itself. If anger were a non-cognitive entity Jesus' statement would not make sense.

We should also comment on Jesus' lack of anger in the passion narratives. Jesus does not become angry at those who arrest him, his accusers, his judge, or those who execute him. Even when those who stand against him are clearly wrong, he does not respond in anger. Instead, his actions and words are those of mercy, love and forgiveness. An offence against Jesus' person does not arouse his anger. This agrees with Matthew 5:43–44: 'You have heard that it was said, "You shall love your neighbour and hate your enemy." But I say to you, Love your enemies and pray for those who persecute you.' This teaching has sometimes been misunderstood. Stachowiak writes,

---

106. Johnson and Buttrick, 'The Gospel According to St Matthew', pp. 163, 294; Hagner, *Matthew 1–13*, p. 116. See also Schnackenburg, *Matthäusevangelium: 1, 1–16, 20*, p. 54.

107. Davies and Allison, *Matthew*, p. 509.

108. Becker, *Jesus of Nazareth*, p. 251.

109. Carson, *The Sermon on the Mount*, p. 47.

110. Keener, *Matthew*, p. 114. See also Chambers, 'Godly Human Anger', p. 25. 'As often Jesus exaggerates to make his point' (France, *Matthew*, p. 120).

'Christ dissolved any possible misunderstanding by absolutely forbidding any kind of hatred.'[111] The lessons of the Sermon on the Mount should be emphasized here. The disciple is not to return hatred and violence for hatred and violence (Matt. 5:38–42; 1 Pet. 2:23).

Hatred

We now move to an analysis of hate in the Gospels. Vine defines hate as 'relative preference for one thing over another' (in passages like Matt. 6:24; Luke 16:13; John 12:25).[112] Friberg agrees '(4) of the opp. of divine election hate, reject, not choose (RO 9.13).' *BDAG* also gives two definitions, one being emotional hatred and one 'to be disinclined to, *disfavor*'. Louw and Nida, to their credit, do not have this as a separate definition. Carson concludes of Matt. 6:24 that hate 'simply means the latter is strongly preferred'. Carson gives no proof for this conclusion.[113] To most commentators the command of Jesus to hate one's father and mother speaks of the supreme importance of the disciples' love for God (Luke 14:26). This use parallels the Old Testament's opposition of love and hate, especially in the wisdom literature. They conclude it is not about emotion. To Marshall it is to 'love less' or 'leave aside'. 'The thought is, therefore, not of psychological hate, but of renunciation.'[114] Does this statement contain an emotional element or is it an expression that means exclusive commitment or a Hebraic contrast?[115]

Michel emphasizes that this is not an emotion.[116] To him the commands of Jesus to 'hate' one's relatives do not refer in any sense to 'a psychologically conditioned shunning of men'. Similarly, the commands to hate evil stress holiness, separation, and the new order of God as opposed to the old order typified by hate. 'The NT overcomes all possible forms of hate between man

---

111. Stachowiak, 'Hatred', p. 354. France argues that this is not emotional (France, *Matthew*, p. 128).

112. Vine, *Hate*, p. 292. Painter seems to downplay hatred as an emotion in John as it is 'the Hebraic sense of choosing and rejecting' (Painter, *The Quest for the Messiah*, p. 47).

113. Carson, *The Sermon on the Mount*, p. 88. See also France, *Matthew*, p. 139.

114. Marshall, *Luke*, p. 592. He follows *TDNT*. Tannehill argues that 'In the ancient world the terms love and hate referred less to emotions than to behaviour that either honored of dishonored someone else.' He offers no concrete proof of this (Tannehill, *Luke*, p. 235).

115. Seebass, 'Enemy, Enmity, Hate', p. 556. See also Michel, '*miseō*', pp. 690–691.

116. Michel, '*miseō*', pp. 690–691.

and man, including religious.'[117] Carr writes that, 'It is here that we find the true key to meaning of (to hate). "To hate father and mother" is not to hate them personally, but to oppose the principles which they represent in opposition to Christ.'[118] Like Jacob's hate of Leah this hatred is 'little more than the contrast produced by preference' (Gen. 29:30–31).[119] To Carr, English 'hate' does not have this meaning.[120] But surely English often has this meaning – we can say 'I hate sausage' without any sense of anger, vengeance or retribution. Remember hate is characterized by the rejection of a fundamental quality of an object. Second, was not Jacob's rejection in the context of a very emotional situation? It was obviously not an unemotional rejection.

Is it possible that these passages do not contain a different meaning of the word hate, but rather hate is used as an example, illustration, or hyperbole? It is used to emphasize the greatness of the love and commitment the disciple is to have for God. Is this meaning, in fact, parallel to the use of hate/love imagery in the Old Testament? To change the meaning of the vocabulary is to rob these expressions of their shock value and power and take the edge and offence from them. This is not the solution to the 'problem' of why hate is used in these contexts. Jesus was making a point. The vocabulary of hate got the attention of his hearers (Luke 14:26; Matt. 10:37).[121] While no-one would argue that hatred of mother and brothers is actual hostility toward them, it is illustrative of the extent of the love of God in the disciple's life. In this context the expression grips the heart and emotions. Shedding all pretence of being merely a figure of speech, the use of hate powerfully illustrates the point. The shock value of the expressions were, in our view, in the mind of Jesus and must be maintained.[122]

It is clear from our analysis of hatred and anger in the Gospels that there are many appropriate reasons to feel angry. Jesus felt angry about injustice and for God's honour. However, anger that divides and fosters personal hatred

---

117. Michel, '*miseō*', pp. 693. See also Hagner, *Matthew 1–13*, p. 159; Schnackenburg, *Matthäusevangelium: 1, 1–16, 20*, p. 97.

118. Carr, 'The Meaning of "Hatred" in the New Testament', p. 156. See also Nolland, *Luke 9:21–18:34*, pp. 762–766.

119. Carr, 'The Meaning of "Hatred" in the New Testament', p. 158.

120. Carr, 'The Meaning of "Hatred" in the New Testament', pp. 159–160.

121. See Luz, *Matthew 8–20*, p. 112.

122. Fitzmyer's comments on Luke 14:21 are appropriate. He emphasizes the shock value of the statement. Fitzmyer, *Luke*, p. 1063. F. F. Bruce sees the shock value in the statement and also argues that hate does not mean 'hate'. Can he have it both ways? Bruce, *The Hard Sayings of Jesus*, p. 120.

against another person is prohibited. Jesus used anger to build God's kingdom, not to tear down relationships. Anger is a dangerous emotion and is most often destructive. If the example of Jesus in having mercy on those who put him to death is followed, anger against another person would be rare indeed.

Anger in the Pauline letters

People's anger

A number of prohibitions against anger appear in Paul's letters. These prohibitions could be seen to be in clear contrast to a cognitive understanding of anger. Anger is not morally neutral, i.e. right when it is based on good thinking and wrong when it is based on wrong thinking. Instead, it is morally objectionable in all contexts. Harrison writes: 'In the NT anger is usually condemned (Gal. 5:19–21; Col. 3:8).'[123] Pokorny sees anger in Colossians 3:8 as 'human emotion' 'in contrast' with the anger of God in 3:6 and Lohse sees it as a prohibition of all anger.[124] Ephesians 4:31 speaks of putting away violent rage and resentment.[125] In what context are we to understand these passages (Col. 3:8; Eph. 4:31; Gal. 5:20)? Anger in Galatians is anger that is from the flesh. Colossians 3:8 is in the context of right thinking, a new orientation, and setting ones mind on 'things that are above' (3:2). The new orientation and thinking leads to new behaviour and emotions. The implication seems to be that the anger that is based on the old way of thinking is not right.

There is further evidence that a prohibition of anger is not advocated. Church leaders are not to be easily angered (Titus 1:7). This verse does not present a prohibition of anger but rather an exhortation to be slow to anger.

---

123. Harrison, 'Anger', p. 48.

124. Pokorny, *Colossians*, p. 168; Lohse, *Colossians and Philemon*, p. 140. See also Pokorny, *Der Brief des Paulus an die Kolosser*, p. 142. Dunn agrees, 'now human "wrath" (in contrast to 3:6), with the implication that what is in view is such a powerful emotion that only God can be trusted to exercise it fairly'. Dunn, *Epistles to the Colossians and to Philemon*, 219. This is an especially interesting conclusion in light of *orgē*, being used for both. The word is used once of righteous anger and once of interpersonal anger against another person. This points to it being a morally neutral emotion.

125. See Patzia, *Ephesians, Colossians, Philemon*, p. 254. Bruce sees it is a prohibition and suggests that its mention 'so soon after v. 26 suggests that to be angry without sinning is as rare as it is difficult'. Bruce, *The Epistles to the Colossians, to Philemon, and to the Ephesians*, p. 364.

Anger is a motivation for Israel to follow the Lord in Romans 10:19 (Deut. 32:21) and in 2 Cor. 7:11 anger (*aganaktēsis*) is a power for good in fuelling change in a believer's life.[126]

Ephesians 4 presents us with the best test case. Many scholars see it as a blanket prohibition. Schnackenburg sees no hint of righteous anger in 26 and emphasizes the general destructive force of anger in both 26 and 31. 'If you work yourself into a rage, do not sin! Or better: Do not sin by getting worked up in anger!'[127] Conzelmann agrees.[128] Lincoln is very strong on this point. Taking his direction from v. 31, which he sees as a broad prohibition of anger, he writes, 'Anger is to be avoided at all costs, but if, for whatever reason, you do get angry, then refuse to indulge such anger so that you do not sin.'[129]

However, it is clear in Ephesians that Paul does not expect anger will never come into the heart of the believer (Eph. 4:26; Ps. 4:4). It is interesting that the prohibition in 4:31 is followed by the reminder of the fact that 'God in Christ has forgiven you'. There is perhaps no better reason to put away anger which comes from being slighted or offended personally.[130] We must agree with O'Brien, 'In the apostle's admonition this expression with its reference to sunset is used as warning against brooding in anger or nursing it.'[131] Wallace makes a good case that the anger in v. 26 is righteous anger that is rightly felt, 'be angry', against sin in the specific community. 'Paul might well be saying, "deal with the cause of your anger immediately".'[132] Best and Hodge both

---

126. Hower, 'The Misunderstanding and Mishandling of Anger', 272–273; Chambers, 'Godly Human Anger', p. 25. In this context it is interesting to note Paul's anger and frustration at the false teachers in Gal. 5:11–13. These are emotionally charged words! See Fung, *Galatians*, pp. 238–242; Guthrie, *Galatians*, p. 133.

127. Schnackenburg, *Ephesians*, p. 207. See also Ernst, *Die Brief an die Philipper, an Philemon, an die Kolosser, an die Epheser*, pp. 366–367; Pokorny, *Der Brief des Paulus an die Epheser*, p. 191.

128. Conzelmann, 'Der Brief an die Epheser', p. 113.

129. Lincoln, *Ephesians*, p. 301. See also pp. 308–313.

130. Bruce, *The Epistles to the Colossians, to Philemon, and to the Ephesians*, p. 361. Hodge sees a distinct difference between malicious anger (p. 31) and righteous anger. Hodge, *Ephesians*, pp. 160–161.

131. O'Brien, *Ephesians*, p. 340. Martin agrees, *Ephesians, Colossians, and Philemon*, pp. 60–61. Martin has excellent comments about the role of knowledge in the passage. Thiselton, *The First Epistle to the Corinthians*, pp. 1052; Lindemann, *Der Epheserbrief*, p. 88.

132. Wallace, '*ORGIZESTHE* in Ephesians 4:26'. See also Gnilka, *Der Epheserbrief*, pp. 235–236.

make significant comments about righteous anger in this context.[133] From a cognitive view of anger we can affirm the interpretation that it probably refers to righteous or legitimate anger.

How are we to interpret the anger in 4:31 that is prohibited? We should not neglect the vocabulary in 4:31 which seems to encompass the full gambit of angry feeling and action.[134] O'Brien writes of 4:31, 'Although v.26 recognizes that in exceptional circumstances one may be angry without sinning, so great are the dangers of this passion that on all other occasions it is to be rooted out comprehensively.'[135] It would seem to be close to impossible for anyone to decide what are the exceptional circumstances where anger is acceptable. Is it not more understandable to see v.26 as speaking of anger that is not morally objectionable and v.31 as anger which is? Certainly the emotion itself can be sin. Just as jealousy is sin if felt for the wrong reasons, so is anger. Therefore, we cannot say that the anger condemned in 4:31 has the same object as that mentioned in 4:26. Instead, to be consistent, we must understand the anger in v.26 as anger that is not morally objectionable, while that described in v.31 is an overall attitude, reinforced by the diverse vocabulary, towards another person which is in itself sin.

Wallace agrees, 'Second, the very fact that Paul distinguishes between anger and sin in v.26 indicates that there is an anger which is *not* sinful.' He continues, 'then it must be concluded that he does not *absolutely* prohibit anger in v.31.'[136] Anger at your car being stolen, a broken promise, or a child's rebellion may fall into the realm of 4:26, while that which is forbidden in 4:31 is hateful anger that wills harm to another person and damages the relationship. We can also see how legitimate 4:26 anger, when nursed and not combined with a forgiving spirit, quickly becomes the anger of 4:31. Just as we have described in jealousy, the morality of the anger is determined by its object. The anger legitimately felt by the believer is to be cleansed by forgiveness and reconciliation and not allowed to become perpetual or turned into hatred.

In legitimate anger, the results are often positive. Anger shows the seriousness of the offence to the offender and may serve to correct future behaviour. (See Chapter one on communication.) How could one raise a child without anger at things like stealing or lying? The child would never

---

133. Best, *Ephesians*, p. 450; O'Brien, *Ephesians*, pp. 349–450.
134. See Best, *Ephesians*, pp. 460–461.
135. O'Brien, *Ephesians*, pp. 350–351. See also Pokorny, *Der Brief des Paulus an die Epheser*, p. 195.
136. Wallace, '*ORGIZESTHE* in Ephesians 4:26', pp. 363–364.

understand the destructive nature of these things. After a strong exegetical article, Wallace concludes, 'In Eph. 4:26 Paul is placing a moral obligation on believers to be angry as the occasion requires . . . As God himself does not dwell in anger, neither should we.'[137]

Finally, notice the references to thinking and understanding in 4:17–20. The foundation for right feeling is right thinking. Love, we are reminded in 1 Corinthians 13:5, is not easily angered or upset (*paroxynomai*),[138] but it does not say never.

The strong argument for legitimate anger should not lead us to overlook the destructive force of anger. Beyond the negative references we have mentioned, anger was not to be a characteristic of relationships in the church (2 Cor. 12:20; 1 Tim. 2:8). Paul's preaching sometimes had an angry response (Acts 19:28). We could say that anger is a general characteristic of the character of the ungodly while it is rare and more difficult to arouse in the godly. Christ came to overcome hostility between men (Eph. 2:14, 16).

Next, we can make a few comments on hatred and anger at sin. In Romans 7:8–15, 24 Paul says that he does what he hates. Sin is something that he hates. This is even stronger in Romans 12:9 where believers are to 'hate what is evil'. Negative emotion with evil as its object is a characteristic of the believer.[139] Cranfield writes, 'Christians are to abhor, to hate utterly, that which is evil.'[140] In 2 Corinthians 12:21–13:7 a humble repentant heart is in view. To Carson humility, hating sin, and the emotions of repentance are essential in the process of reconciliation.[141]

Paul has harsh words for his enemies. His attitude toward them is not said to be angry but is undeniably emotionally charged (2 Cor. 11:13–20; Gal. 1:8; Phil. 3:18).[142] Galatians 5:12 is an emotional statement meant to elicit

---

137. Wallace, '*ORGIZESTHE* in Ephesians 4:26', p. 372.

138. Louw and Nida, pp. 88, 189.

139. Piper argues that this is part of loving the enemy because sin is what makes them enemy. Love hates evil and loves good. Piper, *Love Your Enemies*, pp. 129–130, 133. See also Tasker on Paul's hate for sin. Tasker, *The Biblical Doctrine of the Wrath of God*, p. 42.

140. Cranfield, *Romans*, p. 631. The language used is especially strong. Edwards, *Romans*, p. 292; Dunn, *Romans 9–16*, p. 740.

141. Carson, *From Triumphalism to Maturity*, p. 178.

142. Belleville, 'Enemy, Enmity, Hatred', p. 237. Prov 3:32. 'Paul's godly anger fights the Corinthians' sinful anger; he abhors their snobbery and their surly disrespect for one another.' Chambers, 'Godly Human Anger', p. 301.

emotion. Paul does not feel indifferent toward sin or heresy – he hurts or is angered over it.[143] On the other hand, hatred for another person is condemned, even hatred toward the backsliden or unbeliever (Titus 3:3; 2 Thess. 3:14).[144]

Paul also has ideas similar to the Old Testament about the negative emotions of the wicked. Those who are enemies of God have negative emotion (enmity) toward him (Rom. 8:7, *echthra*). We see that the mind set on the wrong things often hates God. There is also the idea in Paul that friendship with the world is hostility toward God or to be an enemy of God (Rom. 5:10; Col. 1:21, where *echthros* may be translated 'hostility'). Satan is seen as the enemy or hater of God.[145] Further, hatred and anger are characteristics of the wicked (Gal. 5:20; Titus 3:3).[146] False beliefs lead to destructive emotions.[147] Loving evil is to hate God. The same beliefs inform both emotions.

God's anger

Paul features the anger of God prominently in his writings. God's anger against sin is justified and is displayed against sin and sinner (Rom. 1:18; 2:5, 8; 3:5; 9:22; Eph. 5:6; Col. 3:6; 1 Thess. 2:16). All sit under God's wrath (Eph. 2:3).[148] C. H. Dodd is the most frequently cited advocate of the view that God's wrath is not emotional. He writes of Romans 1:18: 'I would therefore be in place here if to Paul "the Wrath" meant, not a certain feeling or attitude of God towards us, but some process of effect in the realm of objective facts.' Dodd concludes: 'In the long run we cannot think with full consistency of God in terms of the highest human ideals of personality and yet attribute to Him the irrational passion of anger.'[149] This is a good place to consider the anger of God in general. Is God's anger an emotion?

---

143. Carson, *From Triumphalism to Maturity*, p. 125; Longenecker, *Galatians*, p. 234.
144. Foerster, '*echthros, echthra*', p. 815.
145. Foerster, '*echthros, echthra*', p. 814.
146. Belleville, 'Enemy, Enmity, Hatred', p. 235; Fung, *Galatians*, p. 258.
147. Foerster, '*echthros, echthra*', p. 814. See also Seebass, 'Enemy, Enmity, Hate', p. 554.
148. See Macgregor, 'The Concept of the Wrath of God in the New Testament', p. 102; Lincoln, *Ephesians*, p. 325; Conzelmann, *An Outline of the Theology of the New Testament*, pp. 240–241; Lindemann, *Der Kollosserbrief*, p. 55; Zeller, *Der Brief an die Römer*, p. 54. Cassirer argues that the idea of the anger of God in the Old and New Testaments is identical. *Grace and Law*, p. 100.
149. Dodd, *Romans*, pp. 22, 24.

The roots of this thinking are ancient. Ngien writes, 'Virtually all the early church fathers took it for granted [that God could not suffer], denying God any emotions because they might interrupt his tranquility.'[150] The Christian God was not like the unpredictable and often vile gods of the Greeks who were often compelled by their evil passions.

Origen writes:

> And now, if, on account of those expressions which occur in the Old Testament, as when God is said to be angry or to repent, or when any other human affection or passion is described, [our opponents] think that they are furnished with grounds for refuting us, who maintain that God is altogether impassible, and is to be regarded as wholly free from all affections of that kind . . . But when we read either in the Old Testament or in the New of the anger of God, we do not take such expressions literally, but seek in them a spiritual meaning, that we may think of God as He deserves to be thought of.[151]

Calvin writes: 'Wherefore, as when we hear that God is angry, we ought not to imagine that there is any emotion in him, but ought rather to consider the mode of speech accommodated to our sense.'[152]

The idea of the impassibility of God was strong in much of the Church Fathers' thinking. This was probably due to two major factors. First, was the emotional and irrational behaviour of the pagan gods which they wanted to deny for God and, second, the influence of Later Platonism on early Christian thinking.[153] They wanted the philosophers to recognize Christianity as a strong and logical philosophy in its own right.

---

150. Ngien, 'The God Who Suffers', p. 38. The council of Chaldedon, AD 451 declared that God did not have human emotions. The fathers probably got their idea directly from Philo. Runia, *Philo in Early Christian Literature*, pp. 176, 338.

151. Origen, *De Principiis*, pp. 277–278. See also, Origen, *Against Celsus*, p. 529; Hansen, 'The Emotions of Jesus', p. 43; Heschel, 'The Divine Pathos: the Basic Category of Prophetic Theology', p. 36.

152. Calvin, *Institutes*, translated by Beveridge, 1.17.12.

153. For a rigorous defense of this assertion see Dodds, *Pagan and Christian in an Age of Anxiety*, pp. 127–130. The philosophical influence is stressed by Ngien who presents a good overview of this influence on the early fathers. Ngien, *The Suffering of God*, pp. 8–10. See also *The Testaments of the Twelve Patriarchs*, pp. 25–26; Hadas, *The Third and Fourth Books of Maccabees*, p. 124.

More recent interpreters also agree with Dodd. Lohse writes of Colossians 3:6, 'the concept of "wrath" (*orgē*) does not indicate an emotion of God . . . Rather *orgē* is God's judgment of wrath.'[154] Lindemann agrees.[155]

Stachowiak writes, 'This way of speaking is, of course, metaphorical; it would be quite impossible in view of the loving assent of Yahweh to his creation to transfer to him human hatred in the real sense of the term.'[156] Bultmann concludes: 'That misunderstanding, however, is based upon the false notion that *God's wrath* is a quality, an emotion, wrathfulness – a notion against which the ancient church, under the influence of Stoic thinking, thought it had to defend God. In reality "wrath of God" means an occurrence, viz. *the judgement of God*.'[157]

Another issue is a misinterpretation of what emotion is. Belleville writes: 'It is important when approaching references to God's wrath and hatred in the NT not to read these in light of corresponding human emotions. God, unlike sinful humanity, is not given to vindictiveness, fitful rages or the urge to retaliate . . . divine hatred is intense aversion toward any sort of wickedness.'[158] The emotion itself is not 'vindictiveness, fitful rages or the urge to retaliate'. Rather, the thoughts behind the anger may or may not foster these characteristics. We can counter that the difference in God's anger from sinful man is not a lack of emotion but why he has the emotion. The anger of God is for good reason and has a constructive purpose. In these contexts the disobedient have given God good reason to be angry due to their sin, pride, hatred of God and hypocrisy (Rom. 1–3). This is not the indiscriminate selfish anger of Greek gods – it is anger against sin that deserves punishment. Similarly, parents become angry with their children without exhibiting any of these negative characteristics.

---

154. Lohse, *Colossians and Philemon*, p. 139. Zeisler agrees: 'it certainly does not denote a divine emotion like a loss of temper' (Zeisler, *Pauline Christianity*, p. 81). See also Fitzmyer, *Paul and His Theology*, p. 42; Gnilka, *Der Kolosserbrief*, pp. 182–183. Ridderbos writes, 'the wrath of God there does not so much have the significance of a divine emotion or of a movement within the divine being as indeed of the active divine judgement going forth against sin and the world'. Ridderbos, *Paul: An Outline of His Theology*, p. 108.

155. Lindemann, *Der Kollosserbrief*, p. 56. See also Pokorny, *Der Brief des Paulus an die Epheser*, p. 204.

156. Stachowiak, 'Hatred', p. 352.

157. Bultmann, *Theology*, vol. 1, p. 288. See also Cousar, *The Letters of Paul*, p. 119.

158. Belleville, 'Enemy, Enmity, Hatred', p. 237.

Some have argued that Paul's use of wrath often does not mention God specifically, thus making God's wrath impersonal. Macgregor writes, 'He [Paul] retains the OT conception of the Wrath of God, but he uses it to describe, not so much the personal attitude of God to man, but rather the inevitable process of cause and effect in a moral universe.'[159] Käsemann agrees, 'Hence it is not to be viewed as an emotion nor set within the framework of a moral world view.'[160] Morris counters that when Paul uses wrath without defining it as God's wrath, the context makes it clear that it is the wrath of God. He strongly argues against those who would make the wrath of God impersonal and impassive. God opposes evil totally and personally.[161] The fierce anger of God speaks of the great evil of sin. 'The writers of the New Testament know nothing of a love which does not react in the very strongest fashion against every form of sin.'[162] The violent emotion shows the character of a holy God even as it is exhibited against those he loves. Yet, Morris writes, 'The wrath of God is often confused with that irrational passion we so frequently find in man and which was commonly ascribed to heathen deities.'[163] Unfortunately, instead of differentiating the wrath of God according to its object, Morris has chosen to differentiate it according to its lack of 'irrational passion'.

Cranfield makes a similar assessment: 'he [C. H. Dodd] is begetting the question by assuming anger is always an irrational passion. Certainly it sometimes is; but there is also anger which is thoroughly rational . . . For indignation against wickedness is surely an essential element of human goodness in a world in which moral evil is always present.'[164] Murray agrees, 'It is unnecessary, and it weakens the biblical concept of the wrath of God, to deprive it of its emotional and affective character.'[165]

---

159. Macgregor, 'The Concept of the Wrath of God in the New Testament', p. 105.

160. Käsemann, *Romans*, p. 37.

161. Morris, *The Cross in the New Testament*, pp. 190–192; Morris, *The Apostolic Preaching of the Cross*, p. 182.

162. Morris, *The Apostolic Preaching of the Cross*, p. 210.

163. Morris, *The Apostolic Preaching of the Cross*, pp. 149–153, 176. Morris goes on to make an excellent list of cognitive reasons why God gets angry in Scripture and why God's anger is intensely personal. There are also cognitive reasons why God's anger is averted. See also Tasker, *The Biblical Doctrine of the Wrath of God*, pp. 20, 23.

164. Cranfield, *Romans*, p. 109.

165. Murray, *Romans*, vol. 1, p. 35.

If anger is not by definition emotional, what is it? Carson writes, 'The price of diluting God's wrath is diminishing God's holiness . . . If God is not really angry, it is difficult to see why any place should be preserved for propitiation.'[166] If I never choose peach ice cream I do not necessarily hate it – it is just not my favorite. However, I may genuinely hate chocolate ice cream. My feeling toward peach is not strong. My feeling toward chocolate is strong. This is what differentiates hatred and ambivalence. Anger shows the value and care given to the object; a lack of anger shows indifference. As we have seen in other sections, there are strong arguments to say that God is emotional. God's anger is always legitimate because he is holy and just. Anger in God is directed against sin because God is always offended at sin.[167] Stott rightly explains: 'His [God's] anger is neither mysterious nor irrational. It is never unpredictable, but always predictable, because it is provoked by evil and evil alone.'[168]

God's anger is often part of executing final judgment which is his exclusive domain.[169] We must agree with Luz when he writes, 'A God who only loves but does not pass judgment would be a forgiveness dispenser who could be manipulated at will. A God who only passes judgment but does not love, first and foremost, would be a monster.'[170] In this context, we should not neglect the fact that, according to Piper, 'The argumentation of Rom. 12:19, 20 suggests that the Christian can love his enemy only if he is sure that the future will bring wrath upon those enemies whom he loves.'[171] The assurance that God will punish sin allows believers to freely love.

Pedersen argues that God's emotion is much like ours. God does not love the sinner and is angry at the sin. Rather, God loves the sinner and he is angry at the sinner when he sins, just as I may love my child and still be angry at him when he disobeys. Love and anger are not incompatible. In fact, we are often most angry at those we love because we care most strongly about them. I am angry with my son for disobedience because he is my son; his actions both reflect on me as a parent and I care greatly about what kind of boy he is

---

166. This is in the context of God being emotional, against C. H. Dodd. Carson, *The Difficult Doctrine of the Love of God*, pp. 67–68.

167. Cerling, 'Some Thoughts on a Biblical View of Anger: A Response', pp. 266–267. See also Tasker, *The Biblical Doctrine of the Wrath of God*, p. 14.

168. Stott, *The Cross of Christ*, p. 173.

169. Cerling, 'Anger: Musings of a Theologian/Psychologist', pp. 14–15. See also Schmithals, *Der Römerbrief: Ein Kommentar*, p. 80.

170. Luz, *The Theology of the Gospel of Matthew*, p. 132.

171. Piper, *Love Your Enemies*, p. 117.

becoming. God is like us in his emotions, able to show anger and love toward the same individual.[172] Men also, therefore, can have justifiable anger toward an individual.[173]

We can conclude that if we understand anger as a cognitive emotion the arguments for God's wrath being without emotion are quickly weakened beyond resurrection. Anger is not inherently wrong or irrational. God gets angry and this speaks of his holy and just nature and his love for us, and shows that he is defender of the weak and the wronged.

Finally, we should briefly comment on hatred in Romans 9:13. 'I have loved Jacob, but I have hated Esau.' Is this a Semitic comparison, the language of election and rejection, or genuine emotion?[174] It is worth quoting extensively from Murray. He points out that in the original context Edom had rebelled against God (Mal. 1:1–5).

> The indignation is a positive judgment, not merely the absence of blessing . . . We must, therefore, recognize that there is in God a holy hate that cannot be defined in terms of not loving or loving less. Furthermore, we may not tone down the reality or intensity of this hate by speaking of it as 'anthropopathic' or by saying that it 'refers not so much to the emotion as to the effect'. The case is rather, as in all virtue, that this holy hate in us is patterned after holy hate in God . . .
>
> Esau was not merely excluded from what Jacob enjoyed but was the object of a displeasure which love would have excluded and of which Jacob was not the object because he was loved . . . In accord with what we have found above, however, respecting biblical usage it must be interpreted as hate with the positive character which usage indicates, a hate as determinative as the unfailing purpose in terms of which the discrimination between Jacob and Esau took place.[175]

God hated the sin of Esau and Edom and choose to love Jacob. This hatred portrays the feelings of God against rebellion and his sovereign election (Heb.

---

172. Pedersen, 'Some Thoughts on a Biblical View of Anger', pp. 210–214. Carson strongly agrees: 'Nevertheless the cliché (God hates the sin but loves the sinner) is false on the face of it and should be abandoned. Fourteen times in the first fifty Psalms alone, we are told that God hates the sinner . . .' (Carson, *The Difficult Doctrine of the Love of God*, p. 69).

173. Pedersen, 'Some Thoughts on a Biblical View of Anger', p. 214.

174. Cranfield, *Romans*, p. 480; Zeller, *Der Brief an die Römer*, p. 177; Moo, *Romans*, pp. 580–581.

175. Murray, *Romans*, vol. 2, pp. 22–23.

12:16). That said, we must conclude that this is one of the most difficult passages to ascertain the emotional content of love and hate. It certainly merits further study.

Anger in the later New Testament

James 1:19–20 presents a similar view to Ephesians 4:26. Believers are to be slow to anger. As we saw in Eph. 4, some scholars wish to interpret this as a prohibition. Porter writes, 'human anger is not compatible with the righteousness of God'.[176] Davids writes that anger is 'by nature immoderate and uncontrollable . . . Second, anger is incompatible with the teaching of Jesus.'[177] These seem to be overstatements as v.19 emphasizes the need to be slow to anger, not its prohibition. Moo writes, 'While James does not forbid all anger (there is a place for "righteous indignation"), he does prohibit the thoughtless, unrestrained temper that often leads to rash, harmful and irretrievable words.'[178] Anger against another is clearly not compatible with God's standards. We can correlate this passage with James' emphasis on wisdom.[179]

Perhaps the most important contribution we find in these books is the hatred of sin. Revelation 2:6 reads: 'Yet this is to your credit: you hate (*miseō*) the works of the Nicolaitans, which I also hate.'[180] And in Jude 23 we read: 'save others by snatching them out of the fire; and have mercy on still others with fear, hating even the tunic defiled by their bodies'. Bauckham writes, 'The phrase suggests that Jude's readers, while exercising mercy toward these people, must maintain their abhorrence of their sin and everything associated with it.'[181] Hebrews 1:9 states: 'You have loved righteousness and hated

---

176. Porter, 'Wrath, Destruction', p. 1240. See also Laws, *James*, p. 81.

177. Davids, *James, NIBC*, p. 38. Davids' emphasis is on wisdom and anger in interpersonal relationships. *James, NIGTC*, pp. 92–93. See also Mußner, *Der Jakobusbrief*, pp. 99–101.

178. Moo, *James, TNTC*, p. 78. See also Frankemölle, *Der Brief des Jakobus: Kapitel 1*, pp. 327–328.

179. Verhey, 'Ethics', pp. 350–351. Being slow to anger fits James' theme of moderation. Notice also the emphasis on knowledge in 5:19–20 (Moo, *James*, PNTC, pp. 82–84).

180. 'It is right to hate evil in all its forms' (Beasley-Murray, *Revelation*, p. 75).

181. The language is graphic and probably has connotations of clothes defiled with human excrement (Zech. 3:3–4). Bauckham, *Jude, 2 Peter*, p. 116. 'Once he treats sin as normal and commonplace, he is on the way to betraying the gospel' (Green, *The Second Epistle of Peter and the Epistle of Jude*, p. 189).

wickedness; therefore God, your God, has anointed you with the oil of gladness beyond your companions.'

These passages highlight that the Christian is to reject evil and heresy and
God will judge sin. To Michel the language of a direct hatred for individuals is
avoided, and hate for and rejection of the act itself is stressed.[182] However, is
rejection all that is meant in these passages? It seems that the imagery goes
beyond rejection and expectation of future judgment to hatred for the act
itself. Having this emotion toward evil is a positive attribute of the believer (Jas
4:4). In interpreting these verses we should remember the nature of hatred that
was explained in the introduction to this section. An overarching and abiding
revulsion is in view. We should not neglect that the theme of destruction and
judgment that is often found in the later New Testament creates an emotional
barrier to sin and is a good reason to learn to hate it (Heb. 10:39; 11:28; 2 John
8; 2 Pet. 3:7; 2:1, 12; Jude 10).

The wrath of God plays a prominent role in Revelation (11:18; 12:12; 14:10,
19; 15:1, 7; 16:1, 19; 19:15) We must disagree with Ladd when he writes after
reviewing the vocabulary of 14:10, 'In any case, God's wrath is not a human
emotion; it is the settled reaction of his holiness to man's sinfulness and rebellion.'[183] God's enemies rage against God and his people (12:17). Evil rages at
God and God is angry at evil. This clearly reflects cognitive understanding as
two diametrically opposed value systems collide. In 16:19 and 19:15 anger and
wrath are used together. Porter concludes 'the evidence is clear that wrath and
anger are readily associated with the divine character in a number of explicit
and forceful passages.'[184]

The Gospel and epistles of John also have something to add to our discussion in their contrast of love and hate. We will consider these books
together in order to avoid repetition. Those who hate their brother are not
true believers and do not love God (1 John 2:9; 3:15; 4:20).[185] This hatred is

---

182. Michel, '*miseō*', pp. 691–693.

183. Ladd, *Revelation*, p. 195. Morris sees both man's and God's wrath as anger in 11:18.
    Morris, *Revelation*, p. 149. See also Beale, *Revelation*, p. 615.

184. Porter, 'Wrath, Destruction', p. 1239. See also Aune, *Revelation 6–16*, p. 901.

185. The phrase 'in the light' is filled with cognitive content (2:9) (Johnson, *1, 2 and 3
    John*, pp. 43–44; Smalley, *1, 2 and 3 John*, p. 59; Kruse, *Letters of John*, p. 85). Like Matt.
    5:21–22, hatred is shown to have the same thoughts as murder behind it. See
    Johnson, *1, 2 and 3 John*, p. 83; Kruse, *Letters of John*, p. 85; Stott, *The Letters of John*,
    p. 146. Some writers also refer to Cain's murder of Abel. This brings to mind our
    analysis of the cognitive element in the sin of Cain as seen in the Old Testament.

not seen as a strong emotion by some commentators.[186] However, these pronouncements are informative in terms of a cognitive definition of emotions. The presence of this negative emotion toward another believer is evidence of what they really believe.[187] Hating a brother proves that faith is not genuine and shows a lack of love for God.

John presents us with a strong development of this imagery. The love of God is in conflict with the hatred of the world. They are based on two conflicting world-views and they cannot coexist. Michel writes, 'Both are so exclusive and comprehensive that they disclose the nature of God and the world.'[188] The hater of God expresses outward hostility toward him (John 15:18). However, the believer is not to hate the world. Instead, it is written, 'Love not the world' (1 John 2:15). The one who hates their brother is not living in the light. This hate is based on beliefs that are not compatible with loving God.[189] A proper understanding of hatred as an emotion based on beliefs and values lets us understand the logical force of these statements.

Anger in the New Testament

In thinking about anger, especially legitimate anger, it is important to remember our study of the Old Testament. There we saw that anger is seen as legitimate in many circumstances. The righteous feel anger, often against sin. We hear echoes of this in the New Testament.

God's anger is a response to sin and rebellion. This is also true of Jesus' anger (Mark 3:5). God's anger is for a constructive purpose, that is, to bring people back to righteousness or to execute judgment.[190] At the same time, God is slow to anger and quick to forgive (Isa. 48:9; Dan. 9:9; Rom. 9:22; 2 Pet. 3:9).[191] People's anger is similar to God's in that it has cognitive cause and emotional content. The problem often faced in human anger is that our standards are not God's. Thus our anger is like God's in form, yet we do not have the character to feel it for the right reasons and execute judgment in the right way.[192]

---

186. Klauck, *Der erste Johannesbrief*, p. 125.

187. See Marshall, *The Epistles of John*, p. 191.

188. Michel, '*miseō*', p. 691.

189. See Stachowiak, 'Hatred', p. 354.

190. This is very apparent in the book of Jonah (3:9, see also Jer. 3:12).

191. Hower, 'The Misunderstanding and Mishandling of Anger', p. 270. See also Grudem, *Systematic Theology*, p. 206.

192. Hower, 'The Misunderstanding and Mishandling of Anger', pp. 270–271.

We may say with certainty that some instances of anger and hate are acceptable while others are not. Anger and hate are sometimes sin and sometimes righteous. The prohibitions against anger in the text are in contexts that make clear that it is destructive toward relationships and felt for selfish reasons. The reasons for legitimate anger and hate are few. It is to be felt for those things that offend God or that go against his principles and generally not in response to personal offence even when these offences are not just.[193] We can also say that some anger for other reasons may be appropriate but this anger should quickly be overcome by careful reflection, forgiveness and mercy. These cognitive responses to anger against another person will minimize or eliminate it. Cerling writes:

> God is angry at sin and at human oppression, a result of sin. Therefore, if we are going to say that anger is justifiable, we must make that qualification of the object of anger. Anger is not justifiable if it is a response to personal offence . . . Anger is justifiable as a response to sin and human oppression.[194]

We have no record of Jesus being angered against a personal offence no matter how violent or unjust.[195] The understanding that the person who is persecuting you is created in God's image and loved by God should produce love towards the enemy. Just as God is angered over sin and oppression, Christians should also be angered by them. Separation from sin is not enough, a violent aversion or hostility toward the evil is what is required of the believer. Hating sin may be a key defence in dealing with temptation. As the righteous learn to hate sin, they will be repulsed by it and so their emotions will lead them away from temptation. Further anger shows the severity of the evaluation of the sin, and communicates this to others (Jesus' cleansing of the temple).

Living with persistent, regular anger is not acceptable for the believer. Raging, hostile people are more likely to have heart attacks. In one study, the people with the lowest blood pressure on the job are those who would actively work out their differences with the person who made them angry.[196] The New

---

193. See also Basset *et al.*, 'Helping Christians Reclaim Some Abandoned Emotions'. Chambers presents a good list of the characteristics of godly anger. 'It is not predominant', 'It springs from jealousy for God', 'It is zealous for good deeds', 'It seeks to establish reform', 'It is not violent or murderous', and 'It is always short-lived' (Chambers, 'Godly Human Anger', p. 239).

194. Cerling, 'Anger: Musings of a Theologian/Psychologist', p. 15.

195. Cerling, 'Some Thoughts on a Biblical View of Anger: A Response', p. 267.

196. Bass, *Make Use of Your Anger*.

Testament's hard line against most anger is to be heeded as it can quickly become destructive to others and yourself. Christian beliefs will often eliminate anger or make it short lived in the great majority of cases. If you think the best of someone and keep no record of wrong it makes it more difficult to be angry; if you are quick to forgive, anger dissipates.

We have observed that hatred toward individuals is prohibited in some texts while anger against them is not. This fits a cognitive framework. Hatred which is lasting and is based on an overall negative quality is not to be felt against individuals, whom God made and loves. Anger which is often over a specific offence and is short lived can be felt towards an individual. Believers are to hate sin (Rom. 12:9; Rev. 2:6; Titus 3:3) but not to hate their brother (1 John 2:11; 4:20; Rom. 12:18–20; Titus 3:2) and love their enemies (Matt. 5:44; Luke 6:27; 23:34; Acts 7:60). When speaking of Ephesians 4:26, Calvin sums up the proper position on anger very well:

> There are three faults by which we offend God in being angry. The first is when we are angry from slight causes, and often from none, or are motivated by private injuries or offences. The second is when we go too far, and are carried into intemperate excess. The third is when our anger, which ought to have been directed against ourselves or against sins, is turned against our brethren.[197]

Conclusion

In a sense I have said nothing that goes beyond common sense. This is how we know emotion operates in our own lives. Yet, New Testament studies have most often interpreted emotion not according to common sense but according to a flawed non-cognitive perspective. This has led to a consistent misinterpretation of texts about emotion and the role it is to play in the believer's life.

We find in Ladd an example of the typical mistakes made in interpreting emotion in the New Testament. He agrees that there are, in Paul, strong inner states, but he also strongly argues that they are not emotion:

> He [the Holy Spirit] brings hope that is not merely an optimistic attitude toward the future or a stance of the emotional life but the deep conviction of the certainty of the eschatological consummation of God's redemptive purpose (Rom. 15:13; Gal. 5:5) . . .

---

197. Calvin, *Galatians, Ephesians, Philippians, and Colossians*, p. 192.

Coupled with love are joy and peace (Gal. 5:22; Rom. 14:17; 15:13). These terms may be easily misunderstood and interpreted in terms of human emotional experience: joy is emotional happiness and peace is emotional tranquility. However, these are theological words that carry profound implications for the emotional life but which in themselves convey a far deeper meaning. Joy is primarily a religious sentiment that finds its deepest satisfaction in the Lord. Therefore one can rejoice even when he is sorrowing (2 Cor. 6:10) or experiencing physical sufferings (Col. 1:24) . . .

In the same way peace is not primarily emotional tranquility but a term encompassing the salvation of the whole man . . . Peace is practically synonymous with salvation (Rom. 2:10) and is a power that protects man in his inner being (Phil. 4:7) and which rules in his heart (Col. 3:15).[198]

The emotions are downplayed as forces that are too insignificant to be at the heart of these texts with words like 'merely' and 'far deeper meaning'. What is 'religious sentiment' if it is not emotion? If peace is salvation what is a person to feel? It is far better for us to realize that peace contains a strong element of feeling based on the facts of salvation. The New Testament calls for us to feel joyful celebration, abundant love and strong hope deeply. God created our emotions and he naturally incorporates them into the very core of what it means to be a Christian.

In a cognitive analysis of emotion the mental gymnastics and energy expended to explain these emotion words as non-emotional theological terms, or prohibit negative emotion, or differentiate the meaning of an emotion in different contexts (zeal, jealousy) become unnecessary. A cognitive framework allows the simple understanding of emotional terms to be used. Passages can be understood at face value as they were intended. The supposed problems in interpreting emotion words in the text quickly disappear and the meaning becomes clearer.

The idea that emotion, particularly negative emotion, leads Christians to sin is also a prevalent misconception in popular preaching and in some theology. A good example of this is found in Pesch who argues that passions are intimately connected to sin.[199] It seems clear from his writings that the controlling influence for his ideas are the Hellenistic philosophers. But the biblical view is

---

198. Ladd, *Theology*, pp. 491–492.

199. The overwhelming part of his summary of emotion in the biblical record is devoted to passion as the source of sin. It is to be fought. What the Bible says about emotion is summarized in Gal. 5:24, 'And those who belong to Christ Jesus have crucified the flesh with its passions and desires' (Pesch, 'Emotion', p. 220).

not that emotions are an irrational force that lead believers to sin but rather that they are either morally good or objectionable based on the thinking behind them. The text calls believers to think right and feel right, not to battle irrational emotions.

Romans 12:9–21 presents a powerful summary of emotion in the Christian life and is well worth studying. Notice that emotions are intertwined in a list of actions and attitudes. Emotions are commanded as are other actions. It is clear that Paul sees that emotion can be commanded and that the emotions that one feels show the true state of the heart.

Finally, it is important to emphasize the consistent presence of links between cognition and emotion that appear in the New Testament. There are good reasons not to be angry, not to fear, to be joyful, and to love one another. Many passages that emphasize emotional characteristics also emphasize knowledge and understanding. As in the Old Testament, the righteous can be identified by how they feel.

Hafemann presents a good summary of the emotional emphasis of 2 Corinthians 7, which presents an excellent conclusion to this Chapter:

> All too often the church is likewise emaciated when it comes to experiencing deep and lasting joy in the midst of adversity because we no longer gain our identity by living within the community of faith. What we love, and therefore what we get excited about, is no longer wrapped up with the progress of God's people. The basis of our contentment is not the growing Christ-likeness of our church, but the comfort level of our personal circumstances. Conversely we are famished when it comes to feeling grief over sin because what we hate, and therefore what we feel remorse about, no longer revolves around the reality of who God is in our midst. What makes us sad is no longer the sting of our sin, but the frustration of our failed dreams and the lack of freedom to get whatever we want.[200]

---

200. Hafemann, *2 Corinthians*, p. 322.

6. EMOTION IN THE NEW TESTAMENT: A SUMMARY STATEMENT

There is a necessary connection between the Christian emotions and the Christian story, because emotions are construals, and construals always require some knowledge, and the knowledge required by the Christian emotions is provided by the Christian story. So people who do not want to think of the spiritual life in terms of emotions and feelings because they believe that emotions are subjective and cut off from doctrine and thinking, can lay their fears to rest. Emotions are no less tied to concepts than arguments and beliefs are.[1]

    Robert Roberts

Interpreting emotion in the New Testament from an explicitly cognitive viewpoint is something new. As we have seen, it is not the predominant understanding of emotion in biblical studies. It is only in the last twenty years that a cognitive approach has become a prevalent view in psychology and the effects of this shift must now be felt in the realm of New Testament studies. My task has been not to complete a final analysis of emotion in the New Testament but to open the door. This approach leaves most questions unanswered as to how a cognitive framework will change the interpretation of individual passages where emotion plays a prominent role. We have, in most cases, taken a direct approach dealing

---

1. Roberts, 'Emotions and the Fruit of the Spirit', p. 87.

only with the emotion vocabulary of the text and not emphasized the emotional undertones of the text, how a text was crafted to arouse the emotions of the readers, or the emotional content of those words that are not basic emotions.

Carson summarizes 2 Corinthians 10 – 13:

> These chapters are among the most emotionally intense of all that the apostle Paul wrote. Partly for that reason, they are also among the most difficult. His language is frequently passionate, his rhetorical questions emotive, his sequence of thought compressed, his syntax broken.[2]

Here we see some of the complexity of the study of emotion in the New Testament. The syntax and style alone can show emotion. This kind of analysis has remained in the background of our study. It would play a crucial part in the analysis of emotion in the New Testament in a more exhaustive study. Further, I have not explored the implications of our findings to understanding the emotional life of the early church. This is another area that could be explored further. The role of emotion within the New Testament is a key factor in understanding the early community.[3]

It is my hope that these kinds of issues can begin to receive the attention which they deserve. With a cognitive perspective, emotion is free to play a prominent and influential role in theology and the Christian faith. It no longer needs to be downplayed, explained away, or redefined in order to fit it into our idea of science and reason. Emotion can be understood as an integral and essential part of New Testament theology.

Theories of emotion and the New Testament

Many have characterized the intellect and the emotions as in tension, often at war with each other.[4] We have argued that that emotions are cognitive and that cognitive theory brings emotion and reason together into a unified whole. In the words of Solomon: 'My purpose in this limited essay has been to deflate (once more) a popular but pernicious theory of emotions, and with it, an old and vicious dichotomy between intellect and emotion.'[5] When knowledge is

---

2. Carson, *From Triumphalism to Maturity*, p. 1.

3. See Kee, *Knowing the Truth*, pp. 57–58.

4. Gilpen, 'Reinterpretation in the History of Christianity', p. 3.

5. Solomon, *Getting Angry: The Jamesian Theory of Emotion*, p. 252.

defined as reason void of any emotion it is not the knowledge that is actually operative in us. The New Testament acknowledges this unity with its holistic view of persons as demonstrated in the meaning of the words heart and mind.

It is clear that the New Testament authors generally write about emotion from a cognitive perspective. This is not to say that there was a well informed theory of emotions behind the writings but it is to say that a cognitive view was assumed.[6]

We see this cognitive framework in many areas:

1. Emotion is freely and frequently commanded in the text.
2. In some instances particular emotions for particular reasons are prohibited.
3. People are held responsible for how they feel and judgments are made about a particular emotion in a particular circumstance being right or wrong.
4. Emotions are seen as a genuine indicator of the righteousness or morality of those who profess belief (or if they really believe).
5. Emotions are regularly linked with thinking and beliefs.
6. Emotions in the text have objects, either stated or implied.
7. Emotions are morally neutral and they may be righteous or wicked depending on their object.
8. God has emotions that are felt for good reasons.
9. To change a person's objectionable emotions the solution offered is often to change thinking.
10. Love is the predominate emotion and often motivates other feelings.

We can also see a cognitive emphasis in the unity of meaning between emotions in different contexts, an idea that is often contested in New Testament studies. You can love your brother or love sin. Paul can hope for the coming of a friend or the second coming of Christ. Jealousy can be felt by God, by a person for the law, or for another person's position. A cognitive view of emotion lets us understand how the emotion words are used with the same emotional emphasis in each of these contexts.

---

6. In the words of Käsemann, 'All this shows that Paul undoubtedly has and formulates an understanding of human existence' (Käsemann, *Perspectives on Paul*, p. 16). Even Paul's basic theology must be extrapolated; our task has been to do this with the emotions. See Sampler, 'From Text to Thought World'; Beker, 'Recasting Pauline Theology'.

As we have seen, a cognitive perspective has broad implications. Emotions are a key element in learning, communications, ethics and behaviour. The New Testament treats them as such. The message is delivered with passion. Love, joy and hope are seen as a crucial part of faith and practice. These emotions enable a high EQ, motivating good social relationships, helping us learn and making us productive. The way Paul feels about his fellow believers is a good example of this. He is not ashamed to tell of his fears, sorrows and joys. We see Jesus preaching with passion and emotional examples and stories, eliciting his hearers' emotion. Emotions were understood to be a crucial element in communicating to others and making the teaching understandable and memorable. People's emotions show their moral development and the strength of their convictions. For example, true repentance is evident in genuine sorrow. Finally, action without love is useless; faith without love is not New Testament faith. Emotion plays an important part in the theology and ethics of the New Testament.

We observed in Chapter one that emotions were one of the strongest motives for change and action. They are a stronger force than physical motives such as hunger. We observe this in the New Testament as believers are to have joy in trials, or even because of trials, and love an enemy. Proper emotions, based on unchangeable truth, allows the believer to overcome and survive the pain of life or physical suffering. Our motivation survives through the difficulty. Or, we might be able to correlate the ideas of hatred and love we find in the writings of John with the ideas about emotion supplying us with information like one of our senses. As we feel love for a brother we are perceiving something real in the object before us.

We are often told in church to do the loving thing and the emotions will come. However, we learned that behaviour can change emotion but this is not a necessary result. It depends on how doing the right thing influences or does not influence our thinking. Perhaps this is why the New Testament sometimes does not concentrate on the action but concentrates on having the right emotion. It says 'love your neighbour' not 'act kindly to your neighbour.' If you do not love your neighbour it does not say 'act like it no matter how you feel' but rather calls us to get our thinking right. This was an emphasis we saw repeatedly as those passages that called for having a particular emotion were filled with the knowledge, beliefs and values that would naturally produce that emotion. These are just a few areas that a proper understanding of emotion aids in understanding the New Testament. With more thought and study, many more connections can be made in coming years.

We have seen that the broad academic community has followed the non-cognitive perspective. This has allowed scholars, including those studying the New Testament, to believe that their work is rational, beyond the influence of irrational passions; a false dichotomy has often led to a general disregard for the role of emotion in the text of the New Testament. This belief has led to misunderstandings and faulty interpretations in New Testament studies that must be avoided in the future.

Emotion in the New Testament and its world

There was a choice in the world of the New Testament between a cognitive and non-cognitive understanding of emotion. Platonic philosophy, the poets and pagan religion often emphasized the irrational passions. The ideas of the Hellenistic philosophers about emotion were in large part a reaction against the emotional excess and non-cognitive perspective of Greco-Roman religion and culture that they observed. Emotion was not a raging force unable to be controlled. Instead, it was dependent on thinking and able to be controlled or extirpated with 'healthy' thinking. To others, following Aristotle, cognitive emotions meant that some feelings were healthy and some harmful based on the nature of their objects.

These debates about emotion were part of the New Testament world. Did some New Testament authors understand these philosophical ideas? What evidence for or against this do we find in the text? There have been various attempts to equate Paul with the Hellenistic philosophers in his view of emotion. These usually emphasize that Paul believed in the power of reason and had a healthy distrust of the passions.[7]

First, we should not neglect the indications that Paul was familiar with the content of the Hellenistic philosophers' teachings. He would have known the basic tenets of their teaching just by traveling in Greco-Roman society.[8] Malherbe writes: 'The Paul that emerges from these essays is one who was thoroughly familiar with the traditions used by his philosophic contemporaries . . .

---

7. For a survey see Nash, *Christianity and the Hellenistic World*. For a good summary of the relevance of Hellenistic backgrounds to the New Testament see Alexander, 'The Relevance of Greco-Roman Literature and Culture to New Testament Study'. We should heed the cautions of Barclay in this section. The task of finding true parallels is complex and very often overstated. Barclay, *Obeying the Truth*, pp. 175–177, 222.

8. Malherbe, *Paul and the Thessalonians*, pp. 4, 24–25, 30, 32. He believed Greek philosophy's influence on the New Testament has been passed over too lightly by most in recent years. Malherbe, *Paul and the Popular Philosophers*, pp. 1, 5, 47–48; Fitzmyer, *Paul and His Theology*, p. 29.

He knew these traditions first-hand and not through the mediation of other Jews who before him had come to terms with the Greek experience. Paul's followers and interpreters took his familiarity with moral philosophy for granted.[9] Theissen writes: 'Paul, being a citizen of Tarsus and of Rome, is fully integrated into the political texture of the Roman Empire.'[10] Stowers writes: 'Paul moved and thought in the world of Hellenistic philosophers and moralists.'[11]

There may also be strong links in Acts between Paul and the Hellenistic schools. Luke is careful to present Paul as knowledgeable about philosophy (Acts 17:18; 22:3). Paul is not one of these crazy street preachers but teaches like the philosophers (17:28). The Gospel is, in fact, better than philosophy (Acts 17:21).[12] It would be surprising to find that Paul had many connections with Hellenistic philosophy and knew nothing about the Hellenistic philosophers' ideas about emotion.[13]

However, it is clear that Paul and the Hellenistic philosophers did not have the same world-views. The idea of extirpating the emotions is an idea unknown in the New Testament. Any similarity in vocabulary is not a similarity in idea.[14] The Stoic would not accept or understand either Jesus' or Paul's passionate commitment to the Gospel, to others, or their emotional language. Where the Stoic idea of happiness was a life free from emotion, Paul's joy was an emotional celebration of God and his work of sharing the Gospel.

A good example is seen in 1 Thessalonians 4. Paul and the philosophers both give reasons not to fear death. However, Paul gives the reason of Christian hope for the future where for the philosophers it is reason itself. Malherbe sees affinity here, but the only parallel seems to be that they are both giving cognitive reasons not to fear death.[15] We can conclude that the relation is not one of dependence but that they both have a cognitive understanding of emotion.

---

9. Malherbe, *Paul and the Popular Philosophers*, p. 8.

10. Theissen, *The Social Setting of Pauline Christianity*, p. 36. See also Ladd, *A Theology of the New Testament*, p. 513; Edwards, *Hellenism*.

11. Stowers, 'Paul on the Use and Abuse of Reason', p. 255.

12. See also the philosophical speech in 20:17–35. Malherbe, *Paul and the Popular Philosophers*, pp. 150–152, 158.

13. Fiore, 'Passion in Paul and Plutarch', p. 138; Stowers, *Paul and the Stoics*, pp. 72–73. See also Meeks, 'The Circle of Reference in Pauline Morality', pp. 310, 315–316; Stowers, 'Paul on the Use and Abuse of Reason', pp. 267–270.

14. Lightfoot, 'St Paul and Seneca', pp. 297, 322; Malherbe, *Paul and the Popular Philosophers*, pp. 67–68, 73; Engberg-Pedersen, *Paul and the Stoics*, p. 47.

15. Malherbe, *Paul and the Popular Philosophers*, pp. 65–66. See also pp. 123–136.

Paul does not neglect reason but he fits it into a theological framework. The goal of the Christian life is not to be perfectly rational, but to create community.[16] Paul did not see human emotion as a human frailty. Instead he celebrated them as God given.

There is also evidence for the influence of Greco-Roman philosophy in Hebrews. Nash, who is generally skeptical about Greek influence, writes, 'I think it is clear that if the influence of Hellenistic philosophy can be detected anywhere in the New Testament, it can be found in the book of Hebrews . . . It is clear that the writer of Hebrews knew personally the language and teachings of Alexandrian Judaism. In all likelihood he knew the writings of Philo.'[17] This is especially intriguing for us as Philo held a non-cognitive view of the emotions. Yet Hebrews does not display the same tendencies.

In conclusion, the Stoic exhortation to extirpate the emotions is wholly missing from the New Testament.[18] Aquinas writes, 'Emotion . . . in so far as it is rationally controlled, it is part of the virtuous life.'[19] To Augustine, if they are in agreement with reason 'who will dare to say that they are diseases or vicious passions'.[20]

The New Testament does not say banish fear from your life. Rather, it gives reason not to fear in specific situations. We could make a similar analysis for the other emotions. To control the emotions the Hellenistic philosophers advocated a radical detachment from your surroundings. In the New Testament, emotions are not to be based on a love for the things of this world but they are to be based on a love for God, a radical attachment to fellow believers, and a love for neighbour. Where the Stoic 'joy' had little or no emotional content, joy in the New Testament is a jubilant feeling felt strongly in the heart. Where compassion was not seen as a legitimate motive for moral action for the Hellenistic philosophers, in the New Testament compassion is a good and necessary motivation for action. Both world-views deal with harmful emotions from a cognitive framework but, like Aristotle, the New Testament affirms the positive role of the emotions in a person's life.

Neither does the New Testament battle non-cognitive 'irrational passions'

---

16. Stowers, 'Paul on the Use and Abuse of Reason', pp. 283–286.

17. Nash, *Christianity and the Hellenistic World*, p. 111. Lindars agrees (Lindars, *The Theology of the Letter to the Hebrews*, pp. 21–23). See also Williamson, *Philo and the Epistle to the Hebrews*, p. 4; Chadwick, 'St Paul and Philo of Alexandria'; Sterling, 'Philo', p. 792.

18. See Meeks, *The Moral World of the First Christians*, p. 130.

19. Aquinas, *Summa Theologica*, vol. 19, 1a.2ae.24.2.

20. Augustine, *The City of God*, 14.9.

with religious ritual, magic and appeasement of a deity. Nor does it make war against them as do Plato, Galen, and the later stoics. Instead, objectionable emotions are believed to dissipate as the believer's thinking is brought under the control of the Holy Spirit. The presence of harmful emotion does not negate responsibility as it did in some Greco-Roman writings. People are held responsible for how they feel. Emotions are seen as part of human reason, not as a distinct irrational force. The God of the New Testament does not behave as the unpredictable gods of the Greeks and Romans, nor is he the unmoved aloof God of the Epicureans.[21]

From looking at parallels between the New Testament and Greek philosophy it seems that Christians had regular contact with the practices and beliefs of Greco-Roman culture.[22] After reviewing the similarities between Paul's writings and the Hellenistic philosophers, Malherbe concludes: 'There can no longer be any doubt that Paul was thoroughly familiar with the teaching, methods of operation, and style of argumentation of the philosophers of the period, all of which he adopted and adapted to his own purposes.'[23] We have concluded that, although they had knowledge of this culture, they formed their own distinct view of the emotions. Finally, we should understand that the contradictory opinions and inconsistencies about emotion that we see in church history are often due to an attempt to synchronize the New Testament and the ancient philosophers. These failed attempts clearly illuminate the distinct and consistent nature of the New Testament teaching on emotion.

Emotion in the Old and New Testaments

It is clear that many Jewish writings of the New Testament period took their lead from ancient schools of philosophy. Josephus, Philo, 4 Maccabees and others show either acceptance of these philosophers' perspective or strong evidence of their influence. The Old Testament, in contrast to these Jewish writers, has a strong place for healthy emotion in its faith and in the lives of its characters. It is clear that the New Testament takes its lead from the Old Testament.

The Old Testament was foundational for the writers' of the New Testament ideas about emotion. The righteous are to love and delight themselves in God.

---

21. See Fox, *Pagans and Christians*, pp. 425–426, 475–491, 511, 672, 678–679.
22. Grant, 'The Social Setting of Second-Century Christianity'. For Paul see Becker, *Paul: Apostle to the Gentiles*, pp. 52–56.
23. Malherbe, *Paul and the Popular Philosophers*, p. 68.

Their joy is based on the truths about God and his salvation in history. They are not to fear other nations, but to fear God. Sorrow and grief are naturally felt and expressed over pain. In times of repentance there is to be grief over sin and a renewal of the heart.

We are also struck by the fact that the emotions of the God of the Bible are different from both the pagan deities of the Old Testament and the Greco-Roman gods of the New. He is not influenced by things like the ecstatic ritual of the prophets of Baal nor is he governed by irrational impulses like the Greco-Roman gods. God's emotions flow out of the greatness of his love and his just character. The self description of God in the Old Testament is often about emotion, he defines himself by what he feels. In this context, the New Testament is not ashamed to present us with a God who feels strongly. People created in God's image are naturally emotional.

Baloian summarizes:

> One of the dominant impressions the ascribing of anger to Yahweh has, is to present Him as an intense and passionate Being, fervently interested in the world of humans. There is no embarrassment on the part of the OT of Yahweh's possession of emotion, but rather, it is celebrated (see for example, 2 Sam. 22:8, 9, 16; Ps. 145:8). In fact, His passion guarantees, not only that He is intensely interested in the word, but that He is a person.[24]

In our Chapter on the Old Testament we emphasized the differences in emotion between the righteous and the wicked. This theme is perhaps most closely paralleled by what we see in Revelation. The nations rejoice in the coming of Antichrist, and weep over Babylon's demise. The righteous, however, rejoice over the judgment of God and the victory of the Lamb. Clearly, the strongest influence on the New Testament's view and handling of emotion is the Old Testament.

Emotion in the New Testament: a summary statement

Ethical lists
It is helpful to take a brief look at the ethical lists of the New Testament. They illustrate some of our basic findings concerning emotion in the

---

24. Baloian, *Anger in the Old Testament*, p. 156.

New Testament. First, we will list the passages and what emotions appear. This will include only the basic emotions that we have covered.[25]

Virtue		Vice	
Passage	**Emotions**	**Passage**	**Emotions**
2 Cor. 6:6	Love	Mark 7:21–22	
Gal. 5:22–23	Love, joy	Rom. 1:29–31	Envy,[26] haters of God
Eph. 4:32		Rom. 13:13	Jealousy[27]
Phil. 4:8		1 Cor. 5:10–11	
Col. 3:12		1 Cor. 6:9–10	
1 Tim. 4:12	Love	2 Cor. 12:20–21	Jealousy, wrath[28]
1 Tim. 6:11	Love	Gal. 5:19–21	Envy, jealousy, wrath
2 Tim. 2:22	Love	Eph. 4:31	Wrath, anger
2 Tim. 3:10	Love	Eph. 5:3–5	
Jas 3:17		Col. 3:5, 8	Anger, wrath
1 Pet. 3:8	Love of the brethren	1 Tim. 1:9–10	

---

25. Käsemann sees these lists as influenced by Hellenistic philosophy. Käsemann, *Romans*, p. 49. 'While the form is distinctly Hellenistic, the content is uniquely Christian.' (Charles, 'Virtue Amidst Vice', pp. 126–127). See also Oberlinner, *Titusbrief*, p. 168; Merkel, *Die Pastoralbriefe*; Knoch, *1. und 2. Timotheusbrief Titusbrief*, p. 80; Gnilka, *Der Kolosserbrief*, p. 184.

26. *phthonos*, as are the other uses of 'envy' in this section.

27. This and other occurrences of 'jealous' is a translation of *zēlos*.

28. *thymos*, as are the other uses of 'wrath' in this section.

(continued)

Virtue		Vice	
Passage	**Emotions**	**Passage**	**Emotions**
2 Pet. 1:5–7	Brotherly affection, love	2 Tim. 3:2–5	Lovers of self and money, haters of good, lovers of pleasure not lovers of God
		Titus 3:3	Hating one another, envy
		Jas 3:15–16	Jealousy
		1 Pet. 2:1	Envy
		1 Pet. 4:3	
		1 Pet. 4:15	
		Rev. 9:21	
		Rev. 21:8	
		Rev. 22:15	Loves falsehood

A few observations are in order. In context, the negative emotions in vice lists clearly refer to aggressive anti-social or destructive behaviour. In this we see evidence that the argument that anger and wrath are universally immoral is false. Jealousy is certainly not universally rejected for, as we have seen, jealousy (*zēlos*) is often used in a positive sense. Love is used in both virtue and vice lists. Obviously, the context and the stated or implied object determine if it is a virtue or a vice.

The intermingling of action and emotion as morally objectionable or morally praiseworthy reinforces a cognitive interpretation of the emotions. Both action and emotion can be considered moral or immoral, it is the object behind or reason for the emotion that makes it a virtue or vice. This also reinforces our interpretation that an emotion may or may not be sin. If felt for the wrong reasons, an emotion can be sin. Love for the wrong things, like money, is condemned alongside destructive anger. As a cognitive interpretation implies, emotions were considered controllable just like the other items on the list and believers can be held responsible for them.

The positive virtues are seen as characteristic of the new life of the believer while the vices are usually seen as the attributes of unbelievers or of the pre-Christian state. The new life, new values, and new thinking lead to new emotions, emotions that are fundamentally different from people who are not a part of the new community.[29]

The lists of virtues are typically characterized by the inclusion or centrality of love. We might also say that the vices are often thought of in terms of those things that are in contrast to love.[30] Even those lists that do not mention love specifically, with the possible exception of Philippians 4:8, are in the context of loving relationships. The centrality of love as the central virtue of living in community speaks of its essential and cognitive nature. It is not one virtue of many – it is the cornerstone of Christian ethics.

The Emotions of God, Jesus and Paul

God

Robinson writes, 'In the total biblical portrayal the wrath of God is not so much an emotion or an angry frame of mind as it is the settled opposition of his holiness to evil.'[31] This is a well represented position – God does not have emotion.[32] However, we have found that the Christian God feels and feels strongly. He is not the angry unpredictable Zeus nor is he the unmovable god of the Stoics. God loves for good reason; he created us. He gets angry for good reason; sin and wickedness. Can we say that God's love is love as we know it if it contains no emotion? Why would we be motivated to follow God if he has no feelings for us? Is a man our friend who does not suffer or empathize with us? God suffers for and feels with his people.[33]

---

29. Knoch, *1. und 2. Timotheusbrief Titusbrief*, p. 80; Oberlinner, *Titusbrief*, p. 168; Gnilka, *Der Kolosserbrief*, p. 184.

30. Becker, 'Der Brief an die Galater', p. 73; Furnish, *Theology and Ethics in Paul*, pp. 87–88.

31. Robinson, 'Wrath of God', pp. 1196.

32. For a summary of the major arguments for and against God having emotions see Creel, *Divine Impassibility*, pp. 113–139.

33. Ngien, 'The God Who Suffers', pp. 38–40.

We see many of the characters in the Bible emotionally pleading with God. God is moved by human emotion and often responds to it. Emotion is a valid means of communicating the urgency or depth of a request to God or the validity of repentance. This makes sense in a cognitive view, God responds to emotion because it is based on the beliefs of the heart and intense emotion comes from the belief that the object has great value.

Finally, God loves his people. The death of Christ was the great demonstration of God's love for us (Rom. 5:8; John 15:13; 1 John 3:16; 4:10).[34] The often-used metaphor of believers being God's children speaks of a special relationship of love. We should emphasize that although this thesis has argued that God's love is cognitive, at the same time we should not neglect the fact that it is not earned. In the words of Morris: 'God loves not because the objects of his love are upright and winsome, but because he is a loving God.' We can agree with the first clause. We can also agree with the second clause if it is stressed that God loves for good reason. Unfortunately, Morris and most scholars seem to mean that this implies that God's love is completely unmotivated.[35] God does not love people because they deserve it or have earned his love, but he does love for good reasons. God loves us both because of his own choice and because we are his special creation. As our creator, there may be unique characteristics that he loves about each individual.

God is love. Love is the most basic of emotions, and God gives himself this name. God is personal, God is emotional and God feels all the emotions that love can produce. This is central to the character of God. Our emotions are part of being made in the image of God; they are a good and integral part of human existence.

---

34. Morris, *The Cross of Jesus*, pp. 20–22.

35. Morris goes on to write that natural human love must be different from the love of God for men and the love of men for God because 'in the way we commonly use the term *love* the response cannot be commanded'. Morris, *Testaments of Love*, p. 40. See also Morris, *Testaments of Love*, pp. 138–164, 260, 271. This is one of the classic books on love in biblical studies. This shows how deeply the basic idea of love is misunderstood. Carson gives a good summary of the emotion and emotional love of God and how it is clear that both human and divine emotion have great similarity. Carson, *The Difficult Doctrine of the Love of God*, pp. 48, 67. 'The price is too heavy. You may then rest in God's sovereignty, but you can no longer rejoice in his love. You may rejoice only in a linguistic expression which is an accommodation of some reality of which we cannot conceive, couched in the anthropopapthism of love' (Carson, *The Difficult Doctrine of the Love of God*, p. 59).

Jesus Christ

Jesus presents Christians with a pattern to follow. Warfield begins his essay on the emotions of Jesus: 'It belongs to the truth of our Lord's humanity, that he was subject to all sinless human emotions.'[36] As a man, he set an example for the emotions of the Christian. As God, Jesus shows us the emotions of the creator.[37]

While the Gnostic Christ cures people of their passions, the Jesus of the Gospels is a man of passions.[38] Grudem concludes, 'Jesus had a full range of human emotions. He "marvelled" at the faith of the centurion (Matt. 8:10). He wept with sorrow at the death of Lazarus (John 11:35). And he prayed with a heart full of emotion.'[39] Warfield also points out that Jesus had the physical traits of emotion. He groaned, cried out, sighed, showed physical rage, 'open exultation of joy', and had an angry glare in Mark 3:5.[40] These physical traits point to the fact that Jesus' emotion was like ours.

Many of the merciful acts of Jesus are in response to cries of distress and suffering. Jesus is moved by the emotions that he observes. Brueggemann argues that a pattern of 'crying out' to God as seen in the Old Testament carried over into the ministry of Jesus (Matt. 9:27; 14:30; 20:31; 21:9). Jesus responds to the anguish of the world with compassion.[41] This is in contrast to Jesus' enemies who do not cry out for help. Jesus responds to those who know their own need, as they naturally express that need in their emotions. Further, Jesus gives those to whom he ministers good reason to take heart (Matt. 9:2, 22; 14:27; Mark 6:50; 10:49; John 16:33). His ministry lifts their emotions. He called men friends and

---

36. Warfield, 'The Emotional Life of Our Lord', p. 93. It is interesting to contrast the death of Socrates, as told by Plato, who faced death in peace and Jesus who faced death in agony and sorrow. Jesus certainly did not meet the Greek ideal. See Gnilka, *Das Matthäusevangelium*, vol. 2, p. 415; Morris, *The Cross of Jesus*, pp. 75–78.

37. Hansen, 'The Emotions of Jesus', pp. 43–44; Edwards, *Religious Affections*, pp. 18–20.

38. Balz, '*phobeō, phobeomai, phobos, deos*', p. 219.

39. Grudem, *Systematic Theology*, pp. 533–534.

40. Warfield, 'The Emotional Life of Our Lord', p. 138. Unfortunately, Warfield, after expounding on the emotions of Jesus, emphasizes the control of the emotions. They did not have mastery over Jesus. He treats them as a force to master not as cognitive reactions. Warfield, 'The Emotional Life of Our Lord', p. 142. He also argues that the emotions of Jesus show his true humanity. We have seen that God has emotion and this is not an argument for the humanity of Jesus. Warfield, 'The Emotional Life of Our Lord', pp. 143–144. See also Ernst, *Das Evangelium nach Markus*, p. 428.

41. Brueggemann, 'From Hurt to Joy', pp. 18–19.

seemed to have special relationships with certain individuals. He was like us, in that he was drawn to close relationships with a select group of people.

Jesus called for people to have faith in God and become members of his kingdom. This would transform their emotions. Schnackenburg writes: 'Consequently faith, like repentance, is a "total" attitude, claiming all man's faculties.'[42] Jesus demands wholehearted service with no reservations (Matt. 6:24; Mark 12:30). This is necessarily emotional. The emotional reaction of Jesus' hearers often signifies if they accept the kingdom. Those who see their sin and repent with their heart are welcomed while those who reject the kingdom are emotionally cold or hate Jesus (Luke 7:38–50; 15:20–32).

The parables of Jesus deserve special attention. We have dealt with some specific parables under the appropriate sections in the previous Chapters. The joy of the one who has found the pearl of great price or the joy of the widow who has found the lost coin illustrate the great joy of finding the kingdom. In the parable of the Prodigal Son we have seen that it is the faulty emotions of the Pharisees that are in view. The difference between the emotional reactions of the older brother and the father comes from the differences in their thinking about that individual. The joy of the father is like God's emotion and the jealousy of the older brother illustrates the Pharisees' sinful emotions. Clearly the emotions of the characters reveal whose heart is righteous.[43]

The fact that emotion plays a prominent role in so many of Jesus' stories shows us something about the teacher. Jesus was concerned with how people felt. He was able to respond to both morally upright emotions and people's unrighteous emotions by telling parables that condemned the bad and reinforced the good.

In the passion, the cross without the emotional suffering of God is not the cross as we know it. According to Stott, in the cross we see the great meeting of God's emotions of love and anger. Jesus' great suffering shows the reality of the greatest love.[44]

Emotions in a perfect person cannot be morally objectionable. Jesus Christ is portrayed as a man of deep emotion. Jesus felt in passionate fullness (John 7:37–38).[45] Further, if Jesus was one with the Father this is also good evidence for the emotional nature of God himself (John 10:30; 14:9).

---

42. Schnackenburg, *The Moral Teaching of the New Testament*, p. 34.

43. Jeremias, *The Parables of Jesus*, p. 131; Linnemann, *Parables of Jesus*, pp. 77–80; Wenham, *The Parables of Jesus*, pp. 109–111.

44. Stott, *The Cross of Christ*, pp. 131, 330–332.

45. Hansen, 'The Emotions of Jesus', p. 46.

Paul

The ministry of Paul is characterized by emotional involvement with his congregations. Commenting on Phil. 4:10, Wesley writes, 'St Paul was no Stoic: he had strong passions, but all devoted to God.'[46]

Martin says of 2 Corinthians 6:11: 'In the process of this opening up of his emotions, Paul has revealed the attitude of his inner heart.'[47] Paul loves people. A mutual relationship of love and affection is what he desires (1 Thess. 2:17). Dunn writes: 'The three great fruits of the Spirit, love, joy, peace – whose emotional dimension should not be ignored – he naturally attributed to God. Paul's ministry, in general, was done in great passion. The plight of the unsaved and believers was a source of tears (Acts 20:19, 31).'[48]

2 Corinthians may be the most emotional book in the Pauline writings. The personal attack that he responds to elicits a deep emotional response from him. He was motivated by his sorrow not to visit them (2:1). In 2:14–17 he breaks into a joyful hymn of praise.[49] In chapter 7 Paul speaks of his care and concern for them and how his emotions are tied up in the relationship (1–4). His 'fears within' are calmed by the arrival of a good friend with good news (5–7). His joy is fuelled by their growth and care for him. The fact that they listened to his hard words and that their grief led them to repentance is reason for Paul to rejoice. Here we have a picture of a man whose emotions are tied up in his ministry, the ministry of the gospel of Jesus Christ (2 Cor. 11:28–29).

We also see clearly in this book that Paul was subject to fear and discouragement.[50] Besides all the physical hardship he has endured, Paul's greatest hardship is his anxiety and longing for the churches (2 Cor. 11:28–29). Carson writes; 'Paul seems to view his concern for all the churches as the climax of his trials.'[51]

---

46. *Explanatory Notes Upon the New Testament* (London: Epworth Press, 1976), quoted in Clapper, *John Wesley on Religious Affections*, p. 42.

47. Martin, *2 Corinthians*, p. 185. For Paul's intense love for the Philippians see Friedrich, 'Der Brief an die Philipper', p. 139.

48. Dunn, *The Theology of Paul the Apostle*, p. 48.

49. Evans, 'Interpretation of 2 Corinthians', pp. 22–23.

50. Upon Paul's first visit to Corinth he was very discouraged. Carson writes: 'Paul succumbed to fear and discouragement' (Carson, *From Triumphalism to Maturity*, p. 5). In Acts 18 God answers with a vision. Christ appears to him and tells him that he has many people in the city. What encourages and motivates Paul is the progress of the gospel.

51. Carson, *From Triumphalism to Maturity*, p. 123. See also 1 Thess. 3:1–10.

The advancement of the kingdom of God was his goal. His emotions were tied to the successes or setbacks of this mission. A summary of the emotional nature of Paul's ministry is found in 1 Thessalonians 3:9–10:

> How can we thank God enough for you in return for all the joy that we feel before our God because of you? Night and day we pray most earnestly that we may see you face to face and restore whatever is lacking in your faith.

The book of Philemon presents a very emotional appeal of Paul on behalf of Onesimus. Paul is not afraid of appealing to the emotions of Philemon with strong emotional language. He uses phrases like: an old man, a prisoner, Onesimus my own heart.[52] Dunn writes of v.13, 'Here Paul screws the emotional intensity to a new pitch, calling Onesimus his very heart.'[53] The status of Christian brother brings a new relationship between slave and master, one based on love.

Paul says to imitate him as he follows Christ. He holds himself up as an example (1 Cor. 4:16; 11:1; 1 Thess. 1:6; 2:14; Eph. 5:1).[54] This exhortation can be applied to Paul's emotions. Not only do we see Paul's emotions for fellow believers, he sees that having a godly emotional life is one of the qualities that qualifies leaders for ministry (Phil. 2:20).[55] Paul's emotions are determined by his love for God and his converts. His love for them leads to all kinds of different feelings. 'For I wrote to you out of much distress and anguish of heart and with many tears, not to cause you pain, but to let you know the abundant love that I have for you (2 Cor. 2:4).'[56]

A new way of thinking

With the renewal of the mind comes a new way of feeling and new reasons for feeling. A Christian world-view will ultimately transform the emotions.

---

52. Gnilka, *Der Philemonbrief*, pp. 37–38; Dunn, *Epistles to the Colossians and to Philemon*, p. 327.

53. Dunn, *Epistles to the Colossians and to Philemon*, pp. 329–330. See also Barth and Blanke, *Philemon*; Lohse, *Colossians and Philemon*, pp. 197, 198.

54. For a survey of this see Young, *The Theology of the Pastoral Letters*, pp. 88–89.

55. See Hawthorne's comments on the language used, *Philippians*, p. 110.

56. This 'is the type of anxiety a parent feels for a child, an anguish compounded of worry, fear, and hope, but rooted finally and decisively in love' (Furnish, *2 Corinthians*, p. 160).

Paul Holmer writes:

> Part of the whole sense-making that Christianity provides is a whole panoply of new emotions. Hope, fear of the Lord, contrition about oneself, love – these and more are not just variations of the familiar or permutations of something we already have, they are new affects, new forms of pathos.[57]

Having the right emotions is part of Christianity itself. Further, having knowledge of Christian teaching is to develop the right emotion. Our emotional life is to be ordered and built on our beliefs about the nature of God and the world. 'How can we despair if we remember that God made us and loves us? How can we not have hope when the prospect is eternal life, the cessation of all sorrows, and a kind of blessedness?', writes Holmer.[58]

Romans 12:1–2 speaks of renewing the mind. This renewing of the mind implies a renewing of the emotions, for the emotions are based on how we think.[59] Moo writes, 'This "re-programming" of the mind does not take place overnight but is a lifelong process by which our way of thinking is to resemble more and more the way God wants us to think.' He concludes, 'But Paul's vision, to which he calls us, is of Christians whose minds are so thoroughly renewed that we know from within, almost instinctively, what we are to do to please God in any give situation.'[60]

How we think not only determines what we do but also how we feel (2 Cor. 5:17; Rom. 8:10). We might say that with a renewed mind we will feel instinctively how we should in any given situation. We see in the last half of Romans 12 that a renewed mind leads to both renewed emotion and action. The intermingling of both action and emotion shows that both are dependent on the mind. Christian ethics are based on theology, eschatology, and the person of Christ. We might say the same about Christian emotion.[61]

In Ephesians 2:1–10 the transformation of the believer is in view. Notice all the things that are known to them: the grace of God; the love of God; the new

---

57. Holmer, *Making Christian Sense*, p. 24.

58. Holmer, *Making Christian Sense*, p. 59.

59. See Ladd, *A Theology of the New Testament*, pp. 524–525; Cranfield, *Romans*, pp. 607–611; Dunn, *Romans 9–16*, pp. 714, 718; Murray, *Romans*, vol. 2, p. 114.

60. Moo, *Romans*, pp. 756–758. Ridderbos connects the renewal of the mind with language about the heart and 'nous'. This is significant in light of our analysis of these terms (Ridderbos, *Paul: An Outline of His Theology*, p. 228).

61. Furnish, *Theology and Ethics in Paul*, p. 213.

life in Christ; future blessing, being created for new life. These are all good reasons to have godly emotions. To 'take every thought captive' implies a new emotional life (2 Cor. 10:5). In Romans 15:4 the truth of the Scriptures is a source of hope. Knowledge gives emotion.[62] Wilson writes, 'Christians set their minds, priorities, and whole manner of existence on "what is above".'[63] Bornkamm stresses the fact that Paul emphasizes reason and right thinking in the context of faith. He concludes, 'The admonition to be reasonable and circumspect therefore means the same as the demand for the renewing of the mind.'[64] Another passage worth noting is Colossians 3:9–10, 'seeing that you have stripped off the old self with its practices and have clothed yourself with the new self, which is being renewed in knowledge according to the image of its creator'.

We have also seen the link between loving, hating and knowledge in John's literature. The idea of family is strong in these books. We are God's children. This knowledge fuels the emotions of family.[65] This is also seen in the teaching of Jesus in the synoptics, as the new kingdom breaks into history it transforms the mind of those who follow. Speaking of the motivation of loving enemies in the synoptic gospels Piper concludes: 'The ambiguity of Christian existence leads to the *fourth* common feature, namely, the necessity for a renewed mind which can prove the perfect will of God. *Jesus* called for a transformation so radical that it left nothing in man untouched.' The fruit of this transformation is that the believer can love their enemy.[66]

The *kerygma* and *didachē*, those central tenets of the faith, are what are to inform the emotions. Believing these things forms the foundation for Christian emotions. In the words of Wilson:

---

62. Towner points to a similar inner change in the Pastorals. Knowing the content of the faith forms the basis for ethics (Towner, 'The Goal of Our Instruction', pp. 159, 243, 252–253). '*In principle*, the author views Christian existence, in Pauline fashion, as the integration of faith in or knowledge of Christ and the outward response of love' (Towner, 'The Goal of Our Instruction', 255). Wilson sees a similar idea in Colossians (Wilson, *The Hope of Glory*, pp. 128, 258, 103, 174). For the parallels between Rom. and 2 Cor. 5 see Furnish, *2 Corinthians*, pp. 289–291. Notice also the strong emphasis in 1 Thess. on what they already know (1:5; 2:1–2, 5, 9, 11; 3:3–4, 6; 4:2, 5:2). See also 1 Cor. 2:6 – 3:4; 8:1–7.

63. Wilson, *The Hope of Glory*, p. 148.

64. Bornkamm, 'Faith and Reason in Paul's Epistles', p. 100.

65. See Brown, *John*, p. 563.

66. Piper, *Love Your Enemies*, p. 174.

For former pagans, who would have comprised most or all of our author's audience, conversion to Christianity must have entailed adopting a radically different worldview. We can assume, then, that the process of internalizing a distinctively Christian understanding of reality while separating from previous beliefs must have called for sustained work on behalf of initiates.[67]

A proper understanding of the gospel will lead to a passionate heart. N. T. Wright rightly emphasizes the centrality of having a new heart in the ethical teachings of Jesus. Here, the Old Testament prophesies of God's people receiving a new heart begin to find their fulfilment.[68]

A renewal of the mind will result in the transformation of the believer's emotions. The New Testament insists that with the acceptance of Christ, comes a totally new way of thinking and transformed core values. If this process has genuinely begun, this will naturally result in a set of uniquely Christian emotions.

In this context, it is helpful to think about the renewal of the mind in light of recent advancements in our understanding of the brain. Jeffrey Schwartz has shown that the body actually rewires our brains when we exert conscious effort. Neurological pathways are built and reinforced as a result of what we *choose* to concentrate on. Researchers have successfully taught people to alleviate depression and compulsive behaviour by choosing how and what to think about the truth of the situation. As they focused on the truth, rather than the feeling, they literally rewired their emotional response. He concludes, 'Through changes in the way we focus attention, we have the capacity to make choices about what mental direction we will take; more than that, we also change, in scientifically demonstrable ways, the systematic functioning of the neural circuitry.'[69] By *forcefully* changing our focus to the things of God, we can rewire our emotional responses.

In bringing the connection between authentic Christianity and the transformation of the emotions to light, we stand in a long tradition of saints who proclaimed the fact that without proper emotion, a believer's commitment and even their salvation must be called into question. Wesley writes about the first commandment, 'Hast thou found happiness in God? Is he the desire of thine eyes, the joy of thy heart? If not, thou hast other gods before him.'[70] Of

---

67. Wilson, *The Hope of Glory*, p. 181.

68. Wright, *Jesus and the Victory of God*, pp. 282–286.

69. Schwartz and Begley, *The Mind*, p. 368. The idea that an adult cannot change the physiology of their neural wiring is false (p. 130).

70. *Explanatory Notes Upon the Old Testament* (Salem: Schmul, 1975), quoted in Clapper,

2 Peter 3:18 ('But grow in the grace and knowledge of our Lord and Saviour Jesus Christ'), Wesley writes:

> But grow in grace – That is, in every Christian temper . . . Frames (allowing
> the expression) are no other than heavenly tempers, 'the mind that was in Christ'.
> Feelings are the divine consolations of the Holy Ghost shed abroad in the
> heart of him that truly believes. And wherever faith is, and wherever Christ is, there
> are these blessed frames and feelings. If they are not in us, it is a sure sign that,
> though the wilderness became a pool, the pool is become a wilderness again.[71]

Calvin writes:

> But how can the mind be aroused to taste the divine goodness without at the same
> time being wholly kindled to love God in return? For truly, that abundant sweetness
> which God has stored up for those who fear him cannot be known without at the
> same time powerfully moving us . . . Therefore, it is no wonder if a perverse and
> wicked heart never experiences that emotion by which, born up to heaven itself,
> we are admitted to the most hidden treasures of God.[72]

Emotion in New Testament theology and ethics

The theologies of the New Testament, as we have seen, do not do a good job in incorporating emotion into their framework. As it is in secular ethics, in New Testament ethics and theology emotion is often belittled, trivialized or ignored.[73] The apostle Paul writes, 'For the kingdom of God is not food and

---

    John Wesley on Religious Affections, p. 34. See also, Wesley, *Wesley's Standard Sermons*,
    edited by Sugden, vol. 1, p. 153.

71. *Explanatory Notes Upon the New Testament* (London: Epworth Press, 1976), quoted in
    Clapper, *John Wesley on Religious Affections*, p. 60. Clapper summarizes: 'If one is to be
    a Christian according to John Wesley's standards, the heart must be engaged.
    Specifically, one must have certain affections and shun certain other affections . . .
    anger and hate are to be left behind while awe and love of God, along with love of
    neighbour, are emotional requirements for the Christian' (Clapper, *John Wesley on
    Religious Affections*, pp. 38–39).

72. Calvin, *Institutes*, vol. 1, translated by Battles, 3.2.41.

73. For example, Caird, *New Testament Theology*; Lohse, *Theological Ethics of the New
    Testament*; Guthrie, *New Testament Theology*; Goppelt, *Theology of the New Testament*;
    Griffith-Jones, *The Four Witnesses*. Morris presents a list of major theological works
    that neglect love (Morris, *Testaments of Love*, pp. 5–6).

drink but righteousness and peace and joy in the Holy Spirit' (Rom. 14:17). We have seen that the ethics of the New Testament emphasize heart and motive which must include emotion.[74]

At best emotion is ignored and at worst it is misinterpreted because of a faulty philosophical framework. In longer studies that deal with emotion, in a majority of cases the conclusions that are reached are contradictory and inconsistent both with a uniform theory of the emotions and within the work itself. In the words of Roberts:

> The emotions which make up the Christian life are not inscrutable psychological phenomena mysteriously caused by God, as inaccessible to our understanding as is the origin of the universe. Thus, reflection about the nature of emotion may lead to a kind of self-knowledge which can be applied, in various ways, to the task of becoming and being a Christian.[75]

Both the Pietist and rationalist separate emotion and thinking, one emphasizing one and one the other. They make the same mistake. Neither has a proper integrated view of faith, theology and emotion.[76] Saliers writes:

> To many religious people and to many systematic theologians, the affections do not seem to be the sort of thing susceptible to being clarified by theological reflection. Yet this is precisely my aim . . . Whatever else it may include, the Christian faith is a pattern of deep emotions.[77]

Many major sources that do consider emotion never clearly define it or do not understand it. Even in specific studies about emotion or emotional vocabulary, often there is little or no attempt to define the specific emotion and almost never is there a general understanding of what emotion is.[78] It is time to reverse these trends. When we see emotion as part of reason and not as a primitive irrational force, we are compelled to give them the attention they deserve.

As we have seen, positive emotion words are often said not to be about emotion and are put in quotations ('hope') to say to the reader, 'Don't misunderstand this to be that emotion that you feel in your daily life, this is

---

74. See Theissen, *Sociology of Early Palestinian Christianity*, pp. 77–78.

75. Roberts, 'Emotions and the Fruit of the Spirit', p. 80. See also p. 81.

76. Saliers, *The Soul in Paraphrase*, p. 5.

77. Saliers, *The Soul in Paraphrase*, p. 11.

78. For example, see Outka, *Agape*.

something much more than that.' This is even more surprising in light of the fact that the books of the New Testament were written to a specific audience often facing a specific problem. As we have noted earlier, broad theological concepts must be carefully distilled from this context. It is even more difficult to argue that joy or hope is not emotional when it is realized that the goal of the letter is to encourage and strengthen a specific body of believers, not to write a theology of joy or hope.[79] When it comes to anger, hatred, or sorrow, these are considered to be emotional. It is often argued, in these cases, that it is best to eliminate these altogether from the life of the believer. The supposed discrepancy between the lack of emotional content for positive Christian emotions and the assumed emotional content of destructive emotions is too prevalent to ignore. Certainly this points us to the conclusion that emotions in general are viewed by most biblical scholars in a negative light.

It seems illogical that many Christian scholars believe that Christian love and joy are not emotional and at the same time insist that negative emotions are emotional and should be avoided. How were we to know from the text of the New Testament that we should look at positive emotions in one way and negative emotions in another?

Further, and even more troubling, why would God not care if we have the good feelings of love and joy and leave us to fight the destructive emotions of anger, fear and jealousy with no effective weapons in our arsenal against these destructive passions? Why do I say that we have no effective weapons against destructive emotions? If emotions are uncontrollable forces that are not dependent on our thinking, how do we fight them? We cannot fight destructive emotions except to perhaps take a pill or a warm bath. If non-cognitive theory is correct we have the worst of both sides. We cannot expect to feel love and joy and we need to fight anger, jealousy and hatred.

This does not seem like a fair or good God. Although many have offered 'solutions' to this problem, often insisting that 'feelings will follow the right actions,' or 'joy is a deep inner disposition that sometimes will lead to good feelings,' this does not really help us out of the problem. Love is either an emotion God designed us to feel or it is not. God either requires and desires that our faith is filled with joy, the jubilant feeling, or he does not. You can not have it both ways!

---

79. See Earl, 'Early Pauline Thought: An Analysis of 1 Thessalonians', p. 49; Scroggs, 'Salvation History', p. 220. Schlatter recognized this trend in Christian education (Schlatter, *Die Christliche Ethik*, p. 324).

We would do well to learn from Saint Augustine:

> And generally in respect of all that we seek or shun, as a man's will is attracted or
> repelled, so it is changed and turned into these different affections. Wherefore the
> man who lives according to God, and not according to man, ought to be a lover of
> good, and therefore a hater of evil.[80]
>
> Among ourselves, according to the sacred Scriptures and sound doctrine, the
> citizens of the holy city of God, who live according to God in the pilgrimage of this
> life, both fear and desire, and grieve and rejoice. And because their love is rightly
> placed, all these affections of theirs are right.[81]

Nussbaum comments on Augustine:

> It [Christian love] is similar [to human love] both in structure and in subjective
> experience. But we can now take one further step, following the lead of the anti-Stoic
> arguments of the City of God. Human love and Christian love, human emotions and
> Christian emotions, are not merely two similar stories. They are two parts of the same
> story. There is only one faculty of love and desire in the human being; the only way
> human being changes her love is to redirect that same love toward a new object. It is
> the same love that loves Dido and loves God.[82]

The nature of Christian emotion themselves are not different than the emotions of the world, but rather it is why they are felt and for what they are felt
that sets them apart. This idea has been a major area where we have found ourselves in disagreement with most New Testament scholars.

In this context, it is also important to emphasize that in most cases
scholars' positive conclusions are accurate in passages we have examined.
Our criticisms of specific statements are usually not about what is affirmed
but about what is denied. In many cases we find a uniquely Christian concept
of an emotion that includes theological content. To say that love of neighbour is emotional is not to say that Christian love does not necessarily
include an understanding of who your neighbour is and what actions and
dispositions are authentic demonstrations of that love. This is clearly seen
in 1 Corinthians 13.

Far from being a side note in theology and ethics, in the Christian world-

---

80. Augustine, *The City of God*, 9.6.

81. Augustine, *The City of God*, 14.9.

82. Nussbaum, *Upheavals of Thought*, p. 547.

view God made us with emotions. The objects we value should be determined by the Scripture. Our beliefs and values will, in turn, determine our emotions.[83] Further, if, as we argued in Chapter one, emotions can tell us something true about our world, they can help us to discern the right way to understand a situation. If our beliefs are correct, our emotions become an increasingly reliable guide to right behaviour.

Central to Christian ethics is the fact that they are lived out in community with other believers. Believers are to love one another.[84] The emotional life of the community in worship, in love and in fellowship was a key concern to the writers of the New Testament. The community was socially close and dependent. The books were written to specific communities facing specific problems. This increases the urgency of healthy emotional interactions in the community. When believers are to feel joy, hope and love and share sorrow and grief, these are not cold and dry exhortations to be analysed and broken down into theological constructs. Instead, they are meant to foster a healthy and vibrant emotional life in what were often difficult situations. Certainly, sociological studies of the New Testament should exhibit a greater sensitivity to the emotions of the community and greater care in analysing how the members of the community are instructed to feel.

Love for God, even when it is assumed, is an essential concept throughout the New Testament. Central to theology is the love of God.[85] Emotions are among the important Christian virtues. Christian emotions are based on Christian thinking.[86] Emotion virtues are not based on temporal objects or circumstances but on the relevant theology. Roberts believes that the basic facts of the Christian faith mean that, 'the believer's "circumstances" are always right for gratitude, hope, peace, contrition, and joy'. What makes these virtues uniquely Christian is that they are based on different things than their secular counterparts.[87]

Those virtues that are not emotions are often linked to emotion. For example, in 2 Corinthians 9 the emotional trait of generous person is a 'cheerful giver'. Emotions are part of the Christian virtue of generosity. The

---

83. Roberts, 'Emotions as Access to Religious Truths', p. 90. 'If emotional perceptions are to be in all respects correct, the framework supporting them must also be correct' (p. 92). See also Schlatter, *Die Christliche Ethik*, p. 324.

84. Dodd, *Gospel and Law*, pp. 34–36.

85. Morris, *Testaments of Love*, p. 171.

86. Roberts, 'Emotions Among the Virtues', pp. 37–39.

87. Roberts, 'Emotions Among the Virtues', p. 44.

emotion shows if the giving is generous or if it is based on impure motives such as receiving earthly praise.

Emotion is a major source of motivation for moral action in the Christian life. The love that is to be at the heart of Christian ethics is emotional. For example, Roberts writes, 'anger is based on a concern that justice be done'. When injustice is seen there is the desire to 'see the offender punished'.[88] Anger at sin or grief over sin may be distinctively Christian when they are felt because Christian values are embraced. If they are not felt when they are appropriate it is a character flaw.[89] Having the right emotions is a barrier against sin. To hate wrong and love good leads to right action. We can also conclude from our study that the New Testament requires that emotion match the action. We are to act out of properly felt love and compassion and on occasion jealousy and anger.

Attitudes make a difference. Christians are held responsible for how they feel. To be like Christ is not only to behave like Christ but also to feel like Christ. Christ could act out of his emotions because his emotions were based on the right things. To be conformed to his image is to be able to act out of feelings because the feelings are based on the truth of the gospel. Schlatter agrees.[90] Emotions are frequently commanded.

In general, emotions are not morally right or wrong in themselves. A possible exception to this is envy. The very definition of envy involves desiring something that is not yours. For the other basic emotions, however, morality is not an inherent part of their definition. Anger can be either right or wrong depending on the reason why it is felt. If it is wrong, it is a moral fault for which one can be held responsible. In the view of the New Testament, the anger itself can be sin. On the other hand, even jealousy, under the right circumstances, can be a moral imperative. Joy in another's pain is an evil and love of sin is reprehensible.

It is good to remember that the expression of and intensity of emotion needs to be differentiated from its initial moral content. For an unmarried couple, the unlimited physical expression of love would violate morality in the view of the New Testament. Violent action that is motivated by appropriate anger is most often to be condemned. Similarly, as we have argued in Chapter five, an initial negative and justified response must not be allowed to fester into an overarching sinful attitude towards someone else. The New Testament is

---

88. Roberts, 'The Logic and Lyric of Contrition', p. 201.

89. Roberts, 'Emotions Among the Virtues', pp. 46–49.

90. Schlatter, *Die Christliche Ethik*, p. 340.

clear that anger easily rages out of control and can do great damage to other people. At the same time, emotional intensity may indicate how strongly a belief is held and a consistent lack of emotional intensity in worship of God, for example, may indicate a lack of commitment to him.[91]

We also should not neglect to draw some parallels between emotion in the New Testament and the indicative and imperative. Rosner writes, 'Nonetheless, Bultmann is correct to insist on the centrality of the indicative and the imperative, that what God has done is the basis of what justified believers must do.'[92] We might say, what God has said is the basis of what believers must feel. Rosner continues, 'Just as Paul links theology and ethics so there is a connection in his thought between orthodoxy and orthopraxy, such that good doctrine leads to good behavior.'[93] We might say, just as Paul links theology and ethics so there is a connection in his thought between orthodoxy and emotion. Good doctrine leads to feeling the right emotions. Schnabel finds five major motivations for Christian behaviour: Christological, salvation–historical, pneumatological, ecclesiological and eschatological. Again, we might argue that these same factors form the basis of Christian feelings.[94] In our study we have seen many links between right emotion and right knowledge in the New Testament. Analysing these connections is fertile ground for further study.

Roberts concludes:

> The emotions have a pre-eminent place in the Christian virtues-system because they are the most immediate way in which the gospel at the foundation of the Christian life makes its mark on the human soul and draws into fellowship with God . . . the Christian emotions determine the distinctive character of the whole range of Christian virtues.[95]

Clapper writes:

> Instead, theology is to provide the paradigm, the defining vision, of the essential features of the Christian life, including speech, actions and emotions . . . The goal of

---

91. See Ben-Ze'ev, *The Subtlety of Emotions*, p. 118.
92. Rosner, 'That Pattern of Teaching', p. 19.
93. Rosner, 'That Pattern of Teaching', p. 20. See also Dunn, *The Theology of Paul the Apostle*, pp. 626–631; Furnish, *Theology and Ethics in Paul*, p. 225; Ridderbos, *Paul: An Outline of His Theology*, pp. 254–255.
94. Schnabel, 'How Paul Developed His Ethics', pp. 293–294.
95. Roberts, 'Emotions Among the Virtues', p. 61.

the properly lived Christian life is not to have an unshakable grasp of the meta-language of theology . . .[96]

The idea that emotions cannot be commanded has been one of the major mis-understandings that we have faced in this study. Piper writes:

> The New Testament knows nothing of the philosophical difficulty that affections or desires cannot be commanded. We find commands to rejoice, to be grateful, not to fear or be anxious, etc., all of which demand a change in our affections. The command to love God with all our heart may mean more, but surely not less, than we should delight ourselves in the Lord and desire his fellowship. The reason affections can be commanded is not that they are in our ultimate control but because, given the nature of reality, some affections ought to exist toward God and man and some ought not. To know that a certain affection ought to exist is a sufficient condition for being the object of a reasonable command to experience that affection.[97]

Piper encapsulates one of the essential elements of the argument against the ought implies can principle when he writes, 'To know that a certain affection ought to exist is a sufficient condition for being the object of a reasonable command to experience that affection.' However, we can add to this the argument that emotions can be commanded because they are cognitive. If either of these two arguments is true, it is logical to command emotion. Further, the fact that there is a consistent pattern in the New Testament of relating commands of emotion to correct theological knowledge enforces our interpretation of these passages not as commands to engage in immediate action but as commands to reexamine and change beliefs and values in light of biblical teaching.

Part of the essence of the Christian is how he or she feels. We must recover some of the insight of Jonathan Edwards, Calvin, Augustine and others as they rightly emphasize the role of emotion in the believer's life. With a little work we can come up with a clear idea of the emotional characteristics of the members of the kingdom of God. They love God and each other, they take joy in what Jesus has done in the past and what he will do in the future. They have secure hope that God will triumph. They become angry at sin and injustice and are jealous for God. They embrace the sorrow of the suffering as their own and grieve over sin. But this emotional life is rarely

---

96. Clapper, *John Wesley on Religious Affections*, p. 158.
97. Piper, 'Hope as the Motivation of Love: 1 Peter 3:9–12', p. 216.

glimpsed in our theologies where emotion is not emphasized as a sign of true faith. Not only do Christians live the ethics of the kingdom, they also feel the attitudes and emotions of the kingdom. This is part of the picture that is very clear in the New Testament. These feelings are a result of good theology and are a necessary component of faith.

In a representative statement about Christian marriage, Hays writes, 'the church must recognize and teach that marriage is grounded not in feelings of love but in the practice of love'.[98] Is this all the church has to offer? Certainly, the call to loving action must be heeded and there is no excuse for selfish action within the body of Christ. Yet, how successful can a relationship be that is based on duty? Love, the emotion, communicates value and worth to the partner. Love, the emotion, is based on the fact that the other person is uniquely fashioned in the image of God. Love demands extravagant action to bless the other person, often involving sacrifice. If love is only action, the radical nature of Christian love is lost to doing the legalistic requirements of duty. Love, properly understood as full deep emotion, will stand the test of time. Here, at the very centre of Christian ethics, we have emotion: to love God and neighbour. In fact love, the emotion, is the only thing that is able to motivate the radical action to which Jesus calls us.

A final word

You should now have a good idea of why this work is entitled *Faithful Feelings*. Emotions are a faithful reflection of what we believe and value. The Bible does not treat them as forces to be controlled or channelled toward the right things, but as an integral part of who we are as people created in God's image. Christian emotions should be the most intense, the most vibrant, and the most pervasive things we feel as they are based on the most important things in life: our relationship to God and his great love for us; our eternal future; and the work of Christ. If we are faithful in making our core heart values and beliefs those of the Bible, our emotions will be faithfully conformed to these truths. God requires that we have faithful feelings as he freely commands us to feel as we should, and demands that we change feelings that are contrary to biblical principles. We can faithfully act out of the feelings that God requires. This is what God has intended. Our emotions will show the reality of our faith. You will find believers living from their hearts at the core of the

---

98. Hays, *The Moral Vision of the New Testament*, p. 372.

great moves of God in the New Testament and church history. The new heart we read about in Jeremiah 31 is ours if we have faith in his son Jesus Christ.

Although this work did not find its genesis in the work of Jonathan Edwards, my research led me to esteem greatly his ideas about emotion. I was delighted to find that much of my thinking was in fact a modern restatement of his work on religious affections.[99] Edwards writes:

> We should realize, to our shame before God, that we are not more affected with the great things of faith. It appears from what we have said that this arises from our having so little true religion . . .
>
> When it comes to their worldly interests, their outward delights, their honor and reputation, and their natural relations, they have warm affection and ardent zeal . . . They get deeply depressed at worldly losses, and highly excited at worldly successes. But how insensible and unmoved are most men about the great things of another world! . . . Here their love is cold, their desire languid, their zeal low, and their gratitude small. How can they sit and hear for the infinite height, depth, length, and breadth of the love of God in Christ Jesus . . . and yet be so insensible and regardless! Can we suppose that the wise Creator implanted such a faculty of affections to be occupied in this way?[100]

Emotion is central to the Christian life and is therefore essential in Christian theology and ethics. According to the New Testament, the Christian life is worth living, it is full of hope and joy. Love is its greatest commandment. As all of us know, life without emotion would be a life not worth living. Our greatest experiences are those where we have felt and lived to the fullest. To the Christian, a healthy emotional life must be built on biblical truth.

We should also not be so quick to emphasize the control or mastery of the passions as if the major area Christians are to be concerned about in their emotional life is not to let their out-of-control passions lead them into sin. The values and beliefs behind emotions that lead us to harm are what need to be changed. We are not at war with our emotions but rather with the thinking and

---

99. Edwards presents a logical and well thought out cognitive theory of the emotions and applies this theory to his faith. Unlike many of the other theologians we have looked at, he is consistent and does not contradict himself. He also uses Scripture instead of philosophy as his foundation. This is another unusual element in his writings. These factors make Edward's analysis of Scripture particularly relevant and helpful.

100. Edwards, *Religious Affections*, p. 27.

values of this world. Cherry writes, 'Religious man is not one who subjects passion to the rule of reason, but one whose reason is passionate and whose affection is intellectual.'[101] The New Testament does not emphasize controlling sinful emotions; it requires their *elimination* (remember that we do not consider all anger, jealousy, or hatred to be sin). We are to eliminate emotion that is sin, just like we eliminate greed or adultery. The Christian should have an overflow of love, joy, and hope that spills out to those we touch. Our goal should be to have righteous feelings, to emphasize the harm of out of control emotions without an understanding of the importance of having the right emotions, is to rob the Christian life of its power and vitality.

Our emotions touch God and elicit his response. In the words of the *Shema*, 'Love the Lord your God with all your heart, and with all your soul, and with all your might.' Emotional ecstasy was not the goal, but healthy emotions were the natural outworking of faith. As Calvin, Wesley and Edwards emphasize, faith without passionate affection for God and others is not biblical faith.

Let us also remember the key role that emotion plays in communication and thinking. It is not possible to make logical decisions without emotion serving to order and prioritize thoughts and responses. Without emotion it would be near to impossible to understand what is important to another person. The emotion of the writers of the New Testament about their experience of the risen Christ is what drives the narrative and elicits a response. Emotion is not the opposite of reason and rationality; it is part of reason's very substance. Thus the idea of communicating the gospel in an emotion-free factual manner is a fallacy.

We should not neglect this study's implication for the life of the church. How we love each other has everything to do with how we feel about one another. Love will draw us into fellowship. In an era of churches focusing on professional stage presentations and great music, perhaps some of our churches need to revive the potluck dinner, family night and the church picnic. The church family has the most wonderful reasons to rejoice and joy and laughter should characterize our fellowship together. We are called to enjoy one another's company just as Jesus made best friends. It is only in loving and enjoying one another up close that we will be prepared to bear one another's burdens when the pain and crises of this world come rushing down upon us.

We must also be careful when evaluating the emotional expression and intensity of ourselves and others. People differ in how they express emotion and in many cases this is a function of personality that is neither right nor

---

101. Cherry, *The Theology of Jonathan Edwards*, p. 167, quoted in Hutch, 'Jonathan Edward's Analysis of Religious Experience', p. 125.

wrong. We must seek to understand one another. As our focus, circumstances and environment change, the intensity of emotion toward God or another individual will fluctuate. Seasons of faith and life are natural and these changes should not be seen as sure indicators of the state of your spiritual health.

Unfortunately, the divorce of emotion and theology is often evident in pastoral counselling. Many pastors approach counselling from a psychological viewpoint when it comes to dealing with emotions, neglecting to realize that the text of the New Testament has significant insights to help order the emotional life of the believer. Emotion is an important part of the biblical world view and personal pastoral counselling should reflect this fact. The New Testament insists that a believer should have a particular emotional outlook and it presents ways to eliminate destructive emotions. Clapper concludes:

> Emotion cannot be left exclusively to the province of the psychologist and the pastoral counsellor . . . Both the theologian of the ivory tower and the counsellor concerned solely with 'feelings' are left behind in Wesleyan practical theology. Wesley saw that the normative question of theology ('What is Christianity?') must be brought together with the counsellor's quest for self-knowledge ('How does that make you feel?') if all of the truths of the Gospel are to be embodied.[102]

A final caution is also in order. It has been my aim to understand how emotions are seen to function in the New Testament, not specifically to understand how we can change our emotional life to what it should be. I do not mean to present an easy wooden model as if people's emotions are mechanical machines where one particular input results in a specific emotional output. People are fantastically complex and our emotions reflect this. It has also not been my aim to make a comprehensive statement about the ability or inability of people to work to change their emotions or the role of the Holy Spirit in the process of that change. The road to emotional health can be difficult, sometimes requiring years to relearn harmful responses. There can be much to overcome, and perhaps a change is not even possible for some of us without radical intervention from the Holy Spirit. It is hoped that the concepts in this book will provide us with some idea of a map to understand where we are, where we need to be, and how to start on the road from here to there.

That said, we can affirm that as believers integrate a balanced view of emotion into their theology, faith and ethics, their lives will be enriched. We should celebrate good things and grieve over the pain of life. The New

---

102. Clapper, *John Wesley on Religious Affections*, pp. 170–171.

Testament understands and encourages the natural flow of our emotional lives. Christian hope and joy can be pervasive even in suffering when they are based on Christian values. As the Christian learns to love people because of who they are created to be by God, even the most difficult individual can be shown genuine love. Anger at sin and its destructive effects is reasonable and natural. In many cases this will motivate corrective action. When Christian emotions are not present, or when harmful emotions are pervasive, it is a warning that the belief system which the New Testament presents has not been grasped and valued. When Christians transfer allegiance from this world to the kingdom of God, their emotions will be transformed.

BIBLIOGRAPHY

ADAM, J. (1902), *The Republic of Plato: Edited With Critical Notes, Commentary, and Appendices*, 2 vols., Cambridge: The University Press.

ALAND, K. & ALAND, B. (1988), *Griechisch-deutsches Wörterbuch: zu den Schriften des Neuen Testaments und der frühchristlichen Literatur von Walter Bauer*, Berlin: Walter de Gruyter.

ALAND, K., BLACK, M., MARTINI, C. M., METZGER, B. M. & WIKGREN, A. (eds.) (1993–94), *The Greek New Testament*, 4th ed., Stuttgart: United Bible Societies. (Electronic version found in *BWW*.)

ALEXANDER, L. C. A. (1995) 'The Relevance of Greco-Roman Literature and Culture to New Testament Study', in J. Green (ed.) *Hearing the New Testament: Strategies for Interpretation*, Grand Rapids: Eerdmans.

ALLENDER, D. B. & LONGMAN III, T. (1992), *Bold Love*, Colorado Springs, NavPress.

— (1994), *The Cry of the Soul: How Our Emotions Reveal Our Deepest Questions About God*, Colorado Springs: Navpress.

ANDERSEN, F. I. & FREEDMAN, D. N. (1980), *Hosea: A New Translation with Introduction and Commentary*, New York: Doubleday and Company Inc.

ANDERSON, A. A. (1972), *Psalms*, vol. 1, *NCBC*, Grand Rapids: Eerdmans.

ANDERSON, G. A. (1991), *A Time to Mourn, A Time to Dance: The Expression of Grief and Joy in Israelite Religion*, University Park, Pennsylvania: The Pennsylvania State University Press.

ANNAS, J. (1989) 'Epicurean Emotions', *Greek, Roman, and Byzantine Studies* 30: 145–164.

— (1992), *Hellenistic Philosophy of Mind*, Berkeley: University of California Press.

AQUINAS, ST THOMAS, *Summa Theologica* (trans. T. C. O'Brien, 1965), vol. 26, *Original Sin*, London: Blackfriars.

—, *Summa Theologica* (trans. John Patrick Reid, 1965), vol. 21, *Fear and Anger*, London: Blackfriars.

—, *Summa Theologica* (trans. Eric D'Arcy, 1967), vol. 19, *The Emotions*, London: Blackfriars.

—, *Summa Theologica* (trans. W. D. Hughes, 1969), vol. 23, *Virtue*, London: Blackfriars.

ARISTOTLE, 'From *Nicomachean Ethics* (1125^{b}26–1126^{b}9)' (trans. Jon D. Solomon, 1984), in *What is an Emotion? Classic Readings in Philosophical Psychology*, Cheshire Calhoun and Robert C. Solomon (eds.), Oxford: Oxford University Press.

—, 'From *Rhetoric* (1378^{a}20–1380^{a}4)' (trans. Jon D. Solomon, 1984), in *What is an Emotion? Classic Readings in Philosophical Psychology*, Cheshire Calhoun and Robert C. Solomon (eds.), Oxford: Oxford University Press.

ARNOLD, C. E. 'Magical Papyri', in Evans, C. A. & Porter, S. E. (eds.), *DNTB*.

ARNOLD, M. B. (1960), *Emotion and Personality*, vol. 1, *Psychological Aspects*, New York: Columbia University Press.

— (1994), 'Cognitive Theories of Emotion', in R. J. Corsini (ed.) *Encyclopedia of Psychology*, 2nd ed., vol. 2, New York: John Wiley and Sons.

— (ed.) (1968), *The Nature of Emotion*, Penguin Modern Psychology Readings, Harmondsworth: Penguin.

— (ed.) (1970), *Feelings and Emotions: The Loyola Symposium, Personality and Psychopathology*, New York: Academic Press.

ARNOLD, M. B. & GASSON, J. A. (1968), 'Feelings and Emotions as Dynamic Factors in Personality Integration', in M. B. Arnold (ed.), *The Nature of Emotion*, Penguin Modern Psychology Readings, Harmondsworth: Penguin.

ASMIS, E. (1989), 'The Stoicism of Marcus Aurelius', in *ANRW, II: Principat*, vol. 36.3.

— (1990), 'Philodemus' Epicureanism', in *ANRW, II: Principat*, vol. 36.4.

ATKINSON, R. L., ATKINSON, R. C., SMITH, E. E. & BEM, D. J. (1993), *Introduction to Psychology* (11th ed.), Fort Worth: Harcourt Brace College Publishers.

ATTRIDGE, H. W. (1989), *The Epistle to the Hebrews*, Philadelphia: Fortress Press.

Aufstieg und Niedergang der Römischen Welt: Geschichte und Kultur Roms im Spiegel der Neueren Forschung. Berlin: Walter De Gruyter.

AUGUSTINE, *The City of God* (trans. M. Dods, 1886), in *A Select Library of the Nicene and Post-Nicene Fathers*, vol. 2., repr. Grand Rapids: Eerdmans, 1979.

AUNE, D. E. (1998), *Revelation 6–16, WBC*, Nashville: Thomas Nelson Publishers.

— (1998), *Revelation 17–22, WBC*, Nashville: Thomas Nelson Publishers.

BAER, D. A. & GORDON, R. P. (1997), '*ḥsd*', in *NIDOTTE*, vol. 2, Grand Rapids: Zondervan.

BAILEY, C. (1926), *Epicurus: The Extant Remains with Short Critical Apparatus, Translation, and Notes.* Oxford: The Clarendon Press.

BALCH, D. L., FERGUSON, E. & MEEKS, W. A. (eds.) (1990), *Greeks, Romans, and Christians: Essays in Honor of Abraham J. Malherbe*, Minneapolis: Fortress Press.

BALOIAN, B. (1992), *Anger in the Old Testament*, New York: Peter Lang.

— (1997), 'Anger', in *NIDOTTE*, vol. 1, Grand Rapids: Zondervan Publishing House.

BALZ, H. (1974), '*phobeō, phobeomai, phobos, deos*', in *TDNT*, vol. 9, Grand Rapids: Eerdmans.

BANKS, R. (ed.) (1974), *Reconciliation and Hope: New Testament Essays on Atonement and Eschatology*, Grand Rapids: Eerdmans.

BARCLAY, J. M. (1988), *Obeying the Truth: A Study of Paul's Ethics in Galatians*, Edinburgh: T.&T. Clark.

BARCLAY, W. (1960), *The Mind of Jesus*, New York: Harper and Row.

BARR, A. (1950), '"Hope" (*ELPIS, ELPIZŌ*) in the New Testament', *Scottish Journal of Theology* 3: 68–77.

BARR, J. (1961), *The Semantics of Biblical Language*, Oxford: Oxford University Press.

BARRETT, C. K. (1967), *The Gospel According to St John: An Introduction with Commentary and Notes on the Greek Text*, London: SPCK.

— (1968), *The First Epistle to the Corinthians*, Black's New Testament Commentaries, Peabody, Massachusetts: Hendrickson Publishers.

— (1973), *The Second Epistle to the Corinthians*, Black's New Testament Commentaries, Peabody, Massachusetts: Hendrickson Publishers.

— (1994), *Paul: An Introduction to His Thought*, Louisville: John Knox Press.

BARTH, M. & BLANKE, H. (2000), *The Letter to Philemon*, Grand Rapids: Eerdmans.

BASSET, R., HILL, P., HART, C., MATHEWSON, K. & PERRY, K. (1993), 'Helping Christians Reclaim Some Abandoned Emotions: The ACE Model of Emotions', *JPT* 21: 165–173.

BASSLER, J. M. (1995), 'Centering the Argument', in D. M. Hay & E. E. Johnson (eds.), *Romans*, vol. 3 of *Pauline Theology*, Minneapolis: Fortress Press.

— (ed.) (1991), *Thessalonians, Philippians, Galatians, Philemon*, vol. 1 of *Pauline Theology*, Minneapolis: Fortress Press, 1991.

BAUCKHAM, R. J. (1983), *Jude, 2 Peter*, in *WBC*, Dallas: Word Books.

BAUER, J. B. (1981), 'Heart', in *EBT*.

BAUER, JOHANNES B. ed. (1981), *Encyclopedia of Biblical Theology: The Complete Sacramentum Verbi*, New York: Crossroad.

BAYER, W., DANKER, F. W., ARNDT, W. F. & GINGRICH, F. W., eds. (1999), *A Greek-English Lexicon of the New Testament and Other Early Christian Literature* (3rd edn), Chicago: Chicago University Press.

BEALE, G. K. (1999), *The Book of Revelation*, in *NIGTC*, Grand Rapids: William B. Eerdmans Publishing Company.

BEASLEY-MURRAY, G. R. (1978), *Revelation*. rev. ed., in *NCBC*, Grand Rapids: Eerdmans.

— (1987), *John*, in *WBC*, Waco, Texas: Word Books.

BECK, J. R. (1999), *Jesus and Personality Theory: Exploring the Five-Factor Model*, Downers-Grove: Inter-Varsity Press.

BECKER, J. (1976), 'Der Brief an die Galater', in *Die Briefe an die Galater, Epheser, Philipper, Kolosser, Thessalonicher, und Philemon, NTD*. Göttingen: Vandenhoeck & Ruprecht.

— (1979), *Das Evangelium nach Johannes: Kapitel 1–10*, in *Okumenischer Taschenbuchkommentar zum Neuen Testament*, Gütersloher Verlagshaus.

— (1981), *Das Evangelium nach Johannes: Kapitel 11–21*, in *Okumenischer Taschenbuchkommentar zum Neuen Testament*, Echter Verlag.

— (1993), *Paul: Apostle to the Gentiles* (trans. O. C. Dean Jr, 1993), Louisville: John Knox Press.

— (1998), *Jesus of Nazareth*, Berlin: Walter De Gruyter.

BEHM, J. (1965), '*kardia, kardiognōsthēs, sklērokardia*,' in *TDNT*, vol. 3, Grand Rapids: Eerdmans.

BEILNER, W. (1981) 'Joy', in *EBT*.

BEKER, J. C. (1980), *Paul the Apostle: The Triumph of God in Life and Thought*, Philadelphia: Fortress Press.

— (1991), 'Recasting Pauline Theology', in J. M. Bassler (ed.), *Thessalonians, Philippians, Galatians, Philemon*, vol. 1 of *Pauline Theology*, Minneapolis: Fortress Press.

BELL, R. H. (1994), 'Provoked to Jealousy: The Origin and Purpose of the Jealousy Motif in Romans 9–11', in *Wissenschaftliche Untersuchungen zum Neuen Testament*, Tübingen: J. C. B. Mohr.

BELLEVILLE, L. L. (1993) 'Enemy, Enmity, Hatred', in *DPL*.

BEN-ZE'EV, A. (1987), 'The Nature of Emotions', *Philosophical Studies* 52: 393–409.

— (1990), 'Envy and Jealousy', *Canadian Journal of Philosophy* 20:487–516.

— (1992), 'Anger and Hate', *Journal of Social Philosophy* 23: 885–110.

— (2000), *The Subtlety of Emotions*, Cambridge: The MIT Press.

BERENSON, F. (1991), 'What Is This Thing Called "Love"?', *Philosophy* 66: 65–79.

BERGER, K. (1994), *Theologiegeschechte des Urchristentums: Theologie des Neuen Testaments*, Tübingen: Francke Verlag.

BERTRAM, G. (1974), '*phrēn, aphrōn, aphrosynē, phroneō, phronēma, phronēsis, phronimos*', in *TDNT*, vol. 9. Grand Rapids: Eerdmans.

BEST, E. (1971), *1 Peter*, in *NCBC*, Grand Rapids: Eerdmans.

— (1998), *A Critical and Exegetical Commentary on Ephesians*, in *ICC*, Edinburgh: T. & T. Clark.

BETZ, H. D. (1979), *Galatians: A Commentary on Paul's Letter to the Churches in Galatia*, in *Hermeneia*, Philadelphia: Fortress Press.

— (1995), *The Sermon on the Mount*, in *Hermeneia*, Minneapolis: Fortress Press.

BEYREUTHER, E. (1976a), '*agalliaomai*', in *NIDNTT*, vol. 2, Grand Rapids: Zondervan.

BEYREUTHER, E. & FINKENRATH, G. (1976), '*chairō*', in *NIDNTT*, vol. 2, Grand Rapids: Zondervan.

Bible Works for Windows, ver. 3.0, Big Fork, MT: Hermeneutika.

BLOMBERG, C. L. (1990), *Interpreting the Parables*, Downers Grove, Illinois: Inter-Varsity Press.

BLUM, L. (1980), 'Compassion', in A. Oksenberg Rorty (ed.), *Explaining Emotions*, Berkeley: University of California Press.

BOCKMUEHL, M. (1998), *The Epistle to the Philippians*, in *Black's New Testament Commentary*, Peabody, MA: Hendrickson.

BOICE, J. M. (1976), 'Galatians', in *EBC*, vol. 10, Grand Rapids: Zondervan.

BORNKAMM, G. (1958), 'Faith and Reason in Paul's Epistles', *NTS* 4: 93–100.

— (1960), *Jesus of Nazareth*, trans. I. McLuskey & F. McLuskey, New York: Harper and Row Publishers.

— (1995), *Paul*, trans. D. M. G. Stalker. Minneapolis: Fortress Press.

BOVON, F. (1989), *Das Evangelium nach Lukas*, vol. 1, in *EKK*, Freiburg: Herder.

BOWER, G. H. (1994), 'Some Relations Between Emotions and Memory', in P. Ekman and R. J. Davidson (eds.), *The Nature of Emotion: Fundamental Questions*, Series in *Affective Science*, Oxford: Oxford University Press, 1994.

BROWN, C. (1976), '*phileō*', in *NIDNTT*, vol. 2, Grand Rapids: Zondervan.

— (ed.) (1975–78), *The New International Dictionary of New Testament Theology*, 4 vols., Grand Rapids: Zondervan.

BROWN, M. L. (1997), "*ašrê*', in *NIDOTTE*, vol. 1, Grand Rapids: Zondervan Publishing House.

BROWN, R. E. (1982), *The Epistles of John*, in *AB*, New York: Doubleday and Company Inc.

BROWN, F., DRIVER, S. R. & BRIGGS, C. A. (eds.) (1906), *A Hebrew and English Lexicon of the Old Testament*, Oxford: Clarendon Press. (Electronic version found in *BWW*.)

BROX, N. (1986), *Der erste Petrusbrief*, in *EKK*, Freiburg: Herder.

BRUCE, F. F. (1964), *The Epistle to the Hebrews: The English Text with Introduction, Exposition, and Notes*, in *NICNT*, Grand Rapids: Eerdmans.

— (1970), *The Epistles of John*, Grand Rapids: Eerdmans.

— (1982a), *1 and 2 Thessalonians*, in *WBC*, Waco, Texas: Word Books.

— (1982b), *The Epistle to the Galatians*, in *NIGTC*, Grand Rapids: Eerdmans.

— (1983a), *The Gospel of John: Introduction, Exposition and Notes*, Grand Rapids: Eerdmans.

— (1983b), *The Hard Sayings of Jesus*, in *The Jesus Library*, Downers Grove: Inter-Varsity Press.

— (1984), *The Epistles to the Colossians, to Philemon, and to the Ephesians*, in *NICNT*, Grand Rapids: Eerdmans.

— (1985), *The Letter of Paul to the Romans*, rev. ed., in *TNTC*, Grand Rapids: Eerdmans.

BRUCE, F. F. (1989), *Philippians*, in *NIBC*, Peabody, MA: Hendrickson Publishers.

BRUEGGEMANN, W. (1974), 'From Hurt to Joy, From Death to Life', *Interpretation* 28: 3–19.

— (1997), *Theology of the Old Testament: Testimony, Dispute, Advocacy*, Minneapolis: Fortress Press.

BRUNSCHWIG, J. & NUSSBAUM, M. C. (eds.) (1993), *Passions and Perceptions: Studies in Hellenistic Philosophies of Mind Proceedings of the Fifth Symposium Hellenisticum*, Cambridge: Cambridge University Press.

BRUNT, P. A. (1989), 'Philosophy and Religion in the Late Republic', in M. Griffin & J. Barnes, *Philosophia Togata: Essays on Philosophy and Roman Society*, Oxford: Clarendon Press.

BULTMANN, R. (1951–55) *Theology of the New Testament*, 2 vols., trans. Kendrick Grobel, New York: Charles Scribner's Sons.

— (1964b), '*elpis, elpizō, ap-, proelpizō*', in *TDNT*, vol. 2, Grand Rapids: Eerdmans.

— (1964c), '*euphrainō, euphrosynē*', in *TDNT*, vol. 2, Grand Rapids: Eerdmans.

— (1965), '*hilaros, hilarotēs*', in *TDNT*, vol. 3, Grand Rapids: Eerdmans.

— (1967). '*lypē, lypeō, alypos, perilypos, syllypeomai*', in *TDNT*, vol. 4, Grand Rapids: Eerdmans.

— (1973), *The Johannine Epistles, Hermeneia*, Philadelphia: Fortress Press.

BURGE, G. M. (1997) 'John, Letters of', in DLNT.

BUTLER, R. (1977), *The Meaning of 'Agapao' and 'Phileo' in the Greek New Testament*, Lawrence, Kansas: Coronado Press.

BUTTERWORTH, G. W. (trans.) (1966), *On First Principles* by Origen, New York: Harper and Row.

BUTTERWORTH, M. (1997), '*rḥm*' in *NIDOTTE*, vol. 3, Grand Rapids: Zondervan.

CAIRD, G. B. (1966), *A Commentary on the Revelation of St John the Divine*, in *Harper's New Testament Commentaries*, New York: Harper and Row Publishers.

— (1994), *New Testament Theology*, edited and completed by L. D. Hurst, Oxford: Clarendon Press.

CALHOUN, C. & R. C. SOLOMON (eds.) (1984), *What is an Emotion? Classic Readings in Philosophical Psychology*, Oxford: Oxford University Press.

CALLAHAN, S. (1988), 'The Role of Emotion in Ethical Decisionmaking', *Hastings Center Report* 18: 9–14.

CALVIN, J. (1960) *Institutes of the Christian Religion*, trans. Ford Lewis Battles, vol. 1, *The Library of Christian Classics*, vol. 20, Philadelphia.

— (1965), *The Epistle of Paul the Apostle to the Galatians, Ephesians, Philippians and Colossians*, trans. T. H. L. Parker (ed.), *Calvin's New Testament Commentaries*, Grand Rapids: Eerdmans.

— (1989), *Institutes of the Christian Religion*, trans. Henry Beveridge, Grand Rapids: Eerdmans.

CAMPOS, J. J. & BARRETT, K. C. (1984), 'Toward a New Understanding of Emotions and their Development', in Izard, C. E., Kagan, J. & Zajonc, R. B. (eds.), *Emotions, Cognition, and Behavior*, Cambridge: Cambridge University Press.

CANNON, W. B. (1968), 'The James–Lange Theory of Emotion: A Critical Examination and an Alternative Theory', in Arnold, M. B. (ed.), *The Nature of Emotion, Penguin*

Modern Psychology Readings, Harmondsworth: Penguin. (First published in *American Journal of Psychology* 39 (1927): 106–124.)

CARLSON, N. R. (1993), *Psychology: The Science of Behavior*, 4th ed., Boston: Allyn and Bacon.

CARR, A. (1905), 'The Meaning of "Hatred" in the New Testament', *The Expositor* 12: 153–160.

CARSON, D. A. (1984), *From Triumphalism to Maturity: an Exposition of 2 Corinthians 10–13*, Grand Rapids: Baker Book House.

— (1987a), *Showing the Spirit: A Theological Exposition of 1 Corinthians 12–14*, Grand Rapids: Baker Book House.

— (1987b), *When Jesus Confronts the World: An Exposition of Matthew 8–10*, Grand Rapids: Baker Book House.

— (1991), *The Gospel According to John*, Grand Rapids: Eerdmans.

— (1994), *The Sermon on the Mount: An Exposition of Matthew 5–7*, Carlisle: Paternoster Press.

— (2000), *The Difficult Doctrine of the Love of God*, Wheaton, Illinois: Crossway.

CASSIRER, HEINZ W. (1988), *Grace and Law: St Paul, Kant, and the Hebrew Prophets*, Grand Rapids: Eerdmans.

CERLING, C. E. (1974), 'Anger: Musings of a Theologian/Psychologist', *JPT* 2: 12–17.

— (1974), 'Some Thoughts on a Biblical View of Anger: A Response', *JPT* 2: 266–268.

CHADWICK, H. (1966), 'St Paul and Philo of Alexandria', *Bulletin of the John Rylands Library* 48: 286–307.

CHAMBERS, S. (1996), 'A Biblical Theology of Godly Human Anger', PhD Dissertation, Trinity Evangelical Divinity School.

CHARLES, D. (1997), 'Virtue Amidst Vice: The Catalog of Virtues in 2 Peter 1', *Journal for the Study of the New Testament Supplement Series 150*, Sheffield: Sheffield Academic Press.

CHARLESWORTH, J. H. (1986), 'Jewish Hymns, Odes, and Prayers (*ca.* 167 BCE – 135 CE)', in R. A. Kraft & G. Nickelsburg (eds.), *Early Judaism and its Modern Interpreters*, Philadelphia: Fortress Press.

CHERRY, C. (1966), *The Theology of Jonathan Edwards: A Reappraisal*, New York: Doubleday.

CHESTER, A. (1994), 'The Theology of James', in *The Theology of the Letters of James, Peter, and Jude*, in *New Testament Theology*, Cambridge: Cambridge University Press.

CHILDS, B. S. (1979), *Introduction to the Old Testament as Scripture*, Philadelphia: Fortress Press.

CHILTON, B. (2000), 'Festivals and Holy Days: Jewish', in *DNTB*.

CHILTON, B. & MCDONALD, J. I. H. (1987), *Jesus and the Ethics of the Kingdom*, Grand Rapids: Eerdmans.

CLAPPER, G. S. (1989), *John Wesley on Religious Affections: His Views on Experience and Emotion and their Role in the Christian life and Theology*, in *Pietist and Wesleyan Studies*, no. 1. London: The Scarecrow Press.

CONZELMANN, H. (1968), *An Outline of the Theology of the New Testament*, trans. John Bowden, 2nd ed., New York: Harper and Row Publishers.

— (1974), '*chairō, chara, synchairō*', in *TDNT*, vol. 9, Grand Rapids: Eerdmans.

— (1975), *1 Corinthians*, Hermeneia. Philadelphia: Fortress Press.

— (1976a), 'Der Brief an die Epheser', in *Die Briefe an die Galater, Epheser, Philipper, Kolosser, Thessalonicher, und Philemon*, in *NTD*, Göttingen: Vandenhoeck & Ruprecht.

— (1987), *The Acts of the Apostles*, Hermeneia, Philadelphia: Fortress Press.

CORSINI, R. J. (ed.) (1994), *Encyclopedia of Psychology*, 2nd ed., 2 vols., New York: John Wiley and Sons.

COUSAR, C. B. (1996), *The Letters of Paul*, Interpreting Biblical Texts, Nashville: Abingdon Press.

CRAIGIE, P. C. (1976), *The Book of Deuteronomy*, Grand Rapids: Eerdmans.

CRANFIELD, C. E. B. (1960), *1 and 2 Peter and Jude*, Torch Bible Commentaries, London: SCM Press.

— (1972), *The Gospel According to Saint Mark*, Cambridge: Cambridge University Press.

— (1975–79), *A Critical and Exegetical Commentary on the Epistle to the Romans*, 2 vols., ICC, Edinburgh: T. & T. Clark.

CREEL, R. E. (1986), *Divine Impassibility: An Essay in Philosophical Theology*. Cambridge: Cambridge University Press.

CRENSHAW, J. L. (1997), 'Sirach', in *The New Interpreter's Bible*, vol. 5, Nashville: Abingdon Press.

CROSSAN, J. D. (1991), *The Historical Jesus: The Life of a Mediterranean Jewish Peasant*. San Francisco: Harper.

CULPEPPER, A. R. (1998), *The Gospel and Letters of John*, Interpreting Biblical Texts. Nashville: Abingdon Press.

CYTOWIC, RICHARD E. (1993), *The Man Who Tasted Shapes: A Bizarre Medical Mystery Offers Revolutionary Insights into Emotions, Reasoning, and Consciousness*. New York: Warner Books.

DANKER, FREDRICK WILLIAM ed. (2000) *A Greek-English Lexicon of the New Testament and Other Early Christian Literature*, 3d ed., Chicago: University of Chicago Press.

DAMASIO, A. R. (1994), *Descartes' Error: Emotion Reason and the Human Brain*, New York: Avon Books.

DARWIN, C. R. 'From *The Expression of the Emotions in Man and Animals*', in C. Calhoun & R. C. Solomon (eds.) (1984), *What is an Emotion? Classic Readings in Philosophical Psychology*, Oxford: Oxford University Press. (First published in *Passions of the Soul*, trans. Haldane and Ross, New York: Cambridge University Press, 1911.)

DARWIN, C. R. (1920), *The Expression of the Emotions in Man and Animals*, New York: D. Appleton and Company.

DAVIDS, P. H. (1982), *The Epistle of James: A Commentary on the Greek Text*, in *NIGTC*, Grand Rapids: Eerdmans.

— (1989), *James*, in *NIBC*, Peabody, Massachusetts: Hendrickson Publishers.

— (1990), *The First Epistle of Peter*, in *NICNT*, Grand Rapids: Eerdmans.

DAVIDSON, R. J. (1984), 'Affect, Cognition, and Hemispheric Specialization', in C. E. Izard, Kagan, J. & Zajonc, R. B. (eds.), *Emotions, Cognition, and Behavior*, Cambridge: Cambridge University Press.

DAVIES, D. P. (1997), 'Eschatological Hope in the Early Christian Community – New Testament Perspectives', in edited by F. Bowie (ed.), *The Coming Deliverer*, Cardiff: University of Wales Press.

DAVIES, W. D. & ALLISON, D. C. (1988–97), *A Critical and Exegetical Commentary on the Gospel According to Matthew*, 3 vols., *ICC.* Edinburgh: T. & T. Clark.

DAVIS, C. (1984a), 'Jealousy', in W. A. Elwell (ed.), *Evangelical Dictionary of Theology*, Grand Rapids: Baker Book House.

— (1984b), 'Joy', in W. A. Elwell (ed.), *Evangelical Dictionary of Theology*, Grand Rapids: Baker Book House.

DAVITZ, J. R. (1970), 'A Dictionary and Grammar of Emotion', in M. B. Arnold (ed.) *Feelings and Emotions: The Loyola Symposium, Personality and Psychopathology*, New York: Academic Press.

DE BECKER, G. (1997), 'Listen to Your Fear', *Readers Digest*, 129–133.

DE LACY, P. (1984), *Galeni: De Placitis Hippocratis et Platonis*, 3d ed., vol. 1, books 1–4, *Corpus Medicorum Graecorum*, 5, 4, 1, 2, Berlin: Akademie-Verlag.

DENNEY, J. (1909), 'The Word "Hate" in Luke 14:26', *The Expository Times* 21: 41–42.

DERRYBERRY, D. & ROTHBART, M. K. (1984), 'Emotion, Attention, and Temperament', in C. E. Izard, J. Kagan & R. B. Zajonc (eds.), *Emotions, Cognition, and Behavior*, Cambridge: Cambridge University Press.

DESCARTES, R. (1927), 'The Passions of the Soul', in R. M. Eaton (ed.), *Descartes Selections*, New York: Charles Scribner's Sons.

DESILVA, D. A. (1998), *4 Maccabees*, Sheffield: Sheffield Academic Press.

DE SOUSA, R. B. (1980), 'The Rationality of Emotions', in A. O. Rorty (ed.), *Explaining Emotions*, Berkeley: University of California Press.

— (1987), *The Rationality of Emotions*, Cambridge: The MIT Press.

DIENSTBIER, R. A. (1984), 'The Role of Emotion in Moral Socialization', in C. E. Izard, J. Kagan, & R. B. Zajonc (eds.), *Emotions, Cognition, and Behavior*, Cambridge: Cambridge University Press.

DI LELLA, A. A. (1987), *The Wisdom of Ben Sira*, trans. Patrick W. Skehan, *The Anchor Bible*, vol. 39. New York: Doubleday.

DILLARD, R. B. & LONGMAN III, T. (1994), *An Introduction to the Old Testament*, Grand Rapids: Zondervan.

DODD, C. H., *The Epistle of Paul to the Romans*, New York: Harper and Brothers Publishers.

— (1951), *Gospel and Law: The Relation of Faith and Ethics in Early Christianity*, New York: Columbia University Press.

DODDS, E. R. (1951), *The Greeks and the Irrational*, Berkeley: University of California Press.

DOUGLAS, J. D. *et al.* (eds.) (1982), *New Bible Dictionary*. 2nd ed., Wheaton, Illinois: Tyndale.

DOVER, K. (1974), *Greek Popular Morality in the Time of Plato and Aristotle*. Oxford: Basil Blackwell.

— (1982), *The Greeks*, Oxford: Oxford University Press.

DUNN, J. D. G. (1988a), *Romans 1–8*, in *WBC*, Dallas: Word Books.

— (1988b), *Romans 9–16*, in *WBC*, Dallas: Word Books.

— (1996), *The Epistles to the Colossians and to Philemon*, in *NIGTC*, Grand Rapids: Eerdmans.

— (1998), *The Theology of Paul the Apostle*, Grand Rapids: Eerdmans.

EARL, R. (1991), 'Early Pauline Thought: An Analysis of 1 Thessalonians', in J. M. Bassler (ed.), *Thessalonians, Philippians, Galatians, Philemon*, vol. 1 of *Pauline Theology*, Minneapolis: Fortress Press, 1991.

EASTMAN, B. J. (1997), 'Hope', in *DLNT*.

EASTON BIBLE DICTIONARY. First published in 1897. (Electronic version found in *BWW*.)

EDELSTEIN, L. (1966), *The Meaning of Stoicism*, Martin Classical Lectures, vol. 21, Cambridge: Harvard University Press.

EDWARDS, J. (1959), *Religious Affections*, 1746, in J. E. Smith (ed.), vol. 2 of *The Works of Jonathan Edwards*, London: Yale University Press.

EDWARDS, J. R. (1992), *Romans*, in *NIBC*, Peabody, Massachusetts: Hendrickson Publishers.

EDWARDS, R. B. (1992), 'Hellenism', in *DJG*.

The Eerdmans Bible Dictionary (1987), A. C. Myers *et al.* (eds.), Grand Rapids: Eerdmans.

EKMAN, P. (1984), 'Expression and the Nature of Emotion', in K. R. Scherer & P. Ekman (eds.), *Approaches to Emotion*, Hillsdale NJ: Lawrence Erlbaum Associates.

— (1994), 'All Emotions Are Basic', in P. Ekman & R. J. Davidson (eds.), *The Nature of Emotion: Fundamental Questions*, Series in Affective Science, Oxford: Oxford University Press.

EKMAN, P. & DAVIDSON, R. J. (eds.) (1994), *The Nature of Emotion: Fundamental Questions*, Series in Affective Science, Oxford: Oxford University Press.

ELLINGER, K. & RUDOPH, W. (ed.) (1966), *Biblia Hebraica Stuttgartensia*, Stuttgart: Deutsche Bibelgesellschaft. (Electronic version found in BWW.)

ELLINGWORTH, P. (1993), *The Epistle to the Hebrews*, in *NIGTC*, Grand Rapids: Eerdmans.

ELLROD, R. (1983), 'Emotion and the Good in Moral Development', in A. T. Tymieniecka & C. O. Schrag (eds.), *Foundations of Morality*, vol. 15 of *Analecta Husserliana*, D. Reidel Publishing Co.

ELS, P. J. J. S. "*ḥbʾ*', in *NIDOTTE*, vol. 1, Grand Rapids: Zondervan Publishing House.

ELWELL, W. A. (1984), *Evangelical Dictionary of Theology*, Grand Rapids: Baker Book House.

ENGBERG-PEDERSEN, T. (2000), *Paul and the Stoics*, Louisville: John Knox Press.

ERNST, J. (1974), *Die Brief an die Philipper, an Philemon, an die Kolosser, an die Epheser, RNT*, Verlag Friedrich Pustet Regensburg.

— (1981), *Das Evangelium nach Markus, RNT,* Verlag Friedrich Pustet Regensburg.

— (1993), *Das Evangelium nach Lukas, RNT,* Verlag Friedrich Pustet Regensburg.

ESSER, H. H. (1976), '*splanchna*', in *NIDNTT,* vol. 2, Grand Rapids: Zondervan.

EVANS, J. W. (1989), 'Interpretation of 2 Corinthians', *Southwestern Journal of Theology* 32: 22–32.

EVANS, CRAIG A. (1990), *Luke,* in *NIBC,* Peabody, Massachusetts: Hendrickson Publishers.

EVANS, C. A. & PORTER, S. E. (eds.) (2000), *Dictionary of New Testament Background,* Downers Grove, Illinois: Inter-Varsity Press, 2000.

EVERTS, J. M. (1993), 'Hope', in *DPL.*

FEE, G. D. (1987), *The First Epistle to the Corinthians,* in *NICNT,* Grand Rapids: Eerdmans.

— (1988), *1 and 2 Timothy, Titus,* in *NIBC,* Peabody, Massachusetts: Hendrickson Publishers.

FERGUSON, E. (1993), *Backgrounds of Early Christianity,* 2nd ed., Grand Rapids: Eerdmans.

FIELD, D. H. (1975), 'Envy', in *NIDNTT,* vol. 1, Grand Rapids: Zondervan.

FIORE, B. (1990), 'Passion in Paul and Plutarch: 1 Corinthians 5–6 and the Polemic against Epicureans', in D. Balch, E. Ferguson & W. A. Meeks (eds.), *Greeks, Romans, and Christians: Essays in Honor of Abraham J. Malherbe,* Minneapolis: Fortress Press.

FITZMYER, J. A. (1981), *The Gospel According to Luke I–IX,* AB, New York: Doubleday and Company Inc.

— (1985), *The Gospel According to Luke X–XXIV,* AB, New York: Doubleday and Company Inc.

— (1987), *Paul and His Theology: A Brief Sketch,* 2nd ed., New Jersey: Prentice Hall.

FOERSTER, W. (1964a), '*echthros, echthra*', in *TDNT,* vol. 2, Grand Rapids: Eerdmans.

FORTENBAUGH, W. W. (1969), 'Aristotle: Emotion and Moral Virtue', *Artethusa* 2: 163–85.

— (1970), 'On the Antecedents of Aristotle's Bipartite Psychology', *Greek, Roman and Byzantine Studies* 11: 233–50.

— (1975), *Aristotle on Emotion,* London: Gerald Duckworth and Company.

FOX, R. L. (1986), *Pagans and Christians,* San Francisco, Harper and Row Publishers.

FRANCE, R. T. (1985), *The Gospel According to Matthew,* in *TNTC,* Grand Rapids: Eerdmans.

FRANK, R. H. (1988), *Passion Within Reason: The Strategic Role of the Emotions,* New York: W. W. Norton and Company.

FRANKEMÖLLE, H. (1994a), *Der Brief des Jakobus: Kapitel 1,* in *Okumenischer Taschenbuchkommentar zum Neuen Testament,* Echter Verlag.

— (1994b), *Der Brief des Jakobus: Kapitel 2–5,* in *Okumenischer Taschenbuchkommentar zum Neuen Testament,* Echter Verlag.

FRETHEIM, T. E. (1997), '*yd*ʿ', in *NIDOTTE,* vol. 2, Grand Rapids: Zondervan.

FRIBERG, T. & BARBARA, F. (1994a), *Analytical Greek New Testament Greek New Testament Grammatical Analysis Database,* ver. 2. (Electronic version found in BWW.)

— (1994b), *Analytical Lexicon to the Greek New Testament.* (Electronic version found in BWW.)

FRIEDRICH, G. (1976a), 'Der Brief an die Philipper', in *Die Briefe an die Galater, Epheser, Philipper, Kolosser, Thessalonicher, und Philemon, NTD*, Göttingen: Vandenhoeck & Ruprecht.

— (1976b), 'Der Brief an die Thessalonicher', in *Die Briefe an die Galater, Epheser, Philipper, Kolosser, Thessalonicher, und Philemon, NTD*, Göttingen: Vandenhoeck & Ruprecht.

FRIJDA, N. H. (1970), 'Emotion and Recognition of Emotion', in M. B. Arnold (ed.), *Feelings and Emotions: The Loyola Symposium*, Personality and Psychopathology, New York: Academic Press.

— (1986), *The Emotions*, Cambridge: Cambridge University Press.

FULLER, R. M. (1997), 'Rewards', in *DLNT*.

FUNG, R. Y. K. (1988), *The Epistle to the Galatians*, in *NICNT*, Grand Rapids: Eerdmans.

FURLEY, D. (1986), 'Nothing to Us?' in M. Schofield & G. Striker (eds.), *The Norms of Nature: Studies in Hellenistic Ethics*, Cambridge: Cambridge University Press.

FURNISH, V. P. (1968), *Theology and Ethics in Paul*, Nashville: Abingdon Press.

— (1972), *The Love Command in the New Testament*, Nashville: Abingdon Press.

— (1984), *2 Corinthians: Translated with Introduction*, AB, New York: Doubleday and Company Inc.

GAEBELEIN, F. E. (ed.) (1976–92), *The Expositor's Bible Commentary*, 12 vols., Grand Rapids: Zondervan.

GAMBERONI, J. (1981), 'Desire', *EBT*.

GARLAND, D. (1992), 'Blessing and Woe', in *DJG*.

GÄRTNER, B. (1978), '*paschō*', in *NIDNTT*, vol. 3, Grand Rapids: Zondervan.

GILLIGAN, S. G. & BOWER, G. H. (1984), 'Cognitive Consequences of Emotional Arousal', in C. E. Izard, J. Kagan & R. B. Zajonc (eds.), *Emotions, Cognition, and Behavior*, Cambridge: Cambridge University Press.

GILPEN, W. C. (1992), 'Reinterpretation in the History of Christianity', *Criterion* 31: 2–3.

GNILKA, J. (1968), *Der Philipperbrief*, HTK, Freiburg: Herder.

— (1971), *Der Epheserbrief*, EKK, Freiburg: Herder.

— (1978), *Das Evangelium nach Markus*, vol. 2, EKK, Freiburg: Herder.

— (1980), *Der Kolosserbrief*, EKK, Freiburg: Herder.

— (1982), *Der Philemonbrief*, HTK, Freiburg: Herder.

— (1986–88), *Das Matthäusevangelium*, 2 vols., HTK, Freiburg: Herder.

— (1999a), *Das Evangelium nach Markus*, EKK, Freiburg: Herder.

— (1999b), *Theologie des Neuen Testaments*, Freiburg: Herder.

GOETZMANN, J. (1975), 'Care, Anxiety', in *NIDNTT*, vol. 1, Grand Rapids: Zondervan.

— (1976), '*phronēsis*', in *NIDNTT*, vol. 2, Grand Rapids: Zondervan.

GOLDSTEIN, J. (1981), 'Jewish Acceptance and Rejection of Hellenism', in E. P. Sanders, A. I. Baumgarten & A. Mendelson (eds.), *Jewish and Christian Self-Definition*, vol. 2, Philadelphia: Fortress Press.

GOPPELT, L. (1978), *Der Erste Petrusbrief*, in *Kritisch-exegetischer Kommentar über das Neue Testament*, Göttingen: Vandenhoeck & Ruprecht.

— (1981), *Theology of the New Testament*, trans. J. E. Alsup, vol. 1, *The Ministry of Jesus in its Theological Significance*, Grand Rapids: Eerdmans.

— (1982), *Theology of the New Testament*, trans. J. E. Alsup, vol. 2, *The Variety and Unity of the Apostolic Witness to Christ*, Grand Rapids: Eerdmans.

GORDON, R. M. (1969), 'Emotions and Knowledge', *JP* 66: 408–413.

GOSLING, J. C. B. & TAYLOR, C. C. W. (1982), *The Greeks on Pleasure*, Oxford: Clarendon Press.

GOULD, J. B. (1970), *The Philosophy of Chrysippus*, in *Philosophia Antiqua: A Series of Monographs on Ancient Philosophy*, vol. 17, Leiden: E. J. Brill.

GRANT, R. M. (1980), 'The Social Setting of Second-Century Christianity', in E. P. Sanders (ed.), *Jewish and Christian Self-Definition*, vol. 1, Philadelphia: Fortress Press.

GRAYSTON, K. (1990), 'Review of *Greek–English Lexicon of the New Testament based on Semantic Domains*, edited by Johannes Louw and Eugene Nida', *Journal of Theological Studies* 41: 198–201.

GREEN, M. (1968), *The Second Epistle of Peter and the Epistle of Jude*, in *TNTC*, Grand Rapids: Eerdmans.

GRIFFIN, M. (1989), 'Philosophy, Politics, and Politicians at Rome', in M. Griffin & J. Barnes (eds.), *Philosophia Togata: Essays on Philosophy and Roman Society*, Oxford: Clarendon Press.

GRIFFITH-JONES, R. (2000), *The Four Witnesses*, San Francisco: Harper.

GRIFFITHS, P. E. (1997), *What Emotions Really Are: The Problem of Psychological Categories*, Chicago: The University of Chicago Press.

GRISANTI, M. A. (1997a), '*gîl*', in *NIDOTTE*, vol. 1, Grand Rapids: Zondervan Publishing House.

— (1997b), '*ḥdh*', in *NIDOTTE*, vol. 2, Grand Rapids: Zondervan Publishing House.

— (1997c), '*śmḥ*' in *NIDOTTE*, vol. 3, Grand Rapids: Zondervan Publishing House.

— (1997d), '*śwś*', in *NIDOTTE*, vol. 3, Grand Rapids: Zondervan Publishing House.

GRUDEM, W. (1988), *1 Peter, TNCT*.

— (1994), *Systematic Theology: An Introduction to Biblical Doctrine*, Grand Rapids: Zondervan.

GUELICH, R. A. (1989), *Mark 1 – 8:26*, in *WBC*, Dallas: Word Books.

GÜNTHER, W. & LINK, H.-G. (1976), '*agapeō*', in *NIDNTT*, vol. 2, Grand Rapids: Zondervan.

GUTHRIE, D. (1957), *The Pastoral Epistles*, in *TNTC*, Grand Rapids: Eerdmans.

— (1973), *Galatians*, in *NCBC*, Grand Rapids: Eerdmans.

— (1981), *New Testament Theology*, Downers Grove: Inter-Varsity Press.

HAARBECK, H. (1976a), '*klaiō, koptō*', in *NIDNTT*, vol. 2, Grand Rapids: Zondervan.

HADAS, M. (ed. and trans.) (1953), *The Third and Fourth Books of Maccabees*, New York, Harper and Brothers.

HAENCHEN, E. (1971), *The Acts of the Apostles: A Commentary*, Philadelphia: The Westminster Press.

HAFEMANN, S. J. (2000), *2 Corinthians*, in *The NIV Application Commentary*, Grand Rapids: Zondervan Publishing House.

HAGNER, D. A. (1990), *Hebrews*, in *NIBC*, Peabody, Massachusetts: Hendrickson Publishers.

— (1993), *Matthew 1–13*, in *WBC*, Dallas: Word Books.

— (1995), *Matthew 14–28*, in *WBC*, Dallas: Word Books.

HAHN, H. C. (1975), '*orgē*', in *NIDNTT*, vol. 1, Grand Rapids: Zondervan.

— (1978), 'Zeal', in *NIDNTT*, vol. 3, Grand Rapids: Zondervan.

HAMILTON, E. & CAIRNS, H. (eds.) (1961), *The Collected Dialogue of Plato Including the Letters*, Bollingen Series, no. 71, New York: Bollingen Foundation.

HANKINSON, J. (1993), 'Actions and Passions: Affection, Emotion, and Moral Self-Management in Galen's Philosophical Psychology', in J. Brunschwig & M. C. Nussbaum (eds.), *Passions and Perceptions: Studies in Hellenistic Philosophies of Mind Proceedings of the Fifth Symposium Hellenisticum*, Cambridge: Cambridge University Press.

HANSEN, W. (1997), 'The Emotions of Jesus', *Christianity Today*, February 3, 1997.

HANSON, A. T. (1957), *The Wrath of the Lamb*, London: SPCK.

HARDER, G. (1978), '*nous*', in *NIDNTT*, vol. 2, Grand Rapids: Zondervan.

HARE, J. E. (1996), *The Moral Gap: Kantian Ethics, Human Limits, and God's Assistance*, Oxford: Clarendon Press.

HARKINS, P. W. (trans.) (1963), *Galen on the Passions and Errors of the Soul*, With an Introduction and Interpretation by Walther Riese, Ohio State University Press.

HARRIS, M. J. (1976), '2 Corinthians', in *EBC*, vol. 10, Grand Rapids: Zondervan.

HARRISON, R. K. (1980), *Leviticus: An Introduction and Commentary*, Tyndale Old Testament Commentaries, Downers Grove, Illinois: Inter-Varsity Press.

— (1984), 'Anger', in Walter A. Elwell (ed.), *Evangelical Dictionary of Theology*, Grand Rapids: Baker Book House.

HAUCK, F. & BERTRAM, G. (1967), '*makarios, makarizō, makarismos*', in *TDNT*, vol. 4. Grand Rapids: Eerdmans.

HAVILAND-JONES, J., GEBELT, J. L. & STAPLEY, J. C. (1997), 'The Questions of Development in Emotion', in P. Salovey & D. J. Sluyter (eds.), *Emotional Development and Emotional Intelligence: Educational Implications*, New York: BasicBooks.

HAWTHORNE, G. F. (1983), *Philippians*, in *WBC*, Waco, Texas: Word Books.

— (1997), 'Joy', in *DLNT*.

HAWTHORNE, G. F. & MARTIN, R. P. (eds.) (1993), *Dictionary of Paul and His Letters*, Downers Grove, Illinois: Inter-Varsity Press.

HAY, D. M. (1993), 'The Shaping of Theology in 2 Corinthians', in D. M. Hay (ed.), *First and Second Corinthians*, vol. 2 of *Pauline Theology*, Minneapolis: Fortress Press.

— (1995), 'Adam, Israel, Christ', in D. M. Hay & E. E. Johnson (eds.), *Romans*, vol. 3 of *Pauline Theology*, Minneapolis: Fortress Press.

— (ed.) (1993), *First and Second Corinthians*, vol. 2 of *Pauline Theology*, Minneapolis: Fortress Press.

HAYS, R. B. (1996), *The Moral Vision of the New Testament: A Contemporary Introduction to New Testament Ethics*, San Francisco: Harper.

HEBBLETHWAITE, B. (1984), *The Christian Hope*, Grand Rapids: Eerdmans.

HEFLIN, B. (1993), 'Hosea 1–3: Love Triumphant', *Southwestern Journal of Theology* 36: 9–19.

HENGEL, M. (1974), *Judaism and Hellenism: Studies in their Encounter in Palestine during the Early Hellenistic Period*, 2 vols., Philadelphia: Fortress Press.

HESCHEL, A. J. (1973), 'The Divine Pathos: the Basic Category of Prophetic Theology', in R. Gordis & R. B. Waxman (eds.), *Faith and Reason: Essays in Judaism*, New York: Ktav Publishing. (First published in *Die Prophetie*, Cracow, 1936.)

HILL, A. E. (1993), *Enter His Courts with Praise: Old Testament Worship for the New Testament Church*, Grand Rapids: Baker Books.

HILL, L. H. (1993), 'Hosea 11: Yahweh's Persistent Love', *Southwestern Journal of Theology* 36: 27–31.

HILLYER, N. (1992), *1 and 2 Peter, Jude*, in *NIBC*, Peabody, Massachusetts: Hendrickson Publishers.

HODGE, C. (1994), *Ephesians*, The Crossway Classic Commentaries, Wheaton, Illinois: Crossway Books.

HOFFMANN, E. (1976), 'Hope', in *NIDNTT*, vol. 2, Grand Rapids: Zondervan.

HOLLADAY, W. L. (1989), *Jeremiah*, vol. 2, Hermeneia, Minneapolis: Ausburg Fortress.

HOLMER, P. L. (1984), *Making Christian Sense*, Spirituality and the Christian Life, Philadelphia: The Westminster Press.

HOLTZ, T. (1986), *Der erste Brief an die Thessalonicher*, EKK, Freiburg: Herder.

HOWER, J. T. (1974), 'The Misunderstanding and Mishandling of Anger', *JPT* 2: 269–275.

HUGHES, P. (1962), *Paul's Second Epistle to the Corinthians*, in *NICNT*, Grand Rapids: Eerdmans.

HUME, D. (1888), *A Treatise of Human Nature*, Oxford: Clarendon Press.

HURTADO, L. W. (1989), *Mark*, in *NIBC*, Peabody, Massachusetts: Hendrickson.

HUTCH, R. A. (1978), 'Jonathan Edward's Analysis of Religious Experience', *JPT* 6: 123–131.

INWOOD, B. (1985), *Ethics and Human Action in Early Stoicism*, Oxford: Clarendon Press.

— (1993), 'Seneca and Psychological Dualism', in J. Brunschwig & M. C. Nussbaum (eds.), *Passions and Perceptions: Studies in Hellenistic Philosophies of Mind, Proceedings of the Fifth Symposium Hellenisticum*, Cambridge: Cambridge University Press.

IRWIN, T. H. (1980), 'Reason and Responsibility in Aristotle', in A. O. Rorty (ed.), *Essays On Aristotle's Ethics*, Major Thinkers Series, Berkeley: University of California Press.

IZARD, CARROLL E. (1972), *Patterns of Emotion: A New Analysis of Anxiety and Depression*, New York: Academic Press.

— (1977), *Human Emotions*, New York: Plenum Press.

— (1984a), 'Emotive-Cognitive Relationships and Human Development', in C. E. Izard, J. Kagan & R. B. Zajonc (eds.), *Emotions, Cognition, and Behaviour*, Cambridge: Cambridge University Press.

— (1984b), 'Cognition is One of Four Types of Emotion-Activating Systems', in P. Ekman & R. J. Davidson (eds.), *The Nature of Emotion: Fundamental Questions*, Series in Affective Science. Oxford: Oxford University Press, 1994.

IZARD, C. E., J. KAGAN & R. B. ZAJONC (1984a), Introduction to *Emotions, Cognition, and Behavior*, Cambridge: Cambridge University Press.

— (eds.) (1984b), *Emotions, Cognition, and Behavior*, Cambridge: Cambridge University Press, 1984.

JAMES, W. (1922a), 'The Emotions', in *The Emotions*, by C. G. Lange & W. James (eds.), Baltimore: Williams and Wilkins Company. (First published as chapter 25 of the *Principles of Psychology*.)

— (1968), 'What is an Emotion?' in M. B. Arnold (ed.), *The Nature of Emotion*, Penguin Modern Psychology Readings, Harmondsworth: Penguin. (First published in *Mind* 9 (1884): 188–205.)

JEREMIAS, J. (1966), *Rediscovering the Parables*, New York: Charles Scribner's Sons.

— (1972), *The Parables of Jesus*, 2nd rev. ed., New York: Charles Scribner's Sons.

JOHNSON, S. E. & BUTTRICK, G. A. (1951), 'The Gospel According to St Matthew', in *The Interpreters Bible*, vol. 8, New York: Abingdon Press.

JOHNSON, T. F. (1993), *1, 2, and 3 John*, in *NIBC*, Peabody, Massachusetts: Hendrickson Publishers.

KAGAN, J. (1984), 'The Idea of Emotion in Human Development', in C. E. Izard, J. Kagan & R. B. Zajonc (eds.), *Emotions, Cognition, and Behaviour*, Cambridge: Cambridge University Press.

KANT, I. (1873), *Kant's Critique of Practical Reason and Other Works on the Theory of Ethics*, trans. Thomas Kingsmill Abbott, London: Longmans, Green, and Co. Ltd.

— (1967), *The Doctrine of Virtue*, trans. Mary J. Gregor, Philadelphia: University of Pennsylvania Press.

KÄSEMANN, E. (1980), *Commentary on Romans*, trans. Geoffrey W. Bromiley, Grand Rapids: Eerdmans.

KEE, H. C. (1986), *Medicine, Miracle, and Magic in New Testament Times*, Cambridge: Cambridge University Press.

— (1989), *Knowing the Truth: A Sociological Approach to New Testament Interpretation*, Minneapolis: Fortress Press.

KEENER, C. S. (1997), *Matthew*, Downers Grove, Illinois: Inter-Varsity Press.

— (2000), *Revelation*, in *The NIV Application Commentary*, Grand Rapids: Zondervan.

KELTNER, D. & EKMAN, P. (1994), 'Facial Expressions of Emotion', in V. S. Ramachandran (ed.), *Encyclopedia of Human Behavior*, vol. 2, San Diego: Academic Press.

KENNY, A. (1963), *Action, Emotion, and Will*, in *Studies in Philosophical Psychology*, London: Routledge and Kegan Paul.

KENT, D. G. (1993), 'Hosea: Man, Times and Material', 36: 4–8.

KIDD, I. G. (1971), 'Posidonius on Emotions', in *A. A.* Long (ed.), *Problems in Stoicism*, London: The Athlone Press.

— (1978), 'Moral Actions and Rules in Stoic Ethics' in J. M. Rist (ed.), *The Stoics*, Berkeley: University of California Press.

KIDNER, D. (1964), *The Proverbs*, Downers Grove, Illinois: Inter-Varsity Press.

— (1973), *Psalms 1–72*, London: Inter-Varsity Press.

— (1975), *Psalms 73–150*. London: Inter-Varsity Press.

KITTEL, G. & FRIEDRICH, G. (eds.) (1964–76), *Theological Dictionary of the New Testament*, 10 vols., Grand Rapids: Eerdmans.

KLAUCK, H.-J. (1990), 'Brotherly Love in Plutarch and in 4th Maccabees', in D. Balch, E. Ferguson & W. A. Meeks (eds.), *Greeks, Romans, and Christians: Essays in Honor of Abraham J. Malherbe*, Minneapolis: Fortress Press.

— (1991), *Der erste Johannesbrief*, EKK. Freiburg: Herder.

KLAUSNER, J. (1989), 'The Sanctity of Yom tov and the Joy of the Festival', *Judaism* 38: 93–102.

KNIGHT, G. W. (1992), *The Pastoral Epistles: A Commentary on the Greek Text*, in *NIGTC*, Grand Rapids: Eerdmans.

KNOCH, O. (1988), *1. und 2. Timotheusbrief Titusbrief*, Echter Verlag.

KOLARCIK, M. (1997), 'Book of Wisdom', in *The New Interpreter's Bible*, vol. 5, Nashville: Abingdon Press.

KONKEL, A. H. (1997a), 'ṣ'q', in *NIDOTTE*, vol. 3, Grand Rapids: Zondervan.

— (1997b), 'śn'', in *NIDOTTE*, vol. 3, Grand Rapids: Zondervan.

KOTESKEY, R. L. (1980), 'Toward the Development of a Christian Psychology: Emotion', *JPT* 8: 303–313.

KRAFT, H. (1974), *Die Offenbarung des Johannes*, in *Handbuch zum Neuen Testament*, Tübingen: J. C. B. Mohr.

KRAUS, H.-J. (1988), *Psalms 1–59*, trans. H. C. Oswald, Minneapolis: Ausburg Publishing House.

KRUSE, C. G. (1993), 'Afflictions, Trials, Hardships', in *DPL*.

— (2000), *The Letters of John*, in *PNTC*, Grand Rapids: Eerdmans.

LADD, G. E. (1972), *A Commentary on the Revelation of John*, Grand Rapids: Eerdmans.

— (1974), *A Theology of the New Testament*, Grand Rapids: Eerdmans.

LANE, W. L. (1974), *The Gospel According to Mark*, in *NICNT*, Grand Rapids: Eerdmans.

— (1991), *Hebrews 9–13*, in *WBC*, Dallas: Word Books.

LANGE, C. G. (1922), 'The Emotions: A Psychophysiological Study', trans. Istar

A. Haupt from the authorized German translation of H. Kurella, in C. G. Lange & W. James (eds.), *The Emotions*, Baltimore: Williams and Wilkins Company.

LANGE, C. G. & JAMES, W. (1922), *The Emotions*, Baltimore: Williams and Wilkins Company.

LAURITZEN, P. (1988), 'Emotion and Religious Ethics', *JRE* 16: 307–324.

LAWS, S. (1980), *The Epistle of James*, Harper's New Testament Commentaries, San Francisco: Harper and Row.

LAZARUS, R. S. (1984), 'Thoughts on the Relations Between Emotion and Cognition', in *Approaches to Emotion*, in K. R. Scherer & P. Ekman (eds.), Hillsdale NJ: Lawrence Erlbaum Associates.

— (1990), 'Constructs of the Mind in Adaptation', in *Psychological and Biological Approaches to Emotion*, in Nancy L. Stein, B. Leventhal & T. Trabasso (eds.), Hillsdale NJ: Lawrence Erlbaum Associates.

— (1994), 'Appraisal: The Long and the Short of It', in P. Ekman & R. J. Davidson. *The Nature of Emotion: Fundamental Questions*, Series in Affective Science. Oxford: Oxford University Press, 1994.

— (1994), 'Universal Antecedents of the Emotions', in P. Ekman and R. J. Davidson (eds.), *The Nature of Emotion: Fundamental Questions*, Series in Affective Science, Oxford: Oxford University Press.

LAZARUS, R. S., AVERILL, J. R. & OPTON, E. M. (1970), 'Towards a Cognitive Theory of Emotion', in M. B. Arnold (ed.), *Feelings and Emotions: The Loyola Symposium*, Personality and Psychopathology, New York: Academic Press.

LAZARUS, R. S., COYNE, J. C. & FOLKMAN, S. (1984), 'Cognition, Emotion and Motivation: The Doctoring of Humpty-Dumpty', in K. R. Scherer & P. Ekman (eds.), *Approaches to Emotion*, Hillsdale NJ: Lawrence Erlbaum Associates.

LEEPER, R. W. (1948), 'A Motivational Theory of Emotion to Replace "Emotion as Disorganized Response"', in M. B. Arnold (ed.), *The Nature of Emotion*, Penguin Modern Psychology Readings. Harmondsworth: Penguin, 1968. First published in *Psychology Review* 55: 5–21.

— (1968), 'The Motivational Theory of Emotion', in M. B. Arnold (ed.), *The Nature of Emotion*, Penguin Modern Psychology Readings, Harmondsworth: Penguin.

— (1970), 'The Motivational and Perceptual Properties of Emotions as Indicating Their Fundamental Character and Role', in M. B. Arnold (ed.), *Feelings and Emotions: The Loyola Symposium*, Personality and Psychopathology, New York: Academic Press.

LEIGHTON, S. R. (1982), 'Aristotle and the Emotions', *Phronesis* 27: 144–72.

LEONARD, R. C. (1993), 'The Numinous Aspect of Biblical Worship', in R. E. Webber (ed.), *The Complete Library of Christian Worship*, vol. 1, *The Biblical Foundations of Christian Worship*, Peabody, MA: Hendrickson, 1993.

— (1993), 'Psalms in Biblical Worship', in R. E. Webber (ed.), *The Complete Library of*

Christian Worship, vol. 1, *The Biblical Foundations of Christian Worship*, Peabody, MA: Hendrickson.

LEVY, R. I. (1984), 'Emotion, Knowing, and Culture', in R. A. Shweder & R. A. LeVine (eds.), *Culture Theory: Essays on Mind, Self, and Emotion*, Cambridge: Cambridge University Press.

LEWIS, A. H. (1972), 'Jehovah's International Love', *Journal of the Evangelical Theological Society* 15: 87–92.

LEWIS, C. S. (1947), *The Abolition of Man*, New York: Macmillan.

— (1958), *Reflections on the Psalms*, London: Geoffrey Bless.

— (1963), *Letters to Malcolm: Chiefly on Prayer*, New York: Harcourt, Brace and World.

— (1975), *The Weight of Glory and Other Addresses*, rev. ed., New York: Macmillan Publishing Company.

LIGHTFOOT, J. B. (1913), 'St Paul and Seneca', in *Saint Paul's Epistle to the Philippians*, 12th ed., Grand Rapids: Zondervan.

LINCOLN, A. T. (1990), *Ephesians*, in *WBC*, Dallas: Word Books.

LINCOLN, A. T. & WEDDERBURN, A. J. M. (1993), *The Theology of the Later Pauline Letters*, New Testament Theology, Cambridge: Cambridge University Press.

LINDARS, B. (1991), *The Theology of the Letter to the Hebrews*, Cambridge: Cambridge University Press.

LINDEMANN, A. (1983), *Der Kolosserbrief*, Zürcher Bibelkommentare, Zürich: Theologischer Verlag.

— (1985), *Der Epheserbrief*, Zürcher Bibelkommentare, Zürich: Theologischer Verlag.

LINK, H.-G. & BECKER, U. (1975), 'Blessing, Blessed, Happy', in *NIDNTT*, vol. 1, Grand Rapids: Zondervan.

LINNEMANN, E. (1966), *Parables of Jesus: Introduction and Exposition*, London: SPCK.

LLOYD, G. E. R. (1983), *Science, Folklore, and Ideology: Studies in the Life Sciences in Ancient Greece*, Cambridge: Cambridge University Press.

LOHSE, E. (1960), *Die Offenbarung des Johannes*, Göttingen: Vandenhoeck & Ruprecht.

— (1971), *Colossians and Philemon*, Hermeneia, Philadelphia: Fortress Press.

— (1988), *Theological Ehtics of the New Testament*, trans. Eugene Boring, Minneapolis: Fortress Press.

— (1995), 'The Church in Everyday Life: Consideration of the Theological Basis of Ethics in the New Testament', in B. Rosner (ed.), *Understanding Paul's Ethics: Twentieth-Century Approaches*, Grand Rapids: Eerdmans.

LONG, A. A. (1968), 'Aristotle's Legacy to Stoic Ethics', *Bulletin of the Institute of Classical Studies of the University of London* 15: 72–85.

— (1974), *Hellenistic Philosophy: Stoics, Epicureans, Skeptics*, London: Gerald Duckworth.

— (ed.) (1971), *Problems in Stoicism*, London: The Athlone Press.

LONG, A. A. & SEDLEY, D. N. (1987), *The Hellenistic Philosophers*, vol. 1, translation of the Principal Sources with Philosophical Commentary, Cambridge: Cambridge University Press.

LONGENECKER, R. N. (1981), 'The Acts of the Apostles', in *EBC*, vol. 9, Grand Rapids: Zondervan.

— (1990), *Galatians*, in *WBC*, Dallas: Word Books.

LOUW, J. P. & NIDA, E. A. (eds.), (1988), *Greek–English Lexicon of the New Testament Based on Semantic Domains*, 2nd ed., 2 vols., New York: United Bible Societies.

LUC, A. (1997), '*lēb*', in *NIDOTTE*, vol. 2, Grand Rapids: Zondervan Publishing House.

LUTER, A. B. (1993), 'Jealousy, Zeal', in *DPL*.

LUTZER, E. (1981), *Managing Your Emotions*, New York: Christian Herald Books.

LUZ, U. (1989), *Matthew 1–7: A Commentary*, trans. W. C. Linss, Minneapolis: Ausburg.

— (1995), *The Theology of the Gospel of Matthew*, trans. J. B. Robinson, Cambridge: Cambridge University Press.

— (1997), *Das Evangelium nach Matthäus*, vol. 3, EKK, Freiburg: Herder.

— (2001), *Matthew 8–20*, trans. J. E. Crouch, Hermeneia, Minneapolis: Fortress Press.

LYONS, W. (1980), *Emotion*, Cambridge Studies in Philosophy, Cambridge: Cambridge University Press.

MACGREGOR, G. H. C., 'The Concept of the Wrath of God in the New Testament', *NTS* 7: 101–108.

MACINTOSH, B. B. (1997), *Hosea*, ICC, Edinburgh: T. & T. Clark.

MACK, B. L & MURPHY, R. E. (1986), 'Wisdom Literature' in R. A. Kraft and G. Nickelsburg (eds.), *Early Judaism and its Modern Interpreters*, Philadelphia: Fortress Press.

MACMULLEN, R. (1981), *Paganism in the Roman Empire*, New Haven: Yale University Press.

MACMURRAY, J. (1962), *Reason and Emotion*, 2nd ed., London: Faber and Faber Limited.

MALHERBE, A. J. (1987), *Paul and the Thessalonians: the Philosophic Tradition of Pastoral Care*, Philadelphia: Fortress Press.

MALHERBE, A. J. (1989), *Paul and the Popular Philosophers*, Minneapolis: Fortress Press.

MANDLER, G. (1990), 'A Constructivist Theory of Emotion', in N. L. Stein, B. Leventhal & T. Trabasso, *Physiological and Biological Approaches to Emotion*, Hillsdale NJ: Lawrence Erlbaum Associates.

MANN, C. S. (1986), *Mark: A New Translation with Introduction and Commentary*, AB, New York: Doubleday & Company.

MARE, H. W. (1976), '1 Corinthians', in *EBC*, vol. 10, Grand Rapids: Zondervan.

MARSHALL, I. H. (1978a), *The Epistles of John*, in *NICNT*, Grand Rapids: Eerdmans.

— (1978b), *The Gospel of Luke*, Grand Rapids: Eerdmans.

— (1980a), *The Acts of the Apostles: An Introduction and Commentary*, in *TNTC*, Grand Rapids: Eerdmans.

— (1980b), *Last Supper and Lord's Supper*, Carlisle: Paternoster.

— (1983), *1 and 2 Thessalonians*, in *NCBC*, Grand Rapids: Eerdmans.

— (1990), 'Review of *Greek–English Lexicon of the New Testament based on Semantic Domains*, edited by Johannes Louw and Eugene Nida'. *EQ* 62: 183–186.

— (1999), *The Pastoral Epistles*, ICC, Edinburgh: T. & T. Clark.

MARSHALL, I. H. & PETERSON, D. (eds.) (1998), *Witness to the Gospel: The Theology of Acts*, Grand Rapids: Eerdmans.

MARTENS, E. A. (1981), *God's Design: A Focus on Old Testament Theology*, Grand Rapids: Baker Book House.

MARTIN, D. B. (1977), 'Paul Without Passion: On Paul's Rejection of Desire in Sex and Marriage', in H. Moxnes (ed.), *Constructing Early Christian Families: Family as Social Reality and Metaphor*, London: Routledge.

MARTIN, R. P. (1974), *Worship in the Early Church*, Grand Rapids: Eerdmans.

— (1982), *The Worship of God: Some Theological, Pastoral, and Practical Reflections*, Grand Rapids: Eerdmans.

— (1986), *2 Corinthians*, in *WBC*, Waco, Texas: Word Books.

— (1988), *James*, in *WBC*, Waco, Texas: Word Books.

— (1991), *Ephesians, Colossians, and Philemon*, Interpretation, Atlanta: John Knox Press.

— (1994), 'The Theology of Jude, 1 Peter, and 2 Peter', in *The Theology of the Letters of James, Peter, and Jude*, New Testament Theology, Cambridge: Cambridge University Press.

MARTIN, R. P. & DAVIDS, P. H. (eds.) (1997), *Dictionary of the Later New Testament and Its Developments*, Downers Grove, Illinois: Inter-Varsity Press.

MATERA, F. J. (1996), *New Testament Ethics*, Louisville: Westminster John Knox Press.

MATTHEWS, G. (1980), 'Ritual and the Religious Feelings', in A. O. Rorty (ed.) *Explaining Emotions*, Berkeley: University of California Press.

MAYER, J. D. & SALOVEY, P. (1997), 'What Is Emotional Intelligence?', in P. Salovey & D. J. Sluyter, *Emotional Development and Emotional Intelligence: Educational Implications*, New York: BasicBooks.

MCCAUGHEY, D. J. (1974), 'The Death of Death (1 Corinthians 15:26)', in Banks, R. (ed.), *Reconciliation and Hope: New Testament Essays on Atonement and Eschatology*, Grand Rapids: Eerdmans.

MCCOMISKEY, T. (1992), 'Hosea', in T. E. McComiskey (ed.), *The Minor Prophets*, Grand Rapids: Baker Book House.

MCDERMOTT, E. A. (1989), *Euripides' Medea: The Incarnations of Disorder*, University Park: The Pennsylvania State University Press.

MCKANE, W. (1970), *Proverbs: A New Approach*, The Old Testament Library, Philadelphia: The Westminster Press.

— (1996), *A Critical and Exegetical Commentary on Jeremiah*, vol. 2, ICC, Edinburgh: T .& T. Clark.

McKEATING, H. (1971), *Amos, Hosea, Micah*, The Cambridge Bible Commentary, Cambridge: Cambridge University Press.

MEEKS, W. A. (1986), *The Moral World of the First Christians*, Library of Early Christianity, Philadelphia: The Westminster Press.

— (1990), 'The Circle of Reference in Pauline Morality', in D. Balch, E. Ferguson & W. A. Meeks (eds.), *Greeks, Romans, and Christians: Essays in Honor of Abraham J. Malherbe*, Minneapolis: Fortress Press.

MEIER, J. P. (1994), *Mentor, Message, and Miracles*, vol. 2 of *A Marginal Jew: Rethinking the Historical Jesus*, New York: Doubleday.

MERKEL, H. (1991), *Die Pastoralbriefe*, in *NTD*, Göttingen: Vandenhoeck & Ruprecht.

MICHAELIS, W. (1967), '*paschō, pathētos, propaschō, sympaschō, pathos, pathēma, sympathēs, sympatheō, kakopatheō, synkakopatheō, kakopatheia, metriopatheō, homoiopathēs, praüpatheia*', in *TDNT*, vol. 5, Grand Rapids: Eerdmans.

MICHAELS, J. R. (1988), *1 Peter*, in *WBC*, Waco, Texas: Word Books.

— (1989), *John*, NIBC, Peabody, Massachusetts: Hendrickson.

MICHEL, O. (1967), '*miseō*', in *TDNT*, vol. 4, Grand Rapids: Eerdmans.

MILLER, C. (1983), *Joy*, Downers Grove, Illinois: Inter-Varsity Press.

MILLER, P. D. (1990), *Deuteronomy*, Interpretation: A Bible Commentary for Teaching and Preaching, Louisville: John Knox Press.

MILNE, B. A. (1982), 'Jealousy', in J. D. Douglas *et al.* (eds.), *New Bible Dictionary*, 2nd ed., Wheaton, Illinois: Tyndale.

MINEAR, P. S. (1972), *The Commands of Christ*, Nashville: Abingdon Press.

MOBERLY, R. W. H. (1997), 'Lament', in *NIDOTTE*, vol. 1, Grand Rapids: Zondervan Publishing House.

MOHRLANG, R. (1993), 'Love', in *DPL*.

MOO, D. J. (1985), *The Letter of James: An Introduction and Commentary*, in *TNTC*, Grand Rapids: Eerdmans.

— (1996), *The Epistle to the Romans*, in *NICNT*, Grand Rapids: Eerdmans.

— (2000), *The Letter of James*, in *PNTC*, Grand Rapids: Eerdmans.

MOORE, B., UNDERWOOD, B. & ROSENHAN, D. L. (1984), 'Emotion, Self, and Others', in C. E. Izard, J. Kagan & R. B. Zajonc (eds.), *Emotions, Cognition, and Behaviour*, Cambridge: Cambridge University Press.

MORRICE, W. G. (1977), *We Joy in God*, London: SPCK.

— (1984), *Joy in the New Testament*, Grand Rapids: Eerdmans.

— (1993), 'Joy', in *DPL*.

MORRIS, L. (1965), *The Apostolic Preaching of the Cross*, Grand Rapids: Eerdmans.

— (1965), *The Cross in the New Testament*, Grand Rapids: Eerdmans.

— (1981), *Testaments of Love: A Study of Love in the Bible*, Grand Rapids: Eerdmans.

— (1984), *The Epistles of Paul to The Thessalonians*, in *TNTC*, Grand Rapids: Eerdmans.

— (1987), *Revelation*, rev. ed., in *TNTC*, Grand Rapids: Eerdmans.

— (1988), *The Cross of Jesus*, Carlisle: Paternoster Press.

— (1992), 'Love', in *DJG*.

— (1997), 'Love', in *DLNT*.

MORRISSEY, M. P. (1986), 'Reason and Emotion: Modern and Classical Views on Religious Knowing', *Horizons* 16: 275–291.

MOULE, C. F. D. (1963), *The Meaning of Hope*, Philadelphia: Fortress Press.

MOUNCE, R. H. (1977), *The Book of Revelation*, in *NICNT*, Grand Rapids: Eerdmans.

— (1991), *Matthew*, in *NIBC*, Peabody, Massachusetts: Hendrickson Publishers.

MUNDLE, W. (1975), 'Fear', in *NIDNTT*, vol. 1, Grand Rapids: Zondervan.

MURPHY, J. G. & HAMPTON, J. (1988), *Forgiveness and Mercy*, Cambridge: Cambridge University Press.

MURRAY, J. (1959–65), *The Epistle to the Romans*, 2 vols., *NICNT*, Grand Rapids: Eerdmans.

MUßNER, F. (1981), *Der Jakobusbrief*, HTK, Freiburg: Herder.

NASH, R. A. (1989), 'Cognitive Theories of Emotion', *Noûs* 23: 481–504.

NASH, R. H. (1984), *Christianity and the Hellenistic World*, Grand Rapids: Zondervan.

NGIEN, D. (1995), *The Suffering of God According to Martin Luther's 'Theologia Crucis'*, New York: Peter Lang.

— (1997), 'The God Who Suffers', *Christianity Today*, February 3, 1997.

NICKELSBURG, G. W. (1981), *Jewish Literature Between Bible and the Mishnah: A Historical and Literary Introduction*, Philadelphia: Fortress Press.

NIDA, E. A. 'Analysis of Meaning and Dictionary Making', *International Journal of American Linguistics* 24: 279–292.

NIDA, E. A. & LOUW, J. P. (1992), *Lexical Semantics of the Greek New Testament*, SBL Resources for Biblical Study, no. 25, Atlanta: Scholars Press.

NOLLAND, J. (1993), *Luke 9:21 – 18:34*, in *WBC*, Dallas: Word Books.

NUSSBAUM, M. C. (1987), 'The Stoics on the Extirpation of the Passions', *Apeiron* 20: 129–177.

— (1990a), '"By Words Not Arms": Lucretius on Gentleness in an Unsafe World', in M. Nussbaum (ed.), *The Poetics of Therapy: Hellenistic Ethics in its Rhetorical and Literary Context, Apeiron* 23, no. 4.

— (1992), 'Tragedy and Self-Sufficiency: Plato and Aristotle on Fear and Pity', *Oxford Studies in Ancient Philosophy* 10: 107–159.

— (1993), 'Poetry and the Passions: Two Stoic Views', in J. Brunschwig & M. C. Nussbaum (eds.), *Passions and Perceptions: Studies in Hellenistic Philosophies of Mind Proceedings of the Fifth Symposium Hellenisticum*, Cambridge: Cambridge University Press.

— (1994), *The Therapy of Desire: Theory and Practice in Hellenistic Ethics*, vol. 2 of Martin Classical Lectures, Princeton: Princeton University Press.

— (2001), *Upheavals of Thought: The Intelligence of Emotions*, Cambridge: Cambridge University Press.

NUSSBAUM, M. C. & HURSTHOUSE, R. (1984), 'Plato on Commensurability and
    Desire', *The Aristotelian Society*, Supplementary, vol. 58.
NYGREN, A. (1953), *Agape and Eros*, trans. P. S. Watson, London: SPCK.
OAKLEY, J. (1992), *Morality and the Emotions*, London: Routledge.
OBERLINNER, L. (1996), *Die Pastoralbriefe Dritte Folge: Kommentar Zum Titusbrief*, HTK,
    Freiburg: Herder.
O'BRIEN, P. T. (1991), *The Epistle to the Philippians*, in *NIGTC*, Grand Rapids: Eerdmans.
— (1999), *The Letter to the Ephesians*, in *PNTC*, Grand Rapids: Eerdmans.
OGILVIE, L. J. (1990), *Hosea, Joel, Amos, Obadiah, Jonah*, The Communicators
    Commentary, Dallas: Word Books.
OLIVER, A. (1997), *"bl"*, in *NIDOTTE*, vol. 1, Grand Rapids: Zondervan.
ORIGEN (1885a), *Against Celsus*, Ante-Nicene Fathers: Translations of the Writings of the
    Fathers Down to AD 325, vol. 4, Buffalo: The Christian Literature Publishing Company.
— (1885b), *De Principiis*, Ante-Nicene Fathers: Translations of the Writings of the Fathers
    Down to AD 325, vol. 4, Buffalo: The Christian Literature Publishing Company.
OUTKA, G. (1972), *Agape: An Ethical Analysis*, New Haven: Yale University Press.
PAIGE, T. P. (1993), 'Philosophy', in *DPL*.
PAINTER, J. (1992), 'Joy', in *DJG*.
— (1993), *The Quest for the Messiah: The History, Literature, and Theology of the Johannine
    Community*, 2nd ed., Nashville: Abingdon.
PALMER, F. H. (1982), 'Love', in J. D. Douglas *et al.* (eds.), *New Bible Dictionary*, 2nd ed.,
    Wheaton, Illinois: Tyndale.
PASCAL, B. (1941), *Pensées and The Provincial Letters*, New York: Random House.
PATZIA, A. G. (1990), *Ephesians, Colossians, Philemon*, in *NIBC*, Peabody, Massachusetts:
    Hendrickson.
PAVELSKY, R. L. (1977), 'The Commandment of Love and the Christian Clinical
    Psychologist', in N. H. Malony (ed.), *Current Perspectives in the Psychology of Religion*,
    Grand Rapids: Eerdmans.
PEDERSEN, J. E. (1974), 'Some Thoughts on a Biblical View of Anger', *JPT* 2: 210–215.
PEELS, H. G. L. (1997), *"qn"*, in *NIDOTTE*, vol. 3, Grand Rapids: Zondervan
    Publishing House.
PELLING, C. (1989), 'Plutarch: Roman Heroes and Greek Culture', in M. Griffin &
    J. Barnes (eds.), *Philosophia Togata: Essays on Philosophy and Roman Society*, Oxford:
    Clarendon Press.
PESCH, R. (1976–77), *Das Markusevangelium*, 2 vols., *HTK*, Freiburg: Herder.
— (1986), *Die Apostelgeschichte*, 2 vols., *EKK*, Freiburg: Herder.
PESCH, W. (1981), 'Emotion', *EBT*.
PETERS, R. S. (1970), 'The Education of the Emotions', in M. B. Arnold (ed.), *Feelings
    and Emotions: The Loyola Symposium*, Personality and Psychopathology, New York:
    Academic Press.

PETERSON, D. (1993), 'Worship in the New Testament', in D. A. Carson (ed.), *Worship: Adoration and Action* Grand Rapids: Baker Book House.

PHILO (1929–62) trans. F. H. Colson & G. H. Whitaker, 10 vols., The Loeb Classical Library, London: William Heinemann Ltd.

PIGDEN, C. R. (1990), 'Ought-Implies-Can: Erasmus, Luther, and R. M. Hare', *Sophia* 29: 2–29.

PIPER, J. (1979), *'Love Your Enemies': Jesus' Love Command in the Synoptic Gospels and in the Early Christian Paraenesis*, Cambridge: Cambridge University Press.

— 'Hope as the Motivation of Love: 1 Peter 3:9–12', *NTS* 26: 212–231.

— (1986), *Desiring God*, Portland: Multnomah.

PITTAM, J. & SCHERER, K. R. (1993), 'Vocal Expression and Communication of Emotion', in M. Lewis & J. M. Haviland (eds.), *Handbook of Emotions*, New York: The Guilford Press.

PLUTARCH (1970), *Plutarch's Moralia*, trans. W. C. Helmbold, The Loeb Classical Library, Cambridge: Harvard University Press.

PLUTCHIK, R. (1968), 'The Emotions, Facts, Theories, and a New Model', in M. B. Arnold (ed.), *The Nature of Emotion*, Penguin Modern Psychology Readings, Harmondsworth: Penguin.

POKORNY, P. (1987), *Der Brief des Paulus an die Kolosser*, Theologischer Handkommentar zum Neuen Testament, Berlin: Evangelische Verlagsanstalt.

— (1991), *Colossians: A Commentary*, Peabody, Massachusetts: Hendrickson.

— (1992), *Der Brief des Paulus an die Epheser*, Evangelische Verlagsanstalt.

POMEROY, S. B. (1975), *Goddesses, Whores, Wives, and Slaves: Women in Classical Antiquity*, New York: Schocken Books.

— (1984), 'Emotions: A General Psychoevolutionary Theory', in K. R. Scherer & P. Ekman (eds.), *Approaches to Emotion*, Hillsdale NJ: Lawrence Erlbaum Associates.

PORTER, S. E. (1993), 'Fear, Reverence', in *DPL*.

PORTER, S. E. (1997), 'Wrath, Destruction', in *DLNT*.

PROUDFOOT, W. (1977), 'Religious Experience, Emotion, and Belief', *Harvard Theological Review* 70: 343–347.

— (1985), *Religious Experience*, Berkeley: University of California Press.

PUGMIRE, D. (1994), 'Real Emotion', *PPR* 54: 105–122.

PURINTON, J. S. (1993), 'Epicurus on the Telos', *Phronesis* 38: 281–320.

PUTNAM, M. C. J. (1990), 'Anger, Blindness, and Insight in Virgil's *Aeneid*', in M. Nussbaum (ed.), *The Poetics of Therapy: Hellenistic Ethics in its Rhetorical and Literary Context, Apeiron* 23, no. 4.

QUELL, G. (1964), '*agapaō, agapē, agapētos*', in *TDNT*, vol. 1, Grand Rapids: Eerdmans.

QUINN, J. D. & WACKER, W. C. (2000), *The First and Second Letters to Timothy: A New Translation with Notes and Commentary*, Grand Rapids: Eerdmans.

RAHLFS, A. (ed.) (1935), *LXX Septuaginta*, Stuttgart: Deutsche Bibelgesellschaft. (Electronic version found in BWW.)

RENGSTORF, K. H. (1964), '*elpis, elpizō, ap-, proelpizō*', in *TDNT*, vol. 2, Grand Rapids: Eerdmans.

RICH, J. M. (1979), 'Moral Education and the Emotions', *JME* 9: 81–87.

RIDDERBOS, H. (1975), *Paul: An Outline of His Theology*, trans. J. R. De Witt, Grand Rapids: Eerdmans.

— (1997), *The Gospel According to John: A Theological Commentary*, trans. J. Vriend, Grand Rapids: Eerdmans.

RIST, J. M. (1969), *Stoic Philosophy*, Cambridge: Cambridge University Press.

— (1972), *Epicurus: An Introduction*, Cambridge: Cambridge University Press.

ROBERTS, R. C. (1984a), 'Will Power and the Virtues', *The Philosophical Review* 18: 227–247.

— (1986), 'Emotions and the Fruit of the Spirit', in S. L. Jones (ed.), *Psychology and the Christian Faith*, Grand Rapids, Baker.

— (1988), 'What an Emotion Is: a Sketch', *The Philosophical Review* 97: 183–209.

— (1989), 'Aristotle on Virtues and Emotions', *Philosophical Studies* 56: 293–306.

— (1992a), 'Emotions Among the Virtues of the Christian Life', *JRE* 20: 37–68.

— (1992b), 'Emotions as Access to Religious Truths', *Faith and Philosophy* 9: 83–94.

— (1993), 'The Logic and Lyric of Contrition', *Theology Today* 50: 193–207.

ROBINSON, B. P. (1966), 'Gethsemane: The Synoptic and the Johannine Viewpoints' *The Church Quarterly Review* 167.

ROBINSON, D. W. B. (1974), 'The Priesthood of Paul in the Gospel of Hope', in R. Banks (ed.), *Reconciliation and Hope: New Testament Essays on Atonement and Eschatology*, Grand Rapids: Eerdmans.

ROBINSON, W. C. (1984), 'Wrath of God', in W. A. Elwell (ed.), *Evangelical Dictionary of Theology*, Grand Rapids: Baker Book House.

ROLFE, J. C. (1931), *Sallust With an English Translation*, rev. ed., The Loeb Classic Library, London: William Heinemann.

RORTY, A. O. (1984), 'Aristotle on the Metaphysical Status of the *Pathe*', *Review of Metaphysics* 38: 521–546.

ROSNER, B. S. (1995), 'That Pattern of Teaching: Issues and Essays in Pauline Ethics', in B. Rosner (ed.), *Understanding Paul's Ethics: Twentieth-Century Approaches*, Grand Rapids: Eerdmans.

— (ed.) (1995), *Understanding Paul's Ethics: Twentieth-Century Approaches*, Grand Rapids: Eerdmans.

— (1999), *Paul, Scripture, and Ethics: A Study of 1 Corinthians 5–7*, Grand Rapids: Baker Book House.

ROSS, W. D. (ed.) (1931), *The Works of Aristotle*, Oxford: The Clarendon Press.

RUNIA, D. T. (1993), *Philo in Early Christian Literature: A Survey*, Jewish Traditions in

Early Christian Literature, vol. 3, Compendia Rerum Iudaicarum ad Novum Testamentum, section 3, Minneapolis: Fortress Press.

SALIERS, D. E. (1980), *The Soul in Paraphrase: Prayer and the Religious Affections*, New York: The Seabury Press.

SAMPLER, P. J. (1991), 'From Text to Thought World', in J. M. Bassler (ed.), *Thessalonians, Philippians, Galatians, Philemon*, vol. 1 of *Pauline Theology*, Minneapolis: Fortress Press.

SANDERS, E. P. (1977), *Paul and Palestinian Judaism: A Comparison of Patterns of Religion*, London, SCM Press Ltd.

— (1992), *Judaism: Practice and Belief 63 BCE – 66 CE*, London: SCM Press.

SANDERS, E. P., BAUMGARTEN, A. I. & MENDELSON, A. (eds.) (1981), *Jewish and Christian Self-Definition*, vol. 2, Philadelphia: Fortress Press.

SANDMEL, S. (1979), *Philo of Alexandria: An Introduction*, New York: Oxford University Press.

SARNA, N. M. (1993), *Songs of the Heart*, New York: Schocken Books.

SCHACHTER, S. & SINGER, J. E. (1984), 'From Cognitive, Social, and Physiological Determinants of Emotional State', in C. Calhoun & R. C. Solomon (eds.), *What is an Emotion? Classic Readings in Philosophical Psychology*, Oxford: Oxford University Press. (First published in *Psychology Review* 69 (1962): 378–399.)

SCHERER, K. R. (1984), 'On the Nature and Function of Emotion: A Component Process Approach', in K. R. Scherer & P. Ekman (eds.), *Approaches to Emotion*, Hillsdale NJ: Lawrence Erlbaum Associates.

SCHERER, K. R. & EKMAN, P. (eds.) (1984), *Approaches to Emotion*, Hillsdale NJ: Lawrence Erlbaum Associates.

SCHILLEBEECKX, E. (1995), *Jesus: An Experiment in Christology*, trans. H. Hoskins, New York: Crossroad.

SCHIMMEL, S. (1979), 'Anger and Its Control in Graeco-Roman and Modern Psychology', *Psychiatry* 42: 320–337.

SCHLATTER, D. A. (1929), *Die Christliche Ethik*, Stuttgart: Calwer Vereinsbuchhandlung.

SCHLOSSBERGER, E. (1986), 'Why We Are Responsible for Our Emotions', *Mind* 95: 37–56.

SCHMITHALS, W. (1988), *Der Römerbrief: Ein Kommentar*, Gerd Mohn: Gütersloher Verlagshaus.

SCHMITZ, E. D. (1976), '*ginōskō*', in *NIDNTT*, vol. 2, Grand Rapids: Zondervan.

SCHNABEL, E. J. (1995), 'How Paul Developed His Ethics: Motivations, Norms and Criteria of Pauline Ethics', in B. Rosner (ed.), *Understanding Paul's Ethics: Twentieth-Century Approaches*, Grand Rapids: Eerdmans.

SCHNACKENBURG, R. (1965), *The Moral Teaching of the New Testament*. New York: Herder and Herder.

— (1980–82), *The Gospel According to St John*, 3 vols., New York: Crossroad.

— (1985), *Matthäusevangelium: 1, 1–16, 20*, Die Neue Echter Bibel, Echter Verlag.

— (1991), *Ephesians: A Commentary*, trans. H. Heron, Edinburgh: T. & T. Clark.

— (1995), *Jesus in the Gospels: A Biblical Christology*, trans. O. C. Dean, Jr., Louisville: John Knox Press.

SCHNELLE, U. (1991), *Neutestamentliche Anthropologie: Jesus, Paulus, Johannes*, Neukirchener Verlag.

SCHÖNWEISS, H. (1975), *'thymos'* in NIDNTT vol. 1, Grand Rapids: Zondervan.

SCHRAGE, W. (1988), *The Ethics of the New Testament*, trans. D. E. Green, Philadelphia: Fortress Press.

— (1991–99), *Der erste Brief an die Korinther*, 3 vols., *EKK*, Freiburg: Herder.

SCHÜRER, E. (1973–1987), *The History of the Jewish People in the Age of Jesus Christ (175 BC – AD 135)*, edited and revised by G. Vermes, F. Millar, M. Goodman & M. Black, 3 vols., Edinburgh: T.&T. Clark.

SCHÜRMANN, H. (1969), *Das Lukasevangelium*, vol. 1, *HTK*, Freiburg: Herder.

SCHWARTZ, JEFFREY M. & BEGLEY, SHARON (2002), *The Mind and the Brain: Neuroplasticity and the Power of Mental Force*, New York: Regan Books.

SCOTT, B. B. (1989), *Hear Then the Parables: A Commentary on the Parables of Jesus*, Minneapolis: Fortress Press.

SCOTT, J. J. (1995), *Customs and Controversies: Intertestamental Jewish Backgrounds of the New Testament*, Grand Rapids: Baker Books.

SCROGGS, R. (1991), 'Salvation History: The Theological Structure of Paul's Thought', in J. M. Bassler (ed.), *Thessalonians, Philippians, Galatians, Philemon*, vol. 1 of *Pauline Theology*, Minneapolis: Fortress Press.

SEEBASS, H. (1975), 'Enemy, Enmity, Hate', in *NIDNTT*, vol. 1, Grand Rapids: Zondervan.

SEGAL, C. (1990), *Lucretius on Death and Anxiety*, Princeton: Princeton University Press.

SENECA, *Moral Essays*, trans. John W. Basore, vol. 1, The Loeb Classical Library. Cambridge: Harvard University Press, 1963.

— (1967), *Ad Lucilium Epistulae Morales*, trans. R. M. Gummere, vol. 1, The Loeb Classical Library, Cambridge: Harvard University Press.

SHERMAN, N. (1993), 'The Role of Emotion in Aristotelian Virtue', *Proceedings of the Boston Area Colloquium in Ancient Philosophy* 9: 1–33.

SILVA, M. (1983), *Biblical Words and Their Meaning: An Introduction to Lexical Semantics*, Grand Rapids: Zondervan.

SIMON, B. (1978), *Mind and Madness in Ancient Greece: The Classical Roots of Modern Psychiatry*, Ithaca, NY: Cornell University Press.

SMALLEY, S. S. (1984), *1, 2, 3 John*, in *WBC*, Waco, Texas: Word Books.

SMITH, D. M. (1995), *The Theology of John*, New Testament Theology, Cambridge: Cambridge University Press.

SNODGRASS, K. R. (1992), 'Parable,' in *DJG*.

SOLOMON, R. C. (1976), *The Passions*, Notre Dame: University of Notre Dame Press.

— (1977), 'The Logic of Emotion', *Noûs* 11: 41–49.

— (1980), 'Emotions and Choice', in edited by A. O. Rorty (ed.), *Explaining Emotions*, Berkeley: University of California Press.

— (1984), '"I Can't Get It Out of My Mind": (Augustine's Problem)', *PPR* 44: 405–412.

— (1988), 'On Emotions as Judgments', *APQ* 25: 183–191.

— (1993), 'The Philosophy of Emotion', in M. Lewis & J. M. Haviland (eds.), *Handbook of Emotions*, New York: The Guilford Press.

— (1995), 'Some Notes on Emotion "East and West."' *Philosophy East and West* 45: 171–202.

SORG, T. (1976), *'kardia'*, in *NIDNTT*, Grand Rapids: Zondervan.

SROUFE, A. L., SCHORK, E., MOTTI, F., LAWROSKI, N. & LAFRENIERE, P. (1984), 'The Role of Affect in Social Competence', in C. E. Izard, J. Kagan & R. B. Zajonc (eds.), *Emotions, Cognition, and Behaviour*, Cambridge: Cambridge University Press.

STACHOWIAK, F. L. R. (1981), 'Hatred', *EBT*.

STÄHLIN, G. (1974), *'phileō, kataphileō, philēma, philē, philia'*, in *TDNT*, vol. 9, Grand Rapids: Eerdmans.

STAUFFER, E. (1964), *'agapaō, agapē, agapētos'*, in *TDNT*, vol. 1, Grand Rapids: Eerdmans.

STEIN, R. H. (1989), 'The Argument of Romans 13:1–7', *NovT* 31: 325–343.

STERLING, G. E. (2000), 'Philo', in *DNTB*.

STOTT, J. R. W. (1986), *The Cross of Christ*, Downers Grove, Illinois: Inter-Varsity Press.

— (1988), *The Letters of John*, rev. ed., in *TNTC*, Grand Rapids: Eerdmans.

STOWERS, S. K. (1990), 'Paul on the Use and Abuse of Reason', in D. Balch, E. Ferguson & W. A. Meeks (eds.), *Greeks, Romans, and Christians: Essays in Honor of Abraham J. Malherbe*, Minneapolis: Fortress Press.

STRIKER, G. (1993), 'Epicurean Hedonism', in J. Brunschwig & M. C. Nussbaum (eds.), *Passions and Perceptions: Studies in Hellenistic Philosophies of Mind Proceedings of the Fifth Symposium Hellenisticum*, Cambridge: Cambridge University Press.

— (1996), *Essays on Hellenistic Epistemology and Ethics*, Cambridge: Cambridge University Press.

STRONGMAN, K. T. (1987), *The Psychology of Emotion*, 3rd ed., New York: John Wiley and Sons.

STRUTHERS, G. B. (1997), *'np'*, in *NIDOTTE*, vol. 1, Grand Rapids: Zondervan Publishing House.

— (1997), *'br'*, in *NIDOTTE*, vol. 3, Grand Rapids: Zondervan.

STUART, D. (1987), *Hosea – Jonah*, in *WBC*, Waco, Texas: Word Books.

STUHLMACHER, P. (1992a), *Grundlegung Von Jesus zu Paulus*, vol. 1 of *Biblische Theologie des Neuen Testaments*, Göttingen: Vandenhoeck & Ruprecht.

— (1992b), *Von der Paulusschule bis zur Johannesoffenbarung: Der Kanon und seine Auslegung*, vol. 2 of *Biblische Theologie des Neuen Testaments*, Göttingen: Vandenhoeck & Ruprecht.

STUMPFF, A. (1964), '*zēlos, zēloō, zēlōthēs, parazēloō*', in *TDNT*, vol. 2, Grand Rapids: Eerdmans.

SUGDEN, E. H. (ed.) (1921), *Wesley's Standard Sermons*, 2 vols., London: The Epworth Press.

SULLENDER, R. S. (1981), 'Saint Paul's Approach to Grief: Clarifying the Ambiguity', *Journal of Religion and Health* 20: 63–74.

TADA, J. E. & ESTES, S. (1997), *When God Weeps*, Grand Rapids: Zondervan.

TANNEHILL, R. C. (1996), *Luke*, Abingdon New Testament Commentaries, Nashville: Abingdon Press.

TASKER, R. V. G. (1951), *The Biblical Doctrine of the Wrath of God*, London: The Tyndale Press.

— (1982), 'Hope', in J. D. Douglas *et al.* (eds.), *New Bible Dictionary*, 2nd ed., Wheaton, Illinois: Tyndale.

TAYLOR, G. (1975), 'Justifying the Emotions', *Mind* 84: 390–402.

TEALE, A. E. (1951), *Kantian Ethics*, Westport, Connecticut: Greenwood Press.

TENNEY, M. C. (1981), 'The Gospel of John', in *EBC*, vol. 9, Grand Rapids: Zondervan.

THEISSEN, G. (1978), *Sociology of Early Palestinian Christianity*, trans. J. Bowden, Philadelphia: Fortress Press.

— (1982), *The Social Setting of Pauline Christianity: Essays on Corinth*, edited and translated by John H. Schütz, Philadelphia: Fortress Press.

— (1983), *Psychological Aspects of Pauline Theology*, trans. J. P. Galvin, Edinburgh: T. & T. Clark.

— (1986), *The Shadow of the Galilean: The Quest of the Historical Jesus in Narrative Form*, trans. J. Bowden, Philadelphia: Fortress Press.

THEISSEN, G. & MERZ, A. (1998), *The Historical Jesus: A Comprehensive Guide*, trans. John Bowden, Minneapolis: Fortress Press.

THISELTON, A. C. (2000), *The First Epistle to the Corinthians*, in *NIGTC*, Grand Rapids: Eerdmans.

THOENNES, E. (1998), 'Godly Human Jealousy: A Fresh Look at Misunderstood Emotion', Paper presented at the annual meeting of the Evangelical Theological Society, Orlando, Florida, November 1998.

THRALL, M. E. (1994), *A Critical and Exegetical Commentary on the Second Epistle to the Corinthians*, vol. 1, ICC, Edinburgh: T. & T. Clark.

TILES, J. E. (1977), 'The Combat of Passion and Reason', *Philosophy*: 321–330.

TOMKINS, S. S. (1970), 'Affect as the Primary Motivational System', in M. B. Arnold (ed.), *Feelings and Emotions: The Loyola Symposium*, Personality and Psychopathology, New York: Academic Press.

— (1984), 'Affect Theory', in K. R. Scherer & P. Ekman (eds.), *Approaches to Emotion*, Hillsdale NJ: Lawrence Erlbaum Associates.

TOOMBS, L. E. (1965), 'Love and Justice in Deuteronomy', *Interpretation* 19: 399–411.

TOWNER, P. H. (1989), 'The Goal of Our Instruction: The Structure of Theology and

Ethics in the Pastoral Epistles.' *Journal for the Study of the New Testament*, Supplement Series 34, Sheffield: Sheffield Academic Press.

TURNER, M. (1995), 'Modern Linguistics and the New Testament', in J. Green (ed.), *Hearing the New Testament: Strategies for Interpretation*, Grand Rapids: Eerdmans.

ULLMANN, S. (1957), *The Principles of Semantics*, 2nd ed., New York: Philosophical Library Publishers.

United Bible Societies and Westminster Theological Seminary (1994), *'Corrected' Biblia Hebraica Stuttgartensia*, ver. 2, United Bible Societies and Westminster Theological Seminary. (Electronic version found in *BWW*.)

The University of Chicago Press (1993), *The Chicago Manual of Style*, J. Grossman (ed.), 14th ed., Chicago: University of Chicago Press.

VERHEY, A. D. (1997), 'Ethics', in *DLNT*.

VINE, W. E. (1984), *An Expository Dictionary of New Testament Words with Their Precise Meanings for English Readers*, in *Vine's Complete Expository Dictionary of Old and New Testament Words*, Nashville: Thomas Nelson Publishers.

VON RAD, G. (1960–62), *Old Testament Theology*, trans. D. M. G. Stalker, 2 vols., New York: Harper and Row Publishers.

— (1966), *Deuteronomy*, Philadelphia: The Westminster Press.

VORSTER, WILLEM S. 'Stoic and Early Christians on Blessedness', in *Greeks, Romans, and Christians: Essays in Honor of Abraham J. Malherbe*, edited by David Balch, Everett Ferguson, and Wayne A. Meeks. Minneapolis: Fortress Press, 1990.

WALL, R. W. (1990), *Revelation*, in *NIBC*, Peabody, Massachusetts: Hendrickson Publishers.

WALLACE, D. B. (1989), '*ORGIZESTHE* in Ephesians 4:26: Command or Condition?', *Criswell Theological Journal* 3: 353–372.

WALTERS, G. (1997), *Why Do Christians Find It Hard to Grieve?* Carlisle: Paternoster Press.

WALZER, R. (1949), *Galen on Jews and Christians*, London: Oxford University Press.

WANAMAKER, C. A. (1990), *The Epistle to the Thessalonians*, in *NIGTC*, Grand Rapids: Eerdmans.

WANKE, G. (1974), '*phobeō, phobeomai, phobos, deos*', in *TDNT*, vol. 9, Grand Rapids: Eerdmans.

WARFIELD, B. B. (1970), 'The Emotional Life of Our Lord', in S. G. Craig (ed.), *The Person and Work of Christ: Christological Studies by Benjamin Brekinridge Warfield*, Philadelphia: The Presbyterian and Reformed Publishing Company.

WARNACH, V. (1981), 'Love', *EBT*.

WATSON, F. (2000), *Agape, Eros, Gender: Towards a Pauline Sexual Ethic*, Cambridge: Cambridge University Press.

WEINER, B. & GRAHAM, S. (1984), 'At Attributional Approach to Emotional Development', in C. E. Izard, J. Kagan & R. B. Zajonc (eds.), *Emotions, Cognition, and Behaviour*, Cambridge: Cambridge University Press.

WEIß, H.-F. (1991), *Der Brief an die Hebräer*, Kritisch-exegetischer Kommentar über das Neue Testament, Göttingen: Vandenhoeck & Ruprecht.

WENHAM, D. (1989), *The Parables of Jesus*, Downers Grove: Inter-Varsity Press.

WENHAM, G. J. (1979), *The Book of Leviticus*, The New International Commentary, Grand Rapids: Eerdmans.

WESTERMANN, C. (1980), *The Psalms: Structure, Content, and Message*, trans. R. D. Gehrke, Minneapolis: Ausburg.

— (1989), *The Living Psalms*, trans. J. R. Porter, Edinburgh: T. & T. Clark.

WHISTON, W. (trans.) (1974), *The Works of Flavius Josephus*, 4 vols., Grand Rapids: Baker Book House.

WILLIAMS, D. J. (1990), *Acts*, in *NIBC*, Peabody, Massachusetts: Hendrickson Publishers.

— (1992), *1 and 2 Thessalonians*, in *NIBC*, Peabody, Massachusetts: Hendrickson Publishers.

WILLIAMSON, R. (1970), *Philo and the Epistle to the Hebrews*, Leiden: E. J. Brill.

WILSON, W. T. (1997), *The Hope of Glory: Education and Exhortation in the Epistle to the Colossians*, Leiden: Brill.

WINSTON, D. (1979), *The Wisdom of Solomon: A New Translation with Introduction and Commentary*, The Anchor Bible, vol. 43, Garden City, New York: Doubleday and Company.

WITHERINGTON, B. (1995), *John's Wisdom: A Commentary on the Fourth Gospel*. Louisville: Westminster: John Knox Press.

WOLBERT, W. (1984), 'Die Liebe zum Nächsten, zum Feind and zum Sünder', *Theologie und Glaube* 74: 262–282.

WOLFF, C. (1989), *Der zweite Brief des Paulus an die Korinther*, Berlin: Evangelische Verlagsanstalt.

— (1996), *Der erste Brief des Paulus an die Korinther*, Berlin: Evangelische Verlagsanstalt.

WRIGHT, N. T. (1992), *The New Testament and the People of God*, vol. 1 of *Christian Origins and the Questions of God*, Minneapolis: Fortress Press.

— (1996), *Jesus and the Victory of God*, Vol 2 of *Christian Origins and the Questions of God*. Minneapolis: Fortress Press.

YOUNG, B. H. (1995), *Jesus the Jewish Theologian*, Peabody: Hendrickson Publishers.

YOUNG, F. (1994), *The Theology of the Pastoral Epistles*, Cambridge: Cambridge University Press.

YOUNG, T. P. (1973), 'Feeling and Emotion', in B. Wolman (ed.), *Handbook of General Psychology*, Englewood Cliffs, New Jersey: Prentice-Hall.

ZAJONC, R. B. (1984), 'The Interaction of Affect and Cognition', in K. R. Scherer & P. Ekman (eds.), *Approaches to Emotion*, Hillsdale NJ: Lawrence Erlbaum Associates.

— (1984), 'On Primacy of Affect', in K. R. Scherer & P. Ekman (eds.), *Approaches to Emotion*, Hillsdale NJ: Lawrence Erlbaum Associates.

— (1994), 'Evidence for Nonconscious Emotions', in P. Ekman & R. J. Davidson (eds.),

The Nature of Emotion: Fundamental Questions, Series in Affective Science, Oxford: Oxford University Press.

ZAJONC, R. B., MURPHY, S. Y. & MCINTOSH, D. N. (1993), 'Brain Temperature and Subjective Emotional Experience', in *Handbook of Emotions*, edited by Michael Lewis and Jeannette M. Haviland, New York: The Guilford Press.

ZELLER, D. (1985), *Der Brief an die Römer*, RNT, Verlag Friedrich Pustet Regensburg.

ZIESLER, J. A. (1988), 'The Role of the Tenth Commandment in Romans 7', *Journal for the Study of the New Testament* 33: 41–56.

— (1990), *Pauline Christianity*, The Oxford Bible Series, rev. ed., Oxford: Oxford University Press.

INDEX OF NAMES

INDEX OF BIBLICAL REFERENCES